Yale Agrarian Studies Series

James C. Scott, series editor

Forests and Peasant Politics in Modern France

Tamara L. Whited

Yale University Press

New Haven & London

Published with assistance from the foundation established in memory of Calvin Chapin of the Class of 1788, Yale College.

Printed in the United States of America.

ISBN 0-300-08227-4

A catalogue record for this book is available from the Library of Congress and the British Library.

The paper in this book meets the guidelines for permanence and durability of the Committee on Production Guidelines for Book Longevity of the Council on Library Resources.

10 9 8 7 6 5 4 3 2 1

For Jean-Yves

Contents

Acknowledgments

It is a pleasure to acknowledge the individuals and institutions that have promoted and improved this book at various moments of its genesis.

A Chateaubriand fellowship from France's Ministry of Culture and a grant from the Society of Woman Geographers permitted me to conduct initial research in France. Funding for subsequent research and writing came from the Mellon Foundation, the Pennsylvania State System of Higher Education, and the Indiana University of Pennsylvania Senate, as well as IUP's Graduate School and Research.

At the outset, conversations with Isaac Chiva, Gérard Collomb, Andrée Corvol, Isabelle Richefort, and Denis Woronoff helped steer this project in positive directions. The staff of the *service de restauration des terrains en montagne* in Chambéry deserve special thanks for ensuring my most satisfying months of research; they shared with me their firsthand knowledge of alpine restoration and constantly outdid one another with hospitality. Jean-Pierre Feuvrier allowed me free rein in the superlative documentary and photographic collections of the RTM Savoie, Jeanloup Boisset and André Col shared technical experience and gave me guided tours of restoration sites in the Maurienne, and Alain Delalune engaged me in philosophical discussions about restoration and provided an excellent set of slides. In Toulouse, Jean-Paul Métailié generously gave me access to his photographic archive and produced prints for me. At the Ecole Nationale du Génie Rural et des Eaux et Forêts in Nancy, Marie-Jeanne Lionnet brought additional printed material to my attention.

From the beginning, I benefited from the insights of skilled readers. Many early drafts faced the humane rigors of Susanna Barrows's duly famous dissertation seminar; I thank David Barnes, Paul Friedland, Megan Koreman, Douglas Mackaman, Katharine Norris, Marc Roudebush, Sylvia Schafer, Vanessa Schwartz, Regina Sweeney, and Matthew Truesdell for their criticisms and encouragement. Later on, Michael Bess played an inspirational role in helping me transmute dissertation into book. James C. Scott supported my work at a critical stage and invited me to present a portion of it to the discerning members of Yale University's Agrarian Studies Colloquium. At Indiana University of Pennsylvania, this book has improved thanks to the eagle eyes of fine and caring colleagues: Lynn Botelho, Irwin Marcus, Elizabeth Ricketts, Holly Shissler, and Wang Xi.

My family has, in inverse proportion to its size, provided enduring love, joy, laughter, and a sense of purpose. My husband, Jean-Yves Boulard, and my mother, Angela N. Whited, have seen me through this project and so much else. I warmly thank Holly, Lynn, and Laurie, whose friendship in the wooded glen of Indiana has been inestimable, and would be anywhere.

Above all, I thank my teachers: Susanna Barrows, who for me and many others has defined mentorship and who gave me the luxury of bathing in her intellectual spirit during my years of graduate school. Carolyn Merchant, *éminence grise* of environmental history, broadened my horizons immeasurably by introducing me to that field and suggesting its many possibilities. I owe a special debt to Peter Sahlins, without whose superb example I never would have had the confidence to work on forest politics in remote regions of France. Peter has shepherded this project from beginning to end.

Abbreviations

ADA	Archives Départementales de l'Ariège, Foix
ADH-G	Archives Départementales de la Haute-Garonne, Toulouse
ADS	Archives Départementales de la Savoie, Chambéry
AN	Archives Nationales, Paris
CNRS	Centre National de la Recherche Scientifique, Paris
INRA	Institut National de la Recherche Agronomique, Orléans
REF	*Revue des Eaux et Forêts*
RFF	*Revue forestière française*
RGA	*Revue de géographie alpine*
RGPSO	*Revue géographique des Pyrénées et du Sud-Ouest*
RTM Ariège	Archives du Service de Restauration des Terrains en Montagne de l'Ariège, Foix
RTM Savoie	Archives du Service de Restauration des Terrains en Montagne de la Savoie, Chambéry

Note on Usage

The adjective *alpine* with a lowercase *a* will refer to characteristics of upland areas of Savoie and Ariège or to upland areas in general; I reserve *Alpine* with an uppercase *A* to designate conditions particular to Savoie or the Alps.

Introduction

In the Pyrenees as in the Alps, the necessities of pastoral life often protest
the artificial separations introduced by politics, inspired by a false
geography.
—*Paul Vidal de la Blache*

For many people from widely varying societies, the idea of reforestation carries a positive resonance. It signals a return to the forsaken gar-
den, a powerful image of ecological health. This book explores the reforestation of alpine France, one of the first efforts of any modern
state to create forest in areas thought to have been deforested within
recent memory. French initiatives to replant the mountains stand out
in the global context of the nineteenth century, an era during which
economic forces induced the clearing of forest on a massive scale in
Asia, the Americas, and the Middle East, followed by tropical rain
forests in Africa and South America. Western Europeans also continued to rely heavily on the forests of the Baltic region for timber, as they
had for centuries, instead of taking stock of their own resources.[1]

Was France critically deforested by the middle of the nineteenth
century? This question leads to the complicated relations between

ecology and perception that have become a major focus of environmental history. In France, a "forest of dreams and that of reality" coexist in popular memory. Since approximately the first third of the nineteenth century, for example, a fear of deforestation has gripped the collective imagination of French officialdom, but subsequently the forest has made one of its gradual comebacks, increasing its share of the national territory by 27 percent in the twentieth century alone.[2]

Ecological patterns and the reasons for them are, of course, rarely self-evident; even with the aid of hindsight, variations over time in the sheer extent of forests raise more questions than they answer. In contrast to the dramatic return of forest following demographic collapse due to the Black Death of the fourteenth century, the forest's fluctuation in modern history has responded to complex human and natural mediations. The absence of forest, for instance, has not always reflected high population densities; in France, the forest has disappeared in places of low human density, such as the west, as well as in more populous regions. But broadly speaking, over the past two centuries the French have relegated their forests to the rocky, sandy, chalky, dry, and clay soils of the country—soils generally acidic and too poor for sustained agriculture.[3]

These early efforts to reforest significant portions of the French national territory nonetheless appear precocious, indeed enlightened. In France, however, enlightened forest management was defined in terms of the purely material interests of an abstract "public," and for this reason among others reforestation was far from a neutral project, much less a "proto-Green" endeavor.[4] It constitutes a major chapter in the broader struggle between peasants and the state for control of the forest during the period from 1860 to 1940. This conflict has been a fundamental dimension of modern environmental history in the Alps and the Pyrenees.

This study weaves the ecological, social, and political threads of the struggles for the forest in the Alps and the Pyrenees, regions deemed in the nineteenth century to be critically deforested. Three overlapping themes provide theoretical springboards for the following six chapters. The first theme treats the differing cultural constructions of the nature of alpine France that framed the debate over reforestation. For foresters influenced by engineering and trained in the techniques of silviculture and forest management, mountains assumed fixed, functional qualities that could be maintained only by the state's intervention in order to avert natural catastrophe; in their view, mountains were destined to be forested. Agro-pastoral peasants living in the mountains perceived their habitats as interpenetrating spaces that shaped a diverse economy marked by

broadly seasonal activities. Alpine peasants did not idealize the mountains—
they often complained of hardships imposed by an exacting environment—
and they harbored their own notions of natural catastrophe. Yet radically different consequences flowed from their constructions, which were based on
lived reality rather than on textbook techniques.

The second theme treats the conflict between legal and customary norms, or,
more narrowly, property and possession. Both sorts of norms created units of
nature in the service of territoriality, a delimitation of boundaries to secure access and resources for some people while excluding others. Property and possession, though, did not share the same legal status. Private property, established as an individual right during the Revolution and further enshrined in
Napoleon's Civil Code, posed the greatest challenge to the maintenance of possession—a realm of rights to land defined narrowly in the Civil Code but em-
bodying a much broader world of access, use rights, and communal property in
the mentalities and practices of peasants. This theme also explores the gradual
transformation of forests into "productive" spaces by the agents of a national
economy. It remained incomplete owing to unexpected triumphs of possession
over property in the late nineteenth and early twentieth centuries.[5]

Third, each side in the struggle for the forest articulated political strategies
to promote its own "forest of dreams." For their part, successive governments
sought to defuse and in fact disguise the struggle by according discretionary
power to the French Forest Administration, known for most of the nineteenth
century as the Administration des Forêts. The major pieces of forest legislation
after 1860 couched the rationale for state intervention in the neutral, universal-
izing concept of public utility, a standard long used with respect to public
works and one theoretically detached from politics. Peasants resisted this standard, their means reflecting centuries-old patterns as well as new opportunities.
Through "devastation," illegal pasturing, petitions, meetings, covert destruction, foot-dragging, force and threats of force, litigation, and voting, peasants
not only pried the administrative state out of its accustomed channels but also
unveiled the inevitably political character of public utility.[6]

The dynamics of contestation have had little place in other accounts of the
state's agenda to reforest alpine France. Written by a diverse body of foresters,
geographers, sociologists, and historians, many French studies of alpine reforestation have primarily judged the Administration des Forêts by its technical
performance. The postwar work of the forester Paul Chabrol retained nineteenth-century conceptions of the anarchic, disorderly nature of the mountains
and their inhabitants and sought to demonstrate how foresters had rectified a

long-lost ecological balance. In the early 1960s, Pierre Fourchy's retrospective of
the first law on reforestation cast the state's initiatives in a history of growing
sensitivity toward alpine ecology. Fourchy qualified a history-of-progress out-
look only by noting the "veritable faith" of nineteenth-century foresters:
"Their work in the beginning was a sort of mission which excuses certain errors, a certain naiveté."[7]

Beginning in the 1980s, sociologists attached to the Institut national de la
recherche agronomique (INRA) brought to light both the technical limitations
of reforestation and the changes in social relations that these policies entailed.
Foresters as well began to admit the ecological errors of zealous reforestation,
above all their predecessors' notorious disregard for the effects of altitude on
the growth of trees. The historian Andrée Corvol has offered the most thoroughgoing critique of the state in what is also the most detailed study of forests
and society in modern France. Yet Corvol's monolithic view of the state, one
that suggests coherent intentions and realpolitik, remains largely uncontested.[8]
No major study has shifted the problem to disputes between rural communities
and the state.[9]

Reforestation would not have occurred when it did in the absence of a powerful Administration des Forêts; Chapter 1 treats its evolution over the two centuries before 1860. More broadly, reforestation belongs to the history of the
French state's provision of infrastructure and economic subsidies. It is thus related to public engineering and the state's penchant for *dirigisme,* especially that
aspect concerned with the spatial distribution of economic activities, referred
to in recent decades as *aménagement du territoire.* "Technocracy" comes immediately to mind, yet it is a strange concept to apply to alpine reforestation.
Foresters believed that they were restoring the mountains to an anterior state,
before the age of technocrats, industry, or even agriculture; the Third Republic's substitution of "restoration" for "reforestation" spoke clearly to this convic-
tion. Assuming that alpine France had once been forested from base to summits required a thorough reenvisioning of the mountains. This conceptual shift
provides the analytical framework for Chapter 2.

An image of fully forested mountains required the erasure of alpine peasants. Along with emigration, reforestation meant the reversal of a trend that
had been in place, with fits and starts, since the beginning of the agricultural
revolution—in western Europe, the gradual formation of a peasantry, at the
expense of forest, as a "closed association over the face of the land."[10] From
the nearer vantage point of nineteenth-century consciousness, many officials
deemed alpine peasants archaic. Napoléon III undertook a vast program of in-

tegrating the majority of peasants into the nation through agricultural modernization, public works, and plebiscites; his republican successors substituted more open electoral politics for plebiscites and rigged elections, continued to support agriculture and finance public works, and facilitated primary education. For practical as much as for ideological reasons, many of these policies bypassed peasants in the uplands. Agricultural modernization, for example, meant shifting production to the plains and away from the thin, erosive soils of the mountains. The plains produced healthier livestock as well; animals there did not grow weak from six months of sequestration in crowded stables, nor tough from months of summer migrations—distinctions of growing importance to urban consumers with more money to spend on food.

For the nineteenth-century urban elite, highlanders themselves were unfit; even recognition of the historically high rates of literacy in the Alps could not dispel images of undersized, prematurely aged, and sometimes cretinous peasants. Most important in the present context, foresters named alpine peasants the primary, if not the only, agents of deforestation. Although it employed some peasants in restoration, the administration did not conceive the regreening of the mountains in their interest, and some foresters openly hoped that reforestation would push peasants off the land. Alpine people did emigrate for many reasons and even inaugurated the nineteenth-century depopulation of rural France. Those who remained became ever more archaic in outsiders' eyes.

Foresters treated the mountains, inhabited for millennia, as ideal, "empty" terrains of experimentation. Clearly the imaginative work this required surpassed that of American explorers, migrants, and bureaucrats on the western frontier, who confronted more lightly populated mountains whose native inhabitants they had never assumed to be part of the polity. To be sure, notions of the idealized, de-peopled mountain were more developed among professors of forestry and makers of policy than among foresters on the ground. Wherever imagined landscapes confronted alpine realities, however, conflict marked the relations between foresters and peasants.

Antagonisms were neither absolute nor permanent. The evidence in this book shows that some representatives of the state did not always play by the rules written by other representatives and that peasants often appropriated the state's language and at times sought their own integration with official structures. It is inaccurate to view unrelieved domination as the primary effect of state policy—perhaps especially in remote alpine borderlands where official power was inevitably stretched thin. Instead, the story yields a less dramatic interplay of forces; to borrow James Lehning's formulation, this was a "process of occasional conformity, occasional resistance, but always negotiation."[11] Such a perspective changes our way of viewing the dynamics of contestation, though not its reality. We gain a far more nuanced understanding of goals, strategies, and outcomes attached to specific struggles.

At its core, the conflict was over the values ascribed to the land of alpine France: abstract, interchangeable space for many professional foresters, specific, meaning-laden places for rural communities. This study is about the politics of this long-term conflict over values. The historiography of rural politics in France points, as a whole, to the transformation of political mentalities from "local" to "national" priorities; most studies have, in one way or another, tried to locate the precise timing and mechanisms of this change. As Maurice Agulhon's essays suggest, the coming of modern politics in the countryside has meant integration with the nation at large, the development of wide conceptual horizons, and the intellectual linking of realities in the village to national currents of thought and action.[12] The achievement of political consciousness has often been an assumed element of modernization, along with certain changes in economy and culture.

Many historians of rural France have argued that, given the sources of modern cultural and economic change, politics too flowed historically from an urban bourgeois setting to a rural peasant one. This "diffusion" model has come under attack in more recent writing, however, for the basic reason that it denies rural people autonomy of mind. Peter McPhee has, for example, sought to place "the rural inhabitants of mid-nineteenth-century France at centre stage" by writing from the premise that rural people could take political initiatives and discriminate among political choices.[13] Moreover, he uncovers four critically weak assumptions underlying the diffusion model: rural people were "stable, unchanging, and immobile"; they lacked any experience with politics prior to 1848, the first year that universal male suffrage was practiced in France; the flow of ideas is unilinear; and the rural context is fundamentally irrelevant. Although these notions have unfortunately framed much of the discussion, McPhee has gone far to prove them untenable.[14]

This book takes issue with a related and prevalent assumption that defines modern politics as the jockeying for representation through an electoral process originating outside the village community. Consequently, the absence of electoral politics can signal only archaism. A more useful definition of politics would include the mobilization of opinions, talents, and strategies in the interest of safeguarding local resources and values. This construction points to the role of locale in collective action: aspects of identity that derive from a sense of place call for profoundly local politics when that identity is threatened. Kent Ryden aptly connects identity with place: "The depth that characterizes a place is human as well as physical and sensory, a thick layer of history, memory, association, and attachment that builds up in a location as a result of our experiences in it."[15] It is not surprising that, invested in so heavily, places can be so ardently defended, and have been in the past. In any case, it is not clear that the

Map 1. Department of Ariège

Eric Leclerc, professor of Geography, University of Rouen.

politics of place has evolved into a thoroughly "modern" form, in the conventional sense; even the advent of national peasant and green parties is no guarantee of its transformation, for mobilization around local issues is typical of both.

The local reference of this book lies specifically in two departments, Ariège in the central Pyrenees and Savoie in the northern Alps (see maps 1 and 2). These departments anchor this study of alpine restoration in its broad strokes; French departments are arguably too large, however, to be named "places" in

Map 2. Department of Savoie

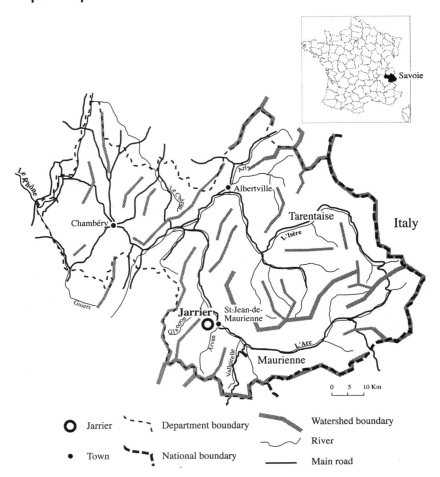

Eric Leclerc, professor of Geography, University of Rouen.

the sense evoked above. The defense of place will be explored through case studies of villages in each department. To begin with the larger scale, Ariège and Savoie suggest bases for comparison that illuminate the range of issues that confronted foresters and peasants in modern France.

MOUNTAINS, FORESTS, COMMUNITIES

Ariège and Savoie are often called *départements forestiers*. With a 39 percent rate of forestation in Ariège and nearly 29 percent in Savoie, they currently rank among the most heavily wooded departments in France, a country whose metropolitan territory consists of about 25 percent forest. Precise definitions qualify the picture suggested in these figures: the French National Forest Office defines forests as areas in which trees occupy at least 10 percent of the surface area, or approximately five hundred saplings per hectare; this is a much broader definition than the international norm for dense forests—a 20 percent ligneous cover—attesting to the extent of sparse woodland in France.[16] While the rates of forest cover increased in these two departments during the nineteenth century, foresters never held Ariège or Savoie to be as ravaged as Provence or the southern Alps.[17] The problems of torrential streams in Savoie and galloping rivers in Ariège, exacerbated by apparently dwindling forests, did not measure up to the critical state of the erosive southern Alps or to certain parts of Hautes-Pyrénées that threatened to collapse onto popular spas. Shared climatic characteristics, described below, assure rapid forest growth in both departments, though more so in Ariège. The historian of Savoie André Palluel-Guillard and the historical geographer of Ariège Michel Chevalier have come to the same conclusion with respect to the "deforestation hypothesis": forests had become profoundly degraded by the nineteenth century but far from denuded.[18] In light of contemporary discussions of deforestation, we could say that degradation had not disrupted the conditions for forest growth.

Nineteenth-century foresters rarely made such distinctions, often interchanging the terms *degradation* and *deforestation* (*déboisement,* more rarely *déforestation*) when referring to forests throughout alpine France, Ariège and Savoie included. Relegated to secondary importance as less deforested areas, these two departments put the state's foresters in the position of having to justify more rigorously the sort of ecological intervention that they deemed imperative for the southern Alps. Ecology in Ariège and Savoie complicated the debate over restoration and forced its principles to the fore.

Inseparable from official perceptions of many alpine forests was the "problem" of pastoralism; that both departments were *pastoraux* as well as *forestiers* explains their inclusion in this book as well as the exclusion of a department from the Massif Central. In that broad region, Third Republic foresters focused their work on the Cévennes, where subsistence had been more purely forest-based than pastoral. Cévenol peasants had, over time, transformed their chestnut forests into less dense orchards and harvested the fruit for human consumption; indeed, the extension of these orchards jeopardized the quality of pasture. This phenomenon reached its height in the early 1800s, but it was not until a full century had passed that soil degradation caused by the thinning of the chestnut forests reached a critical point. Thus, for reasons of both human ecology and chronology, the inclusion of a department such as Lozère would make for a very different, though perhaps no less valid, comparison.[19]

If Ariège and Savoie present similar uses of the forest in a pastoral economy, they are also distinct from each other. Ariège had a reputation loathsome to foresters, for its alpine inhabitants had proved themselves willing to act collectively when the state threatened access to "their" forests. This history is the subject of Chapter 1. In official eyes, Ariégeois peasants treated their woods with disrespect; foresters saw chaotic practices everywhere as well as the alarming indifference of shepherds to the destructive presence of livestock in the forests. Although the notoriety of Ariège was to shape foresters' approaches to restoration, a long history of conflict also shaped their reception in Ariégeois communities.

Savoie, on the other hand, presented foresters with a vast terra incognita owing to its belated annexation to France in 1860. Invaded in September 1792 and soon named the department of Mont-Blanc, the entire duchy of Savoie had participated in the Revolution and remained part of French territory until 1814, when King Victor-Emmanuel I of Piedmont-Sardinia reclaimed it. The French cultural heritage of Savoie argued well for reincorporation, though the annexation constituted a diplomatic swap resulting from French military involvement in the unification of Italy. Nonetheless, Savoie represented a welcome challenge for foresters, who acquired significant jurisdiction over it and who were among the first French officials to open offices in the new territory. From surveying to reforesting, foresters plied their techniques while rediscovering the environment of the northern Alps, little concerned for the opinions or objections of Savoyards.

Paradoxically, geography allowed Savoie a broader opening onto France than it did Ariège; geography reinforced the strategic importance of Savoie and, thanks as well to the nineteenth- and twentieth-century vogue for outdoor recreation, familiarized French people with it long before tourism became critical to the economy of Ariège. This essential basis of comparison calls for a geographical sketch of each department.

Situated just east of the central point of the Pyrenees, Ariège is a famously cobbled department: dividing geographically into the Lauragais plain in the north and the mountains in the south, it also contains an east-west cultural rift, straddling the historically and culturally distinct regions of Languedoc and Gascony. In social and economic terms, the lowland-upland contrast has been the more enduring. One can imagine the tilt of the department by drawing a line on a topographical map from Lézat-sur-Lèze, the northernmost commune in Ariège, to the Pic d'Estats, almost due south of Lézat on the Spanish border: the line would reveal a rise in elevation of nearly three thousand meters over only seventy kilometers. But such simple geometry obscures the fact that very few communes in Ariège boast elevations of more than one thousand meters; it also glosses over the geographical features of Ariège that set this part of the Pyrenees off from the rest.

The Pyrenees, whose central range boasts passes nearly as high as its summits, constitute France's most formidable border. Within this massive barrier formed of schist and gneiss, sandstone and limestone, and granite blocks, Ariège happens to host a particularly complex portion of the Pyrenean topography. Parallel to the central, or axial, zone is a lower series of parallel formations known as the north-Pyrenean range. Its peaks fall between two thousand and twenty-five hundred meters and form a broad barrier in the middle of the department; the central part, known as the massif de l'Arize, separates the prefecture, Foix, from the subprefecture of Saint-Girons. To the north of Foix lies a wide zone called the pre-Pyrenees (named to correspond to the pre-Alps), where summits are less than one thousand meters. Stretching from the Garonne River to the Aude River, these hills detach the Lauragais plain from the mountains. These parallel ranges create a series of east-west valleys unique to Ariège, differing from the transverse valleys that drain the Pyrenees further to the west. Although these valleys may have facilitated east-west communication on a local scale, only the pre-Pyrenean depression bordering Foix is broad enough to have allowed the construction of a major road and railroad. The multilayered Pyrenees of Ariège compartmentalized the department and tended to isolate its communities from the more populous plains of Languedoc.[20]

In addition to higher elevations and broader ranges, the Alps differ from the Pyrenees in their greater accessibility, and the Alpine arc has historically been a crossroad for communication in west-central Europe. The department of

Savoie forms the hub of the northern Alps, whose parallel ranges and valleys march from west to east with a clarity absent in the complex alignment of the southern Alps.

Five calcareous blocks form an avant-garde for the high mountains: these so-called pre-Alps consist of the Chablais-Giffre, the Bornes, the Bauges, the Chartreuse, and the Vercors. Though marked by cliffs hundreds of meters high, portal-like transverse valleys pierce each section of the range. The cities of Annecy, Chambéry, and Grenoble lie in three of these portals, or *cluses*. Behind them, a long depression interrupts the progression from pre-Alps to Alps, forming a continuous plain known from north to south as the Sallanches basin, the Val d'Arly, the Combe de Savoie, and the Grésivaudan. Formed of schists and other "black earth," this valley of unequal elevations is unique to the northern Alps and allowed an agrarian culture to take hold during the neolithic period.

The spinal column of the French Alps rises just to the east, extending from Mont Blanc through the Beaufortain and Belledonne ranges and south to the Romanche and upper Durance Rivers. Continuously high elevations and needlelike peaks bear witness to hard crystalline rock. An interalpine zone extends beyond the central range; this is an area of sustained high elevations but also of deep valleys and immense *alpages,* or summer pastures. Within this zone, the long Tarentaise and Maurienne Valleys, curving outward from each other and separated by the Vanoise range, constitute the heart of Savoie. These two sweeping valleys reflect glacial action in the Alps as a whole: massive glaciers formed in the central range, then punctured, deeply carved, and aerated the Alps, rendering them accessible. In this sense, the "high Alps" of Savoie are its valleys as well, long settled, open to the west, and, in the case of the Maurienne, industrialized since the late nineteenth century.[21]

Ariège and Savoie also have similarities: both departments include lowland and highland, and altitude as well as comparable positions within their respective mountain ranges have created corresponding patterns of forest. Subject to both Mediterranean and Atlantic fronts, Ariège receives heavy precipitation, especially the western part of the department known as the Couserans. Similarly, the Alps create a convergence zone between Atlantic, Mediterranean, and continental weather patterns. Overall, however, climate is mild in both departments given average altitudes. In Ariège, warm, dry winds from the southeast ease temperatures in the winter, and the absence of true glaciers allows relatively mild temperatures in the high Pyrenees.[22] The pre-Alps and central range of Savoie absorb thorough soakings in the milder months and heavy snows in winter, but the interalpine zone, by contrast, is relatively sheltered and remains considerably drier throughout the year.

From one zone to the next in both Ariège and Savoie, the forest changes according to variations in relief, altitude, and climate. Deciduous trees dominate in the lowlands and montane zones, mix with conifers up to subalpine levels, and then give way entirely to fir, pine, and larch. Above the forest lie broad alpine pastures—the alpages of the Alps and the *estives* of the Pyrenees, covered with grasses, gentians, asphodels, and other plants in the summer.[23]

The somewhat wetter climate of Ariège provides ideal conditions for the growth of deciduous trees, which make up 85 percent of the department's forest cover. Beech is the dominant species, thriving up to 1,700 meters in most places south of the oak-covered pre-Pyrenees. In much of Ariège, however, beech mixes in a patchwork with conifers. Nearly a quarter of the coniferous content in Ariège derives from nineteenth-century reforestation with nonnative species: spruce, Silvester pine, Austrian pine, and larch, to name a few. The roughly sixteen thousand hectares of solid fir stands grow primarily in the upper Ariège and Quérigut Valleys, yielding, at around three thousand meters, to the hardier *pin à crochets* (*Pinus montana*).[24]

In Savoie, the dense forests of the rainy pre-Alps thin out in stages to become the sparser forests of the drier interalpine zone. Oak dominates in the lower areas, up to six hundred meters on slopes with northern exposures. Ascending from montane levels in the central range, the forest begins with beech and ends, passing through a mixed zone, with stands of fir and spruce. In the interalpine zone these species share the terrain with varieties of pine. At the subalpine level spruce gives way to *Pinus montana* in the external zone and to Cembra pine with larch in the internal zone. Although the forests of Savoie meet the national average for surface area, covering 151,800 hectares, more than a quarter of the department, Savoie and Haute-Savoie, are home to an extraordinary floristic richness that overshadows the mere quantity of forest cover: between the two departments one can find approximately 2,080 species of plants, or half the flora of France.[25]

Geography, climate, and vegetation in the uplands framed the possibilities for human settlement. Alpine communities worked with the resources and limitations of field, forest, and pasture to forge an agro-sylvo-pastoral economy. This trio of interpenetrating ecosystems ran the gamut from wild to domesticated. The forest, harboring a greater diversity of plants and constituting the primary alpine habitat for animals, was more wild than the field; pastures lay somewhere in between. But alpine communities integrated the three into a working economy, transforming them into a rural space in conjunction with the forces of relief, climate, soil, and water.[26]

Central to rural space was the community. Ariège hosted two of the three dominant settlement patterns in France—agglomerated villages and dispersed hamlets, with very few isolated farms. As in other districts of the Mediterranean Pyrenees, clustered villages lay in the uplands, though more markedly in the Ariège River corridor than in the Couserans. Dispersed hamlets characterized the pre-Pyrenees and the middling altitudes, such as the Massat Valley, but also, exceptionally, the high-altitude Salat basin between the western *pays* of Castillonnais and the central Vicdessos. Upland villages, corresponding to more ancient settlement, tended to contain large unenclosed commons, whereas hedge-enclosed prairies surrounded the dispersed settlements and reflected individual clearings in the Middle Ages and later. Until the last few decades of the Old Regime, roughly twenty-four enormous "valley communities"—areas grouping anywhere from two to thirty villages, with or without hamlets— dominated most of the uplands and some of central Ariège. The coherence of valley communities derived from use rights to forest and pasture enjoyed by all inhabitants of the valley. The communities became subject to partition after the mid-eighteenth century, owing to immemorial antagonisms between villages and to class hatreds; peasants in outlying hamlets, for example, clamored for separation from the *messieurs* in the central *bourg*. Some valley communities did survive, notably in districts of dispersed habitat.[27]

Villages and hamlets also characterized human geography in Savoie, in contrast to the high proportion of isolated farms in the Germanic Alps. Most single villages had outlying hamlets; even within geographical unities such as the Maurienne, only a few self-contained villages lie at the uppermost end of the valley. In both Ariège and Savoie, security from avalanches played an important role in determining villages' sites and shapes; whether drawn out along a single road, grouped around a church or square, or perched on a slope, villages and hamlets grew out of complex natural, cultural, and historical circumstances.[28]

Surrounding villages and hamlets, fields, forests, and pastures constituted the productive spaces in most of the western European ecological zone, but their unique configuration in the mountains derived fundamentally from the challenges of farming on slopes. Thin, rocky soils given to erosion required heavy fertilization—the first justification of alpine pastoralism. Too poor and subject to impossibly short growing seasons, soils at higher elevations could still support trees, their understory, and the many edible and nonedible plants of open areas. High-elevation agriculture was far from negligible: in Ariège, productivity per hectare in alpine cantons outstripped that of lowland cantons, since peasants in the uplands tended to restrict crops to the choicest parcels and cultivate them intensively. Harvests remained modest but, owing primarily to greater use of animal dung, made gains in the nineteenth century: by the early Second Empire, peasants in the alpine cantons of Ariège had doubled wheat production from six hectoliters per hectare in 1812 to twelve hectoliters. An agricultural survey undertaken in Savoie in 1866 reported the surprisingly high figures of sixteen hectoliters of wheat and even higher figures for rye, oats, and barley. These latter grains, all hardier than wheat, were cultivated in both departments through mid-century. Peasants began to be persuaded of the potato's agricultural and caloric merits in the early nineteenth century in Ariège and somewhat later in Savoie, where corn also competed with the traditional grains.[29]

In the zones lying above cultivated areas, the "right" proportion of forest to pasture, as well as their location with respect to each other, were subjects of geographical debate in the nineteenth and twentieth centuries. Many nineteenth-century foresters viewed alpine pastures as deforested areas whose proper destiny was to "return" to a forested state. But peasants did not experience forests and pastures as qualitatively opposed spaces: harboring many resources, alpine forests gave rise to multiple uses and overlapping interests. Because of their floristic diversity, forests articulated the many elements of an agro-sylvo-pastoral economy. An image of perfect equilibrium, however, would be false: though an essential provider of nutrients, shade, and water for livestock, which in turn produced vital fertilizer for fields, the forest also threatened agriculture by encroaching and had to be burnt back.[30]

Alpine peasants used many forest resources for domestic purposes rather than commercial gain. Sizeable quantities of firewood topped the list, given the rigors of winter and the requirements of cheese-making in the summer. Wood composed the primary building material in upland areas, where climate as well as fire necessitated frequent repairs. The forests supplied medicine chests and additional sources of food, not to mention trees and woody plants that furnished particular woods for tools and domestic implements.

Forests functioned crucially in pastoralism as well, and more so in Ariège than in Savoie. The forester Etienne Dralet described Pyrenean forests dense with livestock in the early nineteenth century; many commentators recognized their role as linchpin in the pastoral economy. In order to limit the duration of winter stabling, shepherds used forests as intermediary pastures, protecting animals from exposure on the high pastures during inclement moments of autumn and spring. Rarely far from high pasture in Ariège, swatches of forest provided respite from heat and summer storms during pasturing season as well. The typically sparse forests allowed enough light to promote the growth of edible grasses.[31]

Until the nineteenth century, Ariégeois and Savoyard peasants enjoyed extensive access to forests, despite contrasting property regimes. In France as a whole, private ownership accounts for two-thirds of all forested areas, whereas only about one-third of the forest is in private hands in Ariège and Savoie. The latter department was a stronghold of communal property; up to 73 percent of forest belonged to communes in the duchy's alpine zone in 1738, according to the Sardinian cadastre; the proportion of communal land under the forest regime in Savoie was 58 percent in 1912.[32] Communes, then, determined access to the forests, along with the occasional, and sporadically enforced, regulation emanating from the Sardinian capital of Turin.

A deeper imprint of feudalism in Ariège had resulted in a far greater proportion of seigneurial property, followed by bourgeois acquisition of much of it after the Revolution; not until the late nineteenth century did falling land prices allow peasants to buy parcels of the great domains. The largest single proprietor by far was the state, which in 1876 owned 48 percent of the Ariégeois forest.[33] Yet hardly a forest in Ariège remained untouched by use rights. Though the term can apply to rights in forests under any property regime, use rights touched mostly the seigneurial and state forests of Ariège.

Jurists separate use rights into two categories—"forest" rights and "rural" rights. The former include gathering firewood and wood for construction and repairs, and pasturing animals in the forest, whereas the latter apply exclusively to pasturing rights in nonforested areas, namely, the right to graze on fallow or harvested land, or *vaine pâture*. Peasants regarded their rights as a single and coherent set, and their invocations of "immemorial rights" had concrete meaning: use rights had in many cases existed de facto since Carolingian times and become codified beginning in the thirteenth century. These medieval charters, which "granted" rights over large territories to one or more village communities, structured popular memory for centuries and cemented an identity between community and place. Although subject to regulation by the municipality, use rights helped ensure social and biological reproduction while infusing the notion of property with a meaning akin to possession, before the rigid separation of the two terms under the Civil Code.[34]

In high pasturing season, peasants grazed their livestock mostly on nonforested terrain; this, again, was more the case in Savoie, where peasants had long preferred to cut and burn forest to extend their grassy areas rather than pasture their animals in the forest.[35] Despite the crucial place of forests and the human energy monopolized by alpine agriculture, pastoralism in the Alps and the Pyrenees not only perpetuated agriculture but also provided the chief link to local and regional markets via annual livestock fairs and the production of butter and cheese for sale. Peasants devoted more space to pasturing than to farming, and this spatial preponderance deeply colored images of alpine ways of life for lowland consumption and critique.

In the spectrum of ways to raise domesticated animals, pastoralism differs, first, from sedentary modes, which require intensively irrigated pastures used year-round and proximity to villages. Second, it differs from nomadism—the migrations of entire human groups with their animals over large but well-defined territories—as well as from transhumance—the long-distance migration of large herds along with shepherds between summer and winter pastures, for example, between Provence and the southern Alps. Pastoralism involves migration to and from summer pastures, led by family members or by shepherds, but the migration takes place within a region or even within the space of a single commune. This is especially true of Savoie, where alpine communes, some of the largest in France, tend to incorporate secondary valleys and stretch to the summits.[36] Unlike transhumants, animals raised in a properly pastoral system spend the winter in stables. Although transhumance certainly touched economic life in both Ariège and Savoie, it declined rapidly during the nineteenth century and implicated fewer members of village communities than pastoralism itself.

The centrality of pastoralism is revealed in regional dialects. Throughout the French Alps, local usage defined *montagne,* synonymous with *alpe,* as a high-altitude pasture; thus *mountain* was coequal with its primary function.[37] The words *pasquiers, pla, calms,* and *estiba* commonly designated high pastures in the Pyrenees, yet *montagne* was not unknown, as a forest inspector noted of the Massat Valley in the 1840s: "what in the local speech they call 'mountains' is as follows: Massat, Ercé, Aulus, etc., possess on the sides of the great ridge and above their forests considerable stretches of uncultivated land which serve to pasture their numerous flocks." The inspector also remarked that the rigorous climate might make reforestation of these areas very difficult, and the inhabitants' opposition could undo it.[38] Though they might be fiercely defended, the high pastures remained tenuous, impermanent agro-ecological entities. They were, in effect, always works in progress. Peasants in the Pyrenees recreated their high pastures by burning them annually; areas whose dominant vegetation consists of tough, inedible plants—ferns, heather, broom, and gorse, to name a few—required artificial maintenance. Fire, the most effective method, absorbed the least labor in the task of reviving grasses for livestock's consumption during the spring and summer.[39] Savoyard peasants, for their part, burned the edges of their ever-creeping forest.

Pastoralism existed in hundreds of forms in alpine France, forms differing according to ownership of pastoral lands, management of the flocks, species and varieties of livestock raised, and rhythms of seasonal migration. A diversity of pastoral systems existed in both Ariège and Savoie, but, for the sake of clarity, they can be broken into a few broad contrasts within each department.[40] In the upper Ariège River corridor, communes organized summer pasturing, whereas associations of livestock owners, usually several per commune, regulated pasturing in the Couserans. Exceptionally, peasants in the area around the large commune of Auzat, located in the upper Vicdessos basin, had created a privatized pastoral system by gradually transmuting use rights into property rights. In the lowlands of Ariège, sedentary modes structured the raising of livestock. Hybrids of all these systems had a place in Ariège, including the unique practices found in the Massat Valley, discussed in greater detail in Chapter 4.

Throughout the department, sheep and cows shared the pastures. Sheep dominated in the upper valleys, outnumbering cattle at the end of the eighteenth century by five to one; even in areas of high dairy production, such as the Massat Valley, sheep enjoyed a three-to-one advantage over cows. Differences in breeds of livestock reflected the cultural contrasts between the western and eastern halves of the department, but all major varieties of cattle were small, rustic animals bred for work.[41] Livestock played a significant role in local subsistence, with few Ariégeois cheeses enjoying the wide reputation of a Savoyard *tomme* or *gruyère*.

The green northern Alps earned the epithet *montagnes à vaches,* "cow mountains," in opposition to the drier *montagnes à moutons,* "sheep mountains," of the south. Yet the contrast between cattle- and sheep-producing regions lay within Savoie, coinciding in many cases with a difference in pastoral management. Predominating in the pre-alpine Chartreuse, the central Beaufort and Belledonne ranges, and the interalpine Tarentaise Valley was a system known as the *grande montagne,* in which several families grouped their livestock, mostly milk cows, under the management of cooperatives that hired shepherds or individual entrepreneurs; in either case, communes generally owned the pastoral lands. In the interalpine Maurienne, the *petite montagne* separated livestock, mostly sheep, by family, leaving young family members to care for them. This system, which necessitated a greater human population on the summer pastures than did the more collective grande montagne, also played itself out on communally owned pastures. Both systems demanded more or less complex migrations before, during, and after the pasturing season.[42]

To capture alpine peasants' sense of place and its various boundaries, a loose analogy might be drawn between the imbrication of forest and pasture, more characteristic of Ariège than of Savoie, and the overlapping of property and use. The dominance of use rights in Ariège and the contrasting pastoral systems involving communal property in Savoie exemplify this overlapping and point to the primordial role of possession. Perhaps no one grasped the relations between environment, possession, and property better than a nineteenth-century historian of Ax-les-Thermes (Ariège), H. Castillon, who can be forgiven a bit of exaggeration:

> For the highlander, who lives far from all established government, in the liberty of primitive nature, the wood of these forests is, like the grass of the pastures . . . , the property of whoever comes to take it. There is something which speaks to him high in his heart: it is necessity. Nature caused him to be born in a district where work is insufficient to feed him, but where vast, uncultivable terrains offer him providential resources, and he concludes the right to profit from them. The only property he recognizes in these mountains is communal property, and that in itself is founded upon the extent of local needs and limited only by them.[43]

The seasonal nature of pastoralism reinforced a form of possession dictated by necessity: the geographer Vidal de la Blache wrote of pastoral possession as an activity, an annual ritual of reclaiming the summer pastures.[44]

This *longue-durée* history of peasants' access to forest and pasture set the stage for the reception of French foresters in the peripheral mountain ranges in the first half of the nineteenth century. Collective action to defend rights of access in 1830 and 1848 defined the moments of greatest intensity in the struggle for the forest. Beyond Chapter 1, this book covers the period that followed these high points of popular resistance. Chapter 2 treats the Second Empire's approach to reforestation and its reception in both Ariège and Savoie. Chapters 3 and 4 present case studies drawn from within each department in the context of alpine restoration under Third Republic governments. In both cases, peasants responded to restoration in complex ways. Resistance was both overt and anonymous, collective though seemingly individual. It combined old tactics with new opportunities afforded by electoral politics, emigration, which left remaining villagers with more resources, and growing literacy. Chapters 5 and 6 alternate between national and departmental scales as they uncover continuities but also changes since the late nineteenth century in the arenas of legislation, ecology, and associational culture.

This is not, then, a simple tale of winners and losers in a conflict over nature. Over time, depopulation permitted forests to cover more of alpine France, rendering state-sponsored restoration less urgent. But in its heyday the politics of restoration was refracted through a prism of antithetical values, perceptions, and cultures. Remarkably, a few of the state's representatives "on the ground," namely foresters, allowed their own politics to become influenced by the particularities of locales. If, however, I have placed more emphasis on the actions and responses of peasants, it is because of a captivating artfulness in their defense of places.

Chapter One Forests, the State,

and Alpine Communes:

Authority and Conflict,

1669–1860

Our oaks no longer proffer oracles, and we no longer ask of them the sacred mistletoe; we must replace this cult by care; and whatever advantage one may previously have found in the respect that one had for forests, one can expect even more success from vigilance and economy.
—*M. Le Roy*

FROM POLICING TO PROPERTY

From the late eighteenth century through the first half of the nineteenth, the status of forests in France changed dramatically. Nowhere was the change more apparent than in alpine regions; no longer shunning the barely accessible backwaters with their threatening inhabitants, foresters began to think they could take the alpine forests in hand by formulating technical problems and setting out to solve them. Developments in law, administration, and scientific forestry all contributed to this impetus. The experience of revolution strengthened foresters' resolve and reaffirmed their assumptions about alpine populations. Conversely, peasants' experiences of revolution made them wary of state models. In tracing the background of foresters' schemes of alpine transformation, this chapter will discuss Ariège more than Savoie, the latter having been reincorporated into France only in 1860. It will focus most of all on the state: in the pursuit of longue-durée history, it is hard to find a more appropriate state structure than the Eaux et Forêts. A reasonable starting point is Louis XIV's Forest Ordinance of 1669, a harbinger of later change.

The ordinance itself had many precedents—eighteen recorded edicts pertaining to forests since 1215. Philippe-Auguste instituted the special jurisdiction of Eaux et Forêts in 1219; by 1346, a general staff of *maîtres et enquêteurs* assumed the authority that local bailiffs had enjoyed over royal forests. In the early sixteenth century Francis I issued many regulations pertaining to the conservation of royal, ecclesiastical, and even private forests; in 1537, for example, he prohibited sales of high forest without prior approval of a *parlement*. By Louis XIV's reign, four and a half centuries of sporadic attempts to decree the uses of the forest had left a voluminous, unwieldy record that stood in need of rationalization. In a standard account, the 1669 ordinance achieved this immense juridical task; it also linked jurisdiction with administration, thereby serving as a key model for the Forest Code of 1827.[1]

Michel Devèze has called the edict, prepared under Colbert in the course of eight years, "essentially a police ordinance," and this is correct insofar as "police" is understood broadly as a claim to jurisdiction, which in the case of forests refers to the control of specific territories.[2] The ordinance presented panoramic claims: forests belonging to the monarchy, the church, communities, parishes, and individuals fell under its purview, as did navigable rivers and the practices of hunting and fishing anywhere in the realm. Both the civil and the criminal aspects of jurisdiction lay in the hands of the maîtrises, whose officers carried both judicial and administrative authority. The fourth part of the ordinance, relating to "police and conservation of forests, waters, and rivers," best reveals the document's judicial scope: among other things, it prohibited the sale of royal forests and banished wood-dependent industries such as tanning and shoe- and charcoal-making from all forests. Other parts of the ordinance were prescriptive, detailing the appropriate ways to conduct surveys, cuts, and auctions of wood. Some of the better-known clauses established the number of mature seed-bearing trees (*baliveaux*) that would be left to stand after a cut, a number that differed according to property regime; others sanctioned the traditional method of exploiting deciduous forests known as *tire-et-aire*—the division of a forest into a certain number of areas, cut annually and consecutively, a method based on the time needed for a forest's regeneration.[3]

Inevitably, questions concerning who could do what in the forests and what could be taken out of them implicated the status of use rights. In the two major categories of forest rights, pasturing and wood-gathering, the ordinance again made sweeping claims. It confirmed the principle of refusing new use rights in the royal forests (established in the thirteenth century) and suppressed existing rights to firewood in return for indemnities—given only if possession of such rights could be proved to have existed since at least 1560. Regarding forests belonging to communities and parishes, the ordinance allowed partition between a seigneur and a community if the latter possessed the forest by virtue of the seigneur's gratuitous concession; this mechanism, called *tiercement* (also *triage;* one-third to the seigneur, two-thirds to the community) foreshadowed *cantonnement,* the widely practiced nineteenth-century method of clearly demarcating property bereft of use rights. Finally, Colbert's redactors took the bold step of forbidding the pasturing of sheep and goats in all forests, and pasturing of cattle and pigs was to be tightly regulated.[4]

The Ordinance of 1669 far overstepped the limits of the possible. In defining a global jurisdiction over French forests, it had neglected the monarchy's escalating needs for revenue as well as the entrenchment of local custom. For example, the plan to reimburse holders of newly banned use rights foundered on the treasury's financial straits at the end of Louis XIV's reign; throughout the eighteenth century the monarchy even continued to sell its forests in order to raise money, despite the emphatic prohibition of royal alienations in Colbert's ordinance. Special commissioners, hired to verify titles to use rights, effectively secured the rights of those who managed to get their names on the proper lists. Most famously, the forester Louis de Froidour, who carried the grand title of *Commissaire Général Réformateur* for the grande maîtrise of Toulouse, did not enforce the ordinance in the Pyrenees following his observation that severe penury necessitated use rights in the mountains. Until 1684, Froidour issued reforms that maintained the use rights of Pyrenean communities; confirmed by the Conseil d'Etat, the derogations applied to both seigneurial and royal forests.[5]

Froidour had also noted the blurred distinctions between use rights and property in the Pyrenees: inhabitants seemed to enjoy rights to the forest "as masters," an observation based as much on the confusion inherent in written titles as on the practices of the people themselves.[6] Beyond its failure to establish the state's jurisdiction in the mountains, the Ordinance of 1669 did not effectively substitute a single concept of jurisdiction for these overlapping meanings. After more than a century of intense pressures on the forests paralleled by growing scientific interest in them, Revolutionary legislators again confronted the problem of communities' jurisdiction and its merely theoretical basis in property. But first came reform at the top.

By the end of 1790, the Constituent Assembly (1789–91) had terminated the criminal jurisdiction of the Eaux et Forêts, abolishing the maîtrises and assigning the prosecution of forest crimes to normal district courts. The assembly toyed with the idea of local control over all forests but in the context of vast new acquisitions of forested lands: the nationalization of ecclesiastical forests in 1790 added close to 800,000 hectares to the state's domain. In 1793 the National Convention (1792–95) confiscated an additional 640,000 hectares of forest from émigrés. Two crucial laws of 1790 had already restricted the alienation of state forests. Although somewhat loosened under the Directory (1795–99), and decried throughout the Revolution by would-be purchasers, the laws placed state forests in a separate category from other nationalized property, effectively preventing their privatization. As early as 1791, the assembly dropped the notion of local management by formally integrating forests confiscated from the church into the newly defined realm of the state's *régime forestier.* The Conservation Générale des Forêts also came into being; though short-lived, it served as the model for the forest service of the nineteenth century. Far from constituting a break with the Colbertian system, the reforms of the Revolution created an enlarged state domain under even firmer jurisdiction.[7]

Still, the state did not own all public forests, for communes had gained recognition of their property rights. They had won significant protections for collective rights in the Rural Code of 1791 and recognition of property by the law of 28 August–14 September 1792. This measure gave legal favor to communes rather than seigneurs in questions of ownership of common lands, adopting as national principle the legal tradition of southern France—*nul seigneur sans titre,* no lord without title. The victory for communes came in the wake of intense debates over the origins of communal property: one theory posited the feudal origins of use rights, allegedly granted by the nobility in the interests of keeping land productive and retaining labor; another put forth the idea of "native property," a communal patrimony that had preceded and been degraded by use rights. What is most clear from these debates is that national legislators were moving toward rigid distinctions between use rights and property rights, a distinction alien to the people of alpine France.[8]

In the process of revolution, however, communes appropriated vast tracts of land, in particular state forests, rationalizing these acquisitions through the existence of use rights. Though the movement paralleled the many individual appropriations that were part of the great revolutionary property shuffle, the state began to retaliate under Bonaparte in Year Nine, winning back forested lands in countless legal operations. In Ariège and Haute-Garonne alone, the state stripped communes of 50,862 hectares of forest, cementing a frustration in many districts that would be recalled in the nineteenth century. Communal forests, that is, those recognized by the state, did largely remain intact, for they had been exempt from the decree of 10 June 1793 that allowed partition of the commons at the request of one-third of a commune's inhabitants. In any case, partitioning the commons, rarely hailed with enthusiasm outside the Paris basin and the eastern plains, was especially ill-viewed in alpine areas dependent on extensive grazing lands.[9]

The Revolution changed the status of forests in another important way besides legal reforms of property codes. Leaving thick traces in popular and official memory, the Revolution bequeathed an image of "devastation" to the nineteenth century: peasants had ravaged the forests as they had châteaux, for state control of forests had long symbolized Old Regime authority in general. The highly evocative term *devastation* appeared in many official reports from the period as a code word for several different activities. The most common forest crime of the Revolution was stealing wood, referred to as "pillage," an act hardly unknown in rural France but rendered thoroughly banal by the events of 1789 and after. Second, peasants took to pasturing their sheep in the younger stands of forest officially off limits to them. But most worrisome to authorities was the extension of *défrichement,* clearing the forest for agricultural purposes, much of which took place on fragile mountain slopes. These clearings often followed the usurpation of property, and they had been effectively decriminalized by a reform of September 1791 that legalized the clearing of privately owned woods.[10]

Devastation was limited largely to the Midi and to the years 1789–90, the winters of 1794 and 1795, and the end of the Directory—times of acute political tension and subsistence pressures.[11] But many contemporaries did not know of or did not heed these specificities in time and place, and *devastation* became coequal with *Revolution* in the administrative analysis of rural, especially alpine, France. What is more, the legacy of "devastation" had far-reaching consequences for nineteenth-century forestry. In the conservative Administration des Forêts of the mid-nineteenth century, reforestation found its historical justification in deforestation, whose origins foresters attributed time and again to the Revolution, occasionally including the last few decades of the Old Regime. It is one thing to evoke the great clearings of the late Middle Ages, which Marc Bloch established as the high years of forest clearance in France, or to emphasize the accelerating degradation of forests during the whole eighteenth century, constantly at the mercy of an expanding royal navy, flagrant sales of royal forests, growing cities built of wood, and famines and other population pressures. But this longue-durée history of the forest has become conventional only in the twentieth century; many foresters and politicians in the nineteenth took a markedly short-term view, one fraught with consequences for forests and peasants alike.[12]

The Revolution was thus two-sided in its effects on the forest. A dark legacy of destruction with impunity paralleled an enlightened legacy of privileging property and enacting reform. In that respect, the Revolution accomplished what the Ordinance of 1669 had stood for in theory—jurisdictional clarity. Now state, communal, and private property would structure the uses of the forest[13] Yet in spite of its Old Regime taint, in spite of the abolition of the maîtrises and the practical work of "pillagers," the 1669 document was never abrogated. It remained the basis of forest law and the point of departure for its reform. The postrevolutionary imperative lay in correcting and filling gaps in Louis XIV's edict from the new, seemingly secure basis of property.

GERMAN SILVICULTURE

The gaps were actually more akin to a vacuum of authority; private property did not, in itself, compensate for the power invested in the Eaux et Forêts before the Revolution. Instead, the state's foresters began to elaborate a new system of referents for authority based on technical knowledge. Silviculture and *aménagement* had acquired sufficient prestige during the Revolution to provide those referents. Aménagement is quite close in meaning to "forest management," an aspect of forestry concerned with organizing a forest for a specific purpose, taking into consideration economic and financial factors. The defined purpose of a forest—firewood, lumber, or soil protection—helps determine the location, extent, and periodization of cuts. In American forestry, the two broad types of forest management are even-aged and uneven-aged, the creation, as the terms suggest, of large stands of homogeneously or heterogeneously aged trees.[14] The French term *aménagement* (which can be used in contexts other than forestry) strongly evokes the arrangement and transformation of space. Its etymology dictates the sense of exploiting for the needs of the *ménage*, or human household, and the term strongly suggests the importance of order, as well.[15]

Silviculture, on the other hand, means the "art and science of growing trees," and as such is a field of applied biology akin to agriculture and horticulture.[16] Whereas *aménagement* is a medieval term, figuring in the 1669 Ordinance in its present meaning, silviculture emerged as a science in the eighteenth century. In practice, of course, these two aspects of forestry have much to do with each other—foresters speak of adapting silvicultural systems to the needs of forest management—even though one aspect is more concerned with growing trees, the other with cutting them. Moreover, it is not clear that the two terms designated entirely separate concepts in eighteenth-century France, especially as the novelty of silviculture began to infuse old notions of aménagement.

Silviculture was to a large extent a German import. In both France and the German states, jurists had written tracts and treatises on forests since the sixteenth century; the Germans broke first from the juristic mode, gradually developing a vision of the forest defined by algebra and geometry and aimed at refining technique.[17] A century after Colbert's ordinance—which had said little about technique and entirely neglected questions relating to the growth of conifers—Frederic II created the first German forest academy, in Berlin. Arguably, practical silviculture already existed in France; earlier in the eighteenth century, the naturalists Réaumur and Buffon had published studies on the growth of forests in terms of volume, concepts translated into actual calculations of cubic meters of wood after the Revolution. But because of the schism between practice in the Eaux et Forêts and theoretical science, French ideas found their first audience in the German states.[18]

During the Revolution and First Empire in France, Prussian scientists wrote what are still considered the classic works of German forestry while founding schools of silviculture throughout the German states. By the early nineteenth century, the reigning principles of the German school comprised progressive conversion of low to high forest, planting conifers, and management based on calculations of surface area or of volume. These tenets pointed toward a single ideal: the creation of uniform forests, consisting of single species and identically aged trees.[19] Each of these concepts had been tested on the ground in France in one way or another, but in an atmosphere of empiricism, not through their scientific elaboration followed by dissemination to professionally trained foresters.

The Revolution allowed the reintroduction of this ensemble of principles to France, now in sophisticated, scientized form. With the invasion of the left bank of the Rhine in 1792 and its full occupation by the end of 1794, a generation of French foresters became exposed to German silviculture. Not only did the left bank, its territory 25 percent forest, become a showcase for Prussian methods, but a number of acclaimed German foresters also chose to serve the French state. Foresters such as H. von Cotta, Adam Dressler, Friedrich Ostler, and Albert von Schultz taught the trade to those who would attain powerful positions in the French administration; they also advocated the founding of a school of forestry in France. The Alsatians Bernard Lorentz and his son-in-law Adolphe Parade, both of whom became leaders of the nineteenth-century Administration des Forêts, and Jacques-Joseph Baudrillart, founder of the *Annales forestières*, sought to institutionalize the new silviculture and adapt it to the natural and political conditions of France.[20]

Hardly the reality in eighteenth-century Prussia, the homogeneous forest was even less of a reality in France. But the long-term impact of German methods and the powerful ideal of the rationalized, homogenous forest can hardly be overestimated, as James Scott has recently illustrated. Viewing, growing, and harvesting forests according to mathematical logic reinforced the state's old fiscal approach to forests by better assuring constant yields of timber. Thus forestry provides a keen example of how state-building and the "logic of commercial exploitation" developed together. Once science had honed techniques of measuring and assessing forests, then the scientized forest (single-species, even-aged) could be created, a space that would lend itself perfectly to the use of those very techniques—and to commodities, revenue, and surveillance. In parts of Germany this sort of forest, with its "radical simplicity" and consequent vulnerabilities to insects, diseases, and storm-felling, was created, and it was no place for peasants.[21]

Though the French fully adopted silviculture only under the Restoration, standard German methods remained among the common systems of French forest management into the twentieth century. One method, the calculation of allowable cuts based on surface area, shared a history with (or was derived from) the traditional French practice of tire-et-aire, but by the nineteenth century the prestige of German science was improving its reputation. By contrast, the vernacular practice of *jardinage* never received the imprimatur of German silviculture. Although another German method, calculating cuts on the basis of volume, gained a following among French foresters, the latter continued to couch debates over management in terms of a choice between the two older approaches. A brief foray into the French debate over tire-et-aire versus jardinage provides a further clue to the threat posed to customary uses of the forest.

Several accounts designate tire-et-aire as perhaps the oldest and simplest way of managing a forest.[22] To obtain the measure of an allowable yearly cut, the surface area of a forest is simply divided by the length of its revolution, or number of years needed to grow the species of tree (presumed to be only one) to a desired height and girth; a one-hundred-hectare forest allowed to grow for twenty-five years yields the "possibility" of four hectares per year. This portion is the *aire,* or area; the term *tire* refers to the practice of cutting adjacent parcels from one year to the next. Cutting, in this system, generally meant clear-cutting the aire, though some seed-bearing trees might be left to help regenerate the parcel. Thus, tire-et-aire lies in the category of even-aged management. Approved in royal edicts since the sixteenth century, this rational and geometric method of dividing up the forest remained the basis of official aménagement in the nineteenth.[23] By then, it had also received the sanction of German silviculture.

Jardinage, on the other hand, was a method that sprang from below. Long associated with forests subject to use rights and with coniferous forests in general, jardinage—"gardening"—meant culling a prescribed number of individual, fully mature trees throughout an entire forest. After a jardinage, a forest would look much the same as before, with nearly mature trees left to shade and protect younger ones. Peasants in both the Alps and the Pyrenees who pastured livestock in the forests relied on jardinage as a protective measure against their animals' teeth: if the whole area had to regenerate, animals would chew the saplings. We could call this uneven-aged management, or, as many contemporaries viewed it through the nineteenth century, a dangerous and disorderly approach. Authorities had a difficult time identifying illegal cutting in a forest subject to jardinage; at the very least, the method threatened jurisdictional boundaries. The "gardened" forest also created aesthetic disorder, to the point where some observers confused it with "devastation."[24]

Jardinage has a paradoxical history: though execrated in edict after edict, it became domesticated. Foresters had long observed that tire-et-aire could be disastrous when applied to the coniferous forests of the mountains, given the erosion and degradation that resulted from the presence of sizeable bare areas. Huffel believed that jardinage had been practiced and officially approved in the Vosges as early as the fifteenth century. Froidour himself prescribed jardinage for the pine forests of the Pyrenees, and its sanctioned use spread to the Massif Central, namely the Cévennes, in the eighteenth century.[25] Royal foresters might adapt jardinage to their purposes, but it remained largely identified as a peasant practice until the early twentieth century. Etienne Dralet, Froidour's distant successor as chief forester for the Pyrenean region during the First Empire, inveighed against the peasants' use of "this disastrous jardinage." Peasants cut trees wastefully, slashing and discarding the lateral branches of young oaks until they reached the most vigorous one, taking out whole young pines to make a single *sabot:* referring to years of the Revolution during which Pyrenean communes had usurped state forests, Dralet wrote, "two pines were necessary to supply a man with shoes, six for the year, 2,000 for a village of a hundred families." For Dralet, quelling the "disorders" in the Pyrenees meant using all means from reason to armed force in order to wean peasants from their profligate uses of the forest; disorderly themselves, peasants invariably left devastated forests in their wake.[26]

In any case, German silviculture did not favor jardinage. Bernard Lorentz, the first director of the Ecole Nationale des Eaux et Forêts (see below), introduced a scientific variant of tire-et-aire from Germany called natural regeneration.[27] The adoption of a glorified tire-et-aire as silviculture sat well with the many foresters who, unfamiliar with alpine forests, had always looked askance at jardinage. As the prestige of German silviculture in France began to grow in the early nineteenth century, it became defined in opposition to peasants' uses of the forest. The Alsatian Philippe Hermann, future forest conservator of Colmar, had already explained the purpose of silviculture in 1790, which was to exploit woods not "'according to the interests of users [*usufruitiers*], but [according to] the possibility of reproduction from one revolution to the other.'"[28]

Silviculture, though enhanced by the general prestige of science as well as territorial conquests during the Revolution, could not come into its own without a corps of organized and trained practitioners. Napoleon Bonaparte created the Administration des Forêts in January 1801, the first of three steps toward national forestry achieved in the early nineteenth century, followed by a school of forestry and a new forest code. The revamped administration included structural elements from both the Old Regime corps and the Conservation Générale des Forêts of 1791, but only a symbolic shade of the Eaux et Forêts' legal jurisdiction remained: the right of foresters to stand next to the public prosecutor in correctional courts. But the reason for a new administration had much to do with jurisdiction in that the state had to establish its authority over the former ecclesiastical and seigneurial forests—almost a million hectares. Bonaparte also needed a corps of foresters to extract revenue from these lands; he linked the financing of several major institutions, including the Senate, to revenue from the state's forests, keeping his forest administration under the Ministry of Finance, where it remained until 1877. Above all, he needed a forest administration because he needed a navy, another Old Regime inheritance. A good sailing ship still required roughly six thousand oaks in the early nineteenth century, and the impact of revolutionary "devastation" had not been lost on the First Consul.[29]

At the top of the pyramidal hierarchy stood five general administrators, who oversaw a maximum of thirty conservators. The successors, in loose terms, of the Old Regime grands maîtres, the conservators were distributed in provincial posts where they managed from two to eight departments. Their major duty entailed negotiating between prefectorial and judicial authorities, and they had the last word on the size of annual cuts and lumber sales. Finally, each conservator also donned the hat of forest inspector in the districts that served as headquarters for his region. Most technical functions devolved upon two hundred inspectors assisted by three hundred subinspectors; many members of these ranks retained positions held under the Old Regime and the Revolution. Finally, approximately five hundred general guards took on the chief policing roles, while an enormous corps of eight thousand *gardes particuliers* saw to daily surveillance in the forests of the state.[30]

The Administration des Forêts instituted a system of promotion based on experience; it also retained a percentage of income for retirement pensions before the Ministry of Finance enacted a retirement system for all of its personnel. Despite the incipient meritocracy and social protection, the salary structure favored top administrators, who earned hefty salaries of ten thousand francs; this sum represented fifty times what the poorest-paid guards in the state forests made, a yearly income less than that of most urban workers.[31] Hierarchy was reinforced in another way: until the end of the nineteenth century, the Administration des Forêts cultivated multiple links with the army and based its uniforms, discipline, and mandatory *esprit de corps* on military traditions. During the Consulate and the Empire, the administration recruited its upper echelons largely from the ranks of Old Regime officers; after 1803 it drew many of its subaltern personnel from the ranks of wounded soldiers, whose reemployment became mandatory in 1811.[32] The evolving uniform of the state's foresters served the double purpose of providing visible distinctions among ranks and setting the forester of whatever status apart from the people he would encounter while on duty. Because all elements of the uniform had to be purchased by the employee, details in dress changed according to rank: the tight-fitting green suit and all its accoutrements were reserved for the elite. Yet even the incomplete uniform that guards could afford—a bandoleer slung across the torso, a cap, and good shoes (they were given muskets in the 1840s)—provided ample distinguishing signs.[33] At a glance, a forest guard would never be confused with a peasant (figure 1).

Figure 1. Officer of the Administration des Forêts in full uniform, 1885. Negative by Kuss. ADS.

The military recruitment of much of the corps collided with increasing technical demands on foresters. Influential agents in the upper ranks, many of whom received their training in the German states, bemoaned the fact that most of their inferiors did not possess the slightest knowledge of forestry. A new administrative structure had not magically produced qualified foresters, but the founding of France's first national forestry school in 1824 relieved many fears of structural incompetence. One of the youngest of the *grandes écoles*, yet the first established in a provincial city, the Ecole Nationale des Eaux et Forêts was located in Nancy, it has been argued, because of the city's proximity to German-speaking Europe and to the varied forests of eastern France. With the initial cost of tuition, room, and board fixed at twelve hundred francs per year for the two-year program, the school recruited its students from aristocratic and bourgeois backgrounds, by means of a national exam, for much of the century. Similar to those of the grandes écoles that preceded it, the school's founding charter defined its mandate as training the personnel of a national administration. The first three directors at Nancy, Alsatians imbued with the German science, resolved that silviculture would be the basis of this training. By 1837, Lorentz and his son-in-law Adolphe Parade, who directed Nancy from 1838 to 1864, had produced the first French textbook of forestry, *Cours élémentaire de culture des bois*.

Founded to teach silviculture, not policing, the "Ecole de Nancy" nevertheless reinforced the military ethos of the Forêts. Hardly fortuitous was the dispensation from military service that students at Nancy received in 1826. Required to board at the school beginning in 1839, students also wore uniforms and submitted to rituals of discipline and obedience. After the Franco-Prussian War, students not only received some military instruction at Nancy, but they also had to spend a year in an infantry regiment or battalion of riflemen after their two years of study. Less formally but just as crucially, students received instruction in an ethic: like their counterparts at military schools tutored in patriotism, the Nancéens were taught to "love the forest with passion," and the forest, after all, was a large part of the *patrie*.[34]

Both militarization and the very existence of Nancy bore heavily on the lowly forest guards, for these phenomena intensified rifts in the internal hierarchy. A graduate of Nancy could land a job as *garde général* or, at best, subinspector. Thousands of gardes particuliers continued to emanate largely from military ranks, even after the founding of three schools for forest guards in 1863. The unspoken similarity between the upper and lower echelons of foresters—military backgrounds in the latter, much quasi-military training among the former—did not prevent savage condescension on the part of the forestry elite.

Along with the countless guards of communally owned forests, who were not assimilated into Eaux et Forêts ranks until 1919 and depended for their meager salaries on municipal councils, the gardes particuliers of the state's forests became true outsiders: demeaned by their superiors for their ignorance of forestry, they were commonly hated throughout the countryside for resembling gendarmes and incarnating the state's jurisdiction over forests. Like peasants themselves, forest guards had to supplement their livelihoods with the forest's fruits. Authorized by the administration to keep two cows, gather a certain amount of wood, and cut grasses, they often competed for limited resources. Yet it was not this as much as their previous training in the arts of repression that assured their execration in rural France.[35]

THE FOREST CODE OF 1827

Within three years of the founding of Nancy, however, even the least paid forest guard could derive some status from enforcing the organic set of laws known as the *Code forestier* of 1827—the first significant revision of Colbert's ordinance. The new Forest Code became the linchpin in the reformed system of state forestry: it resolved the remaining jurisdictional confusion of the previous thirty-eight years and dealt with forest management in ways that reflected the growing influence of the Nancy school. Still, by rationalizing the criminal aspects of forest law, it echoed the Ordinance of 1669 and set the stage for a new era of contestation between the state and users of the forest.

Many of the code's 225 articles found precedents in the older document, yet M. de Martignac, Minister of State for Charles X and spokesperson for the code, accented its liberal, lenient, and fair qualities. Martignac deliberately placed the code in the line of legal reforms since the Revolution, proclaiming that "[t]he word 'arbitrary,' in effect, has been forever crossed out by our kings from French legislation."[36] For the corporal punishment, multiple rationales for incarceration, and heavy fines of the previous era, the new code substituted a system of far lower fines for most crimes committed in and against the forests. Leniency certainly described the code's prescriptions for private forests, too, in keeping with the protection given private property in Napoleon's Civil Code and with the political clout of the large owners of property who supported the regime of Charles X. Private owners could manage their forests as they wished, notwithstanding the single noteworthy restriction that forbade clear-cutting, for the subsequent twenty years; even this restriction excepted young forests, small forests, private gardens, and parks.

The spirit of liberalism did not extend to the articles pertaining to communal forests. In the context of communal property, the code achieved a striking union of the concepts of jurisdiction and management: as article 90 stated, "[There] shall be submitted to the forest regime . . . the low and high forests belonging to communes and public establishments, which will be recognized as liable to management or exploitation on a regular basis."[37] The phrase "liable to management" (*susceptible d'aménagement*) received varying interpretations in the nineteenth century, yet what is clear is the linking of a jurisdictional category—the forest regime—with management. To manage was also to control, after all, as would become more evident once the implications of silviculture began to play themselves out during the century. By extension, article 90 cast communal authorities as bad managers of their forests. One of the code's promoters clarified this assumption as follows: "The state is taking over control of communal woods only in order to assure their perpetuation via regular management. . . . [It is] impossible for *communalistes* to administer their woods by themselves and to assure proper surveillance."[38] The Forest Code thus defined communes as legal minors with respect to their forests, suggested that public interest was something other than communal interest, and partially undid the gains made during the Revolution toward the recognition of communal property.

In the communal forests "liable to management," the state established jurisdiction by giving foresters the right to mark trees and officiate at sales of wood. The state's heaviest imprint on communal forests bore upon pasturing: no longer would sheep or goats be tolerated in these forests, a measure that also harkened back to 1669. The center had in effect designated *pâturage* as a space, by definition outside the forest, erasing its vernacular meaning as the practice of pasturing animals in a variety of environments. By the law of 1827, only the Minister of Agriculture could allow exceptions to the rule. But the larger difference between the two codes lay in what followed: Pyrenean communities, for example, did not receive special derogations from the code of 1827 as they had from the Ordinance of 1669.[39]

The articles pertaining to communal forests unveil the elements of order and control that lay behind principles of management. In the early nineteenth century, however, the state first had to create jurisdiction over its own forests by clearly delimiting state property. In order to resolve the problem of superimposed uses by creating a neat fabric of juxtaposed properties, legislators had recourse to cantonnement, the legal means of converting use rights into property rights, a measure legislated in 1790 theoretically to protect communal property.

The Forest Code also allowed private and communal owners of forest to initiate the procedure, illustrating that cantonnement was more than an expedient
measure allowing the state to control its own forests.[40]

For cantonnement involved not only property lines: to reorganize a forest
through cantonnement meant, in fact, to rewrite its value in the language of
capitalism. As worked out in the years after 1827, the first step in any cantonnement involved calculating the "users' capital" (*capital usager*), that is, the
capitalized value of the use rights. Titles to use rights, by contrast, had never attached a monetary value to them; such a designation would have departed
from the tenet of perpetual rights freely granted. If a commune, for example,
possessed use rights to a given forest, the commune's annual needs for firewood
and lumber, figured in cubic meters, would be multiplied by the respective
market value of each kind of wood; this figure, in turn, would typically be
multiplied by twenty to obtain the capitalized value of the use rights. Similarly,
the capitalized value of the forest itself—now characterized by the "immobile
capital" of its land and the "mobile capital" of its trees—required calculation
in order to see how the value of the rights would map onto the value of the
land. If the former figure outweighed the latter, an adjudicator's conclusion
would be that use rights were weighing too heavily on the forest, outdistancing
its "possibility." In most cases of cantonnement, however, the use rights translated into roughly two-thirds of the value of the forest, and communes consequently obtained titles of property to two-thirds of the area in question.
Though often left with a mere third of its former domain, the Administration
des Forêts deemed these arrangements advantageous, for the state's forests
could then be managed scientifically, and the state could increase revenue
by no longer having to pay guards' salaries, while collecting taxes, on the other
two-thirds.

The articles on cantonnement thus completed a paradox in which the Forest Code helped create more communal property while undercutting its importance by submitting it to the forest regime. Offered fewer use rights and
more property of dubious integrity, communes often engaged in long legal disputes over cantonnement. The municipal council of Ax-les-Thermes (Ariège),
for example, delayed its cantonnement for twenty-seven years by repeatedly
refusing the administration's proposals, addressing letters to the Minister of Finance that warned of local rebellion, texturing complaints with historical references to immemorial use rights, and otherwise winning last-minute concessions. Although litigation was not a novelty for alpine communes, the case of
Ax reveals the adoption of new vocabularies by literate members of the com-

mune in order to beat the state at its own game. Contests over cantonnement helped create a new element in the evolving repertoire of popular protest: a foot-dragging use of bureaucracy woven into an older repertoire of violent direct action.[41]

Finally, the Forest Code of 1827 lay well within the framework of Colbert's ordinance by virtue of its title 10, which pertained to the "policing and conservation of woods and forests." The articles in this section defined explicitly the forest crimes that had not been defined implicitly in other sections of the code. They set forth in meticulous terms the plants that could not be extracted without permission, the sorts of tools permitted in the forest, where one and one's livestock could appear in the forest (only on obvious roads and paths), and the distances to be respected for the building of houses and industries near forests. Alongside each prohibition appeared the corresponding fine.[42]

Titles 11 and 12, pertaining to judicial action and penalties, gave teeth to the category "forest crime." These sections of the code restored some of the judicial power of the former Eaux et Forêts. Foresters could once again initiate legal proceedings against suspects, who might be pursued simultaneously by the administration and by a state prosecutor. Bearing witness to acts or evidence of criminal activity, forest guards also had authority to draft reports while under oath, which stood as official evidence if written and submitted according to formal prescription. If correctly done, the reports of forest guards established guilt until proof of innocence, regardless of the potential penalty for the crime in question. Forest guards also received authority to seize animals caught pasturing illegally as well as to confiscate illegally cut wood. Fines increased geometrically for each decimeter of a tree's circumference, and a range of fines per type of livestock comprised the penalties for clandestine pasturing. In the original code, the guilty could not be sentenced to prison for a forest crime per se, but by a law of 1859 a term of between three months and two years was meted to those found guilty of falsifying the tools foresters used to mark trees—the signs of their jurisdiction.[43]

For decades to come, local and regional authorities as well as peasants denounced the Forest Code for its severity and for its neglect of the vital differences between forests of the plains and those of the mountains. Officials in the Restoration (1815–1830) and July Monarchy (1830–1848) governments never disproved a common contention that the code had been drafted hastily and—like the 1669 ordinance—in consideration of the forests of the Paris basin, the quintessential plain.[44] Twenty-three years after passage of the code, a justice of the peace from Ax-les-Thermes framed his complaints in terms of order and chaos. The chaos of the mountains deeply contradicted the rational lineaments of the Forest Code:

> It is easy to understand, in effect, that woods of the plain . . . could be submitted to the forest regime. But how is one to understand that alpine woods, situated in a different climate, subjected to rigorous inclemency, to enormous masses of snow; that these woods, I say, which vary with each step like the soil; which are interspersed with empty lands [*vacans*], grasses, bizarrely wooded rocks, precipices, ravines, communal and private pastures, passages for livestock . . . encumbered by the miserable local population with a multitude of imperious needs attached to their agricultural industry, or better said their existence; [how is it that these woods] could be subjected to the theories of the forestry school, which has never understood these needs and which has never calculated the difference between the difficulties of managing woods in the mountain and those on the plain?[45]

Two revolutions, no less tumultuous in the Pyrenees than in Paris, had transpired since 1827, but the local official turned arguments for order upside down by upholding the chaotic "nature" of mountains and their inhabitants.

CONTESTING THE CODE

In a broader context, the code exacerbated social and economic realities that had already begun to erode peasants' access to the forests. The population of alpine France grew rapidly in the early nineteenth century; in most districts of the Pyrenees, falling mortality rates had launched a demographic transition in the eighteenth century. Ariège had experienced a doubling of population between 1741 and 1846, and the department set a record along with Hautes-Pyrénées of a 10 percent rate of natural increase in the decade 1821–30, significantly above the national average of 7 percent. The later and more gradual demographic transition in the Alps caused mortality and fertility to decline only after 1850. In the first half of the nineteenth century, however, population growth in the Maurienne (Savoie) kept pace with that throughout Ariège: both populations grew by 27 percent between 1801 and 1846–48.[46]

Population growth heightened needs for wood and other forest products while compelling peasants to clear more forest for the planting of rye and potatoes on mountain slopes. More people also acquired more cows, sheep, goats, and pigs, squeezing pastoral resources; numbers of livestock increased even more rapidly than the human population of the mountains in the first half of the nineteenth century, owing to heightened demand for meat from the cities.[47] Greater densities of livestock and consequent overgrazing struck keenly at ecological balance in Savoie. The quantity and quality of forest declined. Extended cultivation carved into the lower limits of forest but even more into the lower, irrigated pastures; to compensate, peasants extended the alpine pastures by cutting into the forest from above.[48]

An additional element complicated matters in Ariège, for agriculture and stock-raising had begun to compete with a local industry that stood to wreak the most havoc on the forests. The development of catalan forges in the late eighteenth century had created state-of-the-art metallurgy, a more decentralized and more efficient technology than large blast furnaces.[49] A hydraulic system, the catalan forge permitted the transformation of iron ore directly into malleable ingot iron, thus avoiding the stage of pig iron. Ariège was rich in the two primary materials needed for iron production—iron ore and trees, the latter transformed into wood and then charcoal to power the forges. Catalan-forge metallurgy took off in the first half of the nineteenth century, reaching its peak in Ariège in 1853. It took an acute toll on the forest: in 1840 alone, the department's fifty-seven forges consumed 240,000 steres, or cubic meters, of wood. Although this figure represented greater efficiency since the beginning of the century, many foresters and departmental authorities continued to castigate the forge owners for their greed, predicting irreparable degradation and permanent emigration from alpine communes.[50]

Changes in the regime of private property also curtailed peasants' access to forests. Wealthy bourgeois purchased a number of large, formerly seigneurial forests early in the century, and the new owners sought to restrict use rights on their lands, many of which they then sold or leased to ironworks. Large owners of livestock engaged in similar pursuits, encouraging the less wealthy to exercise use rights on lands owned by the state and communes, and not on their own. Coupled with these growing restrictions on private lands was a collapse in the early nineteenth century of the old consensus surrounding the commons: appropriations and usurpations from both high and low in rural society became the norm throughout the Pyrenees. If many of the alpine communes most dependent on pastoralism were able to prevent loss of the commons, consensus did not necessarily return: poorer peasants clamored for partition of common lands while the state and bourgeoisie pushed for their sale. Municipal councils passed ever-more-stringent regulations on use of the commons in an effort to preempt usurpations, yet many mayors were themselves large landowners content to let their poorer constituents wage war over communal property. All of these tendencies tore at the coherence of the always precarious pastoral world. The Forest Code exacerbated tensions by further squeezing access to pastures and forests, favoring private property, extinguishing use rights, expelling sheep and goats from the forests, and restricting the few privileges that remained.[51]

Forest crimes escalated in such circumstances. Though it acted with more rigor after 1840, the government of the July Monarchy made enforcing the Forest Code a priority from its inception.[52] The number of criminal convictions in the alpine *arrondissement* of Saint-Girons (Ariège) increased steadily throughout the 1830s, from 415 in 1827 to 2,340 in 1844. Arrests increased notably for the most minor forest crimes, such as gathering firewood from the forest floor or pasturing a single cow in areas off limits. The fines dictated by the code, putatively light and rational, were onerous for peasants in the Pyrenees: at a time when pasturing fines alone represented up to half the value of each animal, many cases of insolvency resulted in jail sentences of between two weeks and two months. Peasants resented the excessive powers placed in the hands of forest guards, authorized to seize livestock and send delinquents to court for the least infraction. A prosecutor in Toulouse believed in 1830 that peasants had begun to attribute their misery to the Forest Code.[53]

Philippe Vigier analyzes forest crimes, as banal in the Alps as in the Pyrenees, as "the logical extension of the essential role played by wood and its different uses in the existence of traditional rural communities."[54] In other words, taking wood, pasturing in the forest, and clearing for agriculture were traditional activities that the state had criminalized. Jean-François Soulet, discussing the Pyrenees, nuances this view by distinguishing a "delinquency of misery," which fluctuated with the subsistence crises of the early nineteenth century, from a "quasi-institutional delinquency" widely practiced for commercial purposes and often linked to communes heavily involved in smuggling. These forest crimes included the fraudulent cutting of wood for speculative sale to forge owners—a practice by no means condoned by all members of the village community.[55]

But the dizzying increase in forest crimes after 1827 clearly stemmed from the double vice of the Forest Code, which restricted access to the forest while providing for efficient repression of forest crimes. By defining forest crimes as individually punishable acts, the law blinded authorities to the possibilities of collective action. Indeed, the state could hardly have been less prepared for one of the most celebrated of all nineteenth-century revolts—the "War of the Demoiselles," which took place throughout Ariège from 1829 until 1832. This "war" consisted of a series of autonomous, guerrilla-like actions in which small bands of men armed with various implements or guns repossessed the forests by threatening, chasing, and sometimes attacking forest guards and charcoal makers, thus targeting at once the state and the bourgeois owners of forest and forge. The men adopted an abridged, or caricatured, disguise: pulling out their white shirts and tying them at the waist, darkening their faces, and donning a kerchief or perhaps an animal skin for the head, to some extent (especially if barely glimpsed through the forest and at night) they passed themselves off as women—hence the name "Demoiselles."

Though condemned by the department's bourgeoisie, the War of the Demoiselles unified heterogeneous Ariège in a geographical sense: beginning at the western tip of Ariège in the forests of Saint-Lary, the revolt spread eastward, especially into the Massat Valley and the Haute-Ariège, eventually involving the whole department. The revolt also changed character in 1830, coinciding with the overthrow of the Restoration monarchy in Paris. Before July, the Demoiselles had extended their attacks from the persons of guards and charcoal makers to the properties of local notables, reviving scenarios from the Great Revolution that included appropriating legal documents pertaining to immemorial rights as well as sacking and burning châteaux. Hearing the news from Paris, the Demoiselles began to use the rhetoric of liberty to underscore their attacks on property and claims to the forest; during approximately the last half of 1830, the insurgents abandoned their disguise, fully adopting the "transparent" language of revolution. Yet by the spring of 1831, they once again dressed as demoiselles.

This deft handling of old and new vocabularies has given rise to a number of interpretations that seek to place the War of the Demoiselles in the vast context of European popular revolt. Among recent authors, Soulet depicts the war as singular but not original; the pursuit and expulsion of forest guards, the later episodes of *jacquerie*, the use of disguise and carnavalesque folklore, and the elements of organized revolt formed part of the larger repertoire of Pyrenean contestation during the eighteenth and nineteenth centuries.[56] For John Merriman, the War of the Demoiselles verges on the anachronistic; although he allows the revolt a political character, defining its politics as a "local issue—the forests, and who had rights to them," he concludes that it represented the last gasp of a losing battle: "[The Demoiselles] were a colorful but tragic vestige of an old world."[57]

Most recently, Peter Sahlins has recovered the symbolic dimension of the revolt in order to explain not only its particular timing and the use of disguise but also, and more broadly, how popular culture infused politics in 1830. The Demoiselles, Sahlins argues, self-consciously used traditions such as the festive calendar and the feminine symbolism of the forest, dramatizing their grievances as well as their ideals. Moreover, the years 1829–32 saw a remarkable exchange of threads of political culture between Ariège and the distant center of Paris; Ariégeois peasants used the "Parisian" rhetoric of liberty after July 1830, while the peasant practice of *charivari* came back to Paris and other urban centers in both journalism and action. These instances contributed to a long history of such exchanges. Through this illustration, Sahlins builds bridges between Old Regime and nineteenth-century France, dispelling the argument for "anachronism" or even "vestige." His central claim for a self-conscious use of repertoire casts doubt on the major assumptions concerning peasants in modernization theory.[58]

All histories of the Demoiselles, however, show a reluctance to draw connections to subsequent struggles. Sahlins suggests that popular opposition to the Forêts endured through different means, namely, individual delinquency and legal action. But during the next major episode of the struggle, the Revolution of 1848, peasants combined these tactics with the older tradition of "devastating" the forest and the novelty of electoral politics. Gone were lightly disguised guerrillas and the politics of charivari. The Second Republic provided the mold for future conflicts over the forest.

The forest troubles of 1848 were the most dramatic elements in the great peasant conflagration that mobilized significant portions of the southwest, the southeast, and the center of France. Scenes of extraordinary violence resulted from the massive misery of the small peasantry, hit by one of the worst subsistence crises of the century: potato and grain harvests failed from 1845 to 1847, causing the last famine in France's history. Small proprietors and sharecroppers also targeted the inroads made by capitalist agriculture, destroying modern implements such as ploughs and threshing machines. If, as for Albert Soboul, peasant sedition in 1848 reflected "the permanence of old reflexes," it occurred in a unique conjuncture of crop failure, deepening capitalism, and population pressure that was most critical in the Pyrenees.[59]

In that region, the crisis centered around reduced access to an increasingly depleted forest. The traditional safety net with its store of acorns, beechnuts, berries, and edible plants, the forest had less to give by 1845: as early as 1830, the effect of tariffs on foreign iron had begun to tell upon the forests of Ariège, as forge owners allowed their wholesale consumption in a spate of iron production. Fifteen years later, fifty-seven forges pounded in Ariège, and the price of charcoal had risen so high it "frightened the sellers themselves."[60] Simultaneously, the Forêts began to overturn the peasants' victory of 1830. The Demoiselles had won limited pasturing rights and a general amnesty by September 1830; officials had even extended these privileges beyond the confines of Ariège. But the pasturing rights had been granted on a temporary basis and had to be renewed each year; the royal favor had done nothing to diminish the uncertainty into which the code had thrown Pyrenean peasants. In September 1846 the Forêts suddenly reduced the grazing privileges granted in the Cerdagne and the Capcir (Pyrénées-Orientales), an act that reverberated in nearby Ariège.[61]

From the Atlantic to the Mediterranean, the Pyrenees ignited once Parisians had overturned the July Monarchy. By February 28, whole villages in the Quérigut, the isolated eastern extremity of Ariège, had begun to pursue forest guards and local "capitalists"—the principal usurers of the canton. Repressed by line troops in the first week of March, the revolt then metamorphosed into massive delinquency in the forests. Simultaneously, peasants in the Barousse Valley (Hautes-Pyrénées) launched a revolt against forest guards and tax collectors, pillaging houses, holding notables for ransom, appropriating legal documents, and pillaging the château of Luscan. Of seven hundred to eight hundred participants, only sixteen—manual workers, peasants, and artisans—were inculpated. Other regions in Basses-Pyrénées and Hautes-Pyrénées remained in a state of "permanent insurrection" from March to August.[62]

Beyond these organized revolts, the most common collective action in Ariège harkened back more to 1789 than to 1830: peasants repossessed their usurped commons and forests with violence, pillaging and burning large sections of communally as well as privately owned forest. Fires began in the spring of 1848, concentrating in forests of the upper Ariège and upper Couserans basins. The heaviest destruction occurred in a forest belonging to a notable, M. Bergasse-Laziroule of Saurat, a village on the road between Tarascon and Massat; between February and May peasants cut or mutilated more than 12,000 trees. By October, the conservator of forests in Toulouse placed the estimate of illegally cut trees in the department at 70,574, not including the forests of Quérigut, Ax, and Mérens, and lamented that it would be fifteen or twenty years before the forests of Ariège would begin to recover. The administration would eventually estimate the damage done to them at more than 2 million francs.[63]

The frequency of pillage and fire, as opposed to the direct confrontations of the Demoiselles, suggested to authorities that individual delinquency had taken on staggering proportions, while collective action had been abandoned. The general prosecutor in Toulouse was still thinking in terms of "forest crimes" in May when he complained that malefactors would have to be prosecuted individually since they had not been seen in any gatherings. Outsiders were often unable to tease out the collective element in "devastation," so blurred had the traces of collusion become. Yet clues were hardly lacking. After the destruction in Saurat, brigades of gendarmes and a detachment of troops descended on the region, arresting two locals; inhabitants rioted, demanding the prisoners' liberty and shooting and throwing stones at the troops, wounding three gendarmes and several soldiers.[64] Though unable to locate the exact nature of the troubles on the sliding scale between individual and collective action, the national government opted for swift repression—undertaken several months before the June Days in Paris. From February 1848 until December 1849, roughly nine thousand soldiers were dispatched to the Pyrenees uniquely to repress the *troubles forestiers;* even more troops tried to quell revolts over tax collection and city tolls in the region. Flames in the Pyrenean forests demanded a full 18 percent of the entire repressive force dispatched throughout France during the Second Republic.[65]

That regime is of course most remembered for the political apprenticeship allowed by universal male suffrage practiced under a republican constitution. The voting record of the Ariégeois must be judged in light of the legal repression that preceded the elections of 1848 and 1849. Toward the end of March 1848, the ministers of interior and finance in the provisional government instructed prefects to annul all derogations to the laws in force, to pursue crimes vigorously, and to support the Administration des Forêts. Radical demands from the Capcir and Cerdagne called for the abolition of the Forêts; the government responded in the spring by reinstating the forest guards who had recently been revoked or expelled. Early abandonment by the Republic, which many assumed would bring clemency and reform of the forest regime, became a lasting fact. An antirepublican movement would appear to be the obvious consequence, but the electoral picture was more complicated. The mountainous arrondissement of Foix returned the smallest percentage of votes cast in the central Pyrenees for Louis-Napoleon in the presidential election of December 1848; while the neighboring departments of Hautes-Pyrénées and Haute-Garonne favored the right in the legislative elections of 1849, Ariège returned 49.8 percent of its votes to republican candidates. Sixty-five percent of voters in the canton of Castillon, hotbed of the Demoiselles, voted for the left in 1849. Some historians interpret this voting as an act of faith consistent with peasants' memories of revolution: they voted republican because the republic had once meant freedom in the forests. By 1851, however, disappointment with the regime bore fruit.[66]

In the plebiscite following the coup of 2 December 1851, both Ariège and Pyrénées-Orientales voted heavily in Louis-Napoleon's favor, as did France as a whole; all voting results of the 1851 plebiscite must be held at arm's length, however, given the atmosphere of repression in which it was conducted. The two departments show a partial contrast in their participation in the revolt against the coup: whereas Pyrénées-Orientales furnished perhaps ten thousand insurgents, Ariège was virtually unmoved, hosting a single unarmed demonstration in the lowland town of Pamiers. A deeper similarity emerges from the fact that the alpine regions of both departments remained quiet. Relatively remote and geared to subsistence, these regions contrast with areas of the Midi that did stage armed insurrections: in Ted Margadant's well-known analysis, an economy increasingly based on cash-cropping and crafts and thus vulnerable to market fluctuations, tight village-town interdependencies, and secret societies with a broad social basis created the conditions for republican mobilization in the face of counterrevolution.[67] Louis-Napoleon's amnesty of 15 January 1852, for all who owed fines or were serving sentences for forest crimes, can be viewed as a reward for alpine quiescence.

Ariège, then, provides a fit example for Margadant's warning that "ideology needs to be distinguished from collective action." But if republicanism was not to die for by 1851, electoral politics had left a mark, in the context of violence. Frustrated by patterns of voting that differed from canton to canton, Soulet dismisses the Pyrenean forest revolts as "primary," that is, nonpolitical. Such a statement overlooks the early marriage between elections and violence; Yves-Marie Bercé's concept of political violence, which he frames as the common ground between revolt and revolution, does more justice to the events of 1848 in the Pyrenees. By 1849 some members of the Ariégeois elite had begun to realize that the road to peasants' ballots led straight through the forest.[68]

One would-be politician sought a constituency precisely by championing traditional forest rights. Latour de St.-Ybars, an Ariégeois poet, set forth his opinions in a pamphlet, "De la Question forestière dans l'Ariège," which also announced his candidacy for the legislative elections of May 1849. He pointedly turned the tables on the Administration des Forêts by arguing that it was the Forest Code itself and foresters' "vicious systems of management" that were destroying the beech and fir forests of Ariège. Asserting that the greatest prosperity of the forest had coincided with liberal use rights, St.-Ybars set 1848 against 1793, a calm year for the forests: "In '93 . . . there was no emotion in our mountains, no havoc in the forests, not a tree cut by these same men who today would like to destroy the woods, so exasperated are they with what they have suffered." Discussing jardinage, forest crimes, and rural poverty, he concluded that the forests had lost their public purpose and served only the administration and its personnel; why else would they be the only ones defending the Forest Code? His platform demanded immediate amnesty for all those convicted of forest crimes and the institution of communal management over all forests. Nothing less would conform to the spirit of 1848: "When all French people [*sic*] have the faculty of naming their representatives and the president of the republic, it is supremely absurd to deny a certain number of citizens the right to manage the commons."[69]

The pamphlet elicited not only derogatory comments from the regional conservator of forests but also a detailed riposte from a local forester who was not an electoral rival. Attacking St.-Ybars for his ideas concerning silviculture, the anonymous forester spoke from the basis of professionalism, a position conquered over the previous half century by the Forêts. This, too, was politics: who could best represent Ariège by speaking most credibly about its forests and its people? The forester accused St.-Ybars of being an outsider, a man of the plain not versed in the ways of mountain people. But his own estimation of the Ariégeois rested on assumptions current among French foresters since the Revolution: these people had let their culture degenerate. Alluding to "the time when the patriarchal customs of the rural inhabitants were far from having degenerated like today," the forester implicitly ranked the degraded peasants with their degraded forests, in words reminiscent of Dralet's. He cast doubt on his own subsequent statement of sympathy with the peasants, proclaiming their common bond of Frenchness. Above all, the anonymous retort took issue with St.-Ybars' account of deforestation. The forester countered St.-Ybars' historicizing of 1793 with a narrative describing the decline of the forests due to abuse by peasants just as much as forge owners: "This sad state of affairs dominates in all alpine communes. The inhabitants' lack of foresight has converted rich forests full of resources for pasturing and heating, into heaths, arid rocks, or sterile grasses dotted with a few remnants of ruined woods. Is that, M. Latour, the result of the vices of exploitation by the Administration des Forêts?"[70] Among foresters, this narrative retained its currency, and it was only bolstered by the devastations of 1848.

ENTER SAVOIE

This context of administrative reform, repression, revolt, and voting structured official and popular memory by the time the Second Empire took on the project of transforming the landscape of alpine France. Although this memory did color perceptions in and of Savoie, its analysis applies most fully to Ariège. For in the context of alpine restoration, the history of Savoie differed greatly in that it once again became a French department in the very year that foresters began to remodel the mountains.

On 22 and 23 April 1860, under the gaze of the occupying French army, men in Savoie voted overwhelmingly in favor of annexation to France as the two new departments of Savoie and Haute-Savoie.[71] Napoleon III had not been eager to allow the plebiscite, but Camillo Cavour, once again premier of Piedmont-Sardinia, had insisted on it in the Treaty of Turin signed on 24 March; the plebiscite allowed Cavour to justify the cession to King Victor-Emmanuel II. The latter was reluctant to part with the Sardinian dynasty's duchy of origin, and since the Restoration of 1814 Savoyards had shown themselves rather loyal subjects in the Sardinian realm.

Napoleon III soon touted the plebiscite as a triumph of nationalism, but as late as March 1860 he attributed the importance of absorbing Savoie only to the duchy's strategic position. Facing the growing strength of a northern Italy finally free of the Austrians, France had to secure the western slopes of the Alps, especially since the Piedmontese controlled the passes.[72] Little nationalist sentiment greeted the Treaty of Turin, and the Savoyards had hardly chosen the timing of their entry into France; the plebiscite was the ultimate result of war and diplomacy far beyond the control of Savoyards. Instead of popular sovereignty, the plebiscite represented only the reversal of 1814, or, in Paul Guichonnet's words, a "Bonapartist sort of ratification of a territorial cession, constituting a swap in a closed diplomatic game between Paris and Turin."[73]

Beyond the official propaganda, French bureaucrats had to assess the "Frenchness" of Savoie for themselves as they began to impose new laws and regulations on the people of the annexed territory. The record was ambiguous, for despite the French linguistic and cultural heritage of Savoie, few Savoyards had openly contested Sardinian hegemony during the forty-six years of the Restoration. Several historians suggest strong support of the absolute monarchy (1814–48) on the part of the reactionary nobility and clergy in Savoie, who held a secure monopoly of local power. Without question a repressive regime incarnated by the Piedmontese *carabinieri,* the Sardinian monarchy nevertheless treated Savoie with relative clemency in the form of light taxes and economic protection from French products. Savoie had gained the especial favor of King Charles-Felix in 1821 following military seditions in Piedmont; the local ruling class had kept the area "loyal" in the eyes of the monarch, in spite of the 163 Savoyards implicated in the affair.[74]

The Revolution of 1848 had left an ambiguous record as well. Those who invoked nationalism in Savoie came in several stripes: some demonstrated in favor of Italian unity, others raised the flag of the short-lived cisalpine republic of the Jacobins, and still others argued for annexation to Second Republic France.[75] The Fundamental Statute granted by Charles-Albert, similar to Louis-Philippe's Charter, found enthusiastic reception among Savoyard liberals, but the terror occasioned by the *Voraces* ("voracious") and the ensuing massacre dealt a blow to republican sympathies. More than fifteen hundred Savoyard workers in Lyon, expelled by the provisional government in Paris and joined by members of a Lyonnais revolutionary association, marched on Chambéry in early April. Most of the Sardinian troops had left Savoie, and the Piedmontese governor retreated along with most of his staff to the Maurienne upon the arrival of the Voraces. After three days, ten thousand peasants responded to the alarm sounded largely by the clergy and routed the Voraces from Chambéry, killing an unknown number of them. Chambéry's "April Days" squelched further revolution in Savoie.[76]

The constitutional monarchy of 1848 allowed Savoie a substantial electoral privilege: the property qualification for voting was half what it was in the other Sardinian states.[77] With, in addition, the highest rate of electoral participation, Savoie seemed well incorporated in the new constitutional arrangement in northern Italy. Nevertheless, the seventy-nine Savoyard deputies in Turin formed an opposition hostile to the liberal transformation of Piedmont; during the 1850s the conservative Savoyards shifted their allegiance away from Cavour, enemy of the Pope and no great friend of Savoie. The greatest obstacle to assuring Savoie's allegiance was of course the *Risorgimento,* a movement that made little room for a non-Italian culture on the other side of the Alps but that was rapidly Italianizing Piedmont; in the 1850s, Tuscan replaced the Piedmontese dialect, and French fell out of favor at the court of Turin. Finally, economic depression endured in Savoie through the mid-1850s, and France seemed to promise greater prosperity. Here, too, Cavour alienated the Savoyard bourgeoisie by promoting an industrial corridor along the axis linking Turin with Genoa, leaving Savoie far to the side.[78]

On balance, then, the regime in Piedmont-Sardinia repelled some Savoyards at least as much as France attracted them. Although the Second Empire was an acceptable regime to the largely conservative network of local power, the strongest political emotion to be found in Savoie in 1860 grew in response to a movement in the northern pays of Faucigny, Chablais, and Genevois (today part of Haute-Savoie) to attach the northern Savoie to Switzerland. Petitioners gathered more than twelve thousand signatures in favor of the drive organized by the Savoyard colony in Geneva; the northern communes were more anxious to maintain their commercial relations with this city than to become part of France. Thus, the *parti français* in the rest of Savoie was galvanized primarily by the threat of a splintered homeland.[79]

If the Frenchness of Savoie remained problematic, Savoyards were, for their part, relatively well acquainted with France. In 1860 nearly eighty thousand Savoyards lived seasonally or permanently in Paris, working as porters, dockers, *garçons de boutique,* chimney sweeps, and servants. In most mountain villages, accounts of life in the French capital could be heard during the spring and summer when migrants came back to work on their farms. Savoyards had a reputation for ranging widely, and nearly every part of France, save other remote alpine areas, had some contact with them in the first half of the nineteenth century.

Yet the converse was far less true: not until the years following the annexation did French officials fully grasp the facts of Savoyard life. Napoleon III acquired a territory where birth and death rates were markedly higher than in France as a whole; where conscripts were shorter on average than their French counterparts; and where poor nutrition, especially iodine deficiencies, led to widespread goiter and cretinism. The Sardinian regime had done little to develop the regional economy, and protectionism had effectively isolated it. Agriculture had expanded in one sense only—upward. Cultivated fields reached altitudes of twenty-five hundred meters and beyond in the inner ranges, competing with both pastures and forests. Given the short growing seasons and poor soils, alpine agriculture could not support a galloping increase in population; seasonal and permanent emigration remained a part of life in Savoie even after the annexation.[80]

Several historians have commented on the hostile reception of French officials in Savoie, who "arrived there as for a tour of duty in the colonies."[81] But in the early years the theme of the *bon peuple savoyard* was used to effect by French administrators who descended on Savoie. In a circular to Savoyard mayors explaining the importance of the recent laws on reforestation and reclamation (see Chapter 2), Prefect Hippolyte Dieu expressed confidence that the government would not have to resort to coercive means of enforcement: "I take pleasure in believing that municipal administrations in Savoie are too enlightened and convinced of the benefits of these measures not to share the views of the government with enthusiasm."[82] The forestry corps had, however, to walk a fine line between praising the locals and acknowledging the sorry state of their forests; the departmental conseil général reported bluntly at the end of 1860, "The communal forests of Savoie are almost entirely exhausted by a negligence which was driving them to certain ruin."[83]

The rhetorical answer lay in blaming the inefficacy of the Sardinian regime, not the Savoyards. By several accounts, the Sardinian government did largely neglect the forests of Savoie. Despite a code of regulations, authorities tolerated overpasturing in the forests, abusive cutting, and unchecked sales of timber. Forest guards received meager salaries and little support from the powers in Turin, who rarely knew the exact boundaries of forests putatively under their care. Many indebted communes had alienated considerable sections of their forests to creditors who had financed much construction during the later years of the Sardinian regime.[84]

Rising demand for wood had intensified neglect. Beginning in the mid-eighteenth century, industry (namely, the Pesey-Mâcot mines at Conflans), public works, and the urban centers of Lyon and Geneva had contributed to thinning the forests of the northern Alps. Like many Pyrenean forests, those in Savoie had been impoverished if not destroyed, causing many to fear a general shortage of wood by the early nineteenth century.[85] French foresters in 1860 asserted that the damage could be traced to improper management and that they had come to heal the degradation that the Sardinian regime had caused. Their reluctance to examine the forest practices of the inhabitants themselves stands in contrast to the decades of blame heaped upon the Ariégeois for both the nonenforcement of the Forest Ordinance of 1669 and the difficult application of the Forest Code of 1827. Politics in the Savoie of 1860 had a rather different cast: integration of the department into the nation demanded that the new regime demonstrate the industry, foresight, civic-mindedness, and other exemplary French qualities of the Savoyards, who had already proven their "loyalty" in the plebiscite.

Such political imperatives might have led to a hands-off approach in the annexed territory, yet they clashed with an image of Savoie that particularly enticed foresters: for many French officials, Savoie posed as a place without history and thus a laboratory for relatively free experimentation. Ultimately, assimilation brought intervention in many forms. French military service, application of the Falloux law on primary and secondary education, and the imposition of the Forest Code all made their mark in Savoie but hardly received universal welcome there.[86] The latter was perhaps the most difficult to introduce, given the large number of communally owned forests. Assimilation *à la française* also meant surveillance through a police-state apparatus. Even as the

Second Empire won over large segments of the rural population of France, officials believed they had reasons to be wary of all people in the uplands. Government reports from Ariège and Savoie bear witness to vigilance, not complacency.

Theories of recent deforestation eventually implicated the northern Alps as much as the southern Alps and the Pyrenees. Most important, the foundations of the state's authority over the forests—the administration, the code, and the school of forestry—had survived the convulsions of 1830 and 1848. Powerful structures remained in place from which foresters launched the most ambitious policy of the second half of the nineteenth century: alpine restoration.

One final current of change made reforestation possible by 1860: a conceptual shift that began to write peasants out of the picture. In the eyes of foresters, mountains, forests, and plains became abstract entities, analyzed in a closed circle that erased the complexities of real human habitats. Institutions such as the Administration des Forêts and the Forest Code had in many ways been defined with reference to threats from the people closest to the forests. As Chapter 2 will show, however, the first law on reforestation carried none of the implicit recognition of peasants as actors, albeit delinquent actors, in spite of the accompanying rhetoric of "public utility." Offered up as a technical issue whose object of concern was land, not people, reforestation contained misapprehensions that were to backfire. Alpine communes responded with a rich and varied arsenal of tactics to combat the refiguration of the mountain.

Chapter Two "A Question Almost Political": Reforesting and Reclaiming Alpine France, c. 1760–1880

Human will is no small thing when, doubled with intelligence, it supplements the forces of nature in order to steer them toward a given end.
—*Alexandre Surell*

But if plantings are imposed, if their immediate and forced consequence is the complete privation or even diminution of use-rights founded upon immemorial tolerance or upon law, there is no reason to doubt that the inhabitants will be unanimously in favor of destroying what you hope to create.
—*Anonymous*

Stories of deforestation require the naming of the guilty. From the late eighteenth century, foresters became steeped in scorn for peasants' ways of managing and using forests and horrified by the revolutionary moments that had brought insubordination and devastation: by the beginning of the Second Empire foresters had both named the guilty and acquired the legal, institutional, and technical means of restoring France's forests.[1] The new regime affirmed the importance of forests, first implicitly by building more railroads and opening new shipyards, then explicitly by promoting green spaces in cities and undertaking the full reforestation of the Landes and the Sologne.[2] Why and how foresters and legislators of the Second Empire conceived of alpine reforestation, and the reception of their schemes in Ariège and Savoie, constitute the subject of this chapter. Neither a conscious will to punishment nor the result solely of status and expertise put into practice, alpine reforestation grew out of a reimagining of alpine nature itself. Twin pieces of legislation in 1860 were the fruit of arguments that posited the absolute, functional differences between mountains and plains: they embodied new images of nature and dealt with the guilty by omitting them.

"RIVERS, LIKE REVOLUTION"

Foresters had not been the first to highlight the differences between plains and mountains with respect to the forest question; as seen in Chapter 1, critics of the Forest Code had pointed to the document's profound inapplicability to the alpine regions of France. If the state remained unable to counter this biting criticism, foresters took the distinction between upland and lowland and brilliantly refigured it in terms of equilibrium. The notion of equilibrium did not require denying the contrasts between plains and mountains; on the contrary, it heightened their opposition, in terms of function, natural tendencies, and, most important, hierarchy. Mountains, because of their tendencies toward disorder and destruction, had to be mastered to the utmost possible extent in the interests of protecting the useful, productive parts of the landscape—plains. The real "equilibrium" to be sought was thus one defined by service and subordination. A concept that foresters drew from engineering, equilibrium fit well with foresters' ideas of aménagement; both required the imagining of large spaces and their relationships.

Before these relationships took conceptual shape, mountains had acquired new aesthetic references. In his classic study of eighteenth-century French nature writing, Daniel Mornet traced the formation of an alpine aesthetic through the travel literature that began with the "discovery" of the Swiss Alps and ventured westward to the French Alps, the Jura, and ultimately the Pyrenees. Privileging the writings of Rousseau and Ramond, Mornet documented a sizeable literature of the sublime published between 1760 and the Revolution.[3] More recently Simon Schama has shown that the "oxymoron of agreeable horror," the basis of the alpine aesthetic and indeed of Romanticism, coexisted for much of the eighteenth century with quite another sensibility, the conquering, "imperial" ethos of mountaineering. Fear and awe, the staples of Romantic alpine experience, could of course accompany a scientific bent and a desire to scale peaks, as they did in Saussure's *Voyages dans les Alpes*. However one reacted to it, the powerful lesson of the sublime was that mountains were "*active* forces of nature, protagonists of calamity."[4] The new sensibility had, by the late eighteenth century, even filtered into the essays of students within the national engineering corps, the Ponts et Chaussées: alongside an older, strictly rationalist view of mountains as barriers and accidents of nature stood the sublime aesthetic that cast the magnificence of mountains as a standard to which the engineer's artifices should measure up.[5]

It is no accident that this complex vision coincided with a dominant strain in eighteenth- and early nineteenth-century geology—catastrophism. Leading scientists such as Georges Cuvier, his collaborator Alexandre Brongniart, and Cuvier's pupil Léonce Elie de Beaumont established along with British geologists the doctrine that mountains had been built during moments of sudden, cataclysmic uplift. Catastrophists also posited that mass faunal extinctions could result from such abrupt geologic change, as Cuvier's research on the strata of the Paris Basin appeared to show. For some catastrophists, past and present geological forces were not the same; they theorized a "greater expenditure of geotectonic energy in earlier times."[6] Other catastrophists preferred the notion of ongoing forces acting sporadically with "catastrophic intensity," whereas "actualists" such as Elie de Beaumont staked out a third position, arguing that extraordinary forces still acted in the present, on occasion. What the variants of catastrophism held in common was that sudden energies caused both the uplift of mountains and their destruction—both their existence and the deep ravines in them, for example.[7]

Catastrophist doctrine eventually retreated before the uniformitarianism of Charles Lyell and other geologists, who hypothesized a far longer time scale for gradual geologic change as well as the continuity of such forces as volcanic activity, earthquakes, and erosion. Though isolated in the scientific community by the mid-nineteenth century, catastrophists extended a long-lasting metaphor that the Romantics had invented. Mountains were disorderly and convulsive. Popular catastrophism placed more emphasis on degradation—and its present reality—than did the catastrophism of geologists: torrential streams and their effects were, after all, visible; the serious flooding of the 1770s and 1780s in the Pyrenees had already unveiled the calamitous degradation of alpine regions, and one could also witness avalanches and landslides in one's own time. In the administrative mind, popular catastrophism forced one of the crucial intellectual links between upland and lowland through the idea of risk. Nature could be conceived more globally, as a set of interdependent regions. The unhappy marriage between mountain and plain favored the "administrative non-separation of distinct geographic areas."[8]

Institutionally, it was foresters, not engineers, who were to use catastrophism to justify intervening in alpine nature. Engineers had reached broad agreement on the importance of examining entire watersheds in efforts to control flooding, but their practical attention remained fixed on damming, diking, and channeling downstream watercourses. Foresters, on the other hand, looked at the uplands, where they had always been more of a physical presence than engineers. As presented in Chapter 1, the Revolution had also bequeathed to the conservative corps the metaphor of stabilizing what was disorderly, convulsive, and threatening.[9]

That forests could help stabilize volatile mountains became virtual dogma through two developments. The first grew indirectly out of the opposition between plain and mountain, via concerns about land clearance. Eighteenth-century physiocrats had promoted a dualistic vision of French nature—the cultivated versus the uncultivated. Their defining economic theory, one that grounded a nation's prosperity in the productivity of its agriculture, led to a struggle against *inculture,* the state of swamps, marshes, fallow land, pastures, and even forests, to name a few of the many kinds of land that fell under the single rubric of "uncultivation." Broadly speaking, the sharp dualism pitted foresters against the physiocrats, who made no distinction between *défriche-ment* (clearing) and *déboisement* (deforestation). Not until the Revolution did local officials and agronomists, who witnessed forest appropriations and clearances from the summer of 1789, voice qualms about the acceleration of défrichement or take issue with the oversimplified notion of inculture. Although clearing land for agriculture had been dethroned as an absolute good, succeeding regimes continued to anchor the social, economic, and moral compass of France in agriculture.

Déboisement was ultimately defined as a concept distinct from défriche-ment, due to the images of revolutionary devastation examined earlier.[10] Forests, in other words, emerged from the category of *terres vaines et vagues* as not merely distinct but also useful spaces, acquiring a status in tandem with the reaffirmed status of foresters. If plains would continue to host agriculture, forests could at least grow abundantly in the mountains. The government of the Second Republic first concretized the assumption: faced with the decision of whether to extend the temporary restrictions on all tree-cutting under the Forest Code, the National Assembly voted in 1851 to relax restrictions for the

plains, in order to stimulate agriculture and in recognition of the growing substitution of coal for firewood in the northern and eastern departments. The
law's spokesman left nothing opaque in his concise explanation: "The plain for
agriculture, the mountain for forest and pasture." But before this ideal spatial
arrangement could take effect, the land of France had to be divided into zones
and classified as plain or mountain by commissions at the level of the *arrondissement*—a little-known task undertaken during the Second Republic.[11]

Second, and in contrast to this neutral relegation of forest to the mountains,
several influential studies cast forests as the only solution to the problems of
alpine torrentiality and erosion. In the forefront of these studies was Alexandre
Surell's *Etude sur les torrents des Hautes-Alpes,* a work that crystallized ideas cir-
culating among engineers and foresters since the late eighteenth century.[12]
Published in 1841, the book received the acclaim of the Academy of Sciences
the following year. Surell, a young engineer in the Ponts et Chaussées, traced
the relation between deforestation and torrents, the unpredictable headwater
streams that began as trickles in the highest alpine valleys, then gathered speed
and much debris along the way until they disgorged their contents into villages
lying in their paths or threw themselves into rivers, whichever came first.

Had he written his work after the floods of the 1840s and 1850s, Surell probably would have tightened the connection between torrents and large-scale flooding, though it is implicit from the first page of his book. Surell began by depicting the hydrographic basins in the department of Hautes-Alpes; the countless
torrents (and, after a heavy rain, their tons of mud and rocks) fed the Durance,
the Buëch, and the Drac, and these rivers flowed into the Rhône. After acknowledging the influence of geology and climate on the formation of torrents,
Surell then hit upon a correlation that was to frame his proposals for restoration:
"Everywhere that one finds new torrents, there are no more forests, and everywhere that the ground is deforested, torrents have formed, such that the same
eyes that have seen forests falling on mountain slopes have witnessed the formation of an incontinent multitude of torrents."[13] Gradually, peasants had deforested Hautes-Alpes, robbing the mountains of their most natural covering.
Surell believed that forests propagated endlessly, all over the world, wherever humanity had not interfered; recognizing that the plains of France had been largely
deforested for the sake of agriculture, he, too, argued that the country's mountains had become the proper and "natural" province of forests, whose presence
there was indispensable to agriculture on the plains. He grasped the importance
of alpine forests mostly in terms of their role in conserving soil, and to a lesser
degree in terms of their capacity to store and regulate water.[14]

Doubtful that alpine communes would have either the will or the money to invest in reforestation, Surell called for national legislation that would mandate this "new sort of public works." Bernard Lorentz, former director of the national forestry school at Nancy, published a more general report on the Alps and the Pyrenees the following year, heightening the impact of Surell's impassioned book. Lorentz seconded Surell's ideas of causation, called for the same bold intervention by the state, and held to a similarly catastrophist vision of the Alps and the Pyrenees. Three years later the director general of the Administration des Forêts, V. Legrand, paid his own dues to Surell, reiterating the key themes and announcing the formula, "the plain for agriculture, the mountain for forest and pasture," used verbatim by the spokesman for the clearance law of 1851.[15] The head of a traditionally rival administration echoed the conclusions of Surell—the engineer—sealing the harmony between the Forêts and the Ponts et Chaussées over the issue of reforestation.

From the catastrophic mountain to the fully forested mountain, elite formulations left out the complexities of the agro-sylvo-pastoral mountain. Only when the alpine ideal included pastures along with forests did the vision implicate pastoralists, but in the discussion the latter posed only as deforesters whose presence in the future landscape would be problematic at best. In seeming corroboration of all these ideas, large-scale flooding began to plague lowland France in the 1840s—catastrophism made manifest. For more than half of the nineteenth century, France suffered floods whose scale and frequency have not been seen since. Many contemporaries believed they were living through a period of heightened environmental degradation, revealed in landslides and avalanches that wiped out entire alpine villages, and shown in the vagaries of the Loire, Garonne, and Rhône Rivers, whose turbulence recurred every few years and menaced major cities. Andrée Corvol asserts that floods became the "scourge *par excellence*" after mid-century and that the "crusade for reforestation was thus confused with moral awakening."[16]

The late eighteenth and the late nineteenth centuries appear to historians of climate as exceptional periods in which the intensity and frequency of torrential rains caused "catastrophic crises." The major floods of the twentieth century in France—1952, 1977, and 1982—pale by comparison. According to one study of the Garonne, floods statistically formulated as "once a decade" or "once every thirty years" occurred frequently toward the late eighteenth and nineteenth centuries, and those dubbed "once every one hundred years" happened several times in each century. Unlike that of the late eighteenth century, the climatic crisis of the nineteenth did not intensify with time; rather, it lasted longer—from 1855 to approximately 1910—and became a continuous series of abnormal years barely punctuated by calmer times. Some years brought heavy spring rains after cold, snowy winters, providing the conditions for flooding throughout the spring and summer. In other years exceptionally heavy summer and autumn rains followed normal winters and springs, a pattern common near the Mediterranean but unusual and cruel in mountainous interiors.[17] The disasters that followed brought national attention to the degradation of the mountains.

The floods of 1855–56 comprised some of the worst of the century: in two consecutive years, three major rivers, the Garonne, the Loire, and the Rhône, overflowed with torrents of water and tons of debris from the highlands, cutting off bridges and roads, destroying crops, and flooding towns. The Garonne was the first to flood in May 1855, but the worst came in the late spring of 1856, when the Rhône inundated Lyon as well as many towns down to the Mediterranean, submerging the Vaucluse plain and turning the Camargue into a giant lake.[18] Several days later, the Loire flooded Orléans, Blois, Amboise, and Tours. Having promptly left Paris to console victims and observe relief efforts, Napoleon III returned to study numerous proposals for the prevention of future disasters. Some called for the fortification of levees, others for the construction of barricades in the upper valleys, and still others for the reforestation of the mountains. The exigency of controlling unpredictable nature resounded in the emperor's words as he opened the parliamentary session of 1857: "By my honor I promise that rivers, like revolution, will return to their beds and remain unable to rise during my reign."[19]

Napoleon III well understood the stakes involved in controlling floods, for the French state faced a growing imperative to respond to natural disasters. By definition local, or regional in the case of a major flood, natural catastrophes acquired national dimensions apace with the state's investment in provincial infrastructure. As more state revenue paid for the construction of roads and bridges—particularly vulnerable to damage from floods—funds for their repair or replacement would have to come from the same coffers. In addition, the nineteenth-century state shouldered more responsibility for protecting towns, many of which were busy dismantling fortifications and extending suburbs. The imperative to protect agriculture was most decisive: not only did the renovation of the primary sector hold a key place in Napoleon III's scheme of economic modernization, but the seemingly natural and necessary role of alpine forests had already convinced many in top administrations.[20]

The first French law on alpine reforestation passed the Corps Législatif on

20 July 1860, by a vote of 211 to 1—a majority typical of parliamentary voting during the authoritarian period of the Second Empire; Napoleon III signed it on 28 July.[21] In the same year as the commercial treaty with England, the acquisition of Nice and Savoie, and the first measure to liberalize the political system of the Second Empire (reinstating the Corps Législatif's annual address to the emperor), the law on reforestation might have passed unnoticed. For hundreds of communes in France, however, its short-term implications far outweighed those of the other momentous laws and treaties of 1860.

The pet project of Eugène Chevandier de Valdrôme, a liberal engineer who later became interior minister under Emile Ollivier, the law laid out the modalities and financing of reforestation in fourteen articles. The phrase "public utility" appears in the legal text as a central standard, but it shows a certain distance from clean definitions formulated during the Enlightenment—the interests of all, including those of posterity. Applying to property belonging to communes, private citizens, and public entities, but not to forests owned by the state, the law encouraged voluntary replanting through subsidies in money or in kind (seeds and seedlings), while also providing for mandatory projects. The latter were potentially most burdensome for individuals and communes. Article 4 stipulated that by imperial decree the state could designate the "public utility" of reforesting a specified area. The few words used to define public utility—"in consequence of the state of the soil and the dangers posed to lower lands"—betray the limitations placed on the concept. The alpine public remained unmentioned.[22]

In exemplary administrative fashion, several procedures would, however, have to precede the decree: these consisted of a public inquiry in the interested commune(s); deliberations by the municipal council(s); the opinion of a special commission composed of the prefect or his delegate, a member of the department's Conseil Général, a member of the arrondissement council, an engineer from the ministry of public works, a forester, and two property owners residing in the commune(s); the opinion of the arrondissement council; and, finally, the opinion of the Conseil Général. At the end of the administrative tunnel, an imperial decree would designate the perimeter of the lands to be reforested. The law then presented private owners with an option: either reforest themselves or consent to expropriation "by reason of public utility." In case of expropriation, a private owner would receive an indemnity but could regain his title to the property only after reimbursing the state for the indemnity as well as for the costs, in principal and interest, of all expenses related to reforestation. He could exonerate himself from reimbursing the state by an outright cession of half the land.

Mandatory reforestation could also apply to communes, though article 8 carefully excluded the term "expropriation" with regard to communes that refused or could not afford to reforest. Yet the article essentially echoed the measures applicable to private owners: the state would either make a "friendly acquisition" of lands slated for reforestation or else reforest them at its expense, managing and profiting from them until full reimbursement by the commune. Here, too, communes could avoid reimbursement by ceding half the land to the state. Whether or not a commune had reimbursed the state, it could exercise pasturing rights on reforested lands as soon as the Forêts deemed them *défensables,* able to withstand the effects of animals' hooves and teeth. Finally, article 10 narrowed the scope of the law by stating that no more than one-twentieth of a commune's lands could be reforested in a single year; once reforested, however, the portion might not be deemed défensable for a number of years, and the law placed no limit on the total amount of communal land that could remain indefinitely off limits to pasturing.

Twenty years earlier, Surell had predicted the significance of denying property rights for the cause of reforestation. In his call for strong legislation, Surell had reminded his audience that expropriation would hardly be novel in itself; the state had long invoked it every time a public authority wished to build a road. As in instances of road-building, the state would have to justify expropriation for the planting of trees by the test of "public utility."[23] And this would require two leaps of the imagination: first, it would mean convincing alpine peasants that trees on *their* lands were vital to the protection of crops and cities in the far distance. Second, the state would have to link the need for expropriation not only to the circulation of goods but also to production, a link in the economic chain more clearly associated with private profit: "Reforestation thus appears as a great work of public utility. . . . In order to judge it well we must depart from our habitual routine of attributing public utility only to lines of communication, that is to say only to works whose object is to facilitate the circulation of products. Does not agriculture, which produces goods, have its own right to public works, everywhere that it cannot do without them to prosper or simply to survive?"[24] Though Surell and the legislators of 1860 tried to accent the "public" nature of production, the validity of the claim still depended on the law's reception in the mountains. In theoretical terms, notions of depeopled, functional mountains had helped to warp the idea of public utility by justifying reforestation in light of downstream interests and private production.

The order and clarity at the heart of the plain-mountain dichotomy lay as well in the law's measures for financing alpine reforestation. The state would cover subsidies for voluntary replanting by selling national forests located on the plains up to a value of 5 million francs and allow special cuts of timber, also on the plains, to the tune of another 5 million francs. Forest would subsidize forest. Yet this seeming circularity responded to the instrumental purpose of a law that had nothing to do with increasing the total forest cover of France. As Surell and others had argued, forests belonged to the mountains in order to protect the plains.

A simultaneous imperial initiative sheds additional light on the reforestation law. Also signed and sealed by Napoleon III on 28 July 1860, the law on the reclamation of marshes and uncultivated lands belonging to communes portended even more sweeping consequences for communal property. This companion law targeted "uncultivated" plains, degraded mountains, and many areas in between: it represented no less than a full assault on communal lands the state deemed unproductive. Applicable only to communes, in contrast to the law on reforestation, it nevertheless echoed the latter in several ways.

Article 1 of the law on reclamation contained the major directive: "Marshes and uncultivated land belonging to communes or sections of communes, for which reclamation shall have been deemed useful, shall be dried and rendered proper for cultivation or planted with trees." Departmental prefects, as clarified in article 2, would be empowered to "recognize the utility" of such improvement, but they would have to consult the municipal councils on the precise parcels to be reclaimed, the modes of reclamation, and the thorny question of finance. Articles 3 and 4 paralleled the coercive measures in the law on reforestation: should a commune refuse to consider a prefect's judgment in favor of improving a piece of the commune's property, an imperial decree could declare the improvement necessary if preceded by the assent of the departmental Conseil Général. In any case, communes were to pay all costs of reclamation. If unable to do so, the state would advance the sums, to be reimbursed in principal and interest by means, if necessary, of a public sale of part of the improved lands. Article 5 held out the option for a commune to cede half of the improved lands to the state in order to free itself from debt as well as from any further obligations to reclaim its remaining property.[25]

The reclamation law did not touch the question of partitioning communal lands, a project legislated back in 1793, suspended in 1796, and anyway greeted with inertia in pastoral areas. Even in 1860, imperial legislators would not tamper with this important inheritance from France's past. The president of the Council of State, M. Baroche, defended this omission by declaring that the bill would have to contain an "encyclopedia" of legal steps in order to allow partition. One member, the marquis de Sainte-Hermine, complained that the omission constituted a serious weakness in the bill, but it did not prevent the nearly unanimous vote (215 to 4) that saw the bill through passage.[26] The vexing question of partition had become irrelevant: the two laws of 1860 provided an armory of possibilities for the state to interfere with the management and the ownership of communal lands deemed unproductive. In the new era of partially free trade with England, the state was taking steps to advance productivity without entangling itself in the legal complexities of communal property.

Dodging the question of partition was only one way of focusing the debate on questions of technique rather than rights to property. Sainte-Hermine himself opened the debate by vouching for the legislators' unanimous opinion that "this considerable and almost sterile part of the French territory" should be made more productive. The old physiocratic dualism clashed with the fantastic diversity of the lands in question. They comprised "sterile moors, foul swamps, sand dunes, denuded rocks," but also "magnificent prairies, excellent plains, forests, and ponds around which rich and industrious people throng." Clearly, no single set of measures could apply to all these lands, but Sainte-Hermine's point suggested that even the latter category—the healthy commons—should be subject to reclamation.[27]

Only one legislator, M. Guillaumin, sought greater specificity in the law by pointing out the difference between marshes and other uncultivated land. Whereas marshes covered approximately 58,000 hectares in France and, not generally coveted by communes, lent themselves well to "coercive means" of improvement, other uncultivated land extended over 2,700,000 hectares—a full 5 percent of the national territory. Their improvement would call for a colossal short-term investment of at least 2 billion francs in the form of subsidies for drains, irrigation systems, animals, and fertilizers. More important, uncultivated land consisted largely of pastures and played a key role in the rural economy. Guillaumin cautioned his colleagues against tampering with pastoral communities' practices: "We should meddle with them only with extreme reserve. That is an almost political question. We must not exert too great a pressure on [the communes]; we should leave them to their own ways, and come to their assistance through councils, subsidies, and improved communications, not through laws."[28] In a similar vein, Charles de Ribbe, jurist and owner of forest in Provence, had criticized in 1857 the discourse of reforestation, which did not take into account the singularities of real places and their inhabitants.[29] Unheeded in 1860, both warnings reverberated through the end of the century, to the chagrin of foresters, agronomists, and other would-be improvers of the commons.

Although not explicitly linked in the course of legislative debate, the two laws on reforestation and reclamation thus interlocked in several ways. Each underscored what were becoming reified differences between the functions of plains and of mountains. The centerpiece of one law and a stated means of reclamation in the other, reforestation ultimately dissolved the old assimilation of forests with uncultivated land. The economically marginal forests, the sizeable areas of sparse woodland and scrub, would become prime targets of reclamation, to be converted into the densely packed, homogeneous stands of conifers that fed foresters' dreams.[30] In mountainous areas, reclamation did often take the form of reforestation after 1860. Having carried out a survey of 77 communes in Ariège (out of the total 336), a public works engineer concluded in 1862 that the reclamation law would apply to 27 of them, 23 by means of reforestation and 4 by conversion to agriculture.[31]

Above all, the logic of nineteenth-century French forestry linked the two laws of 1860. This logic went beyond the avenue for reforestation provided in the law on reclamation. Viewing with horror the practices of agro-pastoral communities in alpine France, whose residents seemed bent on eradicating trees, foresters tended to see potential forests in every degraded pasture. Consequently, richer grazing land—improved through subsidized reclamation— would facilitate a transition toward more intensive pasturing, and peasants would abandon land that could then be planted in trees. Together, reforestation and reclamation would create the sort of landscape demanded by a modernizing Second Empire: for the plain, agriculture; for the mountain, forest.

ECOLOGICAL ERRORS

This imagined rationalization of plain and mountain—the beginning of *aménagement du territoire*—came at a high price for alpine communities and professional forestry alike. François Combes, former chief of alpine restoration in Savoie, has written that nineteenth-century reforestation efforts were "born of a misunderstanding."[32] The policies written into the 1860 law (and into some of its revision in 1882) consisted, rather, of a series of disparate misunderstandings, economic and social as well as ecological. From observations of erosion to assumptions about agro-pastoralism, untested assertions fed the campaign to reforest, impeding its success, arousing hostility from alpine communes, and ultimately tarnishing its reputation in the twentieth century.

Initially conceived as the ultimate remedy for flooding and erosion, reforestation was fraught with misconceptions both about planting at higher elevations and about the capacity of forests to act as sponges. To begin with the latter, a typical late twentieth-century understanding of the problem emphasizes the hydrological functions of forests, among the many protective services they render. Trees, especially conifers that retain their needles, can intercept between 15 and 40 percent of the water in a normal rainstorm, thereby hindering the formation of torrents. Similarly, alpine forests store snow, curbing the speed of melting. Perhaps most important, forests reduce superficial runoff through the retentive capacity of the forest floor and the soil beneath; the dead organic material on top can absorb up to ten times its weight in water.[33] Today's science would broadly sanction the attention paid by Alexandre Surell and others in the 1840s to the hydrological functions of forests.

Like all sponges, however, forests have their absorptive limits. A dense forest may regulate runoff from a short, heavy storm, but the longer the duration of the rain, the more marginal becomes the forest's efficacy. At the point of saturation, water runs off as it would from a tilted pane of glass. Long, often unrelenting rainstorms characterized the precipitation that led to many of the devastating floods of the nineteenth century. The faith of foresters and legislators that more trees and only more trees would extinguish devastating torrents embodied what Combes calls their "first fundamental error."[34]

But reforestation presented an attractive solution to flooding because it seemed possible everywhere. The identity of the terms *alpine pasture* and *former forest* in the minds of foresters had grown in part because no institutional knowledge suggested that forests could *not* prosper above a certain elevation. Surell himself had boldly declared that the vast "natural" province of the forest knew no constraints from altitude: this was a huge zone, "including in width all the space between the mountains' rocky summits and the middle portion of their slopes, and extending in length over the whole range."[35] Surell, the Public Works engineer, spoke as well for his counterparts in the Forêts.

The forestry corps' collective faith that trees could prosper up to the tops of summits presents a problem relating to the diffusion of scientific understanding. Foresters did not begin to study the effects of altitude on vegetation until the first quarter of the twentieth century, yet the French scientific community knew of, and contributed to, such studies from the early nineteenth century. Several of the most renowned botanists of the time devoted themselves to studying why certain species and communities of plants grew where they did. Beginning with Alexander von Humboldt's *Essai sur la géographie des plantes* (1807), the problem of plant distribution by latitude and hemisphere as well as altitude preoccupied botanists. Humboldt, a disciple of the great botanist

Georges Louis Buffon, formulated the idea that a mountain was a "hemisphere in miniature," where each altitudinal zone replicated the vegetative zones found in each hemisphere according to latitude. In other words, altitude was a crucial element of the environment that determined the natural occurrence of specific plants in specific places.[36]

In the field of biogeography, Humboldt passed the baton to Augustin de Candolle, a Swiss naturalist who had studied medicine in Paris, then botany under Lamarck. Candolle moved away from Humboldt's hemispheric generalizations and focused his own work on the smaller distribution patterns of plants; however, he carried on Humboldt's ideas about altitude in his essay *Mémoire sur la géographie des plantes de France, considérée dans ses rapports avec la hauteur absolue* (1817). With Candolle, the idea that each species of plant required a precise set of environmental conditions became an organizing premise of the field of botany.[37] Candolle's ideas remained easily accessible to the French reading public.

In this light, it seems that planners in the Forêts were out of touch with the botanical thinking of their day. At the national forestry school in Nancy, students received no special training in problems pertaining to the mountains.[38] Just as the agriculture bureaucracy, part of Public Works until 1869, existed in large part to increase France's agricultural productivity, the Administration des Forêts existed to promote the growth of forests. At the very least, botanical knowledge and administrative knowledge circulated through different conduits, and in this sphere, little collaboration among experts took place.

It may be disingenuous to hold nineteenth-century foresters to the standards of late twentieth-century knowledge; the comparison does, however, highlight the working concepts within professional French forestry during both eras. The notion of a tree line, for example, was quite fixed for Surell and his successors, whereas foresters today acknowledge that the upper limit of alpine forests is a highly variable line dependent on microclimates. In the Andorran Pyrenees the tree line can vary from one thousand to twenty-five hundred meters within the space of a few kilometers.[39] General agreement also reigns over the artificially low upper limit of forest in the major mountain ranges of Europe, which nineteenth-century foresters themselves assumed. Where they fell short, however, was in imagining the ancientness of the estives and the alpages. Deforestation, for them, was a recent phenomenon, intimately related to revolutionary upheaval. On the contrary, scientists now posit that millennia of pastoralism have caused microclimatic changes in the uplands that make reforestation in many places virtually impossible.[40]

It took several decades of growth for foresters to realize that, when seedlings survived at all at high elevations, they produced "bonsai" forests, patchy and vulnerable.[41] But even where foresters aimed at lower elevations, as they generally did in the Pyrenees, their efforts contravened both the patterns of agro-pastoralism and the realities of alpine ecology. Not only was silviculture at stake; in Ariège in particular, pastoral improvements were calculated to go hand in hand with reforestation. Foresters and agriculture officials, responsible for reclamation, applied the two laws of 1860 by neatly dividing the Pyrenean uplands in a manner that seemed to correspond to the natural function of the terrain. They sought to juxtapose new forest and improved pastures wherever they could show the degradation caused by the archaic practices of alpine peasants.

Applying this scheme to the Pyrenees, foresters and agronomists ignored the priorities that conditioned agro-pastoralism. As discussed earlier, peasants devoted more space but less labor to raising livestock than to growing crops in the Alps and the Pyrenees; livestock monopolized little of the peasant's time but still provided the bank of fertilizer crucial to maintaining subsistence-level production of grains. For most pastoralists, animals served agriculture and provided intermittent commercial returns. Swayed by the visible level of degradation on Pyrenean slopes, agronomists carried the banner of reclamation to the communally owned estives, the high summer pastures above twelve or thirteen hundred meters in altitude. Ignorance of the economic logic at work in the mountains largely doomed the effort; regrassing the estives, putting in drains, and burning off weeds and brush required a long-term commitment on the part of local peasants, who were fundamentally unwilling to turn their labor away from agriculture on their own lands. The wealthy owners of large flocks and the poorer peasants who owned few or no animals saw little advantage in improving the estives.[42]

The drive to restore alpine pastures also failed through foresters' misapprehension of alpine ecology. A composition of grasses and moors covered with heather, ferns, broom, and gorse, as well as rhododendron on the damper slopes and juniper in the drier parts, covered the high Pyrenean pastures. Comparisons of nineteenth- and twentieth-century photographs reveal the remarkable stability of these plant communities—a "biological inertia" that contrasts sharply with the more volatile communities at lower elevations. By rotating their flocks and periodically burning the plants too tough for animals to eat, Pyrenean shepherds had adapted to relative ecological stasis. These key elements of extensive pasturing responded to both the ecology of the estives and the minimal labor peasants could allocate to pastoralism. Foresters, however, interpreted the fibrous plants of the Pyrenean estives as evidence of degradation, and they attempted to extirpate them through massive burnings and mechanical removal. In order to foster intensive pasturing, they also tried to give the grasses an edge through irrigation, but their efforts came to naught; every few years the broom, heather, and ferns grew back.

Earmarking the high pastures for reclamation, foresters deemed the pastures on the lower slopes suitable for trees. The concept of degradation more aptly depicted these pastures; closer to villages, used intensively from fall to spring, and raided of their least shrub for firewood, many lower pastures had entered into full erosion, providing the "self-destructing" image of the mountains held by many travelers and scientists. Many foresters believed them to be beyond regrassing and salvageable only if reforested.[43] Though not an ecological impossibility, this scheme came face to face with rural resistance and ultimately failed. To do justice to this story on a local level, a closer look at Ariège and Savoie is in order.

AMBITION IN ARIÈGE

Louis-Henri Vicaire, director general of the Administration des Forêts, put much of his energy into reforestation during the 1860s. The project incorporated the sanction of law, the glamour of novelty, and a moral sense of mission. Within less than a year, Vicaire had seen to the creation of dozens of nurseries, appointed thirty-two specialized foresters, and launched "inquiries of public utility" in areas of potentially mandatory reforestation. A flurry of experimentation accompanied the first attempts: whether to plant seeds or seedlings (only seedlings survived in Ariège and Haute-Garonne, whereas seeds germinated well in Provence) and which species to privilege were questions answered gradually through trial and error.[44] A sense of urgency often surfaced in the director general's reports. Summarizing the first annual conferences on reforestation, Vicaire criticized foresters who had assigned ten to twenty years for the completion of their work: "The administration has had to point out to its agents that such a delay is incompatible with the speed necessary, from all points of view, to proceed with the task; it has reminded [them] that, when reforestation with definitive species is not immediately possible, the soil should be covered with plants of lower orders."[45] The pressing task of buttressing the mountains with vegetation could, ironically, hardly await the gradual growth of a new generation of trees.

Most of the early reforesting in Ariège came through voluntary efforts. Not only did the administrative process slow down mandatory projects, but Vicaire encouraged voluntary planting in order to avoid as many expropriations as possible, given the expense of indemnities. In his first circular to prefects in August 1860, Vicaire stressed that the success of reforestation would depend on the "general sympathies" of local people; it was up to the prefects to dissipate apprehensions and enlighten people as to their "true interests."[46] Although Vicaire's staff laid plans for mandatory reforesting in twelve departments in 1861, most involved the highly eroded slopes of the Durance basin and the area around Barège, a major thermal station in Hautes-Pyrénées. None initially concerned Ariège or Savoie.

When it came, reforestation met with objection in Ariège ranging from passive resistance, to delaying tactics, to collective violence. Ultimately, foresters in Ariège accomplished few of the goals outlined in the law of 1860. Warnings had been sounded before then, but, if remembered, they fell on deaf ears once Vicaire set the ambitious project in motion. These early warnings had taken diverse forms: there was, for example, the forest guard who had written to his superior in Foix in 1843 to tell him why he thought reforestation in his district would be inappropriate as well as impolitic. The guard's description of the local mountains presented the discerning view of one who regularly made his rounds through their forests and pastures: "As far as property of this [uncultivated] nature belonging to communes and individuals, I have noticed no entirely deforested mountains, for all show some forest[;] one notices pastures up above and sometimes lower, forests occupy[ing] the center of the mountains . . . ; thus I believe we need not concern ourselves with them, and all the more because the uncultivated lands [*vacants*] in question have existed as such since time immemorial."[47] This was not the ideal, neatly banded mountain, with improved estives on top giving way to a dense swath of forest followed by fields below, in whose image the administration sought to transform parts of the Pyrenees after 1860. The guard saw the "disorderly" mountain of the peasants, with pastures mostly on top but some further down, and forests perhaps degraded but far from absent. The guard's remark that these "vacant" lands had existed since "time immemorial" hinted at their status in the uplands of Ariège, and at the resistance that might occur should foresters try to impose a new order on them.

Members of the Ariégeois elite, some even representing lowland agricultural interests, criticized aspects of the legislation early on, noting the limited financing available for subsidies and foresters' false sense of security, born of privileging technique over social questions. As the local agronomist Paul Troy warned, "the administration is at risk of maintaining a dangerous security until the moment that protests, still timid and suppressed, will explode all of a sudden." In addition to offering his own land for experimental plots, Troy suggested that foresters begin to build bridges to alpine communities by plumbing the peasants' sense of tree species and where they grew best.[48]

That foresters should profit from local knowledge would not be taken seriously within the Forêts until the twentieth century. At any rate, and defying general expectations, communes throughout France showed more élan in voluntarily replanting their property than did private owners. Of the 3,237 hectares planted in all departments in 1861, communal efforts had been responsible for all but 583 hectares.[49] In 1862 Vicaire singled out Ariège, along with Cantal and Vaucluse, as a department in which substantial numbers of communes had voted subsidies; by contrast, he cited the hesitation of private land owners, for whom expense, surveillance, and lack of knowledge posed obstacles to reforestation. But Vicaire touted a relative victory at best: by the middle of 1863, only forty-nine communes in Ariège had begun to reforest 387 hectares, while private owners had begun to plant 237 hectares, both tiny amounts compared to the roughly 160,000 hectares of forest in the department.[50]

What had seemed to be an auspicious beginning in Ariège gave way to resistance by 1861. For one thing, foresters bent the legal mechanisms to reforest the state's lands in Ariège, both those that had and those that had not yet been freed of use rights by cantonnement. Reforestation in Ariège began to collide with use rights as much as the genesis of the 1860 law had depended upon their partial extinction. By June 1863, foresters had planted approximately twenty-eight hundred hectares of the state's land in Ariège, four and a half times the amount of private and communal land reforested. Vicaire's report of 1864 highlighted the difficulties of reforesting on state-owned lands burdened with use rights.[51] Despite his expressed concern for "general sympathies," Vicaire's administration treated events in Ariège with denial masked by draconian rigor.

The prefect, ever eager to present an image of tranquillity within his domain, sounded a muted alarm in November 1861. All opposition to reforestation had dissipated in his department, he claimed, but the Ariégeois needed special enlightening and reassuring with regard to the foresters' mission. The prefect seconded the Conseil Général's proposal to create commissions in each canton whose function would be to help choose areas to be reforested. Hinting that technical questions were not the only ones at issue, he referred to a "practical side" of the matter that the notables of each canton could help resolve.[52]

The conservator of the region, Michel Subirane, adamantly opposed such cantonal commissions. His arguments ranged from the right of administrative sovereignty to beliefs about the essential pettiness of the Ariégeois. Not only would local commissions compromise the procedures laid out in the 1860 law, but their members could not possibly exhibit independent judgment. Notables in the uplands of Ariège were the largest owners of livestock and would thus oppose reforestation as a threat to their pastures. The conservator leveled more biting criticism at all alpine peasants, notorious for their intercommunal rivalries. They would be fundamentally unable to think in terms of public utility, which of course defined the purpose of reforestation. Finally, it was high time that the Ariégeois learn to live without the unjustified concessions granted them over the centuries: "The department of Ariège has always been considered an exceptional region. This opinion, in fact unjustified, has given rise to tolerances and concessions so large that the users have come to consider the domain's mountains as their property. The creation of cantonal commissions would obviously sustain them in these ideas and would consequently tend to increase their distaste for reforestation."[53] The meaning of possession in Ariège was strong enough to extend to lands where use rights pertained, yet the Ariégeois would have to be weaned from their privileges.

Subirane never changed his mind about cantonal commissions, but he and the prefect reached a compromise a few months later. They agreed to allow purely advisory commissions, composed largely of an administrative elite, to present formal opinions of any local objections to reforestation pertaining to pasturing rights. At one per arrondissement, these advisory boards had less of a local cast than commissions based in each canton; as such the conservator found them palatable and the prefect, referring to them as "family reunions," credited them in 1864 with having prevented further discord in Ariège. On his own initiative, however, the prefect inaugurated cantonal conferences, which in annual meetings would help designate, along with foresters, parcels to be reforested. Subirane did not object, apparently deeming infrequent conferences, as opposed to permanent commissions, an appropriate forum for local opinion. In 1863 the prefect reported favorably on the balance he had struck between administrative directives and local concerns, for both communes and large private landowners had begun to request more subsidies for optional reforestation.[54]

Ariège became the only department in which institutional changes were made to incorporate, at some level, communal needs and values in the enforcement of the 1860 law.[55] What is far less clear is whether these changes actually softened the law's reception in Ariège. For in his 1864 report on reforestation, Vicaire acknowledged that, despite support at all higher administrative levels, municipal councils and the private owners involved in the public inquiries had remained steadfastly opposed to mandatory reforesting, "even while recognizing, nearly everywhere, the utility in principle of the projected operations." Vicaire admitted that the 1860 law had ignored the importance of pastures in the alpine economy. And communes had remained financially unable to apply the law on reclamation, which had provided for no permanent aid by the state.

Vicaire recommended a complementary law on regrassing (*regazonnement*), which in many places might be sufficient to halt erosion while improving pastures.[56] Indeed, a law permitting regrassing was passed later that year and promulgated on 8 June 1864. The legislative commission charged with examining the bill, also submitted by Chevandier de Valdrôme, utterly omitted a political rationale: instead of arguing for the need to conciliate communities hostile to reforestation, the commission approved of the bill simply because it gave the Forêts a necessary tool to combat *dégazonnement*, which had suddenly been recognized as a cause equal to déboisement in the formation of torrential streams.[57] Articulated as a complement to the law on reforestation, the new law allowed the partial or total substitution of grass for trees where the administration believed that grass would suffice to consolidate alpine soils. Communes and private owners could also demand the substitution but would need the prefect's approval if the foresters refused. Otherwise, the law of 1864 departed from that of 1860 only by allowing owners to exonerate themselves from debt by ceding just one-fourth (instead of one-half) of their regrassed lands to the state and by providing communes with "indemnities for temporary privation."[58] Although several historians recognize the 1864 law as a political concession won by alpine people, the new legislation did not necessarily appease those most threatened by even temporary loss of their pastures.[59]

The case of Auzat, a commune in the upper Vicdessos basin (the Vicdessos is a tributary of the Ariège River), shows how local knowledge justified local control in the minds of villagers who, when confronted with the goals of the Administration des Forêts, could not be satisfied by advisory boards, commissions, or even a complementary law. This area of approximately 350 square kilometers forms the part of Ariège most susceptible to erosion. Moraines mark the topography of the Vicdessos; formed by succeeding periods of glaciation and deglaciation, these deposited mountains are fragile and easily undermined by water. According to one thesis, the people of the Vicdessos magnified the effects of natural disasters in the nineteenth century by converting nearly all of the usable land to agriculture and pasturing. Terraces and hedges helped keep the soil in place on cultivated slopes, but the pastures had suffered from overgrazing, and animals had nibbled away at the forest from the estives above, creating an artificially low tree line.[60]

Around Auzat, spring avalanches of melting snow occurred frequently. The Auzatois received the avalanche of 2 March 1853 with fatalism, a typically rural sense of destiny; they had foreseen it but decided not to leave their homes at the first signs of its approach.[61] Many observations had told them that forests did little to stop advancing masses of wet, dense snow, which can often uproot trees and add their weight to the force of the avalanche. Since the recurring catastrophe in Auzat came in the form of avalanches, it is not surprising that the inhabitants saw little purpose in reforesting the meager lands that provided their sustenance.

When in 1862 the Forêts decided to reforest 8,052 hectares of state-owned lands within the commune—about half the communal territory—the Auzatois addressed a lengthy letter of protest to the emperor. The complaint began with a formulaic appeal to the "gift" of the mountains granted more than eight centuries earlier by the counts of Foix, then deftly exploited the rhetoric of paternalism: "We come to the foot of your throne with tears of despair to show Your Majesty the disastrous position into which the proposed reforestation will throw us, [a project] already begun on our mountains by the Administration des Forêts. You are the father of the poor commoners; thus we feel confident that Your Majesty will, once enlightened as to our situation, pity our misery and save us from the peril that threatens us."[62] With passion and lucidity the authors explained that privation of their pastures would inevitably drive them to emigrate: "for without pastures, no flocks, no fertilizer, no harvests, nothing at all in fact, if not flight or death." The fundamental issue of local control surfaced in the Auzatois' argument that, far from hostile to reforestation itself, they believed themselves the only ones competent to choose the parcels of land most fit to be planted. Local understanding of environmental constraints stood in glaring contrast to an image of administrative arbitrariness: "It is in vain that [the administration] seeks to legitimate its vast projects by the considerable surface area of our commune. It will never be able to deny to us that three quarters of our uncultivated lands are bare rock, inaccessible even to animals, and that reforestation cannot take place other than on the limited grassy areas, that is the pastures, around our chalets which henceforth will disappear, for we will no longer be able to exercise our industry." In addition, officials were ignoring the realities of alpine climate: every summer shepherds could expect a snowstorm or two in the upper pastures, causing the flocks to descend temporarily; were the lower pastures to be reforested, the animals would inevitably run into the seedlings upon their descent and then be seized by the forest guards. As the more than one hundred signatures attested (most written in the same hand and followed by an *X*), these facts might be disguised from afar but were irrefutable in Auzat.[63]

Whether or not Napoleon III ever responded personally to the complaint from Auzat, Conservator Subirane obtained a copy of it and sent it along with his summary dismissal of the commune's arguments to the director general in Paris. With the swiftness allowed by numbers, he dodged all of the Auzatois' concerns about autonomy and survival. The state would reforest the 8,052 hectares over the course of thirty years. After the first fifteen years, about half the planted area would be défensable, no longer off limits to animals. Another 5,761 hectares of communal territory belonging to the state could of course be used for pasturing during this time. Thus, after fifteen years the commune would have 9,787 hectares at its disposal; at five sheep per hectare, this amount of land would allow half again as many sheep as currently pastured in the commune. Subirane did not suggest what the inhabitants were supposed to do during the first fifteen years of reforestation, when approximately half of their pastures would be off limits. Nor did he mention the inaccessible, rocky areas that the Auzatois had said constituted three quarters of their commune's land.[64]

Foresters did not follow through with their grandiose designs. They planted only 800 hectares in the entire Vicdessos between 1870 and 1900; natural reforestation accounts for most of the current 6,500 hectares covered with trees (19 percent of the Vicdessos basin).[65] In part, this was due to the administration's revised notion of what it meant to "restore" alpine lands after 1882, a shift discussed in Chapter 3. Before that year, inadequate resources, unsuccessful plantings, and compromise played decisive roles. But if the people of Auzat did not witness the cordoning off of much of "their" land, relations between them and the Forêts remained tense. A curious incident from 1871–72 illustrates that, less than reforestation itself, contention over local versus central administrative sovereignty defined these relations, as it had in cases of cantonnement.

In the early 1870s the municipal council of Auzat decided on its own to plant some trees, presumably taking advantage of the subsidies available for voluntary reforestation. The parish priest, however, believing he was acting in his parishioners' interest, obtained permission from the forest inspector in Foix to allow them to pasture their sheep in the newly planted areas. The mayor, furious at the priest, complained in heated language to the foreman of forest guards, who, instead of reporting the incident to his superiors as the mayor had requested, denounced the mayor to the priest and the police. The mayor, accompanied to court by many sympathetic Auzatois, was acquitted of his verbal offenses against the priest, but an unnamed higher functionary in the Forêts stood by the foreman (the principal witness) during the hearing. Hippolyte Doumenjou, representing the canton of Vicdessos in the Conseil Général, reported the affair to the director general, the conservator, and the prefect; appalled at the foreman's actions, Doumenjou encapsulated the meaning of the incident in a concluding question: "What [official] sanction will in the future give the Administration des Forêts the right to strike at the authorities in this important commune?" The absurdity of the forestry corps supporting a misguided priest and not standing by the municipal council's wish to protect its seedlings showed that the incident had been an affair between mayor and forester, allied with the priest, having very little to do with forestry at all.[66]

Although such skirmishes and posturing were common in much of Ariège, the level of violence in response to reforestation did not approach the violence of 1848; 1871 would usher in some of the old tactics but not the same degree of mobilization. It is all the more surprising, then, that in the 1870s, the Forêts accomplished none of its major goals in Ariège—voluntary reforestation on a large scale (the 1860 law expired after a decade, canceling all plans for expropriation), the conclusion of more cantonnements, or the reduction of the number of forest crimes.

Voluntary reforestation all but came to a halt between 1870 and 1876, and the Conseil Général even ceased to report on it from 1877 to the end of the decade. Some new plantings took place only in 1874 and 1875; a few private owners received subsidies to reforest a grand total of just under eleven hectares.[67] The tenor of the conservator's explanations changed markedly within three years: commenting in 1869 that a few "isolated complaints" would not succeed in halting the momentum, he pleaded for justice and conciliation in 1872: "Let me proclaim, along with an honorable member of the Conseil Général, 'It is time that, if the population is really suffering because of the Administration des Forêts, let [that suffering] be concluded; if, on the contrary, the administration is a victim of unjust sentiments and exaggerated demands on the part of the population, let justice be done to it.' Yes, it is time!" For its part, the Conseil Général allocated no funds for additional reforestation throughout the 1870s, spending money only on maintaining previous plantings.[68] The loudest voices in the municipalities had succeeded in halting the first phase of reforestation.

Second, the forestry corps in Ariège suspended all cantonnements, initially at the prefect's request in 1869. This process of translating use rights into property rights contained no guarantee that economic needs would be met, nor did it have to in the administrative mind. Though the state often added concessions of 30 to 50 percent to the capitalized value of the rights to sweeten the deal, communities continued to refuse the offers, claiming that the amount of forest left to them would not suffice. Significantly, these refusals became reasons for the Forêts to defer; no cantonnements appear to have been forced upon alpine communes in Ariège in the 1870s.[69] Rural obstinacy had not posed an insurmountable obstacle in the 1840s and 1850s, even in lengthy cases such as the cantonnement of Ax-les-Thermes. In January 1869, the upcoming legislative elections were reason enough for the conservator to recommend suspending all cantonnements; Second Empire politics shifted decisively in that year as the regime practically jettisoned its management of elections through official candidates.[70] Just as violence occurred in Paris and other major cities, the conservator feared that hostile parties in Ariège, "with their habitual malevolence," might exploit the situation. By 1874 the new conservator in Toulouse, Antoine Canferra, told the Conseil Général that he would no longer attempt cantonnements in Ariège but rather, "inspired by sentiments of benevolence," would seek only to regulate use rights. This plan took clearer form in 1876: the administration would work toward the conversion of low forest to high forest on the state's lands in Ariège, most of which were still burdened with use rights.[71]

Finally, the numbers of recorded forest crimes remained high, averaging 2,081 offenses in the department for each year between 1867 and 1876. It was in the village of Goulier, high in the mountains near Auzat, that forest crimes first erupted into collective violence.[72] As Conservator Subirane put it, the "unfortunate population" of Goulier had begun to devastate their forests as a matter of habit and had turned forest crimes into a "perpetual industry." By 1868, four hundred to five hundred women were pillaging the forests and demolishing the new plantings in daily or nightly operations. The principal role of women anticipated the participation of both women and men in the dramatic case of Massat (see Chapter 4), in contrast to the very masculine War of the Demoiselles. "With audacity and impudence they brave and sometimes provoke threats of repression," Subirane lamented, concluding the following year that no repressive measures had had the slightest effect, and the situation was becoming less a "forest question" than one of public order. Somewhat desperately, the Forêts loudly proclaimed a new era of good feelings, attributing the violence in Goulier and a few other communes in the Vicdessos to "odious calumnies" and "dangerous incitations" on the part of a few. What was happening in Goulier, which the Forêts insisted was an exceptional commune? How might the elections of 1869 have been related to the violence? Explanation was clearly less important to the conservator than the need to "moralize the consequences" of violence by making the delinquents work for the upkeep of forests and local roads.[73]

That was before 1871, the year forest crimes peaked in Ariège at 2,606, and the year many forest guards in the Pyrenees were mobilized and stationed along the Spanish frontier after the dispersion of the Communards of Paris. In 1871 forest crimes in the Vicdessos took on the "character of devastation," in the conservator's eyes, and seemed to be inspired by a "spirit of destruction and evil."[74] Further west in the Castillonnais, forest crimes mushroomed in Alos, Moulis, and Lacourt. The closest call for a forest guard occurred in the commune of Illartein, when assailants broke the windows of guard Maubourguet's house and entered the room where his wife and children were sleeping, but they injured no one. During the Terrible Year, peasants' repertoires of action against the Forêts included tactics from both the War of the Demoiselles and 1848: villagers masked themselves, routed the few remaining forest guards, and sporadically "devastated" the forest. Political change in Paris again reverberated in the Pyrenees as it had in 1848, for apparently most devastation had followed news of the Republic, in September 1870.[75]

Judges pardoned many of those convicted of forest crimes in the early 1870s, but the conservator refused to grant a general amnesty in 1872, asserting that it would be considered "an act of weakness, and even an encouragement." The cantons of Vicdessos and Tarascon continued to register the most forest crimes, with the commune of Auzat committing the most pasturing offenses. In one of the last echoes of the War of the Demoiselles, masked men from Moulis invaded the forest in 1876, assaulted forest guards, cut down 1,199 trees, and mutilated forty cows and calves, attaching a note to one of the latter that read, "This is a first warning."[76]

Ariège, then, seems to fit the conclusion made by Raphaël Larrère and others that wherever the Administration des Forêts threatened to disrupt the conditions of survival in alpine areas, peasants' resistance sufficed to limit its intervention.[77] But the balance sheet does not end there, for the state's foresters began, after 1860, to alter the rural economy in ways that would intensify with time and reflect other inroads of the state. In a word, the foresters offered wages. In the relatively peaceful year of 1862, the conservator commented to the director general that the Ariégeois living in the uplands were grateful for the administration's presence, since it offered to employ them in the task of reforestation.[78] Ambivalence characterized the atmosphere in the alpine communes, where the poorest members probably welcomed the opportunity to earn wages, a rarity in the alpine economy, and the middling to better-off remained hostile to the idea of projects that threatened communal pastures.

Working for the Forêts and flouting the Forest Code were by no means mutually exclusive acts; the badly paid forest guards notoriously accepted bribes and sometimes participated in forest crimes themselves.[79] Knowing that much illegal gathering of firewood resulted from poor access to "legal" parts of the forest, the administration sought to improve access roads. Here foresters mixed incentive with coercion: by a decree of April 1868, owners of flocks had to contribute a day of work building roads for every twenty-five sheep sent out to pasture. For each day of corvée, peasants could put in a day of labor paid by the state. Most communes accepted this arrangement fairly well, except for those in the Vicdessos, which did not adhere to it at all. Still, the conservator regarded it as an important means of conciliation.[80] Absent from his report was the fact the Forêts had done all the conciliating during the last decade of the Second Empire.

PRUDENCE IN SAVOIE

Reforestation and reclamation awaited their application in the Savoie of 1860, a department whose men had voted for annexation to France just three months before the passage of both laws. Before they could begin to manage the forests of Savoie, officials had to survey them, a long-term task in itself. The last good cadastre had been prepared in 1730, and the Sardinian government of the Restoration had not left a reliable cadastre of its own.[81] Sixteen years after the annexation, only 189 of the 570 communal forests had been surveyed. The director general's decree of 17 October 1860, submitting all communal forests "capable of regular exploitation" to management by the forestry corps, remained a statement of intention for many years in the absence of evaluations and surveys.[82]

With less-than-precise knowledge of its domain, the Forêts nevertheless divided Savoie into manageable units, as other departments had been since the First Empire; Savoie became one conservation district with four inspection areas, and the director general named Charles Jacquot as the first forest conservator. In addition to surveying, attempting to forbid pasturing in the forests, and regulating cuts, the forestry corps devoted some initial attention to reforestation. Modesty characterized their efforts, as did procedures rather different from those implemented in Ariège. Namely, foresters partially blurred the distinction between "optional" and "mandatory" reforestation during the early 1860s: the administration itself submitted reforestation proposals to some eighty-one communes, which were expected to vote on them and receive subsidies if the votes were affirmative. The amount of land in question was, despite the large number of communes involved, minuscule—only about 400 hectares. And the proposals did not, of course, translate directly into results; the balance sheet for 1862 came to a little more than 212 reforested hectares spread over fifty communes.[83]

Departmental authorities also helped finance reforestation during the first years of the French regime. The Conseil Général of Savoie voted six thousand francs annually from 1862 to 1868 to supplement funds from the state, halving the amount in 1869 and 1870. Compared to the one thousand francs voted annually by the Conseil Général of Ariège in the same years, these were sizeable sums, yet they tell little about the overall popularity of reforestation. For a variety of reasons, foresters covered only 2,800 additional hectares with trees between 1860 and 1880, very little when judged against the department's 85,300 hectares of communal forest. Taking cuttings into account, an inspector estimated in 1887 that the forest cover of lands not yet within the forest regime (still 35 percent of Savoie's forest) had diminished by 144 hectares since 1860.[84]

Two decades of lax reforestation in Savoie stemmed in part from the policies of the department's first "god," Prefect Hippolyte Dieu: early in his administration, he sought to enforce the law that promised a measure of economic renewal for Savoie—the law on the reclamation of the commons. By the time Napoleon III had sent Eugène Rouher, minister of industry, commerce, and agriculture, to direct various works in Savoie in late 1861, the imperial government had already poured more than 3 million francs into the building of roads, schools, and churches in the new department.[85] If money could buy cultural assimilation, then surely the state would be well advised to spend on projects designed to develop the flagging economy; in Savoie, this faith initially dictated expenditures aimed at agriculture. Dieu further clarified that improvements would come at the expense of "backward" communal practices: "One of the greatest ameliorations the administration can pursue in the general interest of the region, as in that of the communes, consists of the improvement of their lands. . . . Common use is the fruit of a barbarous epoch; it offends the principle of equality which must preside over the distribution of communal expenses and benefits; it strikes much property with sterility. In the midst of progress noticeable in all sources of wealth, communal property has remained unproductive for the communes and for the region." This of course echoed the primary view of communal property within the Administration des Forêts, as one of the first treatises on reforestation in the Alps reiterated.[86] As if to mitigate his own attitude toward communal property, however, Dieu created cantonal commissions—a forum for local opinion—to "enlighten and advise" the administration on matters pertaining to reclamation in Savoie. Just a few months later the conservator in Toulouse would oppose the idea of such commissions playing a role in reforesting Ariège; softer treatment was the order of the day in the annexed department.[87]

The prefect also had before him evidence of the success of reclamation, namely, the drainage of marshy valleys in Savoie. In 1824 the Sardinian king, Charles-Felix, had inaugurated vast drainage projects in the Combe de Savoie and Faucigny, distributing the cost among the state, provinces, communes, and individuals; in 1845 King Charles-Albert shifted all financing to the state. Marshes became fertile agricultural land sought by many in Savoie.[88] The prefect aimed to continue the enterprise in the 1860s.

Hippolyte Dieu understood the geological and hydrological problems of the mountains also in terms of an overabundance of water; he concluded that the forestry corps would have to drain the mountain slopes as well as the plains before reforesting. Describing the effects of heavy rains on the fragile schists that decomposed following winter freezes, Dieu asserted that an excess of water could turn an entire hillside into liquefied mud that would descend in a torrent and destroy everything in its path, trees included. "The largest boulders dance like feathers," Dieu wrote poetically, arguing that planting trees on undrained soil would perturb the ground even more. In 1861 he requested a credit of fifty thousand to sixty thousand francs from the reforestation budget in order to proceed with preliminary drainage of alpine slopes.[89]

Without prefectorial support, the forestry corps could not push for reforestation on a large scale in Savoie, especially given its other tasks in the new domain. Yet foresters did replant some areas, baring their practices to popular scrutiny. Unlike the focus in Ariège—planting trees on sections of degraded pastures—the forestry corps in Savoie tried to engage communes in an effort to plant the clearings within forests. Municipal councils would have to be assured that by establishing nurseries, foresters did not intend to plant any pastures but rather to fill in the bare areas inside the boundaries of communal forests. Though calculated to please the pastoral interests in Savoie, this policy met with reluctant approval at best. Reporting on it twenty-two years later, Conservator Léopold Bousquier concluded that it had long been "badly viewed in general by the population," who feared the diminution of their pastures.[90] The foresters did not recognize these clearings as pastures, but Savoyard peasants valued them for their grasses and for the protection they provided animals.

Anecdotal evidence suggests that low-level tension, if not violence, defined the relations between peasants and foresters in Savoie during the first decade or so following annexation. Perhaps Conservator Jacquot was expecting as much when he asked the prefect to invite former soldiers to enter the forestry corps as guards, citing their "probity, discipline, and zeal" as appropriate qualities for the job.[91] Contests for authority could turn on seemingly trivial issues, such as who would mark the trees to be cut in the communal forest of Pussy and delivered to the inhabitants of the commune. On a tour of the forest in the summer of 1861, the inspector from Moûtiers found himself and his adjunct surrounded by several members of the municipal council who, addressing him in a "highly vulgar tone," declared themselves to be the masters of their own forests and therefore the only ones with the authority to mark trees. The intimidation worked: the mild administrative response consisted of a solemn reminder, sent to all Savoyard mayors, of the powers invested in the forestry corps.[92]

Fear and rumors also delineated the rapport between Savoyards and the Forêts. A fire lit in the forest of Mâcot, a commune upstream from Moûtiers on the Isère River, elicited a forest guard's comment that people in Mâcot probably suspected the new administration of wanting to extend its sylvan domain beyond what the Sardinian regime had held. Such a rumor, the guard protested, was entirely unfounded: "The administration has but one goal, and that is to preserve intact the domain left to it, and above all to oppose firmly all acts which have the character of devastation."[93] The district inspector of forests responded less charitably. The culprits could not have been more wrongheaded in their suspicion, for the administration intended to subtract some of the forest of Mâcot from the forest regime, parts devastated during Sardinian rule. In his judgment of the presumed arsonists, the inspector contended that such acts, typically overlooked by the Sardinian authorities, were forest crimes, and he deployed language that echoed a full set of assumptions about all alpine peasants: "Besides, the criminal attempt should not be surprising, coming from the inhabitants of Mâcot, a population essentially bad and delinquent." Some Savoyards had lost their innocence. The number of reported forest crimes was nearly as high in Savoie as in Ariège: from 1861 to 1866, more than 2,100 forest crimes annually filled the reports of an insufficient number of frequently venal forest guards. The numbers declined gradually thereafter: 1,798 forest crimes were registered from 1866 to 1870, and 1,676 between 1871 and 1875.[94]

Where fear and rumor existed without criminality, foresters still mixed appeasement with judgment. In 1864 the regional conservator found himself quelling the fears of the agronomist and livestock owner Fleury Lacoste, who penned his concerns that the administration was planning to reforest two thousand hectares of the vast communal pastures of Thuile. Such a course would destroy the sheep industry in the commune, which produced lamb and mutton prized by butchers in Lyon. The conservator responded harshly: Lacoste was abusing his position as a "notable" to spread a false rumor; all reforesting concerned land designated as forest, not pasture, and was proceeding only at communes' requests; far fewer than two thousand hectares would be reforested in Thuile; and the brave forest agents were acting in the interest of livestock owners like M. Lacoste, even willing to bend the law in their favor. But fear in Savoie engaged the administration at the highest level: the director general had already sent Hippolyte Dieu figures and other evidence to defuse two rumors running rampant throughout the department—that the state's foresters had broad plans to forbid all pasturing in the communal forests and that they had fixed the prices of construction wood at artificially high levels.[95]

All in all, an uneasy truce molded relations between foresters and Savoyard peasants in the early years of the French regime. Both the imperative of economic development and the need for surveys sheltered Savoie from a full application of the first law on reforestation: improvement of the plain superseded rationalization of the mountain. Thus, foresters could not immediately begin to reshape the lands that for them had been historically "empty" of the sorts of conflicts inscribed in the forests of Ariège. But where they tried, they did not encounter a compliant people, automatically accepting subsidies to replant their forest clearings as foresters evidently expected them to. In turn, the Administration des Forêts began to use the language of criminality and delinquency with respect to Savoyards who protested most vehemently. This language mirrored the categories long applied to peasants in Ariège.

In that department, foresters came face to face with popular resistance, mostly passive but occasionally open and violent. Their forms of conciliation were as novel as the uplanders' resistance was predictable: district commissions and a new law allowing regrassing instead of reforestation softened this latest, and most ambitious, intervention by the forestry corps. From one perspective, the tempered workings of the administrative state began to soften the application of a law that reflected a punitive approach anchored in the Forest Code: as far as they went, these shifts foreshadowed things to come. More decisively, the Ariégeois had succeeded in keeping a certain concept of "public utility"— which had been formulated to exclude them—within a political arena, thus redefining it. The practical outcome was that visions of functional and depeopled mountains concocted in Paris and Nancy did not prevail over the forested, pasture-covered, and cultivated mountain of the peasants. A decade-long attempt to restructure the mountains fell with the Second Empire; when the new Chamber of Deputies of the Third Republic finally reworked the old law in 1882, legislators jettisoned a coercive and punitive model of legislation that had foundered in alpine France.

Chapter Three Sisyphus in Savoie: Restoration Confronts the Village, 1882–1913

To restore the mountains . . . is to create a pastoral, sylvan, and mineral symphony from contradictory forces and interests.
—*François Combes*

Of the many projects that the Second Empire left the Third Republic to complete, reforestation lay dormant throughout the first era of the new regime. The law on the reforestation of the mountains had become a dead letter before it expired in 1870, yet the Republic's delay in enacting new legislation resulted only in part from the abject failure of the Second Empire's alpine policies: when the law on the Restoration and Conservation of Alpine Lands finally passed on 4 April 1882, the Senate had already rejected it several times since 1877, the year that a constitutional showdown between the monarchist premier MacMahon and the Chamber of Deputies resulted in republican victory. The Senate, however, did not carry a republican majority until 1879, and a new approach to volatile alpine lands represented an inchoate problem for the regime even after its initial monarchist phase. How were alpine peasants—in the eyes of officialdom one of the most culturally autarkic and least economically viable segments of the rural population—to be included within a republican framework of politics?

The final version of the law represented a compromise between deputies' and foresters' proposals; as early as 1873 the Administration des Forêts had appointed a commission to study possible modifications of the 1860 law. The result was a new departure that restricted the state's field of action considerably while requiring it to assume all costs of alpine restoration. The law of 1882 placed greater emphasis on subsidized and voluntary work and addressed the problem of degraded pastures in lenient terms. Forgoing the stick, it appeared to encourage alpine repair with a carrot wrapped in the state's money.[1]

For Andrée Corvol, a leading interpreter of the politics of French forestry, the 1882 departure amply proves the formidable electoral power of peasants during the Third Republic. Maintaining the venerable argument that the Republic's conservatism flowed from the numerical weight of the rural departments, Corvol claims that Parliament now had to submit to the rural will whatever the peasants' social position. At the same time, she writes, peasants "perceived confusedly" the difference between reforestation and restoration and ultimately assimilated the two terms, maintaining all of their previous hostility to foresters' schemes. The key to the contrast between republican legal compromise and hostile reception, she argues, is peasants' understanding of ulterior motives that lurked in the discourse of foresters. State-sponsored restoration was, then, just as "colonizing" as Second Empire reforestation had been.[2]

The new law was both more and less insidious than these claims suggest. It is true that conciliatory restoration did not have the support of leading members of the forestry corps, as this and the following chapter will show. But it is unnecessary to search for ulterior motives in the legal text itself, which did not signal a dramatic shift from Second Empire reforestation: "restoration and conservation" continued to embody deep assumptions about the supposedly natural functions of plains and mountains and about the unconscious destructiveness of alpine peasants. The law spoke of "public utility," and, like its predecessor, did so problematically. The law of 1882 takes on yet another hue if placed in its immediate political context: passed during Charles Freycinet's second term as minister of public works, it arrived in the heyday of *dirigiste* schemes to alter the French landscape. The "Freycinet plan," undertaken four years earlier, resulted in the densest network of secondary rail lines in Europe, not to mention canals and ports built with state subsidies. Alpine restoration was part and parcel of a massive manipulation of nature characteristic of the early Third Republic.

On the other hand, there is little basis to Corvol's claim that alpine peasants reacted mechanically to restoration, showing hostility before they had understood its implications. Restoration projects did not reflect seamless continuity between legal text and real alterations in the landscape. They were not identical throughout France, and at times they fit reasonably well with the values and economic interests of pastoral communities. It is even more questionable to assume along with Corvol that residents of remote alpine communes were fully aware of the veiled utterances and technical writings (emanating from Paris and Nancy) of chief foresters who did intend to undermine the compromise of 1882. Such communes could only judge restoration on its practical merits.

The situation was certainly complex for the poor, pastoral community of Jarrier (Savoie). The residents of Jarrier grasped the new options before them, taking interest in some while rejecting others. This chapter will examine the legalities of restoration, then look closely at what they meant in the context of one alpine commune. Focusing on the intricate relations between upland peasants and foresters, it will show the multivalence of rural political expression and question the image of a neat transition from sedition to electoral politics that is commonly said to have characterized the rural world in the last third of the nineteenth century. Peasants did not relinquish more direct forms of resistance in favor of the ballot box when they perceived their most vital interests to be at stake. The Jarriens' political responses to the Radical Republic of the late nineteenth and early twentieth centuries ranged from voting to withdrawing their children from secular schools to physically destroying seedlings and structures meant to "restore" their land. In this surprising case, last-ditch resistance from a weakened commune sufficed to halt a huge state project powered by administrative momentum and money. Given the odds against this small commune, the outcome raises questions about the "colonization" and integration of rural France under the Third Republic.

DEFINING RESTORATION

Until 1913, the program legislated in 1882 represented the republican approach to the economic and ecological volatility of the mountains. Nowhere in the legal text did the word *reboisement* (reforestation) appear—its very absence a measure of the anathema the word had become to alpine peasants. In its stead figured "restoration" and "conservation," the key words, respectively, in the law's two major titles. As the terms connote, "restoration" stood for what the state would actively undertake to improve the most degraded alpine land, and "conservation" referred to measures designed to preserve less degraded lands without altering their ecological composition.[3]

In no article did the law elucidate what form the *travaux de restauration* (works of restoration, also *travaux de correction*) were meant to take. Yet this, the most significant title, restrained the state in areas given over to administrative discretion under the Second Empire. First, the law characterized public utility through what would become to foresters a notorious phrase: *des dangers nés et actuels,* evident and present dangers. In other words, an instance of degradation, such as a ravaging torrent or a hillside entering full erosion, had to be clearly visible in order to merit restoration. This condition put restoration in relief against the idea of prevention, no longer deemed to be the appropriate attitude toward "open wounds" in the landscape, as the most common metaphor in foresters' parlance depicted them. The necessary existence of "evident and present dangers" effectively restricted public utility, presumably to projects bearing on the most degraded areas that posed a threat to alpine communes themselves (figures 2 and 3).

In another, very practical way, the new measures further tied the hands of foresters. While maintaining much of the previous administrative procedure—public inquiries in the interested communes, the involvement of municipal councils and special commissions—the legislation of 1882 took an important additional step: public utility would be determined only by law. In other words, the Chamber of Deputies would have to debate the worth of restoring each and every degraded patch of land that foresters were to identify, a provision hardly designed to please the Forêts.

The most ambiguous of the major legal changes lay in article 4, which stipulated that the state must acquire, "either amicably or by expropriation," the parcels it wished to restore. The law of 1860 had allowed reforestation through expropriation, if necessary, and the legal owner lost his title to the land until he reimbursed the state for the cost of the work or ceded half of it outright. Now, a clean break would precede restoration: in the event that an individual, commune, or public entity refused to undertake subsidized restoration, the state would purchase the land and proceed to work on it within the broad limits of property rights. And, of course, the state's coffers would pay for the work.[4]

The ambiguity of the state's potential acquisition of marginal land was twofold. Although the new law exonerated public and private landowners financially, in real terms it opened the door to the loss of the commons in particular, or some unknown portion of them on which dangers were deemed "evident and present." A state councilor and enthusiastic supporter commented

Figure 2. Evident and present dangers: a visit by RTM chief Prosper Demontzey at the Gave de Pau Perimeter, Cauterets, Hautes-Pyrénées, 1890. Negative by Dellon. Archives Départementales des Hautes-Pyrénées.

Figure 3. An open wound in the landscape. Haute-Ariège Perimeter, Auzat, Ariège, 1889. ADA.

that, compared to the fundamental expropriation law of 1841, the restoration law would indeed hasten expropriation by reducing the number of public inquiries from two to one. And the "municipal element" on the special commissions would be reduced to a minimum.[5] In addition, direct purchase raised budgetary questions: how much money should the state allocate to acquisitions, how expensive would restoration prove to be, and how much could peasants legally charge for marginal land? Between 1882 and the end of the century, acquisitions proved costly and, at times, even hindered restoration by absorbing available funds. The restoration service, a new general inspection named the *Restauration des terrains en montagne,* or RTM, received ample yearly budgets averaging 3,700,000 francs until the turn of the century. In an administration that had to manage the national and many communal forests, as well as pay the salaries of 7,300 forest guards and 747 higher personnel, the RTM monopolized nearly a quarter of the budget, as reported to the Chamber of Deputies in 1890.[6]

The language of "evident and present dangers," the daunting legal procedures, and the necessity of land acquisitions guaranteed that restoration would be cumbersome and costly. But these novelties, and the concessions to rural interests they partly represented, stopped with the letter of the law. Two opposed continuities were to give restoration its true flavor, especially as legal dictates became translated into actual projects. These continuities relate to the definition of *restoration* as it was hammered out beyond the Chamber of Deputies.

First, by leaving the meaning of *restoration* entirely open-ended, the text appeared to create avenues for new and imaginative solutions to the problems of alpine ecology. In reality, the law of 1882 certified a movement already under way. The synthesis achieved between the deputies and administrators in Paris and the foresters at the Ecole Nationale des Eaux et Forêts officially sanctioned a set of approaches masked by the vague terminology of "correction" and "consolidation of land." Drawing attention away from the causes of erosive torrents and directing it toward their very action, the novel solutions challenged the idea that only nature could repair nature. Senator Chevandier de Valdrôme had advocated the association of reforestation with engineering works, *génie civil,* in 1860, but the former had enjoyed too great a prestige to be combined with the artifices of engineering—structures designed to shore up and at least slow the erosion of degraded slopes.[7] Techniques based more on engineering than on forestry gradually gained popularity during the last several decades of the nineteenth century; they were not born in 1882. In 1871 M. L. Marchand, general forest guard and former pupil at Nancy, submitted a technical treatise on travaux de correction to the director general of the Forêts, a work published in a second edition in 1876. Later in the century, a persuasive theoretical component came with the work of E. Thierry, professor at Nancy, who derived his ideas on artificial buttressing through work in hydrology and geomorphology.[8]

By 1907 the forester A. Fron could include succinct descriptions of the most successful techniques attempted over the previous decades; his *Economie sylvo-pastorale: Forêts, pâturages et prés-bois* is a useful guide to the various travaux de correction. Fron divided these into two categories: those in the form of physical obstacles whose purpose was to slow the rate of erosion, and drains to rid unstable lands of excess water. In the first category, "rustic" and "living" barriers held pride of place. Built, respectively, of stone masonry or wooden stakes and branches, barriers were placed along ravines where torrents might form or had already formed. They transformed ravines from chutes into staircases, both channeling water away from the fragile banks and diminishing its speed, thereby lessening water's erosive action. Simpler barriers for less degraded ravines consisted of *clayonnages,* or wattle fencing, *fascinages,* or bundles of sticks stretched across the ravine, and *garnissages,* simple reinforcements for dry ravines, consisting of branches lying in the direction of the slope, secured with stakes and perpendicular branches. The second category comprised drains of various dimensions, dug into the ground, paved, and lined with stones. Some combination of all these structures would, in theory, stabilize alpine soils and protect ravines from the effects of rushing water.[9]

The legislation of 1882 simply sanctioned the early theoretical work as well as the practical efforts of the forestry corps in the provinces. At least in the case of Savoie, reforestation had already metamorphosed into restoration by 1880.[10] Long before 1882, foresters had discovered that some slopes were too erosive to support trees and had experimented with other techniques on their own. The requirement of evident and present dangers implicitly demanded engineering works, since it directed all action toward the most fragile alpine areas, those least apt to be reforested: without explicitly mandating or even defining them, the restoration law warranted an array of creative approaches designed to attack torrential streams head on.

Given the fragility of slopes prone to evident and present dangers, foresters would in theory be able to plant only select parts of the broad alpine watersheds of torrential streams. One of the most important consequences of privileging engineering over forestry was a potentially minimal effect on the pastoral economy. Barriers lying across ravines and inconspicuous drains would affect pasturing very little and could thus be undertaken without provoking rural protest. Confirmations of this assumption filtered back to Paris with some regularity from foresters sensitive to pastoral interests. Stationed in Annecy, Inspector Charles Kuss, for example, not only gave engineering works his blessing but also played down the overall importance of forests: "In practice, it is indispensable to limit the [restoration] perimeter in order to accommodate it to the necessities of pastoral life."[11]

Notably among theorists and provincial foresters, artificial travaux de correction were already becoming banal by 1882, a point that beckons the second continuity belied by the text of the law. However appropriate in technical and human terms, elaborate alpine scaffolding was less than popular among top officers of the forestry corps. The writings of the first restoration chief himself, Prosper Demontzey, speak eloquently to this attitude. A disciple of Surell who had risen through the ranks as a specialist in reforestation in Alpes-Maritimes, Demontzey became head of the RTM in 1882 at its inception. A second edition of his magisterial *Traité pratique du reboisement et du gazonnement des montagnes* appeared the same year. Originally written in the context of the Second Empire's reforestation law, the second edition concluded resoundingly that that legislation had proved a total success; no mention was made of its political

failure in the mountains. Demontzey's goals, at any rate, remained the same—
to prevent the formation of torrents by consolidating soil through reforestation
and regrassing. Notwithstanding a lengthy analysis of travaux de correction, he
quoted a restorer of another stripe, Eugène Viollet-le-Duc, to support his idea
that engineering works acted as an initial stabilizer so that forests could eventually take hold.[12]

Demontzey's central assumptions clarify his desired relation between nature
and artifice. First, buttressing could be used only in limited circumstances, for
particular kinds of torrents; masonry walls, for example, could diminish the
slope of the torrent and consolidate its bed, but only in areas where torrents
were undermining the soil. On the contrary, some torrents flowed through
beds of solid rock, for which engineering works would accomplish little. Second, only forests could extinguish torrential streams; this assumption came directly from Surell's work of the 1840s and represented no new thinking on the
part of Demontzey. The relation, then, was both hierarchical and chronologi-
cal. In Demontzey's words, forest would eventually substitute "the effect of its
perpetual vitality for that of a series of inanimate fortifications."[13]

If Demontzey did not regard the restoration law as a major revision in its
theoretical aspects, he well understood the new restrictions. Since forests were
not likely to thrive in areas of "evident and present dangers," plantings would
have to be made in the extreme upland areas where torrential streams formed.
The legal justification for such plantings he left unspecified. High-altitude reforestation held great fascination for Demontzey, a fascination embedded in his
theories of alpine ecology. Borrowed, too, from Surell, these held that all alpine
pastures had taken the place of forest, the latter "ruthlessly excluded by the self-
ishness, incapacity, and improvidence of man."[14] For Demontzey, then, restoration had far more to do with returning to an imagined, anterior landscape than
with restoring the economic viability of a region through the best technical
means at hand. How could peppering the mountains with artificial structures
truly fulfill the mission of the RTM? Where forests had been, they could return: this was the only sort of restoration worthy of the name. In so imagining
the past and future of the mountains, Demontzey recapitulated the central ecological errors made by his professional predecessors: the tree line was a fixed entity at uniformly high elevations, and alpine pastures represented deforested
landscapes that could easily be replanted with trees.

The undying vogue for forests was thus one among several factors that
promised conflict over restoration. Expropriation not only lingered from the
1860 legislation, but it became absolute. If unable or unwilling to restore their

fragile land, individuals and communes would be forced to sell to the state. Hippolyte Doumenjou of Ariège's Conseil Général deemed this illegal in the case of communal land as he saw the legislation taking shape in 1877. A representative of a department that had proved its hostility to reforestation, Doumenjou presented a compelling case that the state could not expropriate a common good for the common good: "One can expropriate existing rights to real estate, such as rights of use or passage, in the interest of public utility; but when the expropriation must afflict an entire body of persons who have augmented their rights by developing an industry, is the law applicable? To expropriate in the general interest, an interest of the same nature, is a contradictory act."[15] Restoration, as concretized in the law of 1882, ultimately placed as few safeguards on the status of communal property as had the outwardly more coercive legislation of 1860.

No less disingenuous were the moralistic accretions that dramatized the RTM's mission. An early exposition of the ethos appeared in the *Notice sur le projet de périmètre de l'Arc Supérieur,* drafted by Forest Inspector P. E. Chapelain for Savoie in 1886. Beyond a summary description of the plans to restore the upper Arc River basin, Chapelain laid down a philosophical basis for human intervention in the geological and hydrological cycles of alpine areas. The first pillar of his argument dealt with human responsibility. He attributed the problems of erosion, *glissements,* or bedrock-debris slumps, and landslides, all associated with torrential streams, to the work of countless generations of pastoral peasants abusing the land. The responsibility of the present generation derived from that of previous generations: "the antiquity of the abuses of usufruct, which have brought about an intolerable situation, does not amount to an unassailable position for the proprietors; to adopt the opinion . . . that they cannot be held responsible for the actions of their fathers, would be to deny the natural laws of inheritance." Chapelain nodded to the difficulty of identifying the causes of degradation—hence the slipperiness of "responsibility"—but castigated peasants for attributing all natural calamities to providence and blithely assuming their own impunity. For Chapelain, such responsibility led inescapably to a call to action. In this call lay a determination to sway the course of the most intractable natural phenomena, a sense of will at the heart of the RTM's raison d'être. Chapelain glossed over the discrepancy between the bearers of responsibility and the agents of "correction," however: peasants would in effect suffer punitive damages while the RTM would reap the glory for taming the torrential fury of the Alps.[16]

In practice, restoration was difficult, slow, and sometimes risky work. Local foresters were left with the task of interpreting the meaning of "evident and present dangers," and this phrase became highly elastic in certain circumstances. Actions taken by the RTM depended on the availability of credits, clamor from important towns, and the visions of its own personnel. In the case of Jarrier, a third source of conflict lay in the ethos of the RTM chief for the re-

Map 3. Commune of Jarrier

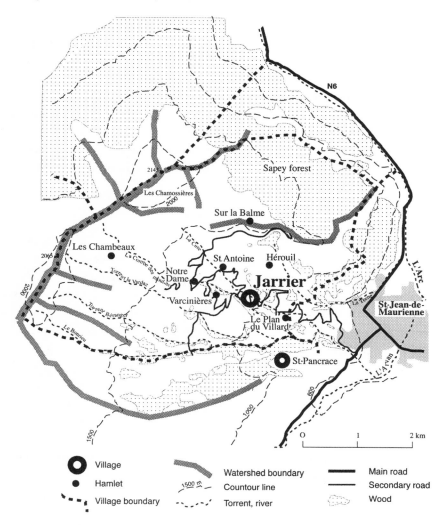

Eric Leclerc, professor of Geography, University of Rouen.

gion, Paul Mougin. Probably the most eminent forester ever stationed in Savoie, Mougin spent twenty years of his career reforesting and correcting torrents throughout the department; foresters still consult and praise his two monumental works, *Les Torrents de la Savoie* (1914) and *Les Forêts de Savoie* (1919).[17] As it happened, Mougin had been formed in Demontzey's school: he, too, dreamed of the vast and even stands of coniferous forest that could alone keep the Alps intact. Yet even with Mougin directing operations, the RTM flailed in its attempt to find objective criteria for restoring the land of Jarrier. Judging Mougin and his corps less on the technical merits than on the human consequences of their project, Jarriens found restoration unacceptable. The Third Republic's invention of restoration brought nothing new to the legacy of blame and the characterization of alpine peasants as unworthy of their lands. Novelty did lie in the fanfare and prestige that greeted the well-financed corps of technicians whose expertise derived from the union of engineering and silviculture. If the RTM represented a modern Sisyphus who would succeed in keeping the mountains intact, then the Alpine version of the legend paled in its modesty. This legend of Sisyphus tells of a shepherd's survivors herding back to the mountaintop the livestock neglected during the shepherd's life; it did not prescribe how to alter the mountain but how to live on it.[18]

RISK AND ADAPTATION IN JARRIER

A few kilometers west of Saint-Jean-de-Maurienne in Savoie lies Jarrier, its many hamlets dispersed over a broad and steep mountain slope (map 3). A vertical sense of space commands one's experience of Jarrier, where no two houses appear to be on the same level (figure 4). The communal territory extends between 800 and 2,173 meters in altitude; this is an extraordinary rise for a commune of only average to small size (1,770 hectares) in the Maurienne (figure 5). Sliced by ravines formed by a series of parallel torrents and streams, the land of Jarrier does not permit the agglomerated settlement pattern found in other parts of France. Instead, scattered hamlets occupy the few relatively stable areas, inhabited, during the nineteenth century, according to season. The census of 1876 showed twenty-seven of these "neighborhoods, villages, or hamlets" constituting the commune of Jarrier; as many as thirty-two dotted the land at different times during the eighteenth and nineteenth centuries, according to local historians.[19]

The extreme dispersion of "neighborhoods, villages, or hamlets" had not, however, created pockets of Jarriens unknown to each other. Families tended to

Figure 4. Hamlet of Le Frégny dessus, Jarrier, 1911. Negative by Paul Noël. No. 2363, Bonrieu de Jarrier, RTM Savoie.

Figure 5. Panoramic view looking north across Jarrier, 1911. Negative by Paul Noël. No. 2438, Bonrieu de Jarrier, RTM Savoie.

own up to three houses, or chalets, in the commune, and with their livestock in tow they ranged widely over the communal territory at precise moments during the year. Jarrier was typical of Alpine communities in possessing alpages, the summer feeding grounds for families' livestock; the *emmontagnage,* or move from winter hamlet to summer chalet, formed the high moment of seasonal migration. Yet the people of Jarrier had created a particularly complex pattern of yearly migration by balancing the conflicting schedules imposed by planting crops, tending vineyards, cutting hay, and pasturing animals.

The summer season began when women, small children, and the elderly packed up a limited quantity of summer provisions on sledges and herded the family's cows and sheep to the alpages. These, named "Les Chamossières" in Jarrier, were communally owned but individually exploited according to the *petite montagne* system typical of the Maurienne.[20] From June to October women, younger children, and elders remained at the family's summer chalet, caring for the animals and making butter and cheese for winter consumption. During these months the men and older children tended crops, principally rye, barley, and potatoes, and harvested hay, stocking it for winter feed in two chalets at lower altitudes, the *maison haute* and the *maison basse* (figure 6). The reason for two houses at differing elevations below the alpages stemmed from the conflicting schedules of pasturing and grape-growing. In early October the human and animal population of the alpages descended to the maison haute, where the animals consumed unharvested hay, often in forest clearings. By the middle of the month, however, the grape harvest demanded the labor of the entire family, so a second autumn migration reunited families, with their animals, in the maison basse.

During the summer, the demands of fields and vineyards competed with hay-cutting for men's labor; a paucity of time, hands, and means of transportation limited the amount of hay that men could take down to the maison basse. Instead, they left a considerable stock in the maison haute, and just before Christmas families would migrate back up the slope so that the animals could feed on the rest of the harvested hay for the remainder of the winter. This particular migration, known as the *remues hivernales,* was a rare phenomenon in Savoie and possibly unique to Jarrier. In April the family moved once again to the principal dwelling, the maison basse. Spring grasses allowed pasturing until June, when the emmontagnage signaled the beginning of another yearly cycle of migration within the commune.[21]

A sizeable communal forest complemented the fruits of farming and raising livestock. Overlooking the scattered hamlets, the 335-hectare forest of Sapey

Figure 6. Descent of winter fodder by mule in Jarrier, 1912. Negative by Paul Noël. No. 2642, Bonrieu de Jarrier, RTM Savoie.

provided Jarrier with resources that rarely left the confines of the commune. The name "Sapey" probably comes from *sapin,* or fir tree, but the forest itself consisted in roughly equal measure of fir and spruce, with a few Sylvester pines and larches, the latter the result of plantings. The architecture of houses and barns demanded a large yearly cut, each house requiring between 180 and 250 cubic meters of wood. Peasants preferred spruce for most carpentry throughout Savoie, though they reserved larch for balconies and pine for floors in both houses and stables. Beyond the yearly cut destined for construction, fuel, and repairs, destructive fires in the hamlets frequently required extra cuts; the incidence of fire began to decrease only in the early twentieth century, as slate replaced thatch on the chalet roofs. The Jarriens depended heavily on their communal forest, for unlike most communes in Savoie, almost no forest was to be found on private property in the commune.[22]

Jarriens regularly swept the floor of the forest, gathering undergrowth, broken branches, and dead wood for fuel. From the less plentiful hardwoods, they manufactured a variety of domestic implements, from tools, cleaning utensils, and baskets to shoes and walking sticks. Gathered in the forest, strawberries, raspberries, juniper berries, and mushrooms seasonally supplemented a diet based on grains, potatoes, and milk. The forest harbored medicinal plants and herbs, in addition to the plentiful fir bark used in an infusion to treat sick animals, as well as the buds from spruce trees steeped to treat sick people and added to hot baths for rhumatics. Finally, the forest provided occasional pasturing and shelter for livestock.[23]

Communal rules mediated families' activities in fields, pastures, and forest; not surprisingly, the overlapping calendars of growing, pasturing, and wood-cutting required delicate synchronization. Municipal decrees from the nineteenth century bear witness to the many points of economic practice regulated, in theory, by the municipality. Holding sway over the communal calendar, the municipal council annually fixed the date of the emmontagnage, traditionally 6 June but variable in case of inclement weather. Pasturing on the commons was not gratuitous; livestock owners paid dues to the commune for each animal, dues fixed in 1885 at thirty centimes per head of cattle and fifteen centimes per sheep or goat. Access to specific pastures and meadows was regulated according to type of livestock.[24] The municipal council also determined the dates signaling the beginning of planting, harvesting, and hay-cutting. Strict regulations concerning fallow lands existed in Jarrier as elsewhere in the thin-soiled Maurienne, where in the highest valleys rye grew for thirteen months before it could be harvested.

The municipality ruled over the communal forest, as well. During the years of the Sardinian administration, the syndics saw to the surveillance of and annual cuts in the Sapey forest, punishing offenders according to communal norms. Reserving the right to sell wood in order to finance various communal projects, the municipality forbade individuals to sell wood outside the commune. The municipality's prerogatives in restricting uses of the forest inevitably pitted the governing body against some inhabitants; nineteenth-century records reveal much tension in the anarchic years of the First Empire, during which Savoie was part of France. In 1834 the council appointed a second guard to increase surveillance in the Sapey forest. The local authorities also imposed obligations, frequently resisted, on residents for the upkeep of both private and communal lands: Jarriens had to dig ditches around their properties to drain stagnant water and, after 1841, to participate in modestly remunerated corvées to repair roads.[25] The commune's social contract entailed much vigilance over an exacting environment.

Moments of celebration and ceremony also marked the communal life of Jarrier, especially pastoral activities and the *tremiado,* the term commonly used throughout the Maurienne to designate the entire yearly cycle of migration. Though perhaps romanticized by local historians (who play down what may well have been the hardships of isolation), cultural life on the alpages had a festive quality. While animals rediscovered the succulent alpine grasses, women and children engaged in the both necessary and ritual cleaning of the alpine chalet and the barn, arranging provisions and lighting the kitchen fire. In contrast to most peasant children, the youngest Jarriens may have enjoyed a relatively carefree time on the alpages, unencumbered by agricultural tasks while older brothers and sisters shepherded livestock and mothers and grandmothers spent their days transforming milk into butter and cheese. But shepherding, too, included songs and games with which to pass the time, and toward the end of summer women organized *veillées,* the long social evenings of singing and telling stories.[26] From the somewhat conflicting evidence of his Savoyard informants, the eminent folklorist Arnold Van Gennep concluded that premarital sexual relations were very likely more common on the summer alpages, as well.[27]

Catholic ritual and summer festival on the alpages combined and culminated in the "benediction of the mountains," a local rite held over three days during the first two weeks of July. In what was in fact a benediction of pasturing livestock, the parish priest ascended to the pastures on a borrowed mule and in the course of two days would bless the animals with holy water at various designated chalets. After each benediction, women offered the priest fresh butter wrapped in aromatic gentian leaves. On the third day, the priest held an outdoor Mass at Les Chambeaux, an alpine pilgrimage site that was the locus of a small chapel. Following Mass, a festive outdoor meal completed the rite; paid for by the priest, the meal usually included the rarities of meat, wine, and fresh bread. A similar though shorter rite known as the "benediction of the harvest" took place on the first or second Sunday in September, the two principal poles of the agro-pastoral economy thus finding their inscription in religion and festival.[28]

Like all communes in the Maurienne, Jarrier had a distinct popular reputation. The interplay of history, oral tradition, and relative isolation in this long Alpine valley had led to a cultural positioning of communes with respect to each other; each possessed a character derived, more often than not, from the belittling perceptions of other communes, a character whose defense or denial could become a basis for conflict. The rather low reputation of Jarrier among visitors and neighboring communes began with the black mud of its paths but extended to the people themselves: Jarriens were thought to be naïvely pious and rather bigoted. People from the adjacent commune of Saint-Pancrace called the Jarriens *gros rats*. More striking was the opinion of the Jarriens current in Valloire, up the valley: Jarriens were, first and foremost, poor. A saying in Valloire depicted the Jarriens as perenially leaning forward; as their families had no plates, they had to eat from a hole carved in the middle of the table, permanently bending their backs. In the Valloirins' hierarchy of poverty, only the people of Saint-Jean d'Arves were worse off, for they had to save their candle stubs. Indeed, one of the most popular songs in Jarrier, performed at veillées or on Sunday afternoons on the alpages, sang the praises of a properly made polenta (with roasted onions), expressing the longing for fine food affordable only on celebratory occasions. Isolation and an endogamy rate of nearly 100 percent through 1939 further defined life in Jarrier.[29]

Migrating from chalet to chalet over the course of the year contributed to the very particular sense of place and time felt by pastoral people in Savoie. In Jarrier, however, a sense of place incorporated the reality of moving land in addition to moving people. Below the surface vegetation, a slope of tightly corrugated metamorphic schist forms a permanent bedrock-debris slump. This is not a matter of loose soil on the surface, for the unstable bedrock of Jarrier descends approximately fifty meters. The parallel divisions between layers of schist make the bedrock vulnerable to infiltration by water; the slopes of Jarrier magnify the problem because the schist runs parallel to the topography. After heavy precipitation the slump may launch a *coulée* or debris flow, a destructive, swift movement of debris down the mountain. Many such flows have been documented in Jarrier's history, and their dates formed landmarks in popular memory. The most notorious dated from 1440 and had become an ominous folktale; caused by a sudden snowmelt, it resulted in the largest of Jarrier's torrents, the Bonrieu, brusquely changing course and destroying much of Saint-Jean-de-Maurienne, the regional capital located in the valley.[30] Debris flows usually occurred on the lower slopes of the commune, leaving large blocks of schist exposed on the upper slopes. Such blocks might not only descend in a violent landslide but, when surrounded by fine, decomposed rock (the result of successive freezes and thaws) and gorged with water, they could also become a fluid mass, producing a debris flow of their own. Over the centuries, enough material had accumulated below Jarrier to form a debris fan; Saint-Jean-de-Maurienne perched atop this fan, continually vulnerable to the violent flows of black mud and rocks from its upland neighbor.[31]

As if unstable bedrock were not enough, five torrential streams slice through much of the territory of Jarrier. Running in parallel lines from northwest to southeast, the Torne, the Cure, the Combe des Moulins, the Vardaz, and the Béranger all flow into the oddly named Bonrieu, or "good rill." This torrent forms the boundary between Jarrier and Saint-Pancrace and flows into the Arvan River, above Saint-Jean-de-Maurienne, the latter river in turn flowing into the Arc (figures 7 and 8). Originating in the high mountains and flowing over uneven beds, the five torrents have wrought considerable destruction on their own, eroding their banks and carrying the suspended material to low-lying areas. In Jarrier and vicinity, the torrents and bedrock-debris slump feed each other's potential for destruction: the Bonrieu and its sources contribute to and direct the contents of debris flows, while a particularly violent flow might gorge and change the course of the Bonrieu, usually to the detriment of Saint-Jean-de-Maurienne. As Paul Mougin wrote in his encyclopedic work *Les Torrents de la Savoie,* "In Jarrier . . . everything descends toward the valley."[32]

The town in the valley had for a long time received more official attention than the village on the mountain slope when it came to debris flows and the Bonrieu torrent. And with good reason: the Bonrieu had virtually destroyed Saint-Jean not only in 1440 but again in 1618. The capital of the Maurienne suffered serious debris flows and flooding in 1715, 1733, and 1740, after which the Sardinian government decided to build a new dike above the town, spreading half the cost among all the parishes in the Maurienne.[33] Yet the importance of Saint-Jean as a regional center of communications and trade obscured the difficulties faced by Jarrier. Although less subject to flooding, the village had, after all, been built along a declivitous slab of bedrock slipping into the Maurienne valley. The instability of the land did not bode well for the built environment, but the Jarriens had adapted with a type of architecture found nowhere else in Savoie: to prevent collapse in times of slippage, they built their houses in the manner of hangars. Men first placed sturdy wooden pillars about three and a half meters apart, then attached the structure forming the roof. Within this perimeter, they built walls of potter's clay or tufa (porous, calcareous rock). Such engineering eliminated points of stress between framework and walls. If one or more pillars slipped, they would simply be lifted back up with the aid of a jack and replaced on their stone foundations. Houses in Jarrier might burn, but rarely did they collapse.[34]

Figure 7. The Bonrieu near Saint-Jean-de-Maurienne, 1911. Negative by Paul Noël. No. 2445, Bonrieu de Jarrier, RTM Savoie.

Figure 8. Confluence of the Arc and Arvan Rivers, Jarrier, 1909. Negative by Paul Noël. No. 2159, Bonrieu de Jarrier, RTM Savoie.

RECEIVING RESTORATION

As in the rest of Savoie, foresters were among the first French officials on the scene in Jarrier following the creation of the new department in 1860. For two decades, however, the Administration des Forêts preoccupied itself with the tasks of surveying and attempting to manage the communal forests, with only limited essays in reforestation. Early exchanges between the municipal council of Jarrier and the local forestry corps related to the "onerous" tax levied on construction wood from the communal forest, Le Sapey. Emphasizing the extraordinary demand for wood to construct and replace the houses' huge pillars and beams, the council achieved its first compromise with the state's foresters in late 1861, who lowered the tax on logs from three to two francs.[35] While the local forest inspector continued to perceive only abuse and profit-seeking in the commune's relation to its forest, municipal council deliberations from the 1860s and 1870s reveal detailed debates preceding regular cuts, extraordinary cuts, and cuts for indigent residents. In the absence of a survey, Jarrier had nevertheless fallen under the tutelage of the forest regime: each time a house burned down (a not infrequent event in Jarrier), the council had to request construction wood from the local forest inspector. And a dramatic shift from the lenient years of the Sardinian government lay in a new regulation that forbade all pasturing in Le Sapey.

The most consequential change followed the arrival of the RTM in Jarrier. By 1880 foresters in Savoie had identified the nine principal torrents that would need attention, six in the Arc River basin, three in the Isère; by 1882 the state had spent 83,000 francs to "correct" two torrents in the Maurienne alone.[36] Not only foresters knew of the torrents in Savoie. Prominent geographers such as V. A. Malte-Brun, secretary general of the Société de Géographie in Paris since 1855, and Elisée Reclus had begun to fashion them into a trademark of the department in short geographical guides to Savoie. To describe them in his 1882 guide, Malte-Brun sought the evocative words of Reclus, the anarchist and Communard for whom torrential phenomena may have held a strong symbolic appeal: "Their bounding waters mine and dissolve the rocks, level the moraines, reduce to sand the living rock of their banks, carry away in their cascades the blocks brought by avalanches of stone and pile them up in enormous beaches all along their course."[37]

Though in many ways a minor commune, and one rarely noticed by geographers, it is not surprising that Jarrier had already captured the interest of state foresters by 1882. Seventeen years earlier, prominent landowners in Saint-Jean-de-Maurienne had introduced French engineers to the sporadic destruction caused by the Bonrieu torrent.[38] Although Saint-Jean had initially sought the attention of the state's engineers and not its foresters, the latter logically took over the project once the law on the restoration and conservation of alpine lands had passed the Senate. The case of Jarrier and Saint-Jean-de-Maurienne recapped the larger alpine problem in miniature: an upland area threatened a relative lowland via a bedrock-debris slump and a ravaging torrent. The Bonrieu, in particular, contributed to both a localized problem and a cumulative threat to the lowlands of France.

Officials of the RTM had, in all cases, to identify the complex set of issues that would both warrant restoration and determine its shape before beginning the actual work. Foresters studied the torrents that fed the Lower Arc River for nearly a decade prior to designating a final "restoration perimeter"—the line demarcating portions of land to be restored. Among these torrents, the Bonrieu, active "from time immemorial," seems to have presented one of the more obvious cases. Early reports on it did not hedge on the reasons for restoration, emphasizing most of all the indirect danger it posed to the state-owned Rhône-Mont Cenis railroad and the National Route Six, both of which linked Savoie to Italy. As for the relative dangers posed to Jarrier and Saint-Jean-de-Mauri-enne, the final report of 1891 did not equivocate: "The Bonrieu is thus a permanent danger for the territory of the commune of Jarrier, but the town of Saint-Jean is even more threatened."[39]

The cause was less obvious. Had it been peasants or the combined effects of geology and climate that had most aggravated torrential conditions in Jarrier? Of interest here is the general reconnaissance report for the Lower Arc, whose authors included Conservator Jean Phal and Charles Kuss, and their parallel report on Jarrier. Drafted in July 1891, the general report placed the destruction of alpine vegetation and the formation of torrents in a broad context: the glacial history of the Maurienne, climatic patterns, the abuse of pasturing, and the overcutting of trees were all to blame. Yet the same authors' specific report on Jarrier made no mention of human causation, simply attributing the degraded soils around the branches of the Bonrieu to "the natural instability of the land."[40] Restoration would begin with unspecified *ouvrages d'art* serving to diminish the angle of the Bonrieu's slope and protect its bed and banks from erosion. These anthropomorphized ouvrages would have to "struggle against the most redoubtable conditions," and their considerable expense and "somewhat artificial character" would not prevent them from being "absolutely indispensable." Only such initial buttressing would permit the second stage, reforestation: young trees required protection so that later they could perform the vital work of fixing the soil.[41] Demontzey, the RTM chief, would have approved.

Restoration perimeters did not represent lines drawn around vast, degraded, and torrential areas. Again, article 2 of the 1882 law required natural dangers to be evident and present and so prohibited the RTM from acquiring limitless stretches of land. The total area included in the first Lower Arc perimeter amounted to a mere 1,984 hectares, only a little larger than the whole commune of Jarrier. Fifteen communes in the lower Maurienne were to contribute land to the perimeter; from Bonvillaret at the northern tip of the Maurienne to Saint-Jean-d'Arves far in the southern uplands, the perimeter "stretched" approximately fifty kilometers yet consisted of many small portions of noncontiguous land. Two of the fifteen communes involved were themselves not contiguous with any other commune in the perimeter.

Such a minute specification of degraded land led each commune to consider its interests separately from those of its neighbors. When the required reports from municipal councils began to reach the administration in late 1892, an overwhelmingly favorable response greeted RTM officials: gone were the grumblings over the planting of forest clearings that had plagued foresters in the last years of the Second Empire. Only three communes—Montgellafrey, Albiez-le-Vieux, and Albiez-le-Jeune—opposed restoration. The council of Albiez-le-Jeune argued their case with economic as well as ecological data. In addition, they protested that their commune had been caught between two perimeters: land had already been "forcibly" taken away from it as part of its inclusion in the Upper Arc perimeter, and enough was enough. A final, provocative question thrown to the RTM rang prophetic: "Why not limit at that [the earlier acquisitions] the barriers, regrassing, and reforesting, instead of depriving this country, already disinherited by nature, of part of its forest and almost all its pastures, if not to augment the state's domain?"[42] The rhetorical question contained a thorough understanding of the opposed interests of the state and the commune; far from confused by the meaning of restoration, Albiez-le-Jeune was one among many communes whose inhabitants grasped the stakes inherent in the agenda.

Jarrier, however, led the majority in its praise for the project. Its "incontestable utility" applied to the "general interest" as well as to the particular interests of the commune. As with most of the twelve communes in favor of restoration, the municipal council of Jarrier concluded with the mild objection that the project's authors had included a bit too much communal pasture within the perimeter. But the council did encourage the RTM to rid the commons of their excess water, though the commune would retain them as pasture. As it stood in 1891, Jarrier's designated perimeter came to just 101 hectares, or less than 6 percent of the communal territory. Although three quarters of the perimeter would consist of pasture, this proportion represented only 15 percent of Jarrier's mostly communal grazing lands.[43]

The reasons for Jarrier's initially open-armed response to the RTM lie not merely in the small amount of its land slated for the perimeter (not small enough, according to the municipal council), but rather in the broader tissue of events that transpired from 1889 to 1897. Relations between Jarrier and the Forêts in fact took a turn for the worse beginning in January 1889, and Jarrier was not alone in conflict: in that and the following year, a rash of forest crimes swept the Maurienne. Though they boded ill for overall relations, these crimes and their aftermath had remarkably little effect upon the Jarriens' contacts with the RTM. They merit a brief examination as an index of this commune's ability to discriminate among contexts as well as the specific actions of civil servants.

The incidents in Jarrier comprised crimes in the Sapey forest, the first committed during the regular absences of M. Georges, the forest guard, another perpetrated, in a subprefect's view, to test the will of a subsequent forest guard. The commune suffered no consequences, even though the latter crime had involved the illegal cutting of 170 "most beautiful and most remarkable" trees in Sapey and the possible collusion of communal officials. (The municipal council, while expressing its deep regret for the crime, decided to use the cut trees to build a new school, a project over which it had wrangled with the forest conservator since the beginning of the year.) The conservator soon dropped his inquiry, and Cyprien Grange, mayor of Jarrier during the last two decades of the nineteenth century, could rest easy.[44]

These crimes were but part of the larger struggle over the forests of the Maurienne, waged over the scarcity of fuel and administrative severity. Officials had not acted so leniently toward the "poor unfortunates" of the upper Maurienne, who, since early 1889, had faced arrest for gathering dead wood in the forests while the perpetrators of "real" and "important" forest crimes routinely escaped judicial action, according to mayors in the canton of Modane.[45] The village named in the Parisian newspaper *L'Autorité* only as "T" (Termignon?) explained that the "veritable band of pillagers and thieves," meaning representatives of commercial logging interests, cut the forests with impunity, unlike the "poor devils guilty of having taken a little wood so as not to perish in the cold." Published in *L'Autorité,* whose slogan "For God, For France" bespoke its antirepublican stance, the letter from T[ermignon] lent a bitter political dimension to the conflict: "And our fir trees, our only wealth, transformed into paper pulp, then shortly afterwards into newsprint in these vast factories which are the veritable tombs of our forests, will publish far and wide the benefits of the Republic."[46]

Poisoned relations between peasants and foresters dominated the two-year period: although antirepublicanism was far from uniform throughout the Maurienne, enmity toward foresters was.[47] The mayors believed the Forêts was refusing to compromise with the petty criminals in revenge for the condemnation of a forest guard who had wounded a delinquent in the canton of Saint-Jean-de-Maurienne. Several arbitrary acts committed by forest guards, claimed the mayors, included the arrest of two young men in the commune of Saint André whose mother had forbidden the local forest guard to continue courting her daughter. And the guards did not appear to grasp the essential problem in the Maurienne—the lack of firewood, exacerbated by the regulation that forbade one commune's sale of firewood to another before it had been marked by a forest guard, that venerable sign of foresters' power. Forest Conservator Jean Phal appeared in Modane in April 1889 to make peace. Phal ac-

ceded to the mayors' request that concessioners of minor forest products be allowed into the communal forests with the necessary tools for extraction and
that the guards dispense with the marking of firewood.[48]

These events continued the pattern of skirmishes, sometimes erupting into
bitter conflict, that had characterized the Savoyard peasants' reception of
French foresters since 1860. But by the 1890s, some familiar as well as some new
players had begun to enact a parallel history. The tense atmosphere of 1889 and
1890 in the Maurienne did not perceptibly influence negotiations between
communes and RTM officials concerning the acquisition of land for the Lower
Arc perimeter. Inhabitants of these upland communes discerned the RTM's
separate sphere of action and, initially, found good reasons to go along with this
latest intervention by the state.

Part of the attraction of the RTM lay in its promised efficacy in the face of
what seemed to be increasing danger. Torrential rains in 1891 and 1892 hit the
Maurienne with floods and landslides once again, automatically casting a favorable light on the new corps of forester-engineers that had been formed to
combat the causes of such destruction. Upland and lowland alike suffered. As
they had in the past, the rains tore into unstable ground in Jarrier and caused
the Bonrieu to roil with water and debris. In August 1891, pounding rain
ejected a ten-meter by two-meter chunk of earth from a field; it descended in
pieces into the torrent, which later in the day took out a bridge, sundering communication between Jarrier and Saint-Pancrace. A little over a year later, the
Bonrieu destroyed the rebuilt bridge.[49]

The importance of the floods of the early 1890s should not be exaggerated;
though fearsome, flooding, landslides, and debris flows lay in the communal
memory of Jarrier as did bad harvests and diseased animals. More important,
the RTM offered communes tangible, novel benefits. Unlike the punitive,
communes-pay-all ethos of the law of 1860, regulations following the 1882 law
stipulated that the creation of a restoration perimeter would free an affected
commune from having to pay the salary of its forest guard. An even greater en-
ticement, highlighted in a letter to the commissioners handling the open inquiry pertaining to the Lower Arc, was revenue: "executing the important
works of restoration will demand considerable expenditures whose benefits
will accrue to the inhabitants of the commune, who, either as workers or as
suppliers, will find a chief source of income."[50] The municipal council of Jarrier insisted on this point in its negotiations with the RTM. In 1894 the council
tied its proposed cession of communal land to the employment of men from
Jarrier for all work carried out within the commune; should the number of lo-

cal workers be insufficient, the RTM should then employ French workers, "to the complete exclusion of workers of foreign nationality"—probably a reference to Italian workers in the Maurienne.[51]

Having voted to do so in 1894, in August 1897 the municipal council of Jarrier formally ceded slightly more than 63 hectares of communal land to the state, citing worsening erosion (landslides had plagued the commune in the spring) as well as Jarrier's straitened finances as compelling reasons. Signaling a shift in expectations vis-à-vis the state, the council affirmed that it was the administration's duty "to prevent [natural disasters] as far as possible." And the council repeated its demand that the RTM hire men from Jarrier to "correct" the Bonrieu. In addition to the communal land, a few private owners sold parcels covering 29 hectares to the state, for the modest average price of four francs, thirty centimes per hectare. With more than 92 hectares of Jarrier's land, the RTM had come close to the 101 hectares it had originally hoped to acquire from the commune.[52]

On 27 July 1898, President of the Republic Félix Faure signed the law declaring the restoration of the Lower Arc basin to be a matter of public utility. Not until the end of 1902 did the state acquire all of the lands within the perimeter, however. The RTM had pushed for the law on the gamble that all of the communes would cede the lands requested, whether freely or for a price, but Albiez-le-Vieux and Saint-Colomban-des-Villards, the two communes that lost the most land to the state, managed to delay their cessions for more than three years.[53] The RTM officials repeatedly acknowledged that timing was crucial; in their minds, peasants who had turned over private or communal land to the state would remain pacified only as long as the RTM made good on its promises. Its record of performance in the Lower Arc suggests, on the contrary, falterings as well as dissension within the corps. Not only had the foresters underestimated the opposition from Albiez-le-Vieux and Saint-Colomban-des-Villards, but they also failed to assure a minimum of resources with which to undertake their work in the remote areas ceded to them. In September 1897 Paul Mougin, then joint inspector of forests stationed in Chambéry, urged his administration to acquire more land quickly and thereby profit from the "great movement of favorable opinion" in the Maurienne, exemplified by the cooperative spirit of the Jarriens. Just five months later, Inspector Charles Kuss sounded an alarm and advised a more cautious approach. A lack of "rational organization" and personnel had prevented any work from being carried out in the Upper Arc and Upper Isère perimeters, where the state had already acquired considerable territory. He feared outcry from the communes: "Let us not deceive ourselves; we would be enticing the population and preparing the most lively opposition, and, we add, the most justified opposition, if we purchased land without being in a position to effect the indispensable works of restoration." Kuss went as far as suggesting that the state not acquire land from the docile commune of Jarrier.[54] His disagreement with Mougin prefigured the larger controversy over Jarrier's portion of the Lower Arc perimeter.

The pace of acquisitions from cooperative communes did not slacken after 1898. Yet only a year after the perimeter's formal creation, pressures from Saint-Jean-de-Maurienne to augment it began to act upon the RTM. Simultaneously, Mougin and others began to bring this specific project into line with their fundamental notion of "restoration," the vision of mountains blanketed with forest that Prosper Demontzey had espoused. Hardly in strict conformity with the 1882 law, their assessments nonetheless reflected the dominant tendency within the RTM.

In 1899 the municipal council of Saint-Jean-de-Maurienne began to lobby the RTM to include a small tributary of the Arc called the Torne in the Lower Arc perimeter. Its confluence downstream from the town, the Torne cut across Jarrier, and the council of Saint-Jean spoke on behalf of its upland neighbor in its repeated requests. At first, several refusals from RTM personnel characterized this particular torrent as less important, the need for its "extinction" lacking "general interest." Such a formulation referred implicitly to the restrictive "evident and present" clause of the 1882 law, but this did not constitute the only reason for excluding minor torrents. Responding to Saint-Jean-de-Maurienne in 1902, the conservator stated flatly that the total area within restoration perimeters had to be limited in order to avert popular protest, which might thwart the entire project.[55]

In the meantime, however, foresters and local officials had begun to assess what the "extinction" of the Torne would require, and their judgments betray Demontzey's more expansive conception of "restoration." This evolution of the RTM's plans for the Maurienne would lead ultimately to a radical revision of the Lower Arc perimeter, one that threatened the livelihood of Jarrier and its tiny neighbor, Saint-Pancrace. A general forest guard for the region who quickly became joint inspector under Mougin after the turn of the century, M. Luze, set forth a new standard in December 1900. Restoring the Torne would demand control of not only the full length of the torrent's banks but also its entire watershed, the countless streams and rivulets that fed into it over a broad upland area. This area was to be put off limits to pasturing, regrassed, then reforested; Luze insisted that reforestation remained the ultimate goal of restoration.[56] By 1904 the RTM had officially changed its opinion of the danger the Torne posed to Saint-Jean-de-Maurienne and National Route Six. Conservator Cochon echoed Luze's analysis as he approved of the Torne's inclusion in the Lower Arc perimeter: the restoration of the Arvan basin would require the full reforestation of the uplands dominating the communes of Villarembert, Fontcouverte, and Jarrier. The limitations of the "evident and present" clause had emerged as reforestation reclaimed its earlier prestige in the new context of restoration.[57]

Both financial and ecological considerations played into the sudden impetus to purchase and reforest vast stretches of upland overlooking the Arc River. Savoie's Conseil Général had estimated in 1901 that perpetually dredging the Torne and building a protective wall along the roadway would prove more costly than simply reforesting the watershed.[58] Mougin, now chief inspector of forests in Chambéry, revealed a financial stimulus of a different order several years later, when the project to enlarge the perimeter was well under way. Mougin asserted that, in the first few years of the century, RTM credits had been siphoned away from the two Arc perimeters in the Maurienne toward ambitious projects in the Tarentaise: only the intervention of M. Deléglise, deputy from the Maurienne, had raised the credits by one hundred thousand francs. The putative necessity of enlarging the Lower Arc perimeter may well have been the deciding factor in accelerating the flow of funds to restoration projects in the Maurienne.[59]

It was also Mougin who in these years made the strongest ecological case for enlarging the Lower Arc perimeter. Training his sight on the Bonrieu torrent in particular, he continually drew connections between its ferment and Jarrier's bedrock-debris slump. The state's acquisitions in the area surrounding the Bonrieu torrent amounted to only 6 percent of the entire basin. Once planted, the area would become only a "thin curtain of forest" that would merely slide along with the moving soil. Arguing for a larger perimeter, Mougin invoked what he believed was the full meaning of "restoration," nothing less than direct intervention in upland ecology through reforestation: "The tasks whose execution the law of 4 April 1882, entrusts to the Administration des Forêts, include the consolidation of alpine lands and later the reforestation of the slopes; in a word, these are works of 'restoration' and not defensive fortifications."[60]

Embedded in Mougin's formulation of the problem was the assumption that a dense forest could in fact halt Jarrier's sliding bedrock. His faith in trees stands in contrast to present-day opinion in the RTM regarding bedrock-debris slumps: François Combes, recent director of the RTM in Savoie, has argued that forests can, on average, anchor the soil up to two meters below the surface.[61] Jarrier's unstable bedrock is fifty meters thick.

By April 1909, Mougin's reasoning had become the sole technical justification for augmenting Jarrier's portion of the perimeter. A representative of the forestry corps successfully argued before the Conseil Général that "ordinary modes of correction" did not apply to the Bonrieu, citing the necessity of a "great mass of forest" to correct the torrent and restore the land.[62] Shortly before the project for a "complementary perimeter" in Jarrier and Saint-Pancrace became law in 1910, Fernand David, then deputy from Haute-Savoie, revised before the Chamber of Deputies the restrictive notion of "evident and present": "Evident and present dangers affecting the land are not only those which appear on the surface in such an obvious way that it is often too late to intervene when we wish to avert them." Jarrier's sliding bedrock had in fact provided the test case in the RTM's bid to circumvent the limitations of the 1882 law.[63]

The complementary perimeter added more than 697 hectares to lands controlled by the RTM in the Lower Arc basin; roughly 29 percent of the total land mass of the two communes, 496 hectares lay within the limits of Jarrier and 201 within those of Saint-Pancrace. During the obligatory public inquiry of 1908 regarding the proposed extension, dozens of protests had emanated from both communes, especially Jarrier, and both municipal councils had expressed dismay and outrage over the new project. The latter appeared during the first major episode of permanent emigration from Jarrier. One-fourth of the 1903 population left the village between then and 1912, following several decades of remarkable stability. Jarriens were participating in the third great wave of rural exodus during the "long" nineteenth century, a wave that most affected the remote regions of France.[64] At a time of dramatic human loss, the new project threatened unconscionable, forced emigration from Jarrier: about fifteen families would have all their land expropriated, another forty families would lose between two-thirds and nine-tenths of their land, and a "large number" of additional families would lose a lesser though still significant portion of their patrimony. The new perimeter would swallow up nearly all of the privately owned and communal pastures in Jarrier; in Saint-Pancrace, whose total communal territory amounted to only 559 hectares, all pastures and chalets would fall within the new boundary. In both communes, increasingly the home of the old, the infirm, and the very young, incapable of hard agricultural labor, livestock raising had become the most remunerative—in many cases, the only possible—industry. The new perimeter would decimate it.[65]

As eloquent as the appeals based on hard material consequences were, equally forceful arguments sought to engage the RTM with its own evidence and assumptions. The municipal council of Jarrier maintained that the commune's pastures were never the site of landslides and thus did not contribute to the Bonrieu's volume of debris. Representatives of Saint-Pancrace respectfully noted that reforestation would remain ineffective in the absence of drainage channels, which they encouraged the RTM to build. Most assertively of all, Jarrier's council brought to attention, with thick underlines, the "LOCAL value of the land."[66] This succinct phrase contained within it a blunt critique of the principles promoted in the Administration des Forêts since the July Monarchy: that the poor alpine inhabitants had become unworthy of their degraded land, which existed for the purpose of protecting the towns, fields, roads, and rails of the plains. The minister of agriculture himself, Joseph Ruau, argued for the extension of the Lower Arc perimeter before the Chamber of Deputies in precisely these terms: "These proportions are high concerning the cultivated areas and pastures, but the agents who prepared the project included only the sites whose restoration is necessary to protect the plain."[67]

Caught up in the promise of more money for RTM projects in the Maurienne and the persuasive style of Paul Mougin, foresters did not heed the appeals from Jarrier and Saint-Pancrace. Ignoring the responses of individuals and the two municipal councils to the public inquiry in 1908, the inquiry's commissioner merely substituted his own opinion in his formal statement, concluding that only thorough reforestation could halt Jarrier's bedrock-debris slump and that the new perimeter, squarely within the "general interest," should be imposed. The commissioner even took the thirty opinions from Saint-Pancrace that favored drainage channels as implicit recognition of the larger project's necessity. His report ended with a concise reference to the impending plight of the inhabitants of Saint-Pancrace: it was, to be sure, "deserving of interest."[68]

Following by just two years the Jarriens' last, gratuitous cessions of land to the state for the original perimeter, the complementary project came as a bitter pill. The municipal council tried again in early 1911 to obtain a reduction in the size of the perimeter, but to no avail.[69] Yet the commune did not bow in resignation to the impending law that would sanction major state acquisitions of both communal and private land. Jarriens resisted encroachment in the only way they could—locally. Vigilance paid off in May 1909, when Mayor Michel Dompnier complained of plantings of spruce and larch in the livestock trails reserved for the commune under the terms of the first perimeter.

Mougin, still the chief forest inspector, acknowledged the unwarranted plantings and promised that the seedlings would be uprooted to the mayor's satisfaction.[70]

Covert resistance provided a further option. As early as 1907, the forest guard Edouard Martin reported the disappearance of markers used to delimit the perimeter. Though initially apt to attribute their disappearance to "meteoric causes," Martin quickly realized that people from Jarrier had been methodically pulling them from the ground. The next year he urged the closing of the perimeter with barbed wire and noted the disappearance of four more markers, adding, "these disappear easily in the perimeter of Jarrier." In 1910, Paul Noël, a general forest guard, estimated that repairing the barbed wire enclosure and replacing more missing markers would require around ten days of labor.[71]

In the years just prior to 1910, an additional source of discord heightened tensions between the Jarriens and the Forêts. In October 1907, Jarrier figured on the new list of communes in several alpine departments that would soon be subject to regulated pasturing. This list related to the "conservation" provisions under the 1882 law on the restoration and conservation of alpine lands. By administrative decree, designated pastoral communes would have to inform the prefect of the "nature and extent" of common lands under pasturing, the paths livestock used to reach the pastures, the numbers and species of animals grazing on the commons, the dates that marked the pasturing season, and the name of the communal shepherd chosen by municipal authorities, as well as any relevant measures of "order and policing" taken by the commune.[72]

Over the next one and a half years, the municipal councils of Jarrier and Saint-Pancrace wrangled with foresters and departmental authorities over the issue of regulated pasturing. The many exchanges that eventually resulted in compromise reveal much about the local meaning of "regulation" and about the values associated with having common pastures, namely, equal access and the safety net they provided the poorest inhabitants. Conversely, the correspondence unveils the tactics of those who held greater power, including belittlement of the communes, admonishment through comparison, and claims to veracity through a higher standard of mathematical precision. For Jarrier's municipal council, a hasty sketch of pastoral practices fulfilled the subprefect's request for a report on communal regulations; for the conservator, the initial report from Jarrier constituted "a negation of regulation, not to mention an irony."[73] But it is doubtful that numerical illiteracy prevented the municipal council from discussing regulation in rigorous terms; more likely, the body was loath to provide foresters with the exact number of animals pastured on the commons: in his own proposal for pastoral regulation, Martin estimated that the Jarriens were allowing five times as many animals to graze on the commons as they should. What is important here is the forester's conception of overgrazing. For Martin and other foresters, a predetermined number of "livestock-days"—considered suitable for the land in question—would be measured against actual pasturing, determined by a simple formula: (number of days of summer pasturing) × (number of bovines) × (fraction of the day spent grazing) + (number of days) × (number of ovines). As the mayor of Jarrier made clear to the prefect, he and his council took many other factors into consideration, including the timing of summer fairs (which greatly reduced the number of livestock) and the different but complementary schedules followed by inhabitants of the various hamlets.[74] Ultimately, regulations largely imposed from above forced the two communes to agree to smaller flocks of cows and sheep on the commons.

Both events—the advent of state control of the commons and the extension of the RTM perimeter—might well have tipped the local economy, already threatened by a first wave of emigration, over the edge. Yet despite the law of 1910 declaring the complementary perimeter a work of public utility, the project exploded within a few years. The end of this story is contained within a 113-page typed report, complete with photographs, written by Paul Noël in 1913. Having risen through the ranks to joint inspector of forests and serving directly under Mougin, Noël echoed his superior on several key issues through 1911, especially Mougin's opposition to allowing livestock onto land within a perimeter.[75] Whether or not his change of heart had anything to do with Mougin's transfer to Valence as conservator in 1911, Noël struck a markedly different tone just two years later. His lengthy report of 1913 stands out as a sustained indictment of the RTM's misguided attempts to restore the land of Jarrier. Most important, his document reflects a genuine appreciation, rare among the majority of foresters in his time, of the narrow options the Jarriens faced. Noël's report led within a year to yet a new perimeter representing a significant reduction of the 1910 scheme.

Noël presented a two-pronged account of why the RTM should abandon the grandiose revision of the original perimeter. His first line of reasoning dealt with the purported menaces to Saint-Jean-de-Maurienne. Yes, one could expect that the Bonrieu would continue to damage the dikes during violent storms, but the threat was surely no greater than the usual dangers to the hamlets of Jarrier closest to the torrent, and, in fact, ample room between the bed of the torrent and the dikes sheltered the town. Arguing against the common assumption that over time accumulating rocks and debris caused torrents' beds to rise, Noël observed that the Bonrieu had dug deeper into its channel, reducing the likelihood that it would suddenly change course, as had happened in 1440. He dismissed the notion of serious danger as adamantly as earlier foresters had advanced it: "it would mean yielding to panic to believe in the possibility, as in 1440 or 1618, of damage to the town of Saint-Jean-de-Maurienne by the torrent. . . . The various alpine hamlets, the town, and the important communication routes, are not the object of any serious menace; in the whole basin and its proximity, only local interests are at stake." These local interests, he estimated, came to 350 hectares under regular threat of torrential destruction and were worth six hundred thousand francs. He compared this figure to an estimate made in 1910 of the cost of the original (1898) project: it had been reevaluated at 3 million francs, nearly the entire annual RTM budget for all of France.[76]

Noël extended his perspective of the Bonrieu to the whole Arc-Isère river system. Since Alexandre Surell's study of Hautes-Alpes in the 1830s, foresters had taken for granted the dire effects of alpine torrents on France's major navigable rivers yet had made few calculations of volume, both water and debris. By Noël's estimate, the Bonrieu dumped around 100,000 cubic meters of "small materials" into the Arvan each year, which in turn discharged 850,000 cubic meters into the Arc. Contributing less than an eighth of the material volume that flowed from the Arvan into the Arc, the Bonrieu hardly merited a restoration of vast expense. Nevertheless, the Bonrieu remained "in terms of surface area . . . the most offensive of all the torrents included in the Lower Arc perimeter."[77] If the most violent torrent in the perimeter were not so dangerous after all, then what did such a conclusion imply for the RTM's schemes of restoration?

Noël's second line of criticism struck at the heart of the RTM's faith in reforestation. The complementary perimeter for Jarrier and Saint-Pancrace would include much of the unstable land found in the communes, and the projects' authors had attributed instability to the slope of the land, the marly nature of the soil, and excessive humidity.[78] Forests, Noël argued, would not suffice to halt or even slow the sliding earth, for in themselves trees could not arrest the constant undermining that water wrought upon the various branches of the torrent. More likely than not, a forest of any extent would be subject to the same forces and over time descend into the valley. Noël commented bluntly, "we know of entire forests that slide."[79] Dismissing forests as too expensive and ineffectual, Noël proposed in their stead a return to small masonry works and wattle fencing to curb erosion from the banks of the Bonrieu and its branches.

Yet even more remarkable than his analysis of real dangers and real solutions—and perhaps more shocking to his readers in the RTM corps—was Noël's evaluation of the role played by the people of Jarrier and Saint-Pancrace in resisting and ultimately nullifying the project for a complementary perimeter. Rare in administrative documents, this aspect of Noël's report presents not only an appreciation of rural resistance but also a forester's newly gained compassion.

Confirming earlier reports of missing markers and barbed wire, Noël criticized the RTM for attempting to close off Jarrier's original perimeter, including the livestock trails that cut across it. Foresters had first put up fencing, and seen it destroyed, in 1906; the peasants' "depredations" reached a crescendo after the complementary perimeter's ratification. Though legal owner of the land contained within the original boundary, the state had effectively lost its possession and become the peasants' dupe.[80] Noël registered no surprise that the new project of 1908 had caused an immediate outcry in Jarrier and Saint-Pancrace. He recounted the municipal councils' protests and their dismissal by higher authorities. When negotiations began in 1910 for the new acquisitions, the peasants' tactics changed: they took their protest to the marketplace and insisted on prohibitively high prices for the parcels that fell within the new perimeter. Proprietors insisted that the new prices, at an average of 3,200 francs per hectare, represented the "real" value of the land, and they admitted to previous deliberate underestimates made in order to pay fewer taxes.[81] Revising the original estimates for the costs of acquisition alone in Jarrier and Saint-Pancrace, the RTM arrived at a figure of nearly 2 million francs. It was at that point that the state simply backed down: "We concluded simultaneously upon the impossibility of making a friendly acquisition and the danger of attempting expropriation. A revision of the 1908 project was called for."[82]

What fears lay behind the phrase "the danger of attempting expropriation"? It remains unclear what Noël and other RTM personnel thought the people of Jarrier and Saint-Pancrace might actually do, but, at least for Noël, there was a greater reason to abandon the project. He could not condone the forced emigration of 300 people, unfortunate examples of the rural population though he felt they were. By 1911 Jarrier's population had dwindled to 769, with nearly 50 percent of the inhabitants either under the age of nineteen or over sixty.[83] In

vivid detail and with a photograph of impoverished Jarriens to illustrate, Noël
spoke for a lingering population that could not emigrate:

> is it desirable, in spite of a current theory which pretends that the restoration of the
> mountain is linked to the expulsion of the highlander? We do not believe so, and we
> really do not see the advantage in transforming into deserts certain regions where the
> inhabitants live without asking for anything, and to which they are profoundly at-
> tached. Besides, what would we do with the evicted people? Colonists for Algeria, for
> Canada? We know that attempts of this sort have been set in motion in Jarrier and
> Saint-Pancrace, but it is necessary to note that some of the inhabitants invited to live
> elsewhere cannot go and colonize. Apart from the able-bodied, there is, in effect, in
> the two communes a dead weight of the elderly, the infirm, and the cretins, unfit for
> serious work, and for a large number of whom the money accompanying expropria-
> tion has no value. The following photograph gives a sense of this sad humanity; it
> shows, in between a girl [*fille*] of forty-five years and a son of eighteen, an old man of
> eighty-one, who takes care of three children. The application of the perimeter pro-
> jected in 1908 would oblige this family to leave [figure 9].[84]

In keeping with his professional duties, Noël concluded his report with a
proposal for a new perimeter. Unlike both the 1898 project, which had included
too little of the Bonrieu basin, and that of 1910, which had covered far too

Figure 9. Inhabitants of Jarrier, 1913. Negative by Paul Noël. No. 2360, Bonrieu de Jarrier,
RTM Savoie.

much, the third attempt would represent 18 percent of the basin and coincide as exactly as possible with the threatened zones. All cultivated and inhabited areas in relatively good shape would be left out. As foreshadowed in his criticisms of the 1908 plan, Noël proposed only a limited role for reforestation and suggested modest rock walls and wattle fencing to stem lateral erosion into the Bonrieu and its branches. Work should proceed gradually, and it could not be completed in less than twenty years. Including acquisition costs, the state would have to spend approximately 920,000 francs. Finally, the joint inspector deferred to his superiors with the subtle suggestion that they abandon this attempt at restoration, as well: "It is up to the administration to decide whether it intends to undertake the expense or, judging it too great and the success too chancy, abandon the restoration."[85]

As the local historians Daniel Dequier and Jean-Henri Viallet describe, the third project for the restoration of the Bonrieu basin became law on 30 July 1914, sixteen years after the first law had addressed the problem. The perimeter incorporated the quantity of land that Noël had recommended. Not begun until the end of World War I, the work took longer than twenty years to complete and included the construction of dikes, walls, and drains and the planting of a small forest named Sur-Les-Bois.[86] What the authors do not mention is that during the war, Jarriens once again showed their hostility to reforestation by destroying previous plantings, pulling up markers and enclosures, and pillaging the foresters' shelter. The restoration begun after the war did not, therefore, build on lasting previous work.[87]

Restoring degraded lands in the Lower Arc perimeter proved especially slow for the RTM. By the beginning of 1928, the state had purchased only 557 of the 2,568 hectares slated for restoration: across ten Alpine departments and sixty-nine perimeters, only the Méouge perimeter in the Drôme surpassed this ratio of land yet to be acquired to land already acquired.[88] Equally important, the RTM had purchased all of the land within extremely few of its perimeters throughout the Alps, forty-six years into the era of restoration. Embedded in the numbers is a history of negotiation and resistance, and rates of acquisition do not tell the whole story, as the case of Jarrier has shown. Because of Jarrier's poverty, sudden and rapid depopulation, centrality to the Lower Arc perimeter, and, despite all, success in redirecting the RTM's ambitions, the case works as a useful prism through which to see other stories of alpine restoration.

Within the prism of this small commune, Jarriens manifested their hostility to the Radical Republic over other issues in the first years of the twentieth century, with methods that place their resistance to the RTM's encroachment in

relief. Specifically, Jarrier proved to be a divided commune in the battle between religious and secular education. Following the Ferry law of 1887, which
required only lay personnel to teach in public schools, the Sisters of Saint
Joseph had closed their girls' school in Jarrier, but they obtained permission to
open a new Catholic school in 1891. From 1901 to 1914, conflict over education
outwardly gripped political life in Jarrier: incidents included a night of win-
dow-breaking and plastering of republican posters at the Catholic school; prefectorial suspensions of two mayors, one of which resulted from Mayor Michel
Dompnier's personal removal of condemned books from the secular school;
the refusal of intransigent parish priests to give First Holy Communion to
young Jarriens from republican households; and a school strike organized by
parents unwilling to send their children to secular school.[89] Electoral politics
reflected this dramatic bifurcation of the commune. Although Jarrier has
leaned increasingly to the right in the major elections of the twentieth century,
voters kept the margin narrow during the Radical Republic: with a rate of ab-
stention noticeably lower than that for the whole Maurienne—12 versus 18 percent—41 percent of Jarriens cast their votes for the left and 48 percent for the
right in the legislative elections of 1902.[90]

By contrast, resistance to the RTM—clandestine and anonymous, on one
hand, economic (through the manipulation of land prices) on the other—lies
in another realm of politics. Direct action made sense in two contexts: not only
did the RTM's complementary perimeter of 1908 represent an objective and
dire threat to the commune's existence, but for those who weathered the first
wave of depopulation after 1903, pastoral lands became at once more available
and more precious, given the developing age profile that Paul Noël poignantly
described.

Local success in tempering the RTM's designs must be counted among the
key reasons why Jarrier remained an agricultural community well into the
1950s, despite its proximity to the valley and to Saint-Jean-de-Maurienne in
particular. It remained so long after hydroelectric domestication transformed
the Arc River into a "staircase with seven steps" largely before World War I, and
after the paper factories and the electrochemical and electrometallurgy industries completed the metamorphosis of the Maurienne into an industrial corridor.[91] Jarrier produced few worker-peasants, the so-called *double actifs* who sta-
bilized social transformation before the development of a purely industrial
workforce by the 1960s.

Aloof from industrial development, Jarrier did not, however, reject all modernization. Its municipal council made electrification a central priority during

the 1930s, and individual property owners took on agricultural modernization as well.[92] Jarrier was one of few communes in the Maurienne to achieve a degree of *remembrement* or consolidation of smallholdings, by 1960. At the same time, the population of Jarrier remained highly dispersed in numerous hamlets (less than 4 percent of the inhabitants lived in the chef-lieu in 1954), and Jarrier retained a high proportion—51 percent—of communal property.[93] The RTM, too, has retained its presence in Jarrier, owning sixty-three hectares on which it planted some trees in the 1970s. But the politics of fait accompli had prevented state-sponsored restoration from deciding the future of the commune; far from becoming a monolithic agent of "colonization," the RTM evolved along with Jarrier.

Chapter Four The Patrimony of the Poor: The Affair of the Mountains of Massat, 1832–1908

Who then told these inhabitants: "the forests belong to you—you are their masters"?
—*Subprefect in Saint-Girons, 1862*

When Louise-Charlotte of Foix, countess of Sabran, died in 1763, the people of Massat (Ariège) had reason to believe that less tumultuous times might lie ahead. During her thirty-year tenure as noble proprietor of the mountains surrounding Massat, the countess had waged war on the inveterate use rights enjoyed by the inhabitants. She had denied the validity of both the charter of 1446 and its confirmation exactly two centuries later by Jean-Pierre Gaston of Foix, documents that testified to the inhabitants' rights to gather wood and pasture animals in the "mountains," a shorthand expression for the ensemble of woods and pastures that ringed the valley.

Years of accusations hurled between the countess and the Massatois had revealed, for the magistrates of the Toulouse Parlement, the steadily increasing deforestation of the Massat valley. Various inhabitants had exploited the forest for the purpose of making charcoal, which fed the local ironworks or was exported to the Vicdessos Valley in exchange for minerals. So, too, had the Sabran dynasty been involved in the local charcoal industry to maintain its own ironworks. The magistrates in Toulouse ultimately banned all charcoal-making in the valley in 1756, yet they did not accept the countess's long-standing argument that the rights of the users should be subordinate to those of the proprietors: in a judgment of 1761 that terminated Louise-Charlotte's case against the Massatois, the Parlement upheld the traditional rights of use enjoyed by the inhabitants in the pastures and forests belonging to the Sabrans and maintained as well the Massatois' right of "property and enjoyment" in their own commonly held lands. The decree allowed limited charcoal production but forbade the cutting of all oak and fir. In order to appease the countess of Sabran, the magistrates condemned the community of Massat to pay her six thousand *livres,* a heavy fine.

Louise-Charlotte died just two years later, but not before she had undertaken another line of attack against what she deemed to be the Massatois' "usurpation" of her lands. In the name of her grandson, Louis-Auguste-Elzéar de Sabran, she initiated the judicial proceedings that would lead to a cantonnement.[1] But the grandson, the new Count of Sabran, became an absentee landlord, preferring Paris to Massat, running up his debts, and eventually representing the nobility in the Estates General of 1789. Before his emigration at the beginning of the Revolution, the count offered to lease all of his rights to the mountains of Massat to the commune for a yearly rent of three thousand francs. Fatally, perhaps, the Massatois refused. Upon returning from exile, the count of Sabran took up his grandmother's project of cantonnement; the Court of First Instance in Saint-Girons accepted his petition in 1806. Like his grandmother the count died before seeing the detailed legal operation to its conclusion, and his beneficiaries, his estranged wife, Lady Champeron, and his daughter Anna de Manas, sold their portions of the mountains in 1814 and 1816, respectively. The new owners were two local notables, Maurice de Roquemaurel and Jean-Jules-Isidore Delpla. In their turn, the new proprietors proceeded with cantonnement. The Court of Foix handed down its definitive judgment in 1824, attributing in full property two-fifths of the "woods, mountains, and pastures" to the commune by virtue of the inhabitants' having exercised use rights and three-fifths of the land in question to Roquemaurel and Delpla, by virtue of their property rights. The mayor of Massat appealed the cantonnement, but the Court of Toulouse upheld the local court's judgment in 1828. After sixty-seven years of withstanding attacks on their use rights, the Massatois were thrust into a new regime of "bourgeois" property that would characterize the nineteenth century. The stage was set for the nearly century-long "Affair of the Mountains."[2]

The Affair of the Mountains of Massat has received very little treatment by historians, though it monopolized official attention in Ariège and, indeed, much further afield in its later phases.[3] In the context of Ariégeois history, the affair neither presents the elements of glamour and mystery evoked by the War of the Demoiselles nor allows for narrative concision. Following the struggle between the Massatois and the Sabran dynasty, the affair evolved into a conflict over property and debt collection, alpine restoration, municipal power, and political legitimacy. It carried the weight of endless financial detail, the foresters' inopportune presence, and a curious mixing of old and new political practices; before culminating at the turn of the century, its various episodes had transpired in fits and starts over many decades. By contrast, the War of the Demoiselles played itself out within a little over two years and achieved stunning short-term success in the form of temporary grazing rights and amnesties. The greatest demonstration of power by the Demoiselles occurred in Massat itself; the town had become the nerve center of the revolt by early 1830 and hosted the largest of the few parades by Demoiselles in January and February of that year.[4]

In a rare evocation of the tensions in Massat around 1900, the historian Philippe Vigier pronounces their absolute difference with respect to the organized violence that characterized the forest question in the earlier part of the nineteenth century: "There is, in spite of everything, no common measure with the mass movements of the years 1830–1840, which correspond to a precise moment in French rural history."[5] But given the amplitude of the affair by 1900, and the questions it raises about rural autonomy and values—the same general concerns for which the Demoiselles had fought—it seems more fruitful to tease out the avenues of both change and continuity in order to pinpoint the nature of forest politics in the early twentieth century. The Affair of the Mountains was in many ways rooted in the War of the Demoiselles. The revolt of 1829–31 became a hovering specter in the minds of property owners, forest guards, and local authorities during many troubling moments of the affair. Who was to say that Demoiselles would not "arise" again, don their curious costumes and, with their superlative ways of moving over the land, once more flout the law and cause terror? Dreadful memories can be read in a subprefect's comment of 1861 as he warned of a "general uprising" of peasants "who still recall the exploits of the Demoiselles, among whom the survivors are highly regarded."[6] The property owners implicated in the affair came to adopt the War of the Demoiselles as a trope, an inevitable reference in their appeals to the au-thorities for protection.[7]

More surprising than these examples from the 1860s is a gendarme's absolute identification of the affair with the War of the Demoiselles in 1897: "For more than half a century, the interested population has grappled with the [C]ivil [S]ociety [of the Mountains of Massat] over this affair. In 1829, the time of the 'demoiselles,' as they were called, a large number of men from the region who were masked and dressed up as women, and armed with sticks, axes and other instruments, came en masse to Massat to protest this affair of the mountains. A detachment of troops was sent to reestablish the order so seriously threat-ened."[8] Although Demoiselles had, in fact, pursued the private forest guards of the Roquemaurel and Delpla families in January 1830—probably in anger over the cantonnement concluded two years earlier—the pursuit took place in the broader context of the revolt;[9] the Affair of the Mountains had hardly gotten under way in 1830 and was not yet referred to as such. Though in error, the gen-darme's assimilation of the two "troubles" is a telling comment about memory and fear.

Thus, Vigier's assumption of "no common measure" is overdrawn. It is only by defining precisely that common measure of rural contestation that one can elucidate the responses of turn-of-the-century uplanders to a basic question that shaped their lives, as it had shaped those of their ancestors: What are the proper uses and meaning of the mountain, in both its sylvan and pastoral guises? Three salient themes provide a set of keys to unlock the meaning of the Affair of the Mountains of Massat. First, throughout this multigenerational conflict, the actors expressed and enacted a focal value: possession. Foresters as far back as Froidour had observed that Ariégeois peasants acted as if all forests and pastures belonged to them, despite the obvious existence of seigneurial and royal domains. The peasant protagonists in the affair retained a traditional meaning of possession, deriving fundamentally from medieval charters grant-ing use rights, but they also fused it to the meaning and status given to posses-sion in Napoleon's Civil Code—a deft welding of local culture to the authority of national law. The rhetoric of possession espoused at the turn of the nine-teenth century was nothing new.

Second, peasants claimed possession by means of an arsenal of tactics that wedded tradition and innovation. Although they employed strategies directly reminiscent of the Demoiselles' practices, the chief actors in the affair also ne-gotiated at carefully chosen moments according to laws governing private property, and they convoked peaceable mass meetings—the latter tactic stretch-

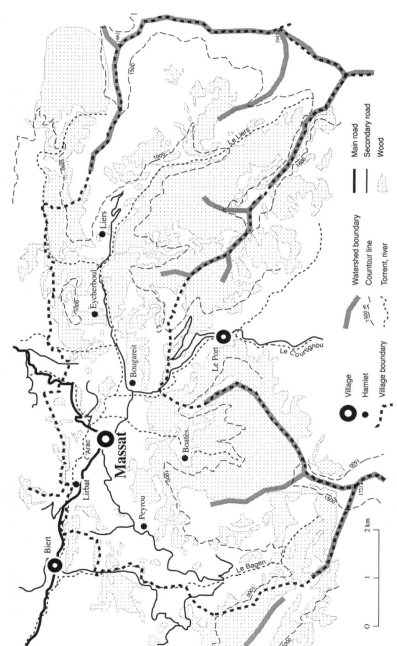

Map 4. Commune of Massat

Eric Leclerc, professor of Geography, University of Rouen.

ing back at least to the late sixteenth century in parts of France.[10] A startling shift in repertoire came with the electoral victory of rural hamlets over the central bourg in May 1900, a victory that would have been inconceivable to the Demoiselles, despite the collusion of mayors in their war. The prefect of Ariège had commented as early as 1834: "The word 'republic' echoes in the spirit of the population." He went on to explain its local translation as the power to become masters of the forests, public and private.[11] Republicanism and possession remained linked in 1900, but the implications of both had changed vastly with the opportunities of electoral politics, a shift whose traces date to 1848.

Finally, the advent of state-sponsored restoration constituted a new element that arrived wholly from the outside. In order to rid their towns of lingering debt, local officials in Massat and two neighboring communes sold land to the Restauration des Terrains en Montagne in 1883. Neither they nor the RTM reckoned that this land, too, would become subject to the justice of inveterate possession. As in the preceding case of Jarrier (Savoie), the rural Massatois managed to thwart an amply financed and well-coordinated state project—one of few restorations attempted in Ariège during the Third Republic. Though not at the center of the Affair of the Mountains, resistance to the RTM symbolized the larger struggle and called forth other elements of a repertoire that was remarkably versatile for a population close to destitution and beginning to emigrate permanently. It played into the Massatois' artful crafting of a long-range vision of collective control (map 4).

THE MASSAT VALLEY

In culturally diverse Ariège, straddling Languedoc and Gascony, the Massat Valley forms a key point of transition. Massat lay just within the historical border of Gascony: its streams are tributaries of the Salat River, marking the frontier, and the town depended on the viscount of Couserans, a vassal politically oriented toward Gascony, despite occasional family alliances with the counts of Foix. Yet the Massatois spoke a dialect of *languedocien:* the town was truly a last outpost of languedocien culture, for in the town of Soulan, just down the Arac River a mere ten kilometers away, the dialect shifted to *gascon.*[12]

Massat was not a minor town, a place where such transition would go unnoticed. It had provided the residence for the viscounts of Couserans and thus constituted a regional capital. In the seventeenth century Massat became a local religious center, hosting a collegiate church with a chapter of six canons. It grew into a town run by doctors, lawyers, merchants, and apothecaries in the eighteenth century and by the Revolution was the largest town in what became Ariège. During the formation of departments and the designation of prefectures under the Constituent Assembly, however, geographical considerations favored Foix, owing to its riverside location and consequent accessibility to both the upper Ariège River corridor and the Pyrenean foothills. Saint-Girons, whose leading citizens lobbied for the creation of a department centering on the Couserans, became a subprefecture in the west, also at the expense of Massat.[13]

The genesis of departmental administration had thus eclipsed Massat, yet the town and its valley remained an important link between east and west, thanks to the easily traversed Port pass. Occupying part of the depression that divides the north-Pyrenean range, the Massat Valley is one of the valleys that run parallel to the Pyrenees and characterize the unique geography of the *Pyrénées ariégeoises*.[14] Glacial erosion created the basin, which extends approximately twenty kilometers on both sides of the Arac River. Other villages and hamlets in the canton, such as Le Port, a leading player in the Affair of the Mountains, cling to steep slopes above the Arac. Typical of the Pyrenees as a whole, Massat's forest ascends through zones of oak partially interspersed with chestnut, giving way to fir mixed with beech, fir alone, and finally pine. Typical as well is the confusion of subalpine and alpine zones; whereas geographers have said that they "naturally" begin at around two thousand meters, the high-altitude pastures, or *estives*, of Massat's alpine zone are as low as eleven hundred meters, bearing witness to an intensive pastoral culture that long sacrificed forest for more pasture (figure 10).[15] But here as elsewhere in alpine France, the forest remained a central element in the pastoral economy: growing in tight proximity to pastures in this mid-altitude region, the forest provided welcome reprieves from the scorching summer sun, as well as grasses, dry leaves, shrubs, and dead branches for animal feed, barn litter, and fuel.[16]

Created by nature and labor, Massat's mountains were jewels of the Couserans. Rich grasses profited from both the damp climate of the area and the fact that the Massatois were irrigating up to 70 percent of their meadows by the mid-nineteenth century. An anonymous source had compared these exceptional mountains to plains and prairies in 1844. Renowned butter came from Massat, though the population did have to rely on a variety of livestock to furnish "work, milk, and meat" for largely local consumption; in nineteenth-century Massat three sheep grazed the pastures for every cow. The Massatois, in addition, devoted 40 percent of their agricultural lands to potatoes, a largely subsistence crop.[17]

Livestock-raising in Massat followed a pattern rarely found in the Ariège up-

Figure 10. Massat, Ariège, c. 1910. No. 315 in L. Labouche postcard series "Les Pyrénées ar-iégeoises." 26 Fi Pyrénées ariégeoises, Archives Départementales de la Haute-Garonne.

lands. The system was known as the *bourdaous,* a word referring to groups of barns situated on individually owned or managed meadows but close to communal pastures. During the summer season, livestock grazed mostly on communal lands, since peasant families harvested hay from their meadows for winter consumption. The location of the bourdaous, usually within sight of villages or hamlets, allowed shepherds to descend each morning with large containers of milk, having spent the night in shelters adjacent to the barns. Transitional between pastoral and sedentary practices, the bourdaous system permitted the shepherds to maintain an existence reasonably integrated with village life during the grazing season and combined aspects of communal and individual exploitation.[18]

In between individualistic and communal forms of managing pastoral lands, the bourdaous system rarely existed in a pure state; associations that oversaw the pasturing of local livestock did exist in the lower part of the Massat Valley.[19] The most individualistic arrangements tended to be linked with transhumant livestock from the lowlands, but local owners of large flocks also contracted with poorer residents who possessed little livestock of their own and resided in the upper hamlets closest to the estives. The bourgeois of Massat had used these contracts, or *baux à cheptel,* at least since the eighteenth century; they benefited the owners enormously while placing all risk of raising the animals with the lessee. Common throughout the central Pyrenees, baux à cheptel remained one of few options for many alpine peasants during the economic squeeze of the early to mid-nineteenth century. Officials decried the contracts for causing local misery and setting in motion patterns of overgrazing and consequent degradation. Within the community, they contributed to a deep social rift that had long separated the bourgeois in town from peasants in the dispersed hamlets. The economic repression following the War of the Demoiselles exacerbated class divisions: the twenty wealthiest inhabitants of Massat had had to pay a fine of 41,600 francs. This antagonism came to the surface again during the Affair of the Mountains.[20]

The sprawling mountains could not, however, provide a livelihood for all Massatois in the nineteenth century. Emblematic of the demographic surge that had taken place over the preceding century, the canton of Massat boasted the highest density in the department by 1846, with eighty-seven inhabitants per square kilometer. Pastoralism, by necessity a low-density occupation, did not suffice for all, nor was there enough arable land for subsistence farming. Social trends inevitably reflected economic penuries: the valley had a reputation for producing "professional" beggars, mostly women, through the end of the nineteenth century.[21] Many Massatois also prevented or deferred permanent departure by becoming specialists in the arts of temporary migration. Women, children, and elders from Massat worked the autumn grape harvests in lower Languedoc and Gers, and the Massatois held a near monopoly of the Ariégeois labor market for harvests of the Lectourois, a rich grain-producing region in Gascony. Traveling masons and railroad workers also came from the Massat Valley. Along with other communes in the upper Couserans, Massat was an important center of origin for traveling peddlers and even traveling distillers. Peddling (*colportage*) as a profession had grown out of seasonal migration, and the activities of the Massatois peddlers, possibly the most diverse in Ariège, ranged from selling wooden gadgets in the Midi to trafficking in vanilla, jewelry, and Chinese vases. Although temporary migration was but a limited palliative to poverty and offset the rural exodus by a few decades at best, Massat nevertheless was able to retain a respectable portion of its inhabitants until the end of the nineteenth century. The town reached its maximum population of 4,157 in 1872 and did not dip below 3,000 until after 1911. In that year, it was still one of only eight communes in Ariège—out of 338—that could boast a population of 3,000 or more inhabitants.[22] Quite different from the profile of Jarrier, the size of and social divisions in Massat were to lend a significant dimension to the struggle of some Massatois for their mountains.

Evidence of poverty and of a dense human population places the value of Massat's mountains in an important perspective: for those who could make a living, or a partial one, from livestock, access to the mountains underpinned economic survival. This group included both the owners of flocks and the holders of baux à cheptel. In this context, the affair began in 1832 with the commune's purchase of the three-fifths portion of land that the cantonnement of 1824 had awarded to the Roquemaurel and Delpla families, the purchasers of the old Sabran inheritance. Eighteen thirty-two marked the end of the War of the Demoiselles, and many property owners feared its recurrence. Roquemaurel and Delpla were probably eager to cut their losses by selling their portion of the mountains of Massat; the forest was nearly exhausted for purposes of metallurgy, as well. The Massatois acquired the 4,350 hectares of land for 130,000 francs, payable in twenty annuities. Taxes on the gathering of underbrush for fuel, a pasturing tax (*foraine*), and a direct tax of 24,000 francs would help liquidate the debt in a timely manner. The commune regularly defaulted on its installments, however, for reasons too murky for the documents to reveal. In 1842, a judge in Saint-Girons ordered Massat to free itself of debt within eighteen months, an order that was never enforced.[23] Decades hence, the Massatois pastoralists were to lose their new property but later regain it, ultimately owning more property than they had after the fated purchase of 1832. The full significance of their triumph can be appreciated by looking at how they handled customary as well as juridical aspects of property and possession.

PROPERTY AND POSSESSION

The many claims made about property during the various phases of the affair must be seen in light of both the Civil Code and popular conceptions of possession. To begin with the Civil Code of 1804, the right to own private property is arguably its centerpiece; article 544 defines it as absolute, fundamentally individual, and, through inheritance, perpetual. In general, restrictions on the use of property required the existence of a text drafted by lawmakers or regulatory authorities in the nineteenth century.[24] This well-known sanctity of individual private property stands in contrast to the Civil Code's prescriptions for collective property. The latter can exist legally in two restricted forms. Through *indivision* (also *copropriété*), individuals possess an abstract fraction of a piece of property, but a co-proprietor may demand formal partition at any time.[25] The second, truly collective, form describes property owned, organized, and regulated in the interest of a "common will." Here the proprietor is a so-called *personne morale,* a legal fiction representing a profit-motivated company, non-profit association, unit of government, or some other administrative structure. Theoretically, this form of collective property cannot be partitioned, since no individual owners exist, yet legal changes, such as the famous decree of 10 June 1793 on the partition of the commons, have attested otherwise.[26]

Apart from both individual and collective property lies the concept of possession. Though certainly not unique to French property law, possession, if proved, carries important juridical consequences in the French system. No general theory of possession exists in the Civil Code; rather, article 2228 defines it briefly, as follows: "Possession is the holding or the use of a thing or of a right that we hold or use by ourselves, or that another holds or uses in our name." Possession reflects the control and use of a thing, but both these objective criteria (*corpus*) and the intention to act as proprietor of the thing (*animus*—highly important in French law) must be present. Possession must fulfill four additional conditions in order to have juridical effects. Use and control of the thing in question must be continuous (without "abnormal interval[s]"), peaceful (entry into possession cannot be made with violence), public (possession cannot be clandestine), and unequivocal (the *animus* must be clear). If possession meets these standards and is in good faith, then the possessor can take civil action in cases of material or legal aggression toward the thing possessed. Most important, the possessor becomes the presumed holder of a property right in case of contest, and possession can itself lead to the acquisition of a property right, generally after a period of thirty years.[27]

"Possession" carried further resonance during the Affair of the Mountains. Residents of the rural hamlets of Massat acted with the knowledge that possession was one legal means of acquiring property; at the same time, they imbued possession with a broader significance: the customary right to *use as one's own* and have that use recognized as a claim to the land. Pastoralists did not make fine distinctions between possession and use rights; the Civil Code did. The Massatois sought possession of the mountains in this broader sense even as they acted within a legal culture that protected possession as well as property rights.

They well knew, however, to which local property regime possession applied. For, as was typical of pastoral communities, two property regimes had traditionally existed in Massat. On one hand, the valley exemplifies Jean-François Soulet's portrait of Pyrenean "microfundia," the regime of small, privately owned parcels that, in all Pyrenean departments, fell markedly below the average plot size in France. The five-to-six hectare parcel retained a remarkable stability in Massat; even depopulation led to little *remembrement,* or combining of parcels.[28] These were the agricultural lands from which families drew their subsistence.

On the other hand, the "commons," whether owned by the state, communes, or local notables, were the primary pastoral lands. What mattered more than ownership here was collective use: the commons were nearly all open to use rights throughout Ariège.[29] The valley of Massat had been exceptional in the Couserans for the aristocratic ownership of pastures and forests. What might be termed a seigneurial mode of production had placed particular stress on the forest in that the owners exploited the woods for charcoal to feed the iron forges, while peasants integrated the forest into their pastoral systems. The commune's purchase in 1832 of the portion of mountains that had fallen to Roquemaurel and Delpla signaled the end of this mode; Massat had merely acted precociously in what would become a general pattern, during the Second Empire, of communal purchases of forests that had been heavily exploited for charcoal production but that still held value for pastoralists. Conversion of property through cantonnement had necessarily preceded these acquisitions, and Massat's had been the first major cantonnement to take place in Ariège.[30] The forest had become pastoral, and property had become collective.

It was an underlying sense of possession, however, with its ambivalent take on property, that framed the conflict to come. Through their purchase of Roquemaurel and Delpla's three-fifths of the mountains, the municipal councilors implicitly acknowledged the property created by cantonnement. Yet in 1830–31, in the heat of the War of the Demoiselles, a prefectorial decree followed by a royal ordinance had opened up all of the mountains to pasturing and instituted a pasturing tax, the foraine. Receipts from this tax would flow to the different owners in the same proportions as the cantonnement—three-fifths to Roquemaurel and Delpla, two-fifths to the commune of Massat. (It will be recalled that, following the purchase of 1832, the foraine was to help pay off the communes' debt.)[31] Thus, the Massatois had regained access to three-fifths of the mountains in 1830; until the 1832 purchase, access was obtained through the foraine. Had the prefect respected, in a limited fashion, the commune's "possession?"

The importance of the prefect's act was revealed later, in the protests that followed the annulment of the sale in 1865. A prelude to that event was a change in administrative structure that split Massat into three communes—Massat, Biert, and Le Port—in 1851. This legislative act from Paris was apparently undertaken to favor the candidacy of General Pelet, partisan of President Louis-Napoleon, but the more rural communities of Biert and Le Port, home to few bourgeois or functionaries, had been clamoring for partition since the eighteenth century and welcomed the escape from the hegemony of Massat. Fracturing Massat necessitated the formation of a collective body to handle the debt. Responding to threats of judicial action on the part of Roquemaurel and Delpla, in 1853 the subprefect in Saint-Girons formed a "syndical commission," composed of select municipal officials, to do so.[32]

Systematic defaulting on debt payments ensued. The three municipal councils sporadically declared the foraine illegal, but were the receipts being embezzled? As early as 1858, the municipal council of Le Port demanded that the foraine be abolished: the livestock owners had been paying it dutifully for twenty-seven years without seeing proof that the syndical commission had been applying the receipts toward the purchase of Roquemaurel and Delpla's three-fifths.[33] Although the president of the syndical commission—also the mayor of Massat—attested in 1855 to the difficulties of finding a responsible collector and in 1862 to the financial shambles caused by Massat's partition a decade earlier (administrative costs had tripled), the full reasons for the commission's abysmal defaults on its payments cannot be teased from these details.[34] What does emerge is that by the 1860s, rumors of illegality and corruption had begun to raise tempers and cause widespread evasion of the foraine.

The creditors soon brought the three communes to trial; in December 1865, the Court of Saint-Girons nullified the 1832 sale and condemned Massat, Biert, and Le Port to give the three-fifths portion of the mountains back to Roquemaurel and Delpla. In his rendition of the affair many years later, the politician and local notable Léon Galy-Gasparrou quoted directly the decision made by the court: among other things, the annulment of the purchase would entail "that the parties be put back in a same and similar state as before."[35] Though ambiguous, could not "before" be interpreted as referring to the arrangement in place between 1830 and 1865, such that the communes would retain their pasturing rights to all of the mountains if they continued to pay the foraine? "Before" might extend as well to the rate of the foraine, yet in the spring of 1867 the recently created Civil Society of the Mountains of Massat (the name of the company to which Roquemaurel and Delpla had technically sold their three-fifths portion of the mountains, but in which they had kept a financial interest) doubled the tax to four francs per cow, two francs per goat, and half a franc per sheep. In addition, the society began to sell off its three-fifths of the mountains in individual parcels, again contravening the sense of "before." It was in this context that in May 1867, twenty or so masked men beat Moustache Ponsolle, Roquemaurel's private forest guard, who died two days later from his wounds. The subprefect attributed the murder directly to the frustration occasioned by the selling of parcels, to which the peasants also responded by invading the pastures and refusing to declare their livestock.[36]

Despite the authorities' fears that armed rebellion would break out, the intransigent residents of Liers, a hamlet of Massat, capitulated and once again agreed to pay the foraine. Nonetheless, Roquemaurel and Delpla pursued punitive judicial action: the Court of Saint-Girons obliged in 1873, condemning the communes to pay more than 80,000 francs to the two owners, a sum calculated as the profits accrued by the inhabitants from more than forty years of using the mountains, their unpaid property. But this debt, too, mounted until it had exceeded 132,000 francs by 1883.

With that, Roquemaurel and Delpla and other members of the Civil Society of the Mountains began to pose as defenders of property rights per se, whose importance stretched beyond their personal interests to define the "true foundation of society."[37] Once peasants began to wrestle with legal distinctions, they opened themselves up to savage belittlement. The imperial prosecutor so chastised the hamlet of Liers in 1867, whose residents had held out the longest against resuming their foraine payments. These peasants had made a "delicate and dangerous distinction" between the right to property and the exercise of the right, yet they possessed "neither intelligence nor sufficient knowledge" to engage in such subtle legal exercises.[38] By then, however, events had paved the way for a more militant alternative to the buying and selling of property.

REFORESTING MASSAT

Into this at times latent, at times open, conflict over property, possession, and tax collection, the Administration des Forêts stepped in 1883. To foresters' eyes, Ariège had remained an exceptional department even into the early Third Republic: Forest Inspector M. Serval opened his comprehensive report in 1882 with the comment, "In Ariège the forest regime presents some absolutely extraordinary characteristics."[39] Of the state's large holdings of "forest" in Ariège, nearly three-quarters consisted of "vacant" land (pastures), still burdened with communal use rights, and communes continued to flout the Forest Code's restrictions on pasturing. The department's Conseil Général favored the transfer of all the state's lands to communes, and many local spokespersons "looking for popularity" had begun to clamor for the exemption of all communal forests

from state management. Both scenarios had, of course, remained unacceptable
to the Forêts, yet the latter found itself far too politically embattled to extend its
authority in Ariège. By the late 1870s no specific projects awaited implementation, and the post of chief reforestation agent for Ariège lay vacant.[40]

Other complaints from foresters included the mediocrity of communal forest guards, the intensification of pastoralism, and the "barbarous" method of
management known as *furetage:* akin to jardinage for high forests, furetage was
a customary method of selecting trees to maintain an uneven-aged low forest.
The larger frustration lay in a sense of slipping opportunity: since the collapse
of catalan-forge metallurgy in Ariège, the forests had begun to recover, and,
if only left to the "forces of nature," would show an "incomparable richness"
in twenty-five to thirty years.[41] Such potential hardened the state's resolve to
maintain its property rights, even if it could not force its own methods of management upon unwilling communes.

The extraordinary flood of 22–23 June 1875 was to give new urgency to reforestation. Unlike the floods of 1855–56, which had wrought the greatest damage in the Rhône and Loire basins and brought national attention to the state of
the Alps, those of 1875 largely affected the watershed of the Garonne. A so-
called centenary flood, the regional inundation touched twenty cantons in Ariège and nearly 14,000 hectares; seventy-eight Ariégeois lost their lives, and the
cost of damage was estimated at almost 6.5 million francs. The disaster brought
Marshall MacMahon to Ariège and with him 1.4 million francs in aid.[42] Destruction was particularly heavy in the Salat basin, where the estimate of damage rose to 1.7 million francs. Massat, Biert, and Le Port were among the affected communes, and the waters intercepted the vital road to Saint-Girons for
more than three kilometers.[43]

A plan for the protection of the Garonne emerged from the Ministry of Public Works in 1880—not until the Couserans suffered more significant flooding
in 1879. Reforestation and regrassing were to be undertaken in order to diminish the flow of debris into the Garonne, halt the rising of the river bed, and ultimately protect the port of Bordeaux. Vulnerable alpine areas were divided
into two categories—"degraded land in movement" and "denuded land." Although the former would be buttressed by "consolidation works" prior to reforestation, and the latter would be subject to replanting, total reforestation
was out of the question. Matching the foresters' vision of the Pyrenees formed
after 1860, the authors of the Public Works report advocated a band of forest to
cover the middle altitudes; individuals and communes would, they insisted, retain their pastures as well as passages through the new forests.[44]

With this mandate, the Forêts initially focused its work in Ariège solely on Auzat, the large commune at the upper end of the Vicdessos basin that had been the object of reforestation in the early 1860s and had since become a center of transhumance.[45] The local drama unfolding in Massat soon gave the Forêts the opportunity to design a large reforestation project for the Couserans as well. Long before, the prefect of Ariège himself had conceived the idea of having the communes sell their two-fifths portion of the cantonnement to the state for purposes of reforestation, as a means of solving their financial difficulties. When the project reached the top in 1863, however, the minister of finance declined to authorize it, citing insufficient public utility.[46] Late in 1883 the Forêts—its credits now swollen since passage of the alpine restoration law of 1882—stepped in to accomplish what it had failed to do twenty years earlier: it relieved Massat, Biert, and Le Port of yet more of their commonly held lands, 804 hectares, and in so doing liquidated just under 100,000 francs of their combined debt.[47] This acquisition by the state left several hamlets entirely cut off from their remaining communal pastures, from sources of income, and from their traditional way of life.

Foresters based in Toulouse drafted their plan for the Couserans by 1887, including Massat, Biert, and Le Port among the six communes in the newly named Salat perimeter. In contrast to the plan for Auzat, the vision for the perimeter included a vigorous campaign of reforestation: the foresters intended not only to fill in existing sparse forest but also to constitute "coniferous forests on ground that is currently pasture." It was clearly a work of public utility to form a "protective zone" above villages and fields, even if it meant encroaching on pastures that, in any case, now belonged to the state; the floods of 1875 amply justified the wholesale creation of coniferous forests in the Couserans.[48] The plan for Massat was more ambitious and intrusive than that for the Garonne River basin as a whole.

François Guary, in his last year as forest conservator in Toulouse, and his two subordinates drafted these plans in the spirit of the legislation of 1860. By 1887, of course, Third Republic legislators had remolded punitive reforestation into the law on the restoration and conservation of alpine lands. This more restrictive law, it will be remembered, allowed restoration only in areas of "evident and present dangers," a hillside entering full erosion, for example. Guary's description of Massat virtually boasted of the "excellent fodder," "good pastures," and ample forests showing a "beautiful vegetation." True, much of the forest in the communal territory of Le Port and Biert was thin, low, and deciduous: they neither pleased foresters' aesthetic sensibilities nor satisfied their assumption that only vast stands of conifers could regulate water. But nowhere in the reports did foresters use the phrase "evident and present dangers," and the scheme of massive reforestation would, in any case, have far exceeded the new limitation.[49] Sixteen years later, when the project had fallen victim to peasants' fires, a new generation of foresters nonetheless justified its lineaments on the grounds that the state had undertaken the acquisition project before passage of the law of 4 April 1882. This was a narrow justification for what would be a palpable failure.[50]

In 1887, local foresters marshaled as many arguments as they could to win approval of the Salat perimeter. Among these figured a solicitude for the economic well-being of the local inhabitants. In Ariège, they noted, which had been struck along with much of the rest of France by agricultural crisis, new salaries paid by the Forêts would be welcomed.[51] They commented on the mendicity, the seasonal migrations, the lack of industry so obvious in an alpine region where "comfort is a rare thing." To that extent, it can be argued that foresters saw themselves as a positive presence in the Massat Valley in the late 1880s. Yet never far removed from paternalism was scorn: Guary, Vaultrin, and Bentajou wrote forthrightly that peasants had no sense of the common good; these particular inhabitants were even "badly placed to appreciate the necessities of public order," for they exaggerated their immediate privations while conveniently forgetting the disasters of the past. And though not responsible for the degradation of land wrought by their ancestors, "it is important to observe that the population has largely benefited from it."[52] Thus, the mandate of 1860 had survived the Third Republic's attempt at conciliation both in practice and in spirit. A venerable rhetoric that accused peasants of neglecting history and refusing foresight, and that equated pastoralism with historical deforestation, lingered through the end of the century. As we have seen, exceeding the limits of the law of 1882 did not characterize foresters' actions only in Ariège: twenty years after the final reports on the Salat perimeter were drafted, Paul Mougin and his associates in Savoie attempted reforestation in Jarrier according to the 1860 model.

This early history of the Salat perimeter reveals, as well, foresters' ways of categorizing and valuing property. Rarely staunch defenders of private forest ownership, they repudiated the wisdom of communal ownership, too. As Inspector Serval had reported in 1882, local demands for the alienation of the state's forests to the communes fell on deaf ears in his administration. Serval understood that all Ariégeois politicians, from municipal councilors to senators, had to pander to the pastoralists' interests, but he and his colleagues rejected time and again the argument that communes would become better care-takers if they held property rights to the large tracts of state forest.[53] In itself this was hardly a new stance on the foresters' part; it does show their insistence on distinguishing between communal and state property. Both were forms of collective property, yet the former was invariably pernicious, whereas the latter represented the only viable means of passing forests on to future generations.[54] Unfortunately for the RTM, these assumptions were to perish in a vortex of lo-cal politics.

LÉON GALY-GASPARROU AND FRANÇOIS PIQUEMAL

Forced to sell to the state, peasants in the Massat Valley now faced a dearth of pastoral land as well as remaining debt. Resentment accumulated below the surface during the 1880s as the Affair of the Mountains reached temporary sta-sis, due in large part to the role played by an aspiring politician, Léon Galy-Gasparrou. Born in Massat in 1850, Galy-Gasparrou came from a family that had long dominated local politics: a Galy-Gasparrou had been first consul of the town in 1761, and another had been mayor in 1832, the year of the ill-fated purchase of land from Roquemaurel and Delpla.[55] With a law degree behind him, Léon Galy-Gasparrou was elected to Massat's municipal council in 1878 and to the Conseil Général the following year. In the early 1880s he became mayor of Massat. Galy-Gasparrou's political fortunes reached their height with his election to the Chamber of Deputies as part of the moderate *gauche démoc-ratique* in 1898, just as the Affair of the Mountains was reaching its apex—and turning against him.[56]

Part of Galy-Gasparrou's initial prestige may have derived from his being the first mayor of Massat following the national reforms of municipal administra-tion in 1882 and 1884. As such, he was the first mayor both to be elected by the municipal council and to hold police powers. As mayor of Massat, Galy-Gas-parrou also automatically became president of the syndical commission of Massat, Biert, and Le Port, the organism responsible for managing the com-munes' debt. He extended this duty to become a prestigious champion of the pastoralists' cause. Beginning in 1887, he led the process of effecting an ex-change of parcels between the state and the communes, personally taking the case to Paris for a meeting with the minister of agriculture. The prefect had paved his way with a flattering letter assuring the minister that Galy-Gasparrou was "one of the steadiest supporters of the Republic in his canton." The latter kept his political clout in mind at each turn, not hesitating to ask the prefect to delay municipal elections in Massat until his commission had concluded the exchange project.[57] Galy-Gasparrou also spoke for all three municipal councils on the issue of taking 160 hectares of collective forest out of the state's forest regime. Fearing abusive pasturing, the conservator of forests refused the request. Galy-Gasparrou had firmly established himself as the pastoralists' champion through his popular stance on the forest question.[58]

As a Radical in Parliament, Galy-Gasparrou stood for a respectably democratizing republic; at home in Massat his constituents looked upon him as fatherly protector of their vital interests. Yet from the mid-1890s, a popular movement to regain possession of the mountains, led by a livestock owner and shepherd named (prophetically?) François Piquemal, variously nicknamed "Francézou" and "Rat," outflanked him. Neither "republican legality" nor the monopolistic style of a political fief holder could carry Galy-Gasparrou through the crisis. In addition, Massat again proved itself a divided community, and, in keeping with his political values, Galy-Gasparrou chose to abandon the most militant of the pastoralists. In return, the followers and supporters of Piquemal developed their own political style, fusing the old tactics of intimidation and threats of revolt with symbols of the Republic as well as the new inspiration of socialism.[59]

That the Affair of the Mountains took a dissident turn in 1895, attracting national attention and raising authorities' fears of armed rebellion, seems odd at first glance. The syndicated communes of Massat, Biert, and Le Port were in fact on the eve of paying off their thirty-year-old debt to the Civil Society of the Mountains; the commission made its last payment in December 1896.[60] For the owners of livestock whose foraine had been collected to pay a debt because previous funds had been mismanaged or worse, the conclusion of debt may only have reinforced the fact that the common lands had been severely truncated. Though freedom from debt satisfied departmental authorities and the bourgeois members of the syndical commission, it hardly softened the temptation among some Massatois to pasture illegally on land that, they believed, remained in their possession.

One such act of resistance provided the spark; the provocateur was none other than François Piquemal. In the summer of 1895, the private forest guard Jean Subra "surprised" Piquemal's livestock on some pastures belonging to the Civil Society. In October of the next year, the Court of Saint-Girons condemned him to pay a fine of fifteen francs for illegal pasturing. At that point, according to a railroad official stationed in the nearby town of

Oust, Piquemal began to mobilize the peasants around Massat: "Piquemal became magnified in their eyes; he appeared to them as an apostle, the defender of their rights; he ran from hamlet to hamlet, holding forth at the veillées, organizing meetings in the course of which he preached revolt against the [C]ivil [S]ociety; the highlanders were so interested in this question that it was easy for him to convince them." Some inhabitants soon refused to pay the foraine and began to pasture their flocks freely on the Civil Society's land. Piquemal's followers pillaged the property of those who had purchased from the Civil Society, and Piquemal himself began to prepare a legal case against it.[61]

But who was François Piquemal? It is likely that he was the same "François Piquemal Rat, proprietor, inhabitant of Massat" (actually resident in the hamlet of Liers) who had unsuccessfully taken civil action against Roquemaurel in 1873.[62] He had achieved notoriety in having his case taken all the way to the Council of State, which had rejected his request that Roquemaurel and Delpla recognize the Massatois' use rights on their land. Descriptions of Piquemal's character come from distant observers who feared the outbreak of disorder; typical is the railroad commissioner's portrait, which he claims is a composite description: "The said Mr. Piquemal, whom I was unable to see, has been described to me by numerous people who know him, as a man of rather obtuse mind whose obstinacy is boundless."[63] In such eyes, Piquemal represented a persistent troublemaker who refused to acknowledge the obvious legality of the cantonnement of 1824, not to mention the succeeding judicial decisions that had effectively stripped the livestock owners and leaseholders of available pastures. The essence, in other words, of an Ariégeois peasant.

Piquemal may have inhabited the uncertain social zone of one who was both an owner of livestock and a shepherd. Not wholly an outsider as were the communal shepherds in other parts of the Pyrenees, Piquemal would have had intermittent contact with village life throughout the pasturing season, as permitted by the pastoral system in the Massat Valley. His nebulous station would also have heightened his dual reception as troublemaker or hero among the Massatois. Piquemal clearly posed a representational problem for the local authorities, for this undeniable native of Massat could not be depicted as an outside agitator. A theory of outside agitation nonetheless appeared often in official reports on the affair. It allowed authorities to deny any grassroots character to the rumblings in Massat, and it also fit with their perceptions of the local peasants' inability to understand complex legal cases while apt to follow herdlike the summons of a simple message. Reports by foresters, in particular, often made no mention of Piquemal's name, referring instead to "certain leaders" (*certains meneurs*): a desire to exculpate the local population was not surprising in light of the RTM's complete dependence on the inhabitants' goodwill in respecting newly afforested areas. Thus the words of General Guard M. Griess in 1898, reporting on the "exalted spirit" reigning in several hamlets of Biert, whose residents had taken to pasturing their sheep in a fledgling forest within the Salat perimeter: "It is beyond doubt, for us . . . that the population's excitement has resulted from pernicious advice."[64]

While preaching revolt, Piquemal lost no time in pursuing legal action against the Civil Society. The prefect informed him in 1896 that he would need approval from his municipal council before undertaking the action; on 20 December, the council of Massat decided one voice short of unanimity not to support Piquemal. Galy-Gasparrou, still mayor of Massat in 1896, evidently marshaled the municipal council against the litigant: he read François Piquemal's request before the council and most likely presented the counterarguments, which rested on the claim that the Civil Society possessed "certain titles" to three-fifths of the mountains. Yet two months later, fifteen members of the municipal council signed a note stating that they had voted "in error" at the December meeting. The statement held that there was reason to support Piquemal verbally and that the commune would run no risks in doing so if he would go to court at his own expense.[65] Stranger still, Galy-Gasparrou stated in his own memoir of the affair that less than a week after the December vote, he intervened personally with the prefectorial council to obtain for Piquemal special permission to plead his case, "in an effort of appeasement." Clearly, François Piquemal's capacities for creating disorder had intimidated even the mayor into allowing the peasant his day in court.[66]

The Court of First Instance in Saint-Girons granted Piquemal two audiences in the summer of 1897. Funds for his trial had come from contributions to a "revolt society" (*société de révolte*) constituted after the municipal council of Massat had refused financial assistance. The only available account of Piquemal's arguments comes from Galy-Gasparrou's memoir, which presents a remarkably flattering portrait of Piquemal drafted by a personal adversary. Years later, however, Galy-Gasparrou may have wanted to conciliate (and suggestively rewrite his own role in the affair). During the audience of 21 July, Piquemal declared simply that the Civil Society was not the legitimate proprietor of any part of the mountains of Massat. On 3 August, however, he presented a more thoroughgoing argument to the court in the form of several astonishing requests:

To allow him to prove that the act of 13 December 1865 and the judgment of 26 May 1866, pronouncing the cancellation of the sale, are void vis-à-vis the communes for lack of proper form, the prescribed formalities assuring the valid representation of the communes in the case not having been observed;

To prove that his adversaries or their spokespersons, parties to the lawsuit concluded by the judgment of 13 December 1865, did not have the good faith required by article 2265 of the Civil Code, when they obtained the cancellation of the sale;

That they did not enjoy peaceable, public, and unequivocal possession, for either thirty or ten years, of the claimed property;

That they were constantly disturbed by the undertakings of the inhabitants of the three communes, [who] were acting as proprietors.[67]

Though Galy-Gasparrou had surely edited Piquemal's words, the latter's highly prepared argument stands as fascinating testimony to a peasant's understanding of the law. Piquemal not only quoted the Civil Code directly, but he also made use of key passages from the code pertaining to possession. In essence, Piquemal argued that the Civil Society had lost its property rights to the mountains because it had lost possession of them. The society had not been able to retain possession's "peaceable, public, and unequivocal" qualities, three of the four conditions required for possession to have juridical effects. This, as Piquemal well knew and even stated at the end ("the undertakings of the inhabitants"), was because over the years the peasants had implicitly questioned the society's proprietorship of the mountains through their own physical acts of possession.

Piquemal's followers—and others intimidated by his threats—began to commit more acts of possession during the trial and afterward. Piquemal had encouraged all of the montagnards to drive their flocks onto forbidden pastures, which many proceeded to do. Another traditional way of claiming possession, "devastating" the forest, came into play during these years. In one instance, two men from Le Port decided to buy some parcels of forest and pasture from the Civil Society in October 1899. The meneurs from Le Port did not forgive them for this act, which was tantamount to recognizing the society's lawful proprietorship; the forest suffered clandestine cutting during the whole month of November and a night of fire. The Civil Society demanded a large sum of money from the communes for damage plus interest, but before the mayor of Le Port could convoke the municipal council, a house that he owned burned down as well.[68]

The Court of Saint-Girons, the Toulouse Court of Appeals, and the Supreme Court of Appeals successively pronounced against Piquemal, all by the spring of 1898.[69] Piquemal and four accomplices propagated the view that the case had been lost because the original vote of nonsupport by the municipal council of Massat had been falsified. At open meetings, they called for the resignation of the whole council. Galy-Gasparrou and the subprefect attended the first meeting in June, but their presence did not cow the insurgents. It was not long before twelve of the twenty-three councilors had been pressured to resign, "either to make common cause with the inhabitants, or out of fear of reprisals on the part of the latter." One councilor, Raymond Piquemal-Cabos, had found a piece of paper affixed to a stick in front of his house; the paper read, "resignation or death." The following Thursday, while Piquemal-Cabos was in Massat on business, a crowd of three hundred people accosted him, demanding the resignation to which he promptly consented. Similarly, Guillaume Dégeilh-Delpeyré resigned after he had found the straw roof to one of his barns missing. The most elaborate intimidation was reserved for the stubborn Galy-Baloué. First a peaceable assemblage at the Grand Hôtel in Massat demanded his resignation; fifty people appeared at his house with the same message the following day. Finally the sinister warning of one Pierrou prompted his resignation: "You've been leading us on for a long time, but if you keep it up, we'll use harsher means." Galy-Baloué signed his letter of resignation at the Café Anselme the next day.[70]

If the politics of direct action had begun to sway the Affair of the Mountains toward a violent course, the shift had happened in a context of electoral politics, not in its vacuum. The alienation of Galy-Gasparrou from many of his constituents had become apparent by the spring of 1897, for one of his political rivals—Paul Pujol, a lawyer in Saint-Lary and hopeful for the legislative elections—had been drawn into the affair and was openly criticizing Galy-Gasparrou's abandonment of the insurgent peasants.[71] Pujol undoubtedly eyed the possibility of dividing Massat and thus eroding Galy-Gasparrou's influence, but the political context stretched beyond personal rivalries. A journalist writing for Toulouse's *La Dépêche* succinctly explained the larger reasons for the "explosion of anger and revolt" in Massat and Le Port. These reasons stemmed from a local awareness of connections between economic misery and politics at the top: "The peasants know in detail how their deputy in the Chamber has voted, and more particularly his votes against fiscal reforms; against tax reductions for small property owners; against progressive income taxes, from which everyone here, without exception, would have benefited; against the Jaurès proposal to lower the price of sugar which, thanks to a coalition of Opportunists and reactionaries, continues to cost us one franc twenty per kilo, while the English pay only fifty centimes." In short, Galy-Gasparrou had voted consistently against a socialist agenda. What might be called "Piquemal's revolt" was thus central to but also symbolic of larger grievances that Galy-Gasparrou, eminent Radical Republican, had ignored. Although the Massatois were far from the only Ariégeois moving toward socialism in these years, their politics had incorporated an older tradition. The journalist from *La Dépêche* brilliantly concluded his article with a warning that tied modern republican politics to a living memory of other roads to justice: "But may our big electors beware. The memory of the 'demoiselles' has not completely faded, and the spirit of independence that one finds at the bottom of our highlanders' hearts could well explode . . . someday."[72]

VIOLENCE, ELECTIONS, AND 14 JULY 1900

During the charged years flanking the turn of the century, the singularity of the Affair of the Mountains continued to lie in the mixing of popular revolt and electoral politics in an effort to secure possession of pastoral lands. The case began to receive more press, yet Toulousain journalists did not grasp the complex political palette in Massat, especially during the violent period of 1899–1900. Typically, a writer for the *Express du Midi* dramatized the "foreignness" of the events in an article with the eye-catching title, "Chronicle in the country of the 'demoiselles.'" Using the device of a companion, an "old highlander" who led him from Saint-Girons to Massat, the writer insisted on the cultural distance between Massat and the rest of France: "Soon, my dear man, you will penetrate a strange country. Even though separated from the rest of the world only by the pleasing corridor that we are presently following, it seems, for those whom destiny condemns to live there, that a great wall of China stands in reality between France and us." With much sarcasm, the writer depicted the canton of Massat as a feudal kingdom that maintained but few formal relations with the French state. Jabbing at Galy-Gasparrou, he remarked that Massat's "representative of the people" in Parliament was in fact a "seigneur" transformed into a deputy, whose presence in the chamber "considerably enhanced the prestige of this assembly in the eyes of other nations." He reduced politics in Massat to the perennial contest over who would promise, in vain, to give the inhabitants free possession of "their" pastures and forests without having to pay taxes on them—an old hope from 1848. In the writer's view, peasants had taken the law into their hands merely because the promise had not been kept after the last election: "Guards are sent to enforce the law: they are greeted by gun shots, and they must take great pains to escape their aggressors, disguised as women and masked, like the former 'demoiselles' of sixty years ago."[73]

The claim that the "aggressors" had revived the costume of the Demoiselles from 1829–31 demands examination: the question of living memory must be weighed against rhetorical references designed to sensationalize. The gatherings of armed people on the mountains during August 1899 and August 1900 provide the most useful test cases; these were the most fraught moments of the entire affair.

The month of August was high pasturing season, the time of year when both shepherds and forest guards concentrated most in the pastures and forests. In May 1899, the president of the Civil Society, Léopold Gaillard, initiated the season by placing a conspicuous poster in Massat. It reminded its readers of François Piquemal's three legal defeats, commanded all livestock owners who had neglected their foraine payments to pay the tax within fifteen days, and ordered them to register their animals at the foraine office before the summer.[74] A rejoinder to the poster appeared in the first few days of August; this placard warned the guards not to attempt a census of livestock and signaled that anyone who tried to take down the placard would be "severely punished."[75] On 9 August the Civil Society's private guards proceeded to count livestock pasturing on the communal territory of Le Port. The population, "assembled and gathered in a mob [attroupée]," assailed the guards, and from the large group emerged five or six individuals who were "disguised, masked, armed with rifles and revolvers." Rushing toward his targets and threatening them with death, one of the men fired upon a guard, but the bullet merely passed through his sleeve. Another small group attempted to cut off the guards' retreat, but the latter escaped by scrambling down a steep ravine.

A similar incident took place nearly a year later. This time, a group of thirty or so people armed with scythes, sticks, pitchforks, axes, and rifles met the private guards on the territory of Massat. Some among the group hid their faces with "white linen." Ultimately pursued by three groups coming from different angles, the guards had an even narrower escape this time and were assailed by stones in the process. Earlier the same day, three gendarmes making a round through Le Port came across three people cutting grass, who, when asked about yelling heard in the distance, responded: "The mountains belong to us; we paid for them. Until now, we have put up no resistance, but today we have in mind to defend ourselves to the last drop of blood."[76]

By the end of August 1900, the Civil Society had requested that gendarmes accompany their guards at all times. A brigade of six gendarmes and one

sergeant were with the guards on 31 August, when at eleven o'clock in the morning the guards came upon and seized ten cows. Soon the sounds of sheep's
horns, shouts, and whistles echoed across the mountains. Within an hour and
a half, residents of the hamlet of Carol, armed with sticks and pitchforks, assembled in front and in back of the guards and gendarmes. The latter loaded
their rifles; this move kept the peasants at a distance and, unable to recapture
their cattle by force, they presented themselves individually to claim their animals and were forced to reveal their identities. In his report the sergeant
claimed that deplorable things would have happened in the absence of the gendarmes.[77]

Thus, beyond occasional "masks" and "white linen," the sergeants made little mention of disguises and no references to the singular costume of the
Demoiselles. In addition, it is unlikely that the groups of peasants were exclusively male, as the Demoiselles had been. For in an earlier incident, thirty-five
women, armed with sticks, had preceded their husbands in jostling and verbally assaulting forest guards on the communal territory of Biert; the women
then recaptured the family livestock, which had been illegally pasturing in a recently planted state forest.[78] While not reincarnating the Demoiselles, the insurgents had manipulated memory of the earlier revolt just enough to suit their
purposes. Using the barest visual signs that bespoke "Demoiselles" to police
and forest guards, they integrated these signs with a more general Pyrenean
repertoire of revolt, from which the Demoiselles themselves had borrowed,
that also included threats of violence, village solidarity, and organization.

Most important, violence remained largely potential, and these shades of
armed revolt were but a part of the spectrum of contestation in 1899–1900.
During both summers, many inhabitants also took part in civil mass meetings,
occasions not only for the expression of grievances but also for debate over
which political tactics—armed rebellion or the ballot box—were most appropriate in the circumstances. The first such meeting, attended by between seven
hundred and eight hundred men, women, and children, took place on a Sunday in July 1899; it lasted for about two hours, and the attendees dispersed without incident.[79] The meetings unveil the importance the peasants attributed to
republican legality and symbolism, and they served to prepare the local voters
for the elections of 6 May 1900.

Local and national identities intermingled at these meetings. At Le Port in
February, five hundred to six hundred people showed up to hear the speeches of
orators who spoke next to a tricolor flag and an inscription that read, "Carol
[hamlet of Le Port], union is force, Equality, Fraternity, R.F.," but they spoke in

dialect. One speaker, Victor Paulin, addressed the question of the mountains, "various other questions whose meaning remained incomprehensible" (to the gendarme reporting), and the Dreyfus Affair. All the orators "preached calm," and the crowd dispersed without a murmur.[80] The tone of the meetings grew overtly political as elections approached. At Biert in March, Michel Laffitte set the agenda that was to prove no less devastating to the entrenched local authorities than the consequences of armed revolt: "Mr. Laffitte Michel of Liers, discussed the affair of the mountains at length; he ended his speech by exhorting the population to remain calm and by inviting them to make good use of the ballot at the next election, the only way to freely lay claim to the mountains, which they must not give up at any price." Likewise, Sieur Rogale, an associate of François Piquemal, exhorted his audience to "open their eyes in order to replace the administrators of the commune of Massat." Significantly, Rogale suggested to the crowd that the violent incidents of the previous summer might have been simulated by the Civil Society's private guards. And Piquemal himself spoke, reviewing the court decisions against him but reaffirming that the disputed lands still belonged to the people.[81]

Vociferous criticism of the municipal councils (despite the forced resignations of 1898) and of Galy-Gasparrou continued to be heard as the frequency of meetings increased during the month before the election. The long-time mayor of Massat and deputy from Ariège could perhaps not have imagined that the restitution of a property regime agreeable to the peasants—deemed illegal by the defenders of private property—would be furthered by a perfectly legal act, a municipal election. But with four additional gendarmes dispatched to keep order in Massat, a rural coalition joined by some residents of the chef-lieu nevertheless swept in a new municipal council on 6 May, evicting political magnate Léon Galy-Gasparrou in a triumph of peasant politics.[82]

Those who immediately disdained the new municipality, composed of Galy-Briulat, Piquemal, and Rogale, gave it the epithet of "government of the peasants." The old urban-rural rift had resurfaced in Massat, for many inhabitants of the chef-lieu had voted for the list of candidates loyal to Galy-Gasparrou. For them, the new mayor and council disgraced the commune. The adjunct mayor Rogale soon began to act as mayor; rumor had it that Galy-Briulat had fallen ill. In the subprefect's estimation, Rogale had not "the least notion of the duties that his function entailed." He had maintained a "provocative attitude," was frequently in a state of "overexcitation," and committed frequent "blunders." He was to be seen at the front of a band of people armed with sticks during the troubling events of 14–15 July.[83] Both the subprefect and Galy-Gasparrou attempted to annul the elections, the latter conniving to obtain a further partition of Massat into several communes. According to *Le Réveil du Saint-Gironnais,* a newspaper subtitled *Mouthpiece of Popular Demands,* these actions announced Galy-Gasparrou's "unqualifiable war" against his commune.[84]

One of the first actions taken by the new municipal leaders was to open negotiations with the Civil Society for the repurchase of the society's three-fifths of the mountains, an action remarkable for its mundane legality. Over the next several years, Galy-Gasparrou did his utmost to vitiate the negotiations. The results of a public inquiry showed that a wide majority of the Massatois favored the idea of repurchase; Galy-Gasparrou in turn sponsored a "counter-inquiry." During this process, Prefect Delanney, himself favorable to repurchase, was transferred out of Ariège, the only prefect in the department's history, according to the journalist for *Le Réveil,* to have experienced a transfer. With such evidence in hand, it appeared that "everything—administration, Conseil Général, Council of State, laws—everything is at the service of the tyrant of Massat!"

More immediately, Galy-Gasparrou and the "government of the peasants" struggled over possession of another sort, the appropriation of republican symbols. Within five days of the municipal election, the defeated mayor had managed to brand the victors as right-wing nationalists and claim that his defeat had been due to the exercise of "anti-republican terrorism" upon the voters. Two years later Galy-Gasparrou made claims of an original link between "the agitator" and boulangist candidates back in 1889.[85] In mid-1900, political struggles shifted to the cultural arena: the final battle for republican legitimacy in this Pyrenean bourg came to be waged over music and culminated in the memorable celebration of the national holiday.

A varied festive repertoire characterized the celebration of 14 July throughout much of France during the Belle Epoque, but the people of Massat borrowed little from it in 1900. There, 14 July saw no artillery salvos, parades, banquets, bonfires, races, theatrical presentations, open-air games, planting of liberty trees, or fireworks.[86] Only hostile gatherings, peripatetic music, and one spontaneous ball marked the occasion, yet these activities began on 12 July and recurred through the fifteenth. The presence of music is not surprising: the number of choral societies and brass bands had mushroomed in Ariège after 1875, and Massat was not to be outdone in having its own *Philharmonique.*[87]

During four consecutive evenings, the opposing parties defined their politics through musical choices. Partisans of the "peasant government" began to gather on 12 July at the Café Claustre, where they sang popular songs, notably one that disparaged Galy-Gasparrou. The following evening, the opposing Philharmonique gathered in front of the church to play the Marseillaise and the revolutionary "Chant du départ," as well as other songs as they sang through the streets of Massat. The performance attracted a large crowd in the central square that "whistled, sang, and uttered loud laughter followed by cries of 'long live the Republic!' 'long live Gasparrou!'"[88] For the moment, Massat's Philharmonique had appropriated the Marseillaise and become the focal point for Galy-Gasparrou's followers.

Bitter political divisions, music, and potential violence came together on the evening of 14 July. The "peasant" mayor set off the holiday by silencing the Philharmonique with a decree requiring municipal approval for all concerts in the commune. That evening, a group of five "foreign" musicians, invited by the mayor, gave a lively peripatetic concert led by the adjunct mayor, Rogale, and children carrying Venetian lanterns. This provocation incited a large and hostile crowd of Galy-Gasparrou's townies to follow the musicians and the mayor's party; an "indescribable brouhaha" ensued until eight hundred or nine hundred people reached the square in front of the church. Surrounded by their opponents singing the Marseillaise "at the top of their lungs," the mayor's party could only duck into the Café Claustre to defame Galy-Gasparrou through song.[89]

The following events highlight the significance that both sides attached to the Marseillaise. Defying the mayor's decree, the Philharmonique soon appeared in the central square, where a spontaneous ball, punctuated by whistles and cries of "Long live Gasparrou!," got under way. Not to be drowned out by the din, the mayor's partisans emerged from the café and, now armed with sticks, formed themselves into columns and marched through Massat, whistling, crying "Down with Gasparrou!," and singing the Marseillaise themselves.[90] Once the two groups encountered each other, violence seemed imminent, with only the presence of gendarmes likely to defuse the hostility. Rogale and his followers carried the night, making a last tour of Massat as they again intoned the Marseillaise. They finally dispersed at one-thirty, not before the gendarmes had caught some among Rogale's group filling their pockets with pieces of macadam and had heard the report of a rifle in the distance. Indeed, everyone in Massat had become "excited by politics."[91]

The struggle over the Marseillaise and 14 July suggests that the meanings of neither the anthem nor the national holiday had become calcified by 1900. Such contested appropriation stands in contrast to the fate of 14 July in much of France during the 1890s, a decade of political discord that stifled enthusiasm for the national holiday.[92] But as the case of Massat shows, both symbols could become transfigured in a crisis of local politics. The peasants had not championed another well-known song such as the Carmagnole or the Internationale. In their fledgling attempts at local government, they snatched the Marseillaise from their opponents and sought the legitimacy it bestowed. Galy-Gasparrou failed to define his opponents as antirepublican agitators. Massat's strange celebration of 12–15 July 1900 also reveals a battle of interpretation: it was important that the Marseillaise and the holiday speak to the "rights of the people" and, perhaps still, revolution.[93] The "peasant government" had to wield these republican symbols if the question of the mountains were to reflect the lofty concept of *égalité*. If the municipality's stance did not represent a scrupulously legal approach to property, the Marseillaise and other symbols might be used to justify the rights of possession.

Claiming the "monstrousness" of a government that did not respect private property rights lay at the center of the Civil Society's next strategy to repossess the mountains. On 5 November 1900 Léopold Gaillard, the society's president, petitioned the Chamber of Deputies and the Senate, hoping to illustrate the proprietors' impotence in the face of insurgence and invite the representatives to put an end to the "violent spoliation" that had victimized them.[94] Not for nothing did the petition begin, "If there is one principle that the Government of the Republic must protect, it is that of the inviolability of property." Though government could regulate and manage regimes of property, government had as well to respect preexisting property rights that could be proved with "titles." Through armed resistance and the usurping of foraine payments, the people of Massat had flouted the sanctity of both government and property. The petitioners made no reference to the municipal council that an election had legally constituted, writing instead of the "revolutionary government in the communes of Massat, Biert and Le Port." Questioning whether the population had been "prompted by theories of socialism," the petitioners reminded the deputies and senators how inadmissible it would be that socialism, "not yet established as a principle of government," despoil rightful owners of their property. Yet the outraged proprietors could ultimately justify some form of intervention from Paris only through a gross exaggeration: whether socialist or revolutionary, the government in Massat had stemmed from an "armed revolt counting thousands of absolutely disciplined people."[95]

Neither appeals to the sanctity of property nor claims of armed rebellion convinced the politicians to defend the Civil Society. Their reticence likely stemmed from the assurances of local and departmental officials, who began to show clemency toward the peasants in 1901. In February the Court of Saint-Girons ruled only against Le Port in the Civil Society's case against the three communes, based on charges of property damage due to "rebellion"; a similar blow to the proprietors occurred a month later when the Toulouse Court of Appeals gave a certain Maurette, implicated in the incident of 1 August 1900, the light sentence of four months in prison. Commenting on the latter case, the subprefect in Saint-Girons (so recently Galy-Gasparrou's supporter) asserted that the protection of private property did not belong entirely with the state and that "the property owners are less important than they say they are, and in their excessive pretensions one could find one of the principal reasons for the commotions that have arisen." He even recommended the official pardon of Maurette, although the prefect would hesitate on that score.[96]

Part of the judicial largesse was perhaps a quid pro quo for the good example set by the "peasant government": disproving the inflamed accusations of the Civil Society, the municipality of Massat had adopted the formal rules regulating the buying and selling of private property (though all the while giving tacit approval to "unlawful" acts of possession). In July 1901 the Civil Society once again agreed to sell its coveted three-fifths of the mountains; the prefect speedily adopted the project, achieving a reduction in the sale price (to 165,000 francs), authorizing a Crédit Foncier loan at 3.8 percent, and extracting an assurance from the mayors that no "regrettable incidents" would recur. Watched by gendarmes, the Massatois voted 549 to 107 in favor of repurchase in a public inquiry held on 3 January 1902. After several more years of delay produced by Galy-Gasparrou's heavy-handed politicking, the communal syndicate of Massat and Le Port became sole proprietor of 3,000 hectares of alpine pasture and 135 hectares of low forest in 1910. It seemed that peace might return in the form of full communal ownership of the mountains.[97]

The Affair of the Mountains did not conclude only with a legal transfer of property, for the Massatois won their struggle for possession as well. Though considerably more extensive, the Civil Society's lands had not been the only stakes in the affair; the 804 hectares purchased by the state in 1883 in view of reforestation had remained a tender issue with the pastoralists and perhaps a worse symbol of outside encroachment. Indicating the level of animosity, a tide of forest crimes had swept Massat, but in these instances as well, the prefect conciliated. Delanney intervened directly with the minister of agriculture and the director general of the Eaux et Forêts in Paris: the latter, assenting in the release of eight "recidivists" detained by the local forest inspector, commended his administration's "tolerance" in easing the "exceptional situation created by the so-called question of the mountains of Massat."[98]

In reality, this tolerance had been harshly exacted by the Massatois pastoralists. It was no accident that in 1903, Forest Inspector Joseph Watier argued to end reforestation in the Massat area, for the state had effectively lost possession of "its" lands there. Between 1886 and 1903, peasants had set roughly thirty-eight fires on the naturally forested and reforested areas of the state's territory and committed "innumerable" pasturing infractions. Watier's minute list of all the recorded fires shows that most had been lit in the months from November to March, the traditional burning season; while promoting the growth of spring grasses, the fires had also assured the peasants' possession of the land. The fires impelled Watier to claim, "The state's property is illusory; to guarantee its respect, it would be necessary to guard it night and day with considerable force and at the risk of provoking the population."[99]

More interesting still, both sides had conflated property and possession vis-à-vis the parcels slated for exchange, since 1890, between the state and the communes. The transfer of property titles had never taken place, for the syndical commission had not seen to the proper delimitation of the areas in question. Yet for the preceding ten years, both sides had "entered into possession as if the exchange were an accomplished fact." By tolerating illegal pasturing on the state's lands, the communes had come into possession of the latter; for its part, the state had made full use of the land still owned by the communes. The confusion of property and possession had become a tacit convention by 1908, a modus vivendi that a reforestation inspector deemed it unwise to reform.[100]

The Affair of the Mountains of Massat set an important precedent for foresters working in the Massat Valley. Their refusal to continue with reforestation was put to a test in 1908. In that year, inhabitants of the hamlet of Arac (Le Port) exposed the danger they faced from frequent winter avalanches that formed on an uncultivated slope belonging to the elderly Alexis Loubet. The Eaux et Forêts declined to acquire the land for reforestation, despite the plea from Arac. Although no one denied the applicability of the 1882 law, forest inspectors made ample reference in their refusals to the Massatois' fires. As Inspector A. Campagne stated bluntly, "It would be delusional to acquire new land in a region where the state's property has always been considered as 'res nullius' and, as such, has been pillaged and plundered mercilessly."[101]

As in the case of Jarrier, the project to restore the highlands ringing Massat stemmed from local foresters' violations of the limited law of 1882: in both cases, the projects called for massive reforestation that fell outside the boundaries of "evident and present dangers." Such overstepping of the law does not, of course, account entirely for the varieties of resistance seen in either commune. Whereas the pastoralists of Jarrier experienced restoration as a single, overwhelming threat to local livelihood, those of Massat, Biert, and Le Port perceived it as an intolerable last straw. Both cases, however, reveal that the abstract and idealized schemes to transform the peripheral regions of France found their real tests not in foresters' treatises but in alpine villages and hamlets. Foresters trained in Nancy grasped imperfectly the local contexts that conditioned their projects; the thickness of the context in Massat sets off this case in degree, but not in kind, from that of Jarrier.

In conclusion, the peasants of Massat linked property, possession, and politics in ways that both accommodated modernity and shaped it to their traditional interests. The prefect's remarks about forests and republicanism in 1834 echoed loudly in 1900, yet the configuration of strategies had changed. The peasants' repertoire of action included playing by the rules of private property as well as manipulating the enduring concept of possession and its sanction in the Civil Code. Likewise, in the same years they put faith in both electoral politics and varieties of popular revolt. Unwilling to give up modes of "self-justice," they also adopted both the trappings and the exigencies of the Republic. Instead of being bled dry by poverty and emigration, the peasants of Massat had mustered the means of shaping a communal existence in the twentieth century.

Chapter Five Old and New in the Eaux et Forêts: Peasants, Forests, and the State in the Twentieth Century, 1898–1937

To attain the goal [of restoration], the agents of the Eaux et Forêts will always need to win the people's confidence: they will even have to possess firmness, loyalty, moderation and tact.
—*Paul Mougin*

In the spring of 1898, Minister of Agriculture Jules Méline decreed that all personnel in the Administration des Forêts would thereafter exercise their duties within the Eaux et Forêts. By changing the name of a major administration within his ministry, Méline restored a rubric from the Old Regime that had given way to the Administration des Forêts with the reorganization of 1801. Though the name of an Old Regime bureaucracy that had existed in one form or another since the twelfth century clearly provoked pride, Méline justified the change in purely functional terms. The management of fresh-water fishing and fish-breeding had been attributed to the Forêts in 1896; thus, on one level, the inclusion of "waters" in the title effectively acknowledged the new service. Yet Méline explained his decree in another way: "Waters and forests are two terms united by a relationship of cause and effect, two words which, joined together, seemed in former times to form but one. Forever have we instinctively felt that close links of reciprocal dependence existed between waters and forests, and that independently of the material products furnished [by trees], forests rendered services of the highest order by regulating atmospheric waters and regularizing the flow of springs, streams, and rivers."[1]

Nineteenth-century science emphatically justified the renaming. Since the publication of Alexandre Surell's *Etude sur les torrents des Hautes-Alpes* in 1841, geographers, engineers, and foresters had awakened to the role of forests in retaining water and stemming floods. The connection had become irrefutable within the Administration des Forêts, and Méline's symbolic act also served to laud the RTM (Restauration des terrains en montagne), formed in 1882 to translate the connection into practical works of restoration. Jules Méline, protector of agriculture by means of the 1892 tariff, now placed his imprimatur on another kind of protection—that of fertile plains from the rushing waters, eroding slopes, and people of the mountains.

The Eaux et Forêts reemerged, however, at a time when voices from inside and outside the forestry corps had begun to attack the RTM. Although the grand title of Eaux et Forêts masked the limited legal role of the RTM (bound as it was to correcting "evident and present dangers"), the official budget report to the Chamber of Deputies in 1890 had revealed that the RTM enjoyed a generous 24 percent of the Forêts credits, a sum that ought to have produced lasting accomplishments. In the first eight years of its existence, the RTM had submitted as many projects for restoration (all in the Alps) to Parliament, comprising 22,569 hectares out of an estimated 100,000 hectares designated for future perimeters.[2] During the 1890s the RTM continually revised the latter figure upward, acquiring by 1900 roughly 163,000 hectares, 70 percent of this land in the Alps, 23 percent in the Massif Central, and just 7 percent in the Pyrenees. The RTM had spent more than 25 million francs to acquire the land and more than 41 million in restoration. These numbers paled, however, in comparison to estimates of future costs: less than half the land earmarked for restoration by 1900 had been purchased. An additional 27 million francs would be needed for the acquisition of another 172,000 hectares, and 86 million francs for their restoration. The RTM's report of 1900 included the sanguine prediction that "for its perfect achievement, the work of restoring alpine lands will require another forty-five years." Still, it was not until 1908 that the Chamber of Deputies demanded to see the accounts of the RTM, in an act of collective skepticism regarding the service's endless and expensive work.[3]

Despite the RTM's proclamation of initial success in 1900, restoration had encountered setbacks both natural and social. As the cases of Jarrier and Massat have shown, schemes of alpine restoration could fail for a web of reasons that included conflicts with local forms of management, silent and open resistance, and extraneous circumstances that foresters either tried to ignore or were ill-equipped to overcome. But critics of the RTM simplified the causes of failure, thereby streamlining their own project: for them, the mediocre results of restoration stemmed from the shortcomings of a law that failed to curb the rapacious tendencies of France's alpine peasants.

This chapter shifts focus from local case studies back to departmental and national scales in order to highlight two contrasting but parallel trends in early twentieth-century relations between the state and alpine pastoralists. First, the state sought to return to what Andrée Corvol calls the "imperialist tradition" in French forestry. Second, however, demands from peasants, economic imperatives, and demographic change brought about a new pattern of engagement, marked by mutual recognition and negotiation, between the state and alpine communes. Legislative gains by the Eaux et Forêts, though important, masked a more gradual process of reconciliation.

FORESTRY'S REASSERTION

Criticisms of the alpine restoration law of 1882 led to legal changes both before and after World War I, and the effects of the war itself combined to alter the Third Republic's original course of action in the mountains. From the 1890s on, the range of criticism marked old territory and broke new ground. A sampling of texts by four leading authorities on alpine restoration, three of them foresters within the Eaux et Forêts, reveals the continuing appeal of Surell's arguments for reforestation as well as new concerns and concepts—namely, the idea of "preventing" natural disasters, a rewriting of the economic role of the forest, and a withering respect for private property.

To begin with the legacy of Surell, S. Guénot, secretary general of the Geographical Society of Toulouse, launched an appeal for reform following the floods of 1897 in several Pyrenean valleys and the Garonne basin. Guénot diagnosed the floods as products of torrential rains, exacerbated by run-off and erosion, which stemmed exclusively from deforestation. Documenting the torrential headwater streams that had plunged into the Garonne, Ariège, Gers, Save, and Adour Valleys, Guénot paraphrased Surell in his double equation: the presence of forest guaranteed the absence of torrential streams, while the absence of forest guaranteed torrential streams.[4] While echoing Surell in ascribing deforestation to the mean ways of the peasantry—"general insouciance" was his preferred phrase—Guénot could also, writing three decades into the Third Republic, point a finger at the democratic process. Public opinion and democracy rewarded those who spoke most eloquently for the narrow interests of a small group, and an "ignorant and unreflective population" could never embrace the interest of all, preservation of the common patrimony. The "reactive" legislation of 1882 had bowed to the tyranny of narrow interests: in this light, Guénot logically equated the enlightened thinking of *bons esprits* with a spirit of prevention. He called insistently for a new law on alpine restoration.[5]

The notion of preventing natural disasters received sharper articulation in the work of Pierre Buffault, a forester educated at Nancy who became an inspector in Barcelonnette in 1905 and later conservator in Aurillac. For Buffault, the flaw in the legislation of 1882 lay in its piecemeal focus on "localized remedies," minute restorations of areas of proven degradation or "evident and present dangers." This curative approach contradicted sound forestry, which by definition looked to the future, not to "past facts." In delineating a program for prevention, Buffault seized upon a word that would be much repeated among foresters in the early twentieth century: the *regularization,* as opposed to the *correction,* of waterways constituted the obvious goal. To regularize the hydraulic cycle implied future continuity, whereas to correct suggested repair on a small scale. Regularization, then, could be achieved only by completely replanting denuded mountain slopes.[6]

Explicitly or not, the new call for prevention referred to a specific geographical context—the Pyrenees. An official "awakening" to the state of the Pyrenees took place among foresters toward the turn of the nineteenth century, yet it followed in the line of periodic rediscoveries of this less traveled alpine region. The foresters Louis de Froidour and Etienne Dralet had previously dramatized the palpable degradation of the Pyrenees in the late seventeenth and early nineteenth centuries, respectively. In his strict focus on law, Buffault noted that the restoration act of 1882 had been written with the Alps in mind: forming easily in the highly erosive soils of the Alps, individual headwater streams might be "corrected" there; conversely, their relative absence in the Pyrenees did not translate into less flooding.[7] Lucien-Albert Fabre, whose career as forest inspector (1894–1912) took him from Bagnères-de-Bigorre to Dijon, cast all of Gascony and the Pyrenees in a narrative of permanent destruction, where "the danger of . . . denudation has been 'evident and present' since the legendary epoque of the first pastoral fire, the date of man's taking possession of the Pyrenees."[8]

It was not really "man's possession" in itself that disturbed Fabre but rather the archaic mode of *pastoral* possession. Fabre readily used the language of possession to herald a positive transformation of the mountains, one that foresters would effect: "The Pyrenees . . . will then be open to the penetration of the *forest idea,* mature for the evolution of their economic role and truly conquered." The state would have to assure this preparation with nothing less than "virility."[9] Whereas the metaphor of a feminine nature conquered by masculine "man" is pan-European and ancient, here the contrast lies between two very different forms of possession, and in two senses. Functionally, the peasants' sense of possession as use rights could not coexist with the property rights to be won by an administrative and economic apparatus coming from afar. Symbolically, the possession of a feminine forest was, in Pyrenean culture, closer to marriage, whereas the possession of which Fabre wrote referred directly to conquest.[10]

This conflict, in its various manifestations, had a venerable pedigree in the Pyrenees. What stands out in Fabre's formulation is his reference to the "economic role" of the Pyrenean forests. He historicized their economic value in terms of three phases. In Colbert's time, these interests had been limited to provisioning the navy with wood, a project that came to little fruition owing to the difficulty of cutting on the steep Pyrenean slopes and the relative absence of navigable rivers on which to transport logs. Next, the "scientific conquest" of the Pyrenees had revealed the connections between deforestation and flooding in the early nineteenth century; these studies had received more attention as the volume of trade and the consequent importance of navigable rivers (the Garonne) and deep ports (Bordeaux) had increased. But the economic interests of the twentieth century would be qualitatively different: "Thus a third period of the Pyrenean economy is beginning with this century, that of the reclamation [*mise en valeur*] of the range, the construction of *living barriers.* This will in large part be the work of 'tomorrow's' foresters."[11] The Pyrenean forests, cast as a "living barrier" to natural calamity, would provoke the economic take-off of the entire region, in addition to providing wood and clean, calm rivers for downstream interests. Fabre's prediction gets at a central ambiguity of twentieth-century forestry: economism *à outrance* forced officials to look at the real economic state of the mountains, in effect leading to a belated recognition of the montagnard and his circumstances.

Fabre's portrait of the new Pyrenean economy involved subsidizing and refashioning the sylvo-pastoral mode of production, a topic treated in greater detail in Chapter 6; to other observers, it became clear that movers of national industry would increase their own demands upon forests in the Pyrenees and elsewhere. An expert on the sylvo-pastoral economy, A. Fron, strongly suggested in 1907 that this economy and way of life could not remain sheltered from external demands and that alpine forests would have to be vigorous if they were to fulfill multiplying needs. Fron's remarks on the consumption of wood in the early twentieth century reveal a surprising conjuncture: exploitation of the forest for firewood, railroad ties, mine shafts, building construction, and the fabrication of numerous small objects—all characteristic of the nineteenth-century forest economy—remained heavy, while new industrial uses of wood, namely, for paper pulp and telegraph poles, were rising steadily.[12] Statistics published after World War II showed that France had ceased to be self-sufficient in wood early in the century, with imports doubling exports prior to 1910. At least one economic historian has noted that France's exports of manufactured goods increased apace with its dependence on outside sources for raw materials, and both in spite of the era of high prewar tariffs.[13]

Once combined, arguments for the prevention of natural disasters and for the shoring up of France's sylvan resources fueled a powerful critique of privately owned forest. Foresters had not abandoned their anxieties over communal forests, but now private owners became subject to similar criticisms, a rhetorical attack unthinkable a few decades earlier. The only defense that Fron could muster for private owners of forest was that their personal interest might be engaged in small acts of restoration, but his comment was purely hypothetical; everything was yet to be done to restore privately owned forest. It bears remembering that most of France's forests have been under private ownership since the Revolution, and that during the past century their proportion of the nation's forest has remained at a stable two-thirds, though their proportion has been significantly lower in alpine departments.[14]

It was Pierre Buffault who most eloquently voiced the alarm over private forests. He analyzed egregious gaps in the Forest Code that effectively allowed private owners to get away with not replanting their cut-over lands and to escape the meager surveillance carried out by overburdened municipal authorities. In a salvo launched at the sanctity of private property, Buffault echoed the arguments his forebears had made about the commons: "The laws which force you [private owners of forest] to prune your trees, to slaughter a diseased animal, to dredge a stream—to take examples only from the agricultural domain— are so many blows to this primordial right. That is a necessary consequence of the state of society, where the right of each ceases where that of his neighbor begins, where the general interest, the public good, require the sacrifice of many private interests, of many individual rights."[15]

Indeed, in a spate of forest legislation just prior to the outbreak of World War I, the Chamber of Deputies first singled out the private forest regime as worthy of reform. The so-called Audiffred law of 2 July 1913, named for Jean Honoré Audiffred, deputy from the Loire, became the first tentative approach to regulating private forests. Tentative it was: while automatically submitting forests belonging to departments, mutual-aid societies, and nonprofit associations to the national forest regime, it merely gave individual and corporate owners the option of having their forests managed by the Eaux et Forêts. This contractual arrangement further allowed private owners to decide which operations the state's foresters would undertake—from basic tasks such as surveying, taking inventory, and determining allowable cuts to the more specialized tasks of regulating use rights and prescribing ways to "improve" the forest. Applied only after 1918, the Audiffred law proved the reluctance of private owners: a modest twelve thousand hectares of private forest came under state management through the law. But its significance must be seen in the long history of limitations on the use of private property. The Audiffred law paved the way for the Pisani law of 1963, which introduced the far-reaching concept of the duty of private owners to "assure the biological equilibrium of the country."[16]

Despite the reference in its title to the "reforestation and conservation of private forests," the Audiffred law carried less weight than the law that followed on its heels a month and a half later. On 16 August, Parliament voted in favor of a major revision of the 1882 law on the restoration and conservation of alpine lands. For some, the inadequacies of the early Third Republic's scheme had been proved by the bad floods of 1910; as seen above, however, the chorus opposing the 1882 legislation had been growing since before the turn of the century. The revision completed a circle from the highly *étatiste* law of 1860, to the compromise of 1882, and back—or nearly so.

Legislators in 1913 kept several of the restrictions as well as enticements formulated in 1882, yet they expunged an entire approach to restoration—and a way of looking at the mountains—by deleting the controversial phrase, "evident and present dangers."[17] Restoration would no longer be limited to lands degraded by *visible* torrential erosion. Instead, the word *reforestation* (carefully kept out in 1882) reappeared in the title and the body of the law, and article 2 stipulated that works of "restoration and reforestation" could be undertaken in view of "the maintenance and protection of land and the regularization of the water regime." Again, to "protect" and "regularize" meant to prevent natural calamities; by shifting to a more global focus, and away from preexisting torrential streams, the law permitted the state to intervene far more fully in the

Massif Central and the Pyrenees. Méline's "Eaux et Forêts" and the analyses of Pierre Buffault and others resonated in the new legislation.[18]

Though signaling a bright green light for the RTM, the important revision of 1913 was not applied until after World War I. Objects of semi-military recruitment during peacetime, the overwhelming majority of foresters were mobilized in 1914, serving in the uniform of the Eaux et Forêts. A skeletal forestry corps remained to oversee the most basic tasks, alpine reforestation not among them. The great war profoundly influenced later directions in reforestation, an appreciation of which demands a look at the effects of the war on the forests of France.

FROM FOREST DEATH TO PROTECTION

No one, not even those who spent their apprehensions on the growing French wood deficit, was prepared for the massive consumption of wood that war with Germany and its allies entailed. The material needs of what has been called the first truly industrial war are more readily conceived in terms of steel and explosive material for heavy artillery, mortars, machine guns, and the first tanks, yet the war's reliance on wood was staggering. Not only had no anticipatory "special provisions" been made, as a postwar report claimed, but the sheer scale of the war effort rapidly disabused those in charge of matériel, who had believed in the sufficiency of existing stocks of wood.[19] Military authorities foresaw the use of wood for barracks, shelters, railroad ties, and pickets, but it was the transformation from battle to trench warfare and the huge use of artillery that both caught planners unprepared and vastly increased the demand for wood. Ten meters of trench required one stere, or cubic meter, of round logs; a single, relatively solid artillery shelter required between forty and fifty steres of untreated logs. Using Paul Fussell's figure of twenty-five thousand total miles (forty thousand kilometers) of trenches built by both the Allies and the Central Powers, mostly in France, wood needed for this purpose alone came to 4 million steres; with perhaps thousands of artillery shelters, as well as barracks and myriads of railroad ties and pickets, the quantity of wood for the war effort hovered around France's average annual production of construction wood.[20]

Clearly these estimates contain a high margin of error, but we do know that the rapid construction of trenches promoted intensive cutting by military authorities, cutting deemed in another postwar report to have been "abusive and defective."[21] It was not until July 1915 that the general director of the Eaux et Forêts orchestrated an entente between the minister of agriculture and General

Joffre, to the effect that a certain number of mobilized foresters, battalion chiefs, and various officers of equal or inferior rank would comprise the SFA (service forestier aux armées). Under the authority of the Général Directeur des Etapes, the SFA became responsible for regulating all cuts in the army zone and for arranging contracts with private forest owners, using the tool of requisition as last resort. The SFA's jurisdiction did not extend to the interior zone, however, where it soon became apparent that the different branches of the army were competing with each other for the best wood at the best prices. Private owners stood to make ample profits, and the rate of cutting accelerated. Consequently, the minister of agriculture created the Comité général des forêts in May 1917, soon to be renamed the Comité général des bois, perhaps reflecting the idea that more "woods" were left than "forests." The new committee was to rationalize and oversee cutting and provisioning in all zones, in liaison with a new General Inspection created to monitor cuts made in the interior for the use of the British and American as well as French armies.[22]

The army's frenetic consumption of wood could be slowed and regulated, but the destruction and degradation of the forest due to warfare itself could not. Much of the eastern and part of the western sector of the western front lay in forest, nearly all of which had been rendered ecologically sterile and economically useless by the end of the war. Roughly 240,000 hectares of forest were in the occupied zone as of September 1917, and another 344,000 hectares lay in the war zone. An article from 1919 measured the extent of forest in "regions struck by battle" at 600,000 hectares, 75 percent of which were destroyed; a survey undertaken in the same year, however, showed "only" 200,000 hectares in need of soil restoration or replanting, and this was to be the Carnegie Foundation's figure for destroyed forest as well.[23] Such figures do not tell the whole story: entire forests had disappeared. High Wood, as the British called a lush forest on the Somme, was decimated in twenty-four hours. Short of obliteration, forests suffered from most of the activities in the war zone: the construction of defenses, encampments, and access roads, the passage of troops, the firing of countless shells and bullets, and "systematic devastation by the enemy" degraded many hectares of forest nearly beyond recognition. Where shells and trenches had ripped into the earth, the very conditions for forest growth had been disrupted. As Minister of Agriculture Fernand David put it at the war's end, "a few years will suffice to restore the Reims cathedral if we devote the necessary means. But whatever the sums of money allocated, it will only be after a century or two that the pine forest of Viel-Armand will recover its former splendor."[24]

On top of heightened exploitation and degradation of France's forests during the war, the massive effort of postwar reconstruction was sure to draw heavily upon stretched resources as well. Director General Dabat estimated in 1917 that France would face annual wood deficits on the order of 1,636,000 cubic meters, deficits caused by wartime degradation alone; in addition, he guessed, the demand for wood could increase by as much as 50 percent as the country sought to rebuild towns, mines, and railroads. Although the government could increase imports of wood from the colonies, Dabat questioned whether the latter could provide enough, and surely France's coniferous forests were inadequate to the monumental task ahead.[25]

Given this harsh set of circumstances, the General Direction of the Eaux et Forêts lost no time in outlining plans for restoration. In a report issued one month after the armistice, forestry officials outlined the four essential tasks necessary to restore the war-torn forests: leveling the soil; reseeding the low forests and cutting down "trees too mutilated to be left standing" (the adjective *mutilé* here removed from its now common context of disabled veterans); reforestation of the utterly destroyed forests and agricultural areas no longer fit for crops; and rebuilding houses, sawmills, paths, and enclosures in the forest. Replanting would constitute the most important part of the work. Calculating the needs for a minimal reforestation of two hundred thousand hectares undertaken over ten years, the foresters estimated an annual need of 48 million seedlings and fifty-six thousand kilos of seed. Another estimate placed all restoration costs at 1.4 billion francs.[26]

If repairing the ravages of northern and northeastern France seemed far removed from foresters' concerns in the Alps and Pyrenees, postwar imperatives to increase the production of timber also implicated alpine forests. Already in 1917, Dabat seemed to have Ariège in mind as he alluded to the probable market for beech for the production of railroad ties: an inevitable rise in prices would place even "certain alpine forests, until now unexploited for lack of commercial outlets," within the orbit of the timber market. But the post-armistice report suggested a different prospect for alpine forests. Instead of focusing on hardwoods, abundant in the Pyrenees, foresters should begin to substitute conifers in the mountainous regions of France, "in order to produce construction wood in place of firewood of little value."[27] This measure, quite logical from a national economic perspective, represented a fundamental threat to the agro-pastoral forest that peasants had largely managed to keep intact, despite fifty-eight years of state intervention in alpine ecosystems in the name of reforestation and restoration.

Ultimately, postwar anxieties over the forests of France did not usher in a new era of ambitious alpine reforestation. The difficulty of propagating conifers in Ariège was already well known, and by 1930 Conservator Jean Salvador would attest to the overall failure of softwood planting as he lamented the roughly seventy-thirty ratio of beech to fir in the department.[28] Coupled with calls to prevent natural disasters (mandated by the legal revision of 1913), this reality helped to focus further debate on the "protective" qualities of existing forests. Protecting major arteries appeared especially urgent in Savoie, whose historical strategic importance had grown apace with improvements in communications. The postwar imagination seized upon France's peripheries with renewed alarm. In his *Les Forêts de Savoie* (1919), the forester and scholar Paul Mougin captured fears of both invasion and destructive nature in a single formula for potential disaster: "Did we not see in July 1914, on the very eve of the formidable conflict which covered Europe with fire and blood, torrents and rivers such as the Charmaix, the Isère, destroy the railroads linking the cities of Modane and Grenoble with Lyon; when the mobilization was ordered, free circulation had not yet been reestablished. Of what consequence would this interruption have been had Italy joined the ranks against us?"[29]

Elements of the prewar critique and postwar imperatives coalesced by 1922. A single piece of legislation concerning alpine restoration enshrined the principle of prevention, introduced a new means of regulating private property, and sealed the official role of alpine forests in the national economy—the protection of major roads and waterways. The Chauveau law "relative to protective forests [*forêts de protection*]" passed the Senate on 29 April. Use of the phrase "protective forests" dated at least from 1906; in that year, a particularly étatiste forester named Reynard had proposed the classification of all forests located above eight hundred meters in altitude as "protective forests."[30] Prior to the war, Mougin himself had traced precedents for the idea to regulations passed by the Sardinian regime during the eighteenth and nineteenth centuries. Making a case for historically strict conservation of forests capable of preventing floods and holding back landslides and avalanches, only briefly did Mougin mention the commonly lax enforcement of these laws, concluding with an appeal to "tradition": "Is there nothing to be borrowed from these institutions of ancient origin, [and from] secular practice, in order to add a new title to the Forest Code of 1827?"[31]

Specious though Mougin's evidence appears, the concept of "protective forests" did have a tradition, but it was both more recent and metaphorical. "Protection" was a concrete mode of "prevention," and the latter term had not only been plugged by foresters since the 1890s, but it could also be relocated in the vocabulary of medicine, lending it greater prestige. Foresters had for some time portrayed degraded mountain slopes as "open wounds," as mentioned in Chapter 3. Prior to 1913, many foresters had also begun to view the 1882 law on alpine restoration as a mere treatment of symptoms, whereas a lasting cure was in order for France's mountain ranges. Louis Tassy, a doctrinaire forester whose career included two posts as conservator in the 1860s, the chief post for forest management in the central administration, and a professorship at the Agronomic Institute in Paris until 1882, judged the restrictions imposed by "evident and present dangers" in these terms: "When an ulcer eats away at a poor devil, do you limit yourself to cauterizing the ulcer? No, you try to act on his entire constitution. That is what we should do for the Alps; we should submit their entire constitution to severe and energetic treatment."[32] Pierre Buffault, the proponent of a "regularized" water cycle, had seized upon the metaphor in the writing of Ernest de Gorsse, a superior in the Eaux et Forêts. Under de Gorsse's pen the metaphor of illness became transparent: "Conservation of the forest is the hygiene of the mountain: if the forest disappears, the mountain falls ill of a general disease marked by localized accidents: torrential streams, erosions, avalanches. So then, following the example set by doctors, it is necessary not only to treat these local manifestations, these ulcers, but also to cure the whole organism by re-establishing the hygiene that is the forest."[33]

Such a fully developed metaphor of human illness, manifested by the ulcer, represents an altered vision of alpine space vis-à-vis the disorderly and destructive mountain of the early nineteenth century. After the war, the new metaphor reverberated with that of "mutilation" ascribed to the trees destroyed on the battlefields. The use of human metaphors was not coincidental; just as disorder had been located in alpine peasants and their ways of life as well as in mountains themselves, the sickness found in the mountains was part and parcel of the sickness of agro-pastoralism and its agents. And that could be related to the generalized illness of war-torn France.

The Eaux et Forêts imposed the Chauveau law as if in fulfillment of Tassy's prescription for "severe and energetic treatment." The institution of "protective forests" has been placed within a progressive narrative of maturing ideologies of conservation. From this perspective, the new category emerged logically after the establishment of the first embryonic national park in 1913, the parc national de l'Oisans near Grenoble, and before a law of May 1930 that allowed the classification and protection of natural sites deemed to have broad cultural and scientific value.[34] Viewed in the context of the legislation discussed above, the creation of protective forests echoed the much older tradition of imperialist forestry in France.

The Chauveau law of 1922 rivaled the seminal laws of 1913 by according even greater discretionary powers to the Eaux et Forêts. In this respect, the law reflected the enlarged presence of the state in economic life established during the war. The classification of "protective" could be given to forests whose "conservation shall be recognized as necessary to the maintenance of alpine lands . . . and to the defense against avalanches, erosion, and invasions of water and sand" (article 2). If classified as such, a forest would fall under a special regime in which the state's foresters would regulate rotations, pasturing, use rights, and cuts—regardless of public or private ownership. Even private owners disobeying the new rules would be considered as having committed forest crimes on someone else's property, and fines could be twice those foreseen in the Forest Code. The path to classification would follow the modes set forth in 1882, including public inquiries and votes by municipal councils, but a decree by the Council of State could nullify local opposition. Finally, the law allowed for indemnities to be paid to private owners or users for loss of revenue, yet the state could also expropriate.[35] The Eaux et Forêts—not Parliament—would oversee the creation of protective forests, and the law left the central concept of protection broadly defined.

PREVENTIVE TREATMENT IN ARIÈGE AND SAVOIE

Both Pyrenean and Alpine forests clearly fell within the scope of the Chauveau law. The greater lushness and faster growth rate of Pyrenean forests argued well for their inclusion in the new mandate, but, accentuating the long-term imperatives discussed above, violent storms had pummeled the upper Maurienne and Tarentaise Valleys in September 1920, assuring the subsequent law's early application in Savoie as well. The prefect's description of "diluvian rains" also proved that the florid manner of depicting floods and other natural disasters, honed throughout the nineteenth century, had not been lost by 1920: "Descending in impetuous cascades the steep and deforested slopes dominating these narrow valleys, the unleashed torrents, carrying away everything in their paths, hurled themselves into these corridors and, in a few instants, provoked extraordinary rises, floods, landslides, flows of mud and gravel which, in a few hours, caused a veritable disaster."[36] What had changed by 1920, however, was that the waters had more to destroy. Flooding demolished some of the factories built in the wake of hydroelectric development, in addition to sections of railroad and national roadway. The prefect's estimate of more than 6,600,000 francs' worth of damage did not even include the partial mangling of the transportation routes.

In the Chamber of Deputies's *session extraordinaire* of 1921, Savoyard deputy Antoine Borrel was quick to establish damage in the Arc River Valley as a national and even international issue: the destroyed roads, rails, and bridges hampered France's communication with Italy and, indeed, compromised the "great [lines of] communications between the Orient and the Occident." Borrel made resounding calls for state aid and preventive measures designed to "maintain the mountains' mantle of verdure." It was high time for the state to understand the value of such measures: the Arc River heralded good (hydroelectric power) as well as evil (violent floods), and humanity, if properly organized, could maximize the river's beneficent side while gradually taming its capriciousness.[37]

During the same session, Borrel's colleague M. Bouvet, deputy from the Jura and president of the "forest group" in the chamber (reconstituted in 1920 after its suspension during the war), echoed the call for preventive measures: he recommended the full restoration of alpine pastures, reforestation to attain a forest cover of at least 30 percent in the Maurienne, and the immediate passage of the Chauveau law—then being debated in the Senate. Bouvet characterized these proposals as "preventive treatment, [the] hygiene, if I may say, of the mountain."[38]

Savoie began to receive preventive treatment in 1925, when officers of the Eaux et Forêts launched public inquiries in the fourteen towns and villages whose forests they had slated for classification. Some of the forests were private, others communal. The formal opinions drafted by the municipal councils in the summer and autumn of 1925 reflected the interests both of individuals who pastured flocks on lands belonging to the communes and of those who pastured on their own lands, depending on local patterns of ownership. Nine of the fourteen municipal councils issued rejections of the proposed classification; the number remained the same during another round of councils' opinions the following spring.[39]

From the municipal councils as well as individual owners and users came similar complaints: familiar themes revealed ways of valuing the land, the peasants' experience of the war, and demographic realities in the uplands of Savoie. Nearly all of the complaints depicted the proposed protective forests as threats to property rights, whether communal or private, and to traditional ways of using and occupying land passed down from ancestors. Furthermore, the new regime would be all the less acceptable given sacrifices of livestock during the war: several individuals recounted the loss of animals due to requisitioning. Forced to sell their sheep to butcheries, they had had to accept prices that did not reflect the value of their milk-producing animals. These were the complaints of pastoralists who had prospered before the war: Simon Victorin, Richard Irénée, and Joseph Favre had, for example, lost between 120 and 190 sheep to the army. They had since reconstituted smaller flocks at far greater expense.[40] Between the lines of these protests lay another sense of sacrifice: whether from the plains, the foothills, or the high Alps, peasants had borne the brunt of the department's casualties during the war. More than half of the Savoyard casualties died in the offensives of 1914–15, the army relying heavily on the reputations and bodies of Alpine riflemen.[41] Though these human losses had improved the market in land for those who remained, heavy emigration following the war had continued to tear at the fabric of agro-pastoral life. Individuals and municipal councils also made frequent, if largely rhetorical, reference to the large families still present in the highlands and to the necessity of further emigration were their pasturing lands to be truncated.

Much of the "forest" in question consisted in fact of *pré-bois*, or meadows interspersed with woods. These were not, then, solid masses of forest slated for preservation under the Chauveau law but transitional ecosystems maintained as such by pastoralists. The municipal council of Bramans, in the Maurienne, claimed that in pré-bois, pasturing actually maintained the forest, for browsing sheep stimulated the regeneration of grasses while inhibiting the growth of inedible bushes such as heather and rhododendron—relatively fast-growing plants that could choke a perennially young forest and eventually crowd it out.[42] This logic did not convince forest inspectors, who continued to promote what would become the largest protective forest in Savoie. Bramans was to lose 612 hectares in the end.

Likewise, the forest inspector in charge of the case of Termignon did not deign to refute its council's detailed arguments rejecting classification. The commune's final appeal, drafted after its protective forest had become a legal fact, appeared to a forest guard as hostile quibbling: the immense commune of Termignon, the largest in the Maurienne, would lose a minuscule forty-eight hectares. Similar to the pré-bois in Bramans, this section of Termignon consisted of "thin" forest with numerous clearings. Rather than criticizing any arbitrariness on the foresters' part, the mayor and council of Termignon protested with a careful description of the specific value of these forty-eight hectares. They formed an important part of the lowest alpine pastures, protected by the communal forest and crucial for late-spring pasturing in times of inclement weather. Removing these parcels from the commune's control would also hinder access to chalets and upper pastures.[43]

Although such arguments had been respected just as little by foresters in the nineteenth century, they had on occasion led to negotiations and even modifications. Such was not the case with the application of the Chauveau law, whose logic of economism convinced many. Though delayed for lack of credits, the final designation of protective forests in Savoie overrode all of the communes' complaints: all fourteen "forests" selected in 1925 received their new classification in 1932.[44] Even Savoie's Conseil Général had favored classification from the beginning, and the location of the communes provides a partial explanation. Aside from Bramans and Termignon in the Maurienne, nearly all of the remaining twelve communes were located along a narrow corridor in the northernmost part of Savoie: in the foothills of the steep Aravis range of the Alps, and along the Arly River, these communes lined an important commercial road stretching from Albertville into Haute-Savoie and ultimately Switzerland. In this area within the economic orbit of both Chambéry and Annecy, pastoralism was becoming marginal, a decline reflected obliquely in the communes' vivid opposition to protective forests. At the upper end of the Maurienne, Termignon and Bramans looked down upon another important road, the gateway to communication with Italy. And two of the five communes that had not voiced opposition—Montmélian and Ugine—were themselves small industrial centers. By the early 1930s, the slowed but continuing rural exodus and the industrial development that was resisting economic downturn more successfully than elsewhere in France had thoroughly redefined the interests of Savoie in the eyes of departmental authorities.[45]

The conflict over protective forests in Ariège yielded an identical outcome but revealed dissimilar dynamics. The Chauveau law implicated more communes in the Pyrenean than in the Alpine department, twenty-three versus fourteen. Yet, as in Savoie, many were concentrated in the same area of the department, on both sides of a river and along an important road: eleven of the twenty-three communes lay within a day's walk of each other along the narrow corridor of the upper Ariège River, following the only road that led out of Ariège into Andorra and Spain. The choice of these communes followed the same logic, then, of protecting major commercial arteries from landslides as well as preventing downstream flooding.

Unfortunately, documents from Ariège do not include the voices of individual rural people, whose reports in Savoie, though scripted, bear witness to their hardships during World War I and a sense that they had already shouldered enough sacrifice. Part of this absence likely stems from a much swifter administrative trajectory in Ariège, from the initial selection of forests to their final classification. Begun in the summer of 1925, the path toward a ministerial decision had been completed by September 1926 for about half the forests; the fate of the remaining forests was sealed one year later. If anything, the experience of foresters in Ariège had proved that time was never on their side.

Yet even with a surprisingly snappy administrative process to contend with, municipal councils made their opinions—largely negative—of protective forests known. Unlike analogous cases in Savoie, communal authorities in Ariège complained explicitly about the foresters' own contraventions of the Chauveau law, the designation as "protective forests" of lands that were in fact sparse forest or, in some cases, not forest at all. The council of Rogalle, downstream from Massat in the Salat River basin, tinged its observation with sarcasm: the thirty hectares of communal forest in question were in fact mostly grassland, "in which trees are so few that it is impossible to see a forest . . . creating a forest which does not exist is not anticipated in the law of 28 April 1922 invoked by the Administration des Forêts [sic]."[46] The parameters of the Chauveau law should have allowed the commune an escape hatch from the tutelage of foresters, given the sparseness of Rogalle's forest. Instead, foresters effectively used the Chauveau law in Ariège and Savoie to promote restoration according to the broad mandate of 1913.[47]

Another surface similarity between the two departments uncovers a deeper contrast. Though the selected forests in Ariège consisted of a similar mix of communal and private parcels, there the private forests were nearly all subject to use rights. These figured as important elements in the complaints of several communes, and the existence of use rights seems to have been the deciding factor in a municipal council's decision whether to defend a private owner from the threat of classification. A member of the Conseil Général, M. Gomma, claimed as much in his comment on local responses: "If it is a question of private forests, the communes complain not because they sympathize with the owners, with whom they are often in discord, but because they fear the limitation of their use rights." In the three communes that voted in favor of protective forests, municipal councils made no mention of use rights on the private lands involved. As seen before in Ariège, it was not so much property as possession that was at stake; the language of possession surfaced even in the words of the consummate politician Léon Galy-Gasparrou, who stood vehemently against "what would be, for the communes, a partial dispossession of their territory."[48]

Galy-Gasparrou's comment reflects the most significant divergence between Savoie and Ariège concerning protective forests—in Ariège, the elected departmental authorities on the Conseil Général stood staunchly by local communities, continuing its unswerving support for pastoral interests since the nineteenth century. This support did not, though, come without a vigorous debate over local sovereignty and local values. The Conseil Général resolved to approve classification only if the "interested collectivities" had done so first. In the following debate, M. Gomma, the one official broadly in favor of protective forests, tempered his enthusiasm by suggesting that foresters implement the scheme gradually in Ariège and only in the face of threats to particular forests. While Gomma upheld the primacy of the "general interest," Galy-Gasparrou retorted with an argument for the wisdom of local use and decision-making, adding a very local observation: the Ariégeois forest had steadily claimed more land over the previous twenty years, and numbers of sheep had decreased.[49] Gomma responded with contempt for "local wisdom" in his paraphrase of the mayor of Castelet in the upper Ariège basin: "'Ask the inhabitants of Castelet if they do not prefer, every seventy-five years . . . to be exposed to certain risks and remain free.' That is what an enlightened and fully informed man told me immediately after a serious disaster."[50] Here was the confrontation of two logics: one that accepted the consequences of the alpine environment in return for maintaining a way of life, and one that faulted the peasants for antisocial behavior toward the world downstream *and* a perceived lack of self-interest. But Gomma's was a minority voice in the Conseil Général of 1926, which concluded its first session by passing the resolution supporting the communes.

By September 1926, decrees from the minister of agriculture and even the President of the Republic had formally placed nine forests in Ariège under the new regime. Soon thereafter, members of the Conseil Général vented their indignation that neither their nor the communes' opinions had been heeded. One councilor, M. Mazaud, summed up what had transpired as a futile gathering of local officials in order for the Eaux et Forêts to notify them, "Nothing you can say will do any good." Calls for the modification of the Chauveau law, and even Gomma's admission that "there are perhaps cases where the administration goes a little far," also betokened futility. The conseil concluded by expressing its surprise that "the decisions it had made have remained ineffectual and inoperative" and insisting that "in the future it [the Eaux et

Forêts] take into account the opinions of departmental and communal assemblies."[51]

The following summer, the minister of agriculture approved the new classification of the remaining forests originally selected in Ariège. With a stroke of the pen, 1,500 hectares of communal and private land fell under state management in the lower Castillonnais, and more than 5,000 hectares in the upper Ariège River corridor. In the latter region, no municipal councils had favored the project. By the end of 1927, protective forests accounted for 12,215 hectares of land in Ariège, by far the largest area in any department, the total area of protective forests in all of France coming to 28,882 hectares. The forester G. Géneau credited the regional conservator with the achievement: "When one knows the strong prejudices that clash with the forest idea in this department, one can only admire the energy and savoir-faire of Conservator Tessier to whom we owe this remarkable record."[52]

In Savoie the smaller number of communes and far smaller amounts of land had rendered the contest over protective forests a hotly symbolic issue. From Termignon had come arguments upholding its immemorial rights to pasturing and watering livestock, and the municipal council had pointedly remarked that these rights predated the annexation of Savoie to France. The forty-four proprietors of forest in the commune of Flumet not only had presented sophisticated descriptions of the inherent instability of the terrain but also had expressed deep resentment of their weakness vis-à-vis the state: "The proprietors . . . know that for a long time still, they will be in the hands of public powers, and [they] dread the state's dominion over their forests."[53]

The threat in Ariège had been more concrete and protest more vehement. Never before had the state been as swift or as sure in its appropriation of large tracts of forest and pasture. In the simplest sense, the Eaux et Forêts had new laws and new economic imperatives on its side, and its personnel acted accordingly. In a broader context, the Eaux et Forêts expanded its ascendancy in a period when other administrations were doing likewise: the interwar years saw the Ponts et Chaussées, Génie Rural, and Electricité de France in control of ever-increasing portions of communal space in both mountain ranges.[54] On the other hand, the designation of protective forests in Ariège and Savoie affected but a handful of communes in each department. Although the state appropriated far more land in Ariège under the Chauveau law than it ever did by virtue of the restoration law of 1882, still the acquisition amounted to roughly only 13 percent of all private and communal forest in the department and 7 percent of all forest.[55] Even if one acknowledges a certain renewal of central administrative power in both the Alps and the Pyrenees, this trend hardly shaped the full relationship between the state and alpine communes in the twentieth century.

SOLICITING THE STATE; RECOGNIZING
ALPINE FRANCE

Beginning in the 1920s, alpine communes started to ply the Eaux et Forêts with requests for services, a change most apparent in Savoie. The documentary weight of such banal requests for subsidies in order to improve the communal forest, repair alpine chalets, irrigate alpine pastures, or protect the commune from a torrential stream signals a definite shift in local perceptions of the potential uses of the state. That the mayor of Montagny should actually invite Eaux et Forêts personnel to inspect the communal territory and then take "all measures of protection and reforestation" necessary to protect a part of the commune from erosive collapse would have been unthinkable at the beginning of the century.[56]

Did communes simply bow to the inevitable, acknowledging as had Flumet their fate "in the hands of public powers," or were their novel requests carefully calculated? In Savoie, new ways of valuing communal forests may have arisen from lighter dependency on them, which resulted from new directions in agriculture. As peasants improved land in the department's well-watered valleys, as emigration from the mountains exacerbated the labor shortage, and as the remaining montagnards began to abandon unprofitable farming of minor grains (rye and oats) on the slopes, less livestock grazed the alpine pastures.[57] Many pastures in middling altitudes were abandoned and over time naturally reforested. No longer needed as much for firewood, construction wood, and intermittent grazing, the forest, too, changed character and lent itself to the logic of preservation.

Testimony from the aptly named commune of Le Bois shows that some communes had begun to appreciate, in their terms, the forest's protective value. In 1937 Le Bois requested significant aid from the Eaux et Forêts to protect the hamlet of Crey (the largest of the commune) from a bedrock-debris slump (*glissement de terrain*). Le Bois made the request not for the usual reasons of foresters, but for its own—as a way of preventing further emigration from the commune: "the exodus of [Crey's] inhabitants, whom we must keep on the land at all costs," would be the price of neglect.[58]

Concerns about emigration reveal an area in which foresters' and communes' priorities were beginning to coincide. The state was becoming an increasingly important source of employment in rural France; for its part, the Eaux et Forêts, and the RTM in particular, had always relied on local labor to carry out many aspects of its work (figure 11). It is easy to imagine that in the twentieth century, the promise of jobs may have swayed more municipal councils in favor of restoration than in the nineteenth; likewise, foresters probably grasped more fully the political benefits to be accrued from hiring locally. The demand for jobs outpaced opportunities, and in 1931 the Eaux et Forêts found itself in the position of justifying to the prefect of Savoie its reasons for not hiring more people during the winter. Foresters, Conservator Sorney explained, needed help mostly in the summer; all he could suggest was that the authorities attempt to revive local arts of tool- and lace-making, repoussé work, and weaving.[59] Tellingly, in the economic collapse of the mid-1930s the RTM received special credits for *chantiers de chômeurs* and, with a vastly increased labor force, achieved some of its most spectacular restorations in the Alps (figure 12).

Even more surprising than new communal uses of the state was the Eaux et Forêts' retreat from some of its most hallowed principles—in stark contrast to the institution of protective forests. The battle for reforestation had always faced two related obstacles: lack of interest or active hostility on the part of pastoralists and the grazing of their livestock. To foresters, rural habits of allowing grazing in forests represented an anathema of the highest order. Just as the Forest Code of 1827 had banished goats from the forest and attempted to regulate the grazing of sheep and cattle in state and communal forests, all grazing in reforested areas had been banned from the beginning. As the principled forest guard Messines, who would make something of a career judging Savoyard pastoralism into the 1930s (see Chapter 6), explained in 1926, "[pasturing] is not compatible with the necessities of reforestation." Though a senator from Savoie had secured pasturing rights in state forests during the drought of 1921, the privilege did not extend to lands within restoration perimeters. It was only after the same senator, M. Machet, correctly pointed out that some of the RTM's land consisted of grassy zones above the tree line, and that grazing would thus not interfere with the growth of new forests, that the regional conservator conceded that exceptional grazing might be allowed in future years of drought.[60] In the dry spring of 1931, Jules Paccalet of Bozel won the privilege of pasturing fifty cows within an RTM perimeter, in an area more than twenty-two hundred meters in altitude; in 1933 Fontcouverte became the first commune in Savoie to acquire grazing privileges within an RTM zone for the residents of its *chef-lieu*. The area was small, the grazing conditions strict, and the land but a "sorry pas-

Figure 11. Local workers sowing larch seeds in the snow. Ubaye Perimeter, Méolans, Basses-Alpes, 1894. Negative by Sardi. Archives Départementales des Alpes de Haute-Provence.

Figure 12. Restoration of the Saint-Julien torrent, Savoie, 1934. Negative by Fevre. ADS.

ture, without a single trace of forest vegetation." Still, some foresters had begun to see parts of the extensive network of RTM lands for what they were—too high and too rocky ever to allow reforestation. In 1932 the conservator had even conceded that the prefect could, in most cases, grant exceptional grazing privileges himself.[61]

Similar exceptions also became the norm in Ariège. Communes that already possessed grazing rights for cattle in state and communal forests won similar concessions for sheep in 1925. Grazing would be limited by "special conditions" and recompensed by a fee of ten centimes per animal or a day of work for the forest service for every thirty animals; a ministerial decision in 1936 reduced both amounts.[62] The readmission of sheep into the Ariégeois forests further weakened the once fraught distinctions between state and communal priorities. It represented an economic advantage for pastoral communes as well as the latest step taken by the state to regulate pasturing. As communal authorities had once done, now foresters collected the fees and controlled the number of animals and seasonal duration of pasturing. In 1936 Forest Conservator Jean Salvador justified the extended grazing rights from both national and local perspectives: he touted the success of reforestation—the young forests could now withstand a certain amount of damage from cows and sheep—and also asserted the economic necessity of promoting the Ariégeois livestock industry during the depression.[63]

The most revealing contradiction in Ariège lay in the survival of the "disorderly" forest, itself partially co-opted by the state. Nineteenth-century foresters had deemed irrational the practices of Ariégeois peasants, who kept an aesthetically and economically "poor" forest by means of jardinage, the maintenance of an uneven-aged forest by culling or "gardening" individual trees throughout the forest. Numerous use rights thwarted the state's plans for management by taking their own toll on the forest. The early 1920s were, again, decisive years of change. A law of 1924 created departmental agricultural councils, one of whose stipulated duties was to codify the "customs and usages of an agricultural nature" that had the force of law in each department. Statements from the highest levels of government now posited local usages and use rights as beneficial to peasants in general and, consequently, useful in combating rural exodus.

In compliance with the law, Léonce Fournié published *Code officiel des usages locaux à caractère agricole ayant force de loi dans le département de l'Ariège* in 1935, a document that testifies to both the new pasturing rights granted in the 1920s and 1930s and the maintenance of older use rights and methods. Fournié's two-hundred-page text codified the use rights common throughout Ariège, those in force in particular cantons, and those, such as *vaine pâture,* that only a few communes had retained. Most revealing is Fournié's characterization of the privately owned forests in which the old methods prevailed: private owners submitted their forests to jardinage as well as *sarclage*—the practice of "weeding" the forest of deformed branches and dead wood for firewood, as well as collecting leaves, mosses, acorns, wild cherries, and apples to feed pigs and turkeys and fibrous plants for stable litter. And private owners still had the habit of cutting light wood in an old moon and dark wood in a new moon.[64]

Not merely juxtaposed with the state's more Cartesian schemes of managing forests, jardinage had been rehabilitated by the state itself and used in many Pyrenean forests under the forest regime. Forest Conservator Charles Broilliard, retired in 1891, wrote of jardinage as a special method of managing fir forests; use rights in such forests posed a problem for him, but not the method itself.[65] But a text by Jean Salvador establishes jardinage as the definitive method for managing Pyrenean forests by 1930. The state's foresters now qualified it as *jardinage amélioré* and promoted it (as well as its companion *furetage* for low forests) as a remarkable way of allowing sufficient shade and protection for young beeches and firs, preventing erosion, and mitigating damage from livestock. Tellingly, Salvador had to appeal to these benefits in order to justify the appearance of forests submitted to jardinage and furetage: "The aspect of a low forest [managed by] furetage produces the impression of a devastation; and yet this method, practiced for centuries along the entire range of the Pyrenees, has assured the conservation of beech forests."[66] Age-old disorder now received its highest consecration.

The creation of protective forests and the surveillance of private forests represented the last great acts in the imperialist tradition of French forestry. These twentieth-century developments deepened old differences between Ariège and Savoie with respect to the forest question: the state increased an already extensive sylvan domain more dramatically in Ariège than in Savoie, and it was in Ariège that departmental authorities remained in league with the communes.

Little by little, however, relationships among peasants, forests, and the state had begun to veer away from the often raw antagonism of the nineteenth century. Unprecedented concessions made by the Eaux et Forêts, new demands from rural communes, and the maintenance of use rights shaped a new playing field. Some of the older bases of conflict grew more nebulous: having their use rights recognized and acquiring grazing privileges and jobs clearly conformed to pastoralists' interests, while these same measures allowed the Eaux et Forêts and particularly the RTM to proclaim their role in helping to diminish rural exodus. The metaphor of human illness that came to characterize alpine environments, a metaphor amplified by the decimation of lowland forests in World War I, carried more than one potential: it justified the "severe and energetic treatment" ministered in the form of protective forests, but it also brought attention to the "sickness" of agro-pastoralism and the need to focus the concept of public utility more locally. Residents of rural communes, acting autonomously with respect to foresters' metaphors, grew bolder in demanding their share of the state's resources. Before the 1920s and 1930s, however, anxieties bearing upon alpine France had spread beyond official circles: twentieth-century relationships between peasants and the state were also forged in the presence of new players, whose own agenda for alpine forests and people is the subject of the final chapter.

Chapter Six The Coercion of Pedagogy: Associations in Alpine France, 1891–1937

What is he and what is he worth, this highlander whose physiographic milieu we have known for so little time? Penetrating his character is certainly more arduous than scaling his mountains.
—*Lucien-Albert Fabre*

The Eaux et Forêts reached the pinnacle of its authority in 1913, a year that saw seminal legislation (discussed in Chapter 5) as well as a historically high complement of foresters in the corps. Five years later, war had killed ninety-four foresters, more than 13 percent of the officers in the Eaux et Forêts. By 1935 only the two highest ranks, general inspector and conservator, had been fully reconstituted. The entire corps had declined by nearly 25 percent of its 1912 numbers.

These figures come from a detailed complaint published in 1935 by Georges Rabouille, forest guard of the Eaux et Forêts.[1] Beyond documenting the decimation of the forestry corps, Rabouille traces the extension of foresters' duties since the late nineteenth century. They had become responsible for regulating fresh-water fishing and hunting within their domain in the 1890s; monitoring water pollution, restocking fishing and hunting areas, initiating legal action in cases of

hunting and fishing violations, and carefully surveying forest land that had recently changed ownership represented burdens added to the fundamental mis-
sions of the corps: management of one-twentieth of the national territory and
alpine restoration.[2]

The twentieth-century twist in relations between foresters and communes,
explored in the previous chapter, further reveals itself in Rabouille's account of
a 1935 gathering of mayors in the Meurthe-et-Moselle. The mayoral assembly
issued a protest to the Eaux et Forêts demanding more foresters to see to the
maintenance of communal forests. Rabouille's overall portrait, then, is that of
a highly trained corps that was overworked, overwhelmed with requests, and
underpaid (he includes a revealing comparison of foresters' and military officers' salaries); foresters had become unable to "hold with dignity the social rank
at which their functions place them."[3]

In light of Rabouille's analysis, it is not surprising that new institutions began to take up the forest question in the twentieth century. This chapter is concerned with associations which promoted popular forestry as a necessary crusade that would compensate for the inadequacies of the state's forestry corps.
Alongside associations whose specific mission was to ignite broad public interest in forestry, various tourist organizations also assumed the role of forest protector. These associations had begun to popularize recreation *en altitude* before
the turn of the century, initially catering to small numbers of hardy mountain
climbers, or "alpinists," as they called themselves, after their preferred mountains. With time, analogous groups represented skiers and lower-elevation hikers. In terms of the forest question, the common ground held by these two
kinds of associations—from membership lists to ideologies and agendas—is of
interest here. The associations also voiced a set of concerns that echoed those
emanating from the ranks of the Eaux et Forêts: they became, to different de-
grees, havens for disgruntled foresters. But for the coercion of law and bureaucracy the associations substituted pedagogy, seeking to uplift refractory alpine
peasants by means perceived to lie beyond the capacities of the state. The goal
of regenerating alpine land and people was no less illusory, however, when approached with pedagogic means.

Pedagogy was undergirded by specific constructions of the mountains of
France and the people who lived in them. While partaking of the forestry corps'
righteous sense of mission, associations channeled their work through other
kinds of objectification. Here the tourist associations provide the best example,
for their collective interest in forestry stemmed from a desire to maintain their
largely bourgeois clients' playgrounds. Their alpine nature had to do, to borrow

Nicholas Green's words, with "leisure and pleasure—tourism, spectacular entertainment, visual refreshment."[4] This implied a complete erasure of the alpine peasantry: instead of insalubrious shepherds' huts, hygienic hikers' shelters should dot the mountain slope. The effort to create this kind of landscape led, paradoxically, to the associations' "discovery" of alpine inhabitants and their ways. Although this chapter is concerned above all with associational discourse, rural resistance echoes in the largely negative response to associational schemes.

THE ASSOCIATIONAL ETHOS

One of the earliest associations, the Société des Amis des Arbres, shows the concatenation of professional forestry, popular forestry, and tourism, for it involved both foresters and a broader public from its inception. The organization was founded in 1891 by a Niçoise doctor, M. Jeannel, author of a treatise on the relation between human mortality and rates of afforestation by department. A small association recruited from the high society of Nice, it expanded in 1894 with Jeannel's decision to move its headquarters to Paris. In the same year, Prosper Demontzey—reforester par excellence and first head of the RTM—became president, and six of the governing council's twenty-four members hailed from the Eaux et Forêts. Several engineers and important members of national agricultural societies were also present. Through its statutes, however, the Société des Amis des Arbres tried to fashion itself as a mass movement, opening membership to children, calling particularly upon women and artists to join, even offering free membership to certain professional groups.[5]

In his first written address as president, Demontzey reached out not only to professionals in horticulture and silviculture but also to the "galaxy of urbanites in love with the countryside, for whom trees constitute the greatest charm."[6] His appeal touched upon the growing aesthetic attraction of the nation's forests; indeed, the society's central goal of voluntary reforestation could only be met if enough of the urban public were to see and appreciate forests for themselves (figure 13). By 1895, the recreative appeal of forests had become firmly established among the bourgeoisie, but the lure of the mountains was just beginning to grow. While the Société des Amis des Arbres championed reforestation throughout France, another impulse combined alpine tourism with reforestation in what became the first mass organization to promote open-air recreation—the Touring-Club de France.

Under the high patronage of the president of the Republic, the Touring-

Figure 13. Foresters and bourgeois: silviculture lesson, 1908. Apremont, Savoie. Negative by Mougin. ADS.

Club was founded in 1890 "to propagate tourism in France." Like other continental touring clubs of the era, the French club militated for improved road surfacing for bicycles and later automobiles, organized trips and provided travel services, and, after the turn of the century, became engaged in the protection of natural sites and monuments—and reforestation. Foresters were prominent on the organizing committee, as in the Société des Amis des Arbres, but the more broadly based Touring-Club grew more quickly: by 1913 more than 132,000 people had paid dues to the organization.[7]

The Touring-Club in part drew a large membership from its particular stance on alpine tourism. Founded significantly after the so-called golden age of alpinism—the period between roughly 1854 and 1880, marked by the spectacular ascents of the great summits of the Alps, largely by British climbers— the Touring-Club had to define itself with respect to the Club Alpin Français, or CAF. Though a late-comer to the group of national alpine clubs throughout Europe, the CAF had been active since 1874 in organizing ascents and disseminating information through its review, *La Montagne*. The CAF not only kept its members apprised of trails, weather, and local accommodations, but it also tutored them in a particular way of appreciating the mountains through the values of action, work, risk, and enterprise.[8] Although the Touring-Club never espoused an alternative to this mode of consuming the mountains, it claimed to work "for the greatest number." The club fixed its annual membership fee at five francs, considerably lower than the twenty-franc rate of the CAF.[9]

As its membership figure of 1913 suggests, the Touring-Club did succeed in opening up recreation in general to a broader public. Yet it gained little support from the working class and, after founding its Committee on Alpine Tourism in 1910, even had to defend itself from accusations of promoting "tourism for the rich": a writer for the club's monthly review protested that skiing required only "a little bit of valor, solid legs, [and] a pair of skis." Ultimately, the Touring-Club maintained a complementary rather than a competitive relationship with the CAF. The two clubs divided up the mountain as they represented different sectors of society: the CAF continued to promote "rope and ice-axe" alpinism, while the Touring-Club concentrated on building trails and encouraging hiking in subalpine regions.[10] Altitude recapitulated social status.

For the Touring-Club, promoting tourism became inextricably attached to the forest question. Its official interest in the latter can be dated from the creation of the Commission on Grasses and Forests in 1904; the following year, a series of articles on the "deforestation of French soil" appeared in the *Revue*. This direction reflects the prominence of foresters on the club's organizing committee: by 1913, twenty of its approximately sixty members were agents from the upper echelons of the Eaux et Forêts. And in that year the Touring-Club organized a major international forest conference held in Paris.[11] The grumblings of foresters frustrated with inadequate laws and insufficient funds can be heard in the variety of lobbying initiatives taken by the Touring-Club in favor of reforestation. Its publications naggingly reminded the Eaux et Forêts of its duties, a stance that could provoke ill relations between associations and the state—not to mention antagonism between foresters who had joined associations and those whose loyalty remained with their corps.

The associations attempted to forge identities through liberal rhetoric that staked out their position in civil society. But given the number of high functionaries that sat on organizing committees, an ethos of private initiative wary of the state was bound to come in a variety of inflections. A vision of public-private reciprocity emerged in the Société des Amis des Arbres, for example: associations could aid an overburdened public sector. President (and RTM chief) Demontzey claimed that the state "must simply second private efforts" in restoring the forests. Reforestation would reflect a consecutive as well as a reciprocal pattern of contributions: the RTM would continue to construct "defenses of the first order," the masonry and wooden structures it had invented to prop up the mountains; then, in their shadow, "the few present forests and those that the volunteers of reforestation will create, shall grow for the greater good of the country."[12] Yet the association would maintain an exclusive goal of "protection and propagation of the tree," leaving long-term management to the Eaux et Forêts.

Defenses of associational initiative reflected discursive positioning more than a state of fact. Encouraging voluntary reforestation by individuals and communes had been one of the cornerstones of the Third Republic's alpine policy, for the law of 1882 had extended the system of subsidies in place since the Second Empire. Clearly, the associations themselves relied on the state for supporting aspects of their agendas, often in a transparent spirit of entitlement. The Association Centrale pour l'Aménagement des Montagnes (ACAM), an organization treated in greater detail below, arrived at the same conclusion as had the Société des Amis des Arbres: its volunteers would plant forests but not manage them thereafter. In 1906 the organization formally requested that the Eaux et Forêts "consent" to managing its fledgling forests. The Touring-Club, for its part, pushed for a strict pastoral regime enforceable by the state.[13] Such encroachment on the foresters' terrain prompted Philippe Bauby, a joint inspector apparently unconnected to any of the major associations he cited, to accuse them of "neophyte ardor" in 1907. That year saw a mass exodus of foresters from the ACAM: the Eaux et Forêts was calling its ranks to order.[14]

If not in the legislative arena, it was in pedagogy that the associations could claim the upper hand over the Eaux et Forêts. Pierre Buffault and others might urge fellow foresters to become comfortable in the classroom alongside the professor of agriculture: had foresters possessed greater knowledge of local forests as well as the ability to communicate it, Buffault reasoned, they would greatly have streamlined the frantic search for wood during the war. And the ongoing wood deficit called for counseling private owners in silviculture.[15] In the era of World War I, though, how could foresters substitute the image of teacher and guide for that of aloof, paramilitary arm of the state while the latter was passing ever more coercive legislation?

Associations seized the pedagogical initiative for themselves. Many of their most outspoken members criticized the state's laxity in teaching the importance of forests to the nation. Their ambitious remedies assumed grand dimensions, for at stake was not only the education of an urban public but also the tutoring of montagnards in wiser use of their resources. Though often masked as benevolent aid, the associations' broader agenda promoted a radical transformation of the montagnards' way of life. Some of their projects, however, crossed urban-rural divisions, and two of these—primary school education and *Fêtes de l'Arbre*—illuminate the associations' pedagogical goals.

The Touring-Club took the lead in propagandizing for the forest before World War I. Its prewar publications for children of primary-school age included the *Manuel de l'arbre* and the *Manuel d'enseignement sylvo-pastoral à l'usage des écoles primaires,* as well as a *tableau mural* that illustrated the benefits of grasses and forests and the disasters caused by their destruction. Primary schools could request these materials from the Touring-Club free of charge. The club also instigated a memorandum from the minister of public instruction, requesting teachers throughout France to present the current scientific thinking in sylvo-pastoral studies and to encourage the foundation of school-based "forest societies."[16] These had first emerged in eastern France with the support of the Société Forestière de Franche-Comté; after 1907, the Touring-Club generously subsidized their expansion in neighboring regions. These school clubs created and maintained nurseries where children dutifully tended seedlings and eventually would replant the commons with them. By 1914 nearly four hundred *sociétés scolaires forestières* existed throughout France.[17]

The associations' greater originality lay in promoting tree-planting festivals, which took pedagogy a step further: such events could unite symbolism and pragmatism in a day of speeches and perhaps a children's parade combined with communal planting. Discussion of a national Fête de l'Arbre dated from at least 1895, and the American, Spanish, and Italian versions of Arbor Day had provided models since 1872, 1898, and 1902, respectively. France, of course, also had a revolutionary tradition of tree-planting to draw upon, although the planting of single oaks—the tree preferred by the National Convention but not the exclusive species of "liberty tree" during the French Revolution—could hardly be equated with reforestation. Oaks, in addition, as the revolutionaries had discovered themselves, grew slowly and would not survive alpine conditions.[18] Equally important, the politics of the liberty tree was of dubious value for those who promoted a patriotic Fête de l'Arbre, especially after World War I.

By 1910, local tree-planting festivals had become popular in parts of France, namely, the Ain and the Ardèche in the southeast. The Touring-Club and the Société des Amis des Arbres occasionally sponsored these rites, and foresters were often on hand to give instructions (figure 14). Not until the late 1920s did plans for a national festival come to fruition, due to the collaborative efforts of the Société des Amis des Arbres and the recently formed Association Nationale et Industrielle du Bois. Created in 1927, the ANIB grouped private owners of

Figure 14. Fête de l'Arbre, 1906. Saint-Julien-de-Maurienne, Savoie. Negative by Mougin. ADS.

forest, merchants, and industrial users of wood in an effort to coordinate voluntary reforestation throughout the country. The organization quickly secured the patronage of five government ministers and reached out to chambers of commerce, agricultural societies, and schools. Within a few months, the two associations had obtained the minister of public instruction's authorization for a national Fête de l'Arbre.[19]

In many ways, the meaning of the first Fête arises from its organizers' chosen date—11 November. The authors of the ANIB's announcement of the festival took pains to justify this annexation of tree-planting to remembering the Armistice. Though they frankly admitted their hesitation regarding the date, the season, at least, had been an obvious choice: November through February was the optimal period for transplanting evergreen seedlings, whose sap then lay dormant. Mentioning the risk of deforming the secular holiday and blurring its "particular character," the authors then insisted that the Fête de l'Arbre would remain a secondary element in Armistice Day ceremonies: it would "adapt itself as narrowly as possible to the usual framework of the ceremonies, and bring only the particular significance that a gesture of piety in honor of the victims of war involves." Indeed, the ANIB had tactfully submitted its plans to the Associations de Combattants et de Mutilés and received their unanimous approval.[20]

It was not difficult to play up the linkages between planting trees and remembering the war. The ANIB's succinct justification included the importance of young trees in improving the national patrimony, secured by the dead of the war; embellishing the ground where the latter had passed their youth; and standing as a "gesture of faith in the future of our country."[21] The ANIB could also draw upon the anthropomorphic image of France's forests as heroes of the war; the forester J. Demorlaine had characterized them as such as early as 1919. Forest cover had greatly aided both defensive and offensive operations (despite the fact that the Germans had benefited equally from French forests), and the nation owed the ravaged forests of the former war zone time and opportunity to "heal their numerous and glorious wounds." The 1920s had already, in fact, been marked by the regreening of the so-called red zone of greatest wartime devastation, and plans to create a *forêt sacrée* as well as a *voie sacrée* had been discussed since 1919.[22]

Because it was published shortly before 11 November, the ANIB's 1927 pamphlet offered only a spare set of suggestions for the ceremony itself. Ideally, schoolchildren would plant one or several trees in the village square, preferably next to the war memorial. Following this act, the mayor, primary school teacher, or veterans' delegate might deliver a speech rendering homage to the war dead, linking reforestation to patriotism, and explaining the benefits of trees, including the "defense" of plains and valleys provided by alpine forests. The ANIB considered this symbolic manifestation appropriate for communes not yet actively involved in reforestation; in places where an initiation had already taken place, the ceremony could include a massive tree-planting by many residents or the inauguration of a nursery.[23]

By 1929, the ANIB had drafted a thorough "how-to" for La Fête de l'Arbre et de la Plantation. Now little emphasis was placed on the ceremonial and more on the practical. The ANIB had reconceived the festival, still scheduled for 11 November, as a day of national reforesting, an ambition evinced in the following calculation: If each of France's thirty-eight thousand communes planted one thousand trees, then the French territory would, in a single day, be newly covered with nine thousand hectares of seedlings. Consequently, the new recipe for the festival included detailed instructions to guide the effort, from preparing the ground to choosing species and planting them. Local organizers could also draw upon the short speech included in the ANIB's pamphlet. Here the authors retained references to the other meanings of 11 November, packing the model oration with associations and metaphors. Now the new forests themselves would play the role formerly reserved for the single or several trees placed near a war memorial: forests would stand for memory itself and even become a "cult of the territory so gloriously defended." Above all, the speaker should play down the mundane aspects of reforestation by drawing upon the emotional content of the day to stimulate planting: "This does not have only to do with planting a tree: the moment has come to associate the memory of the dead from the war to thoughts of our children's future and to provoke a vast movement in favor of reforestation throughout our whole country."[24]

In hopes of assuring participation, the ANIB announced fifty prizes to be awarded to communes that executed the most successful festivals. These ranged from a top prize of three hundred francs to silver and bronze medals as well as diplomas; the ANIB planned to distribute them based on written reports from mayors whose communes had taken part in the prescribed activities. Unfortunately, little evidence of the festival's results remains in the departmental archives of Savoie and Ariège. The prefect of Savoie did, following the ANIB's request, notify all mayors in the department of the upcoming festival in 1927, but only a single commune's response lies alongside other official documents. The testimony of Saint-Marcel, however, speaks to the economic situation of many alpine communes in the 1920s. The municipal council had voted against organizing a tree-planting festival for the following reasons: "The resources of the communes are very limited and major expenses lie ahead; the division of the commune into scattered hamlets does not lend itself to the success of this festival." But what reactions to urban ideas of festival, memory, and forests themselves lay behind this politely crafted answer? The probable lack of response from other communes may bear silent witness to a similar hostility.[25]

In 1931 the ANIB claimed that the number of communes participating in the Fête de l'Arbre had grown considerably since 1927.[26] Whatever the local success of such celebrations, Fêtes de l'Arbre and forest clubs in primary schools clearly did not lead to reforestation on the scale hoped for within bourgeois associations such as the ANIB. And as far as alpine France was concerned, associational discourse continually led back to the problem of the montagnards themselves and their troubling archaism. Related anxieties over alpine people and alpine nature ultimately called for a more severe brand of pedagogy: direct intervention in the highlanders' ways of life. This quite different trend evolved in the writings and efforts devoted to *améliorations pastorales*—pastoral improvements. Such an innocuous phrase masks the dreams of those who adopted it as a program in the early twentieth century: in it would lie the key to the complete social and natural regeneration of the mountains. Understanding the associational approach to améliorations pastorales requires a brief look at initiatives first taken by the state.

THE FAILURE OF AMÉLIORATIONS PASTORALES

The concept of pastoral improvements, originally theorized in the nineteenth-century Administration des Forêts, recognized the need to reinvigorate alpine pastures in order to enhance human life in the mountains and to promote a hard distinction between pastures and forests. As discussed in Chapter 2, the 1860 law on the reclamation of the commons had gone hand in hand with the first law on reforestation; together they signaled an orderly, administrative vision of mountains, with pastures, forests, and fields in distinct zones. The law of 1882 had, in view of regulation, required communes to furnish precise information about their grazing rules to the state. With the creation of a *Service pastoral* in 1884, attached to the RTM, the Administration des Forêts began to subsidize pastoral improvements.[27]

Though legislation had linked pasture to forest, individual foresters commonly distinguished between them. A forest inspector in Ariège had insisted in 1866 that pastoral improvements were not in the classic domain of forestry: "It is especially and above all an agricultural question which interests first and foremost the owners of flocks." But, as foresters eager to improve their corps' reputation in the mountains discovered, an administration that took interest in irrigating pastures, constructing shelters on the alpages, conserving natural springs, and disinfecting barns could garner local approval, reforestation notwithstanding. As early as 1883, some foresters involved in pastoral improvements had even adopted the peasant technique of *écobuage,* the use of controlled fires to rid pastures of unwanted plants and return nutrients to the soil.[28]

Communal reluctance to initiate pastoral improvements quickly became the foresters' standard complaint in the late nineteenth century. Even if built by the forest service, irrigation channels, watering troughs, and shelters required maintenance by local people. In Ariège, targeted early for pastoral improvements, foresters frequently lamented the peasants' indifference, if not active resentment, toward the administration's good works. The Conseil Général of the department voted an annual five-thousand-franc subsidy for irrigation and écobuage of pastoral lands in 1890 but halved the amount three years later; even its cautious subsidies far outweighed the extent of local interest. When the Conseil Général funded the creation of several demonstration sites in 1896,

Conservator Loze noticed a glimmering of local curiosity and reported it with a double negative: the peasants who had participated in the work had seemed "not to misunderstand" its usefulness. Yet Loze's following comment about the local participants betrayed the harsh tutelage that also linked pastoral improvements to forestry: "Is this to say that the moment has come to abandon them to themselves? Far from it."[29]

Throughout the early Third Republic, references to the sloth and incurable apathy of the montagnards, as well as the supposed defects of communal management, appeared in reports and treatises that sought to explain the degradation of alpine pastures.[30] In 1900 the Eaux et Forêts produced a balance sheet of pastoral improvements in Ariège and Haute-Garonne in a report that accompanied the RTM's participation in the Paris World's Fair. Authored by Inspector Campardon, the report did not mark a shift in assumptions regarding peasants and pastoralism. Campardon duly noted the lack of communal initiative and the shepherds' neglect of irrigation channels, even if the one hundred thousand francs funneled into the two departments over the years had purchased a certain amount of good will; a few peasants had willingly contributed their labor to pastoral improvements, and one local association in the Saint-Gironnais (Ariège) had contributed the surprising sum of twelve hundred francs to repair high alpine roads. Campardon's optimism was, however, cautious.[31]

Within a decade, foresters would find confirmation of these traditional attitudes in the rise and fall of *fruitières,* or cooperative creameries. Spearheaded by the state in the 1870s, fruitières in Ariège, Hautes-Pyrénées, Haute-Garonne, and Basses-Pyrénées for a time incarnated pastoral improvements, even though a small minority of foresters actively supported them. The goal was to improve the efficiency of alpine cheese production through the pooling of local resources, year-round fabrication, and the substitution of more productive breeds of sheep and especially cattle for local ones. Such an experiment illustrates a certain tolerance for collective property within the Eaux et Forêts, but by 1910 foresters' reports attested to the failure of fruitières. Beyond the laments, their analyses are instructive: fruitières required more labor as well as more milk than could be furnished locally, peasants rejected the technicity of the project, and women resented their loss of control over the production and transformation of milk.[32]

The Eaux et Forêts' prewar stance on pastoral improvements is best revealed in a hefty three-volume report of the RTM, published in 1911. Exactly one of the work's 878 pages is devoted to pastoral improvements; it simply notes that between 1899 and 1909 the lion's share of the state's modest subsidies had gone to the one successful fruitière, located in Marignac (Haute-Garonne). The best the Eaux et Forêts could do was to remain relatively mute about the outcome of its pastoral project.[33]

Enter the ACAM—the Association Centrale pour l'Aménagement des Montagnes. In a public lecture delivered in Toulouse in 1907, Paul Descombes introduced the young association over which he presided. Typically, it had been founded by a group of engineers and tourists; the ACAM's organizing committee showed an elite combination of state technicians and entrepreneurs in tourism similar to that present in the Touring-Club. Several engineers, foresters, and graduates of the Polytechnique shared duties with presidents of the Bordelais Ski-Club and the southwest section of the CAF.[34] Descombes himself was a very well-connected *polytechnicien* and former director of a state factory. By several accounts he was able to use his connections with foresters, railroad companies, chambers of commerce, departmental councils, and the city of Bordeaux (the seat of his association) to obtain support and subsidies for his alpine projects.[35] The ACAM provided the most significant alternative to state-directed restoration, and especially améliorations pastorales, in the early twentieth century.

The ACAM has been interpreted as a challenge to both the state and other contemporary organizations in terms of a working vision of the mountains. Andrée Corvol paints the ACAM—supported as it was by prominent foresters— as having broken a consensus within the Eaux et Forêts over the primacy of the state's action and the privileging of silviculture. Similarly, Bernard Kalaora and Antoine Savoye depict the ACAM as the organ of a renegade group of "social foresters" whose concept of the preservation of alpine life drew upon the sociology of Frédéric Le Play.[36] In this view, the ACAM stood at great odds with the CAF and the Touring-Club, for example, over the issue of national parks. The latter organizations spearheaded the creation of France's first such park on the communal territory of Saint-Christophe-en-Oisans (Isère) in 1913—the Oisans, ironically, a node of alpine capitalism as a traditional center of departure for wide-ranging peddlers. The park represented a defeat for the ACAM, which had rented lands and attempted restoration in harmony with local interests in Saint-Christophe several years earlier.[37]

Paul Descombes, however, was most concerned to position the ACAM with respect to the Eaux et Forêts, differing in his very identification of the alpine problem—a double urgency to "maintain the mountains' land and people." Descombes and his staff grew fond of graphs that showed correlations between alpine degradation and the diminution of the human and animal population of the Pyrenees. Population decline was conspicuously absent from the Eaux et Forêts' litany of concerns about pastoralism in the prewar era. To the dual problem President Descombes proposed a single solution, the initiative of his association, which, he argued, would surely be more welcome in the mountains than the foresters. The barbs he threw to the forestry corps included references to the "inanity of coercive laws" and "legislation insufficiently adapted" to local conditions.[38] The ACAM explicitly rejected the legal measures that allowed the state to expropriate for reasons of public utility. Its defense of property fit well with the overall project of the ACAM, which was to proceed with restoration in the form of pilot projects on land that it would rent or purchase from communes. Reviewing the ACAM's work in its first five years, member and forester Joly de Sailly formulated the ideal role of the state as mere cooperative partner and supporter of private initiative.[39]

Reports on the ACAM's actual work, undertaken mostly in the Pyrenees, carefully avoided both Descombes' personal characterizations of insouciant alpine peasants and his references to the deficiencies of communal ownership. Instead, the organization's efforts would "enrich the montagnards by showing them that they were the first victims of deforestation."[40] In other words, handing the peasants such images of themselves would ultimately transform them. Yet the pedagogic style of the ACAM combined solicitude with condescension. Descombes gave to his preferred method of alpine restoration the telling name of *Leêons de choses*. By this means, the ACAM secured leases of varying terms for degraded communal pastures and proceeded with conspicuously public demonstrations of how to regenerate forsaken land. In one unidentified area of twenty square kilometers, the ACAM had not only "liberated" the land from summer transhumants but also achieved a "spontaneous improvement" in only five years and at the cost of only five francs per hectare.

This vague description, omitting details concerning local reception and concrete methods of restoration, was thoroughly characteristic of the ACAM. In the decade between 1904 and 1914, the ACAM rented pastures in Alpes-Maritimes, Haute-Garonne, Hautes-Pyrénées, and Basses-Pyrénées, using as its primary experimental pastures land leased for sixty years near the Pic-du-Midi. At the annual congress of 1914, Descombes declared universal success. The "formerly refractory" peasants had shown exemplary collaboration, due to the "simplicity, elasticity, and mildness" of the ACAM's approach. Alpine communes went along with the ACAM's projects only as long as they cost nothing to the communes, however; foresters often claimed that peasants returned to their previous methods after the leases to the ACAM had expired. The organization did not last much beyond World War I; ironically, its remnant fused with the Club Alpin Français in 1924.[41]

The relatively short life of the ACAM can be traced to at least two causes: for one, its goal of stemming rural exodus became overwhelmed by alpine emigration spanning the years of the Great War. Savoie and Ariège lost, respectively, 9 percent and 13 percent of their population between 1911 and 1921, proportionally more people leaving rural cantons. For another, Descombes' idealism and flamboyant style attracted little support in the context of the postwar era's hard-nosed economism. Characteristic of the 1920s and early 1930s were new associations that vigorously embraced not only advances in biogeography and ecology but also the idea that the mountains had distinct functions in the national economy. Although they inherited such a notion from the Administration des Forêts of the Second Empire, their leaders operated under the novel assumption that the state would have to work with associations in order to jumpstart these flagging regional economies: the associations, however, would carry the banner of modernization.

For example, the Société Française d'Economie Alpestre articulated a vision of reciprocity between itself and the Eaux et Forêts after World War I. Founded in 1913, though not functioning until 1919, this association fashioned itself as an umbrella organization that would, in part, channel public funds for pastoral improvements in the Alps more effectively than had the state. Félix Briot, founder, retired Eaux et Forêts conservator, and vehement critic of the Restauration des terrains en montagne, was bound to offend some of his professional cohorts when he claimed that for the RTM, the era of major acquisitions and costly projects was over. But he praised the subsidies allocated under the 1882 law for pastoral improvements, though the state had not always distributed them wisely.[42] In any case, the rhetoric of modernization assured a ready ear in the national administration. A telling article in the society's journal from 1930 identifies the sorts of people who ought to be concerned about the alpine economy—industrialists with interests in hydroelectric power and secure communications, hoteliers trying to attract alpine tourists, and consumers in general who depend on various alpine products. It was for industrial, commercial, and consumer interests at large that the mountains should be tended. Briot, not coincidentally, had once promoted creameries in Hautes-Alpes and attributed the slackness of alpine dairying to communal pasturing.[43]

Such values were salient in a sister organization for the Pyrenees, the Fédération Pyrénéenne d'Economie Montagnarde. Briot himself was present at its founding moment in 1932, but Henri Gaussen inspired its formation. Gaussen's career combined botany, geography, cartography, and photography; he is best remembered for a stunning photographic history of the Pyrenees that stretches from 1900 to 1970. Gaussen attracted a who's who of French administration, industry, and tourism to the federation's *Comité d'Honneur*—high officials within the ministries of agriculture, interior, education, public works, commerce, and industry; chiefs of the Compagnie des Chemins de fer du Midi; and presidents of the Touring-Club and Club Alpin, not to mention academics from Toulouse, various chambers of commerce, and departmental *syndicats d'initiative*. In the first issue of the Federation's *Annales,* Gaussen plainly stated that officials of the Compagnie du Midi railroad had spearheaded the organization and that the company had a direct interest in the economic development of the Pyrenees.[44]

Echoes of the ACAM's pedagogical lessons can be heard in Gaussen's preliminary statement of the federation's role, to "coordinate efforts, give examples and advice." But both the Alpine and the Pyrenean association diverged in practice from the "soft" approach of Paul Descombes, in keeping with the powerful economic interests that backed them: assuming a will to modernize among the remaining peasantry, they sought to harness the alpine populations of France to the mores of the national economy by promoting competition. This strategy took shape as early as 1920 in the first *concours d'alpage* held in Haute-Savoie and sponsored by the Société Française d'Economie Alpestre. Sixteen contestants had to demonstrate efficiency in two general categories— "general management of alpine pastures" and "livestock, personnel, and productivity." Their farms ranged in size from 14 to 240 hectares and fell between 1,300 and 2,400 meters in altitude—typical alpine operations. The Société clearly buttered the event by awarding prizes, monetary awards ranging from three hundred to eight hundred francs, to all sixteen participants, and the prefect, senators, and deputies of Haute-Savoie were on hand to observe their distribution.[45] In subsequent years, competitions would be held in specific regions of Savoie, Haute-Savoie, and Isère, the société garnering departmental funding as well as the technical expertise of Eaux et Forêts personnel, who typically judged the competitions.

For its part, the Fédération Pyrénéenne inaugurated competitions in 1933, beginning with an alpine architecture contest. In this instance, contestants in both Hautes-Pyrénées and Haute-Garonne were to develop prototypes of Pyrenean chalets, traditional in style yet exhibiting high standards of hygiene and the use of electricity. The sort of chalet, in other words, to delight—and not offend—tourists. In the same year, the federation sponsored a competition in alpine agriculture and, most remarkably, one in teaching. The latter engaged female primary school teachers in a demonstration of their skills in teaching household management to girls. A description of the second-place winner for Ariège, one Mme Décamps, reveals the sorts of values that, in the eyes of foresters and their colleagues in civil society, were to inform the alpine peasant woman of the twentieth century. Madame Décamps received praise for her abilities to teach cooking, sewing, ironing . . . and horticulture and arboriculture to girls of post-elementary age.[46]

Through its departmental affiliate in Savoie, the Fédération Française de l'Economie Alpestre continued to sponsor pastoral competitions through 1937; by then, however, the Eaux et Forêts had reduced its subsidy of the event from an average of eight thousand to four thousand francs in 1936.[47] In the Pyrenees, Henri Gaussen's organization ceased to report on competitions in 1935 and had presumably stopped holding them. The real problem, however, was not financial: articles in each society's journal claimed, paradoxically, that traditional alpine life was in large part to blame for the decline of pastoralism. The incentive of competition could not remedy this state of affairs. Their analyses also unveil continuities in the Eaux et Forêts' own stance toward different alpine regions, as the reports of forest inspectors judging the competitions, such as François Rey in Savoie, demonstrate.

Decadence, insouciance, excessive individualism: old patterns and attitudes apparently revealed themselves once again. The Maurienne was "behind" the Tarentaise, the Pyrenees as a whole less advanced than the Alps. François Rey castigated pastoralism in the Maurienne as had foresters of earlier generations: "Excessive individualism is without doubt the principal obstacle to the progress of pastoralism in the Maurienne; it even happens that personal interest is sacrificed to it. Someone who might be disposed to improve a small zone of the commons abstains for fear that his neighbor will benefit; the installation of cables for the taking down of hay is still sometimes impeded by lack of understanding among the interested parties, or by the ill will of one of the proprietors situated furthest down [in elevation]."[48] Rey was referring of course to the petite montagne system of production in the Maurienne in which individual families exploited common pastures, contrary to the grande montagne pattern in the Tarentaise, marked by organized and fully communal management. Tellingly, neither Rey nor his successor Messines allowed their own data to contradict a damning analysis of the petite montagne system. Both foresters admitted, for example, that alpine villages in the Maurienne had suffered more from emigration and lower birth rates vis-à-vis the Tarentaise, the industrialized towns of the Arc Valley benefiting from the drainage of alpine youth. The result on the slopes overlooking the valley had been a return to extensive pasturing, neglected pastures, and little or no regulation of the numbers of animals on the alpages—a state of affairs summarized as "decadence." Rey even credited the more prosperous pastoral life of the Tarentaise largely to a law of 1920 that subsidized the renovation of commonly owned and managed alpine pastures: "Only the collective grande montagne escapes from the crisis [of personnel] thanks to the days of work the members impose on themselves and especially to the financial intervention of the state."[49] In other words, neither writer could argue convincingly that either "individualism" or "collectivism" had much to do with the state of pastoralism in the Maurienne and the Tarentaise, yet outdated images of the solitary and uncooperative highlander continued to blur reality.

By the late 1930s hopes of renewing pastoralism had given way utterly to a cold form of economism. Human abandonment would lead to natural reforestation, and reconstituted forests would attract tourists; tourism emerges as the likeliest means of salvation for the lingering upland population. The associations had once taken pains to distinguish their mission from the *dirigisme* of the state, yet they came to develop a similar conception of *aménagement du territoire*, without, however, matching the Eaux et Forêts' subtle accommodations with the alpine population (discussed in Chapter 5). As Briot, the forester and association founder, wrote in 1937, "Tourism and alpinism will make active life, movement, and well-being hold sway in the alpine regions. Such is the direction in which the highlander must orient himself, using with measure and discrimination, that is to say within the rules of ECONOMY, the goods (forest-pasture) that nature has put so generously at his disposition."[50]

Henri Gaussen articulated the same hope (or fate) for the Pyrenees. Writing of Ariège, he blamed the invasion of heath on degraded pastures on "economic upheaval, commercial folly, laziness, the desire for a broader life." Shepherds could not be counted on to reinvigorate the estives, but they would passively accept scientific improvements effected by outsiders. Gaussen's vision underscored the return to an interventionist approach to alpine ecology, but now to make Ariège fit for tourism. With depopulation abetting natural reforestation, foresters would have free reign to expedite the process. Though not a member of the corps himself, Gaussen urged the return of the foresters' old noblesse oblige: "The foresters are conscious of the nobility of their mission; they render services to the country and to the mountain, and are useful to the montagnard in spite of himself." Professional foresters had simply to keep the faith: "following the formula that [foresters] know well, since faith lifts up the mountains, it can also reforest them."[51]

This geographer who had lived in Ariège since the age of ten reasserted the familiar tropes: "As far as tourism, Ariège lags behind other parts of the Pyrenees, and all the Pyrenees are well behind Savoie, for example." Concretely, the outsider still needed sturdy *sabots* and "an insensitive sense of smell" when passing through Ariégeois villages. For though the inhabitants of the Jura, the Vosges, and Savoie had finally come to understand the proper relation between forests and pastures, the Pyreneans had not: the tragedy of the commons in this part of France had placed the pastoral economy "on the level of that in the Balkans."[52]

The associations' leading members had once recognized that the montagnards themselves would have to play a role in restoring and maintaining landscapes, however aesthetically irrelevant they and their villages were for alpine tourism. This pedagogic approach—whether in the form of education and fêtes de l'arbre, Paul Descombes' style of intervention, or sponsored competitions—had failed by the 1930s, and cynical economism reemerged, echoing older tendencies in the Eaux et Forêts. Yet the disquieting facts, repeated in the now-familiar refrains, continued to haunt professional and amateur foresters, for they implied a human and natural degradation beyond control. To assert that pastoral life in the Pyrenees was "on the level of that in the Balkans" not only underscored, for French people, the degree of ruination but also sounded a new note. Comparisons between France's forests and those in other parts of the world became a dissonant melody in associationist and state rhetoric from the late nineteenth century. These comparisons reveal a more fundamental reason for the failure of the associations than the supposed intractability of peasant mentalities: the discourse that swirled around the alpine peasant was based on unresolved contradictions. At once lazy and improvident (a venerable stereotype by the twentieth century), the alpine peasant suddenly appeared to possess the virtues of martial prowess and fecundity. Most important, an underlying anxiety about deforestation was located in an imperialist view of the world. To pick apart this tangled web of images requires, first, a detour to Algeria, the colony that became a potent reference point in French discussions of deforestation.

MEDITERRANEAN WORLDS

The modern forest history of Algeria began in 1848 with the first concession of land to a Parisian businessman; a statute of 1846 had made this possible by allowing the state to expropriate and transform collective property into state and private property. Forests were declared state property in 1851 and the Forest Code applied to them. David Prochaska underscores the poor fit between law and customary practice by rightly characterizing the code as "based on the assumption that forested areas were uninhabited" and that capitalist relations should govern all uses of the forest in Algeria as in France. In addition, the large concessions during the Second Empire of prime cork oak forest reflect an expropriation of Arabs and Berbers far more brutal than that of French peasants had ever been. Governments of the Third Republic did not alter the trend: between 1871 and 1919, Muslims in Algeria lost access to 7.5 million hectares. No other pretext was needed beyond the state's commercial interest in granting land to concessionnaires. These developments paralleled the growing authority of the Algerian forest service. In stages, the forestry corps secured a jurisdiction separate from that of the military and civilian authorities alike, and the corps became integrated with the metropolitan Administration des Forêts in 1881.[53]

Conflict over the Algerian forests erupted in the early 1880s when structural grievances combined with more recent provocations. The application of the Forest Code had led to skyrocketing violations and costly fines; the advent of phylloxera in France had already caused the clearing of Algerian land for vineyards to accelerate; and the French army had just conquered Tunisia in 1881. Whereas Arabs and Berbers had organized armed resistance to French settlers earlier in the century, that impossible solution had since been discarded in favor of litigation and petitioning, on one hand, and an intensified use of fire, on the other. The conflagration of 1881, possibly the worst in Algerian history, scorched nearly 170,000 hectares, mostly in heavily forested Constantine province. In the years to come, the French government would ascribe most "intentional" fires to *kçar*, the practice of burning forest and brush to clear land for new pasture; the criminalization of kçar can be seen in the heavy fines and further confiscations of land that issued from the government's harsh standard of collective responsibility. The penalties Algerians paid were harsher than those suffered by French peasants, even though the same Forest Code supposedly applied to Algeria.[54] But a parallel rhetoric linked French and Algerian pastoralists in an apparently common culture of insouciance and neglect. Echoes of the older, scathing assessment of the alpine peasants of France can be heard in the vexed appeal to Algerians by one Dr. Trolard, a settler who had founded the League for the Reforestation of Algeria in 1883. Written in both French and Arabic, his pamphlet of that year titled *La Forêt: Conseils aux indigènes* betrayed a hyperbolic and paternalistic style (using the familiar "tu" form of "you" throughout) as it admonished Algerians to respect "the trees of your neighbors and those of the state." Like their French counterparts, Algerian peasants had continued the wasteful ways of their ancestors, lighting pastoral fires (kçar), cutting inefficiently, and grazing goats with their "murderous teeth" in the forest. Despite his mini-lesson on the correlation between forest and regular rainfall, Trolard made a more ominous linkage between France's mantle of forest and strict enforcement of the Forest Code, promising the same for Algeria.[55] Though a softer pedagogy might now be appropriate for the French peasant, repression would continue to take center stage in the colony.

It was an Ariégeois politician and longtime critic of French forestry, Hippolyte Doumenjou, who brought the double standard to perfection. Also writing in 1883, Doumenjou argued within the same short work for the revision of the Forest Code in France and its tightening in Algeria. Reforestation, no longer necessary in France, would make Algeria more like the metropole, and this would bring positive social change (forests would allow native Algerians to become sedentary farmers), political benefits (forests, of course, help inculcate patriotism), and even diplomatic advantages (better to rely on Algeria than on "doubtful" European allies). This mission, already accomplished in France, simply had to be carried across the Mediterranean; as Doumenjou explained in a dazzlingly transparent statement typical of his age, "In Algeria, reforestation is the indispensable condition of colonization."[56]

There was a certain urgency attached to Doumenjou's bold statement, for he went on to describe Algeria as "an admirable colony, almost at our doors." The proximity of Algeria to France was perhaps one of the most troubling features of the colonial relationship, certainly the one that most informed anxieties over deforestation. Trolard, in a florid appeal to the French Senate in 1893, marshaled nearly one hundred quotations from a pantheon of luminaries, including Sully and Chateaubriand, as well as contemporary foresters, politicians, and other self-proclaimed experts on the forest question. If there is a refrain running through Trolard's *La Question forestière algérienne,* it is that deforestation will transform "the Algerian Tell [into] a prolongation of the Sahara," the Tell being the well-watered coastal zones of North Africa, marked by a succession of mountain ranges punctuated by valleys. If the spectre of deforestation were hovering over "France overseas," then might not the northward progress of devastation leapfrog the Mediterranean? If the Tell could become the prolongation of the Sahara, then why not the French Alps, Pyrenees, and Midi as well? Trolard quoted the ominous words of Adolphe Blanqui. This political economist, brother of the anarchist Auguste Blanqui, had noted in an 1840 work titled *Rapport sur l'Algérie,* "devastation takes giant steps."[57]

Michael Osborne, in his study of the acclimatization of exotic plant species in Algeria, outlines the fearsome economic dimensions of the colony's proximity to France. "To make matters worse," he writes, "the two countries grew even closer as the century progressed" owing to technical advances in transportation and communication; the reality, by 1890, that tomatoes could be shipped from Algiers and arrive in Marseilles markets on the same day, gracing Parisian tables the next, posed obvious threats to certain agricultural interests in France.[58] But in forestry circles, the presumed deforestation of Algeria *and its northward creep* surpassed economic or political concerns. By the early twentieth century, it had begun to take on mythic proportions. Rhetoric emanating from associations, in particular, reached a high pitch as it linked theories of ancient and contemporary deforestation to Algerians and, finally, to French highlanders.

Although many writers limited their anxiety over deforestation to thoughts of France's future, their visions maintained a necessary referent: the deforested parts of the world. An irrefutable equation pitted forested lands and civilization, on one hand, against deserts and barbarism on the other.[59] And history could move in one direction only: forests might become deserts, but not vice versa. Some called attention to desertified regions where contemporary cultures apparently struggled to survive: S. Guénot of the Geographical Society of Toulouse had warned in 1899 that the Pyrenees could be brought to the state of Greece, Dalmatia, Palestine, Cyprus, and Central Africa. For the Touring-Club, deforestation and the consequent fall of civilization were most apparent in Sicily, Mauritania, North Africa, and Spain.[60] Just as cultural decline could always be imputed to deforestation, the latter always led to the former.

Facile equations between ancient deforestation and the decline of cultures also became popular, as in this typical formulation from the *Courrier des Bois,* a technical journal of the wood industry: "Forests are indispensable to man and to civilization. Their disappearance precedes by little the decline, then the death of empires. It is in the middle of sandy, rocky deserts that we look today for the ruins of Babylon, Niniveh, Tyre, Sidon, and Carthage. With the last tree, the last man disappears."[61] Trolard's compilation of French wisdom on the forest question similarly warned of desiccation and siltation that would result from deforestation, as it had in the ancient past at various points around the Mediterranean world. Interestingly, the deforestation of Algeria was consistently depicted as very recent and ongoing, with rarely a hint of the ancient catastrophe that had beset North African ecosystems as a consequence of their designation as granary for the imperial capital, Rome. J. R. McNeill has shown that in five Mediterranean regions, deforestation and erosion did accelerate, if unevenly, during the nineteenth and twentieth centuries; however, in the colonial Maghreb "commercial agriculture played a large role in destroying forests over areas wider than the needs of the local population would have done."[62] This sort of assessment never figured in French debates about the Algerian forest question; instead, erroneous theories of the unprecedented, solely peasant-driven deforestation of Algeria bore no small resemblance to those applied to alpine France in the nineteenth century. In the Algerian case, the theory had special uses that, by a circuitous route, would lead back to the French montagnard.

It should by now be clear that cries of alarm over the burning forests of France's oldest and closest colony could be used to further the colonizing mission. But Algeria's "fateful" proximity, entropic decline toward desert, and recent deforestation formed a bundle of assumptions that made integrating an empire—in this case, managing both the forests of the metropole and the deserts and scrublands of the colonies—a supremely difficult task. If France was not to be remade into Algeria, nothing less than a conversion of the French montagnard was needed; civilization's fate lay in his hands. The pedagogic mission, then, acquired astonishingly high stakes. For the associations, two possible narratives hung in the balance: the declensionist story of deforestation and decline, or a story of recovery that told of the transformation of alpine France, allowing forests to flourish through modernized pastoralism, tourism, or industrialization.

But could this be achieved given the situation in Algeria? In 1930 the director of forests for Algeria, V. Boutilly, cited the yearly value of fines imposed on native pastoralists for forest crimes as upwards of 3 million francs. Boutilly justified this enormous sum in the high tones reminiscent of administrative responses to forest crimes in Ariège a century earlier: "if one realizes that most of the deliquents are incorrigible recidivists and that the number of crimes is not diminishing, one will be obliged to deduce that this repression is not sinning through excessive severity."[63] Such an identification of an unregenerate land and people was clearly not without precedent; that this language had long been part of the Eaux et Forêts' rhetorical arsenal has a double importance. For one, its displacement from a French to an Algerian context suggested that the forest question in Algeria was crystal clear: it was all a matter of repressing criminal uses of the land. By contrast, questions concerning the alpine forests of France and the place of highlanders in the nation had become murky. If soft pedagogy gave way to the repressive impulse in practice by the 1930s, it was also because older discourses had long since returned through the back door. In brief, the French highlander could show a dangerous resemblance to colonial pastoralists. Spokespersons for the associations (with their many state connections) came face to face with elements shared between two pastoral Mediterranean cultures. They could not name their discovery as such, however, and their rhetoric ultimately sank under a weight of contradiction as they oscillated between unidimensional views of the highlander as either vicious or virtuous: such blatant contradiction was partly responsible for foiling the associations' efforts at alpine regeneration.

Typical of many foresters who joined associations, A. Fron, analyst of the Restauration des terrains en montagne, wrote of pastoralism in his 1907 *Economie sylvo-pastorale* as follows: it "appears today, such as it is practiced, as the negation of the civilized state and as the residue of destroyed populations."[64] Agreeing that contemporary pastoralism was barbaric, most writers identified alpine people as the destroyers rather than the destroyed. Though hardly born in the twentieth century, this rhetoric became more virulent as certain peasants were seen as behaving more "anachronistically." Even Lucien-Albert Fabre, a forester in some ways sympathetic to the peasants' interests, wrote easily of their "pillaging, ravaging instincts."[65]

Even analyses that granted the alpine peasant a more complex psychology beyond "instinct" proved hardly more charitable. Writings on the alpine peasant from the Association Centrale pour l'Aménagement des Montagnes show how little the organization's key members altered assumptions in the course of twenty years. Paul Descombes, for all of his, at times, astute linking of "pastoral prosperity" to healthy forests, located the most intractable problem in the peasants' "insouciance," a word he was fond of: once this "problem" was solved, "all the others will disappear as if by enchantment." Descombes also echoed the common nineteenth-century premise that peasants lived only in the present, unconcerned for the future, and unaware that they suffered from the "insouciance" of their ancestors.[66] Approximately two decades later, Count Roquette-Buisson, ACAM member and former prefect and paymaster-general of the Treasury, identified the causes of deforestation as improvidence, nonchalance, and ignorance. He proclaimed that the logic of pastoralism itself was based upon a moral failing: shepherds extended their alpine pastures because, being lazy, they found it easier to keep watch over sheep on treeless land. This, too, was the Touring-Club's rendition of alpine shepherds, men who preferred to lounge and "watch the clouds run" rather than execute small tasks to improve the pastures.[67]

Stereotyping of this sort could also arise from ideas of race. In the writing of

Pierre Buffault, a so-called social forester connected to the ACAM, alpine peasants consisted of subgroups that together formed a racial category. The southern location of the Alps, the Pyrenees, and the Cévennes provided a convenient alibi for claiming affinities between the French alpine peasant and the Arab shepherd, whose laziness needed no elaboration: "In particular, in our three great alpine regions, the Alps, the Cévennes and the Pyrenees, we must deal with populations whose apathy and more than southern, quasi-Arab, carelessness, [are] one of the characteristics of the race." The "Béarnais," the "Catalan," and other subcategories within the Pyrenean "race" all shared a preference for contemplation over work, exhibiting nonchalance in their daily activities. Above all, they regarded their grasses and forests as their limitless, collective property.[68] In other cases, racial stereotyping could be casually mixed with environmentalist arguments about character, as in this depiction from the *Courrier des Bois* in 1924: "In the North, man, struggling against all the vicissitudes of existence, loves and respects the woods and forests. It is different with the man of the Midi, whose existence is easier, who feeds himself with less work, and who carries in himself the hatred of woods and forests."[69] Whether emphasizing biological fixity or shifting adaptations to environment, these commentators drew from a stock of peasant stereotypes that had served to stabilize a social order since at least the First Empire.[70]

Embedded in race, environment, or some combination of the two, certain characteristics of the alpine peasantry seemed as static to these twentieth-century writers as they had to many in the nineteenth. To return to an earlier point, foresters and association spokespersons of the early twentieth century had proclaimed the possibility of changing character through benign instruction. Weighing the limitations of the old statist approach to alpine restoration—acting upon the land under the assumption that people would comply—they made peasants themselves the object of action. Thus would the "vicious" alpine peasant be redeemed. Contradiction came with an opposite set of anxieties that competed quite well with fears over the degradation of the mountains. Here a construction of the "virtuous" peasant placed alpine peoples at the center of many debates over France's declining birth rate and the physical "decadence" of the French. Depictions of alpine peasants as sources of national regeneration drew as much upon the vocabulary of race as did portraits of alpine barbarism. The amplitude of these debates grew full enough to catapult the upland population of France into a battle over stereotypes. Insouciant and destructive on one hand, but fecund and robust on the other, the marginal highlander stood in a web of conflicting images.

A dominant theme in the case for the alpine peasant was the purported connection between alpine fertility and pastoralism. This theme had already been sounded in the context of local politics; the Ariégeois Hippolyte Doumenjou argued in 1877 that pastoralism engendered early marriages; the state would drain this fount of population (not to mention morality and piety) by covering pastures with trees.[71] Doumenjou's argument, voiced at a time when falling birth rates were just beginning to become a source of national woe, could be dismissed for its obvious political purpose. But by the early twentieth century, alpine depopulation had continued apace and could no longer be so easily accepted as a beneficial, civilizing trend. Consequently, the myth of the fertile alpine family assumed grander dimensions, and Doumenjou's hypothesis linking the large alpine family to pastoralism received sophisticated support. Anxious now to rehabilitate these peasants, "social" foresters and associations designated both alpine degradation (whose agency they did not discuss) and expropriation by the state as the root causes of permanent emigration from the mountains.

The argument for keeping alpine peasants in the mountains because of their fertility is best examined in a brief foray into demographic history. Well before 1900, peasants had begun to leave the mountains in large numbers; demographic trajectories in part lay behind emigration but were in turn affected by it. As seen in Chapter 1, Pyrenean departments reached their maxima of population before 1850. Epidemics of cholera, smallpox, typhoid, and lung infections weakened the population and spurred emigration in the 1840s and 50s. Relative to the nation, however, death rates dropped precociously before the nineteenth century ended, and marriage and birth rates quickly fell into line: for the whole nineteenth century, rates of death, natality, and nuptiality in three of the four major Pyrenean departments remained nearly consistently below national averages. Although regional and national death rates revealed the largest disparity before 1830, emigration further eroded the birth rate and reduced population growth in most of the Pyrenees after mid-century. Pyrénées-Orientales, with its high birth and death rates, provided the exception. Further, as Jean-François Soulet has shown for the Pyrenees as a whole, the foothills and middle-altitude regions—areas whose economies had diversified beyond pastoralism—had witnessed the greatest rise in human numbers in the earlier part of the century.[72]

The Alps had undergone a similar, though later and less dramatic, demographic transition during the nineteenth century. Pier Paolo Viazzo, whose work integrates the results of the Princeton European Fertility Project, concludes that fertility over the whole Alpine crescent declined to a moderate level after 1850. If marital fertility remained high in the uppermost valleys in the French Alps even after World War II, so did permanent celibacy (a partial effect of emigration); crude birth rates remained the same or lower there than in lower valleys.[73] At the time of annexation, birth and death rates in Savoie significantly surpassed French averages; the death rate fell noticeably only after 1880, and the birth rate also fell into line with the rest of France by 1900, reaching the low rate of 19.7 births per thousand in 1910–13. As in the Pyrenees, population had, in the early nineteenth century, grown more rapidly in the lower areas of Savoie, not in the alpine zones.[74]

Thus, demographic evidence does not point to remarkable alpine fertility in the early twentieth century, nor to a correlation between pastoralism and a population that reproduced itself. Indeed, few could deny the toll that emigration of the young had taken on alpine birth rates. But "social" foresters and association leaders held to the assumption that if only further emigration could be stopped, then the old demographic regime could be restored along with the vegetation and volatile soils of the slopes. The invariable coupling of these two kinds of restoration suggests an ulterior motive behind the argument for population: the unorthodox thought that the presence of peasants was vital to alpine restoration might borrow some of the odd credibility of the fertility myth if the two were simply juxtaposed. The first part of this equation did foreshadow subsequent thinking in the administration, as discussed in the conclusion. In the earlier part of the twentieth century, though, the decline of alpine populations and land degradation appeared as two inextricable sides of the same coin.

Both peasants, the vicious and the virtuous, can be seen for example in the arguments of Paul Descombes of the ACAM. Renewed pastoralism combined with popular silviculture would keep the mountains intact, while reforestation that was sensitive to local interests could be cast as social policy: "[Reforestation is] the only means of conserving a sane and vigorous population of more than a million highlanders, which is decreasing with a distressing rapidity."[75] And this followed by only a few paragraphs Descombes' castigation of his subjects' insouciance. In 1907 Descombes underscored the social crisis of alpine emigration and the dire connection between cultural and natural degradation: "All cities and all departments are equally interested in maintaining the mountains' land and population, if only to reduce the exodus of highlanders, the inevitable consequences of which include their accumulation in cities, the saturation of the work sites, the plethora of hospitals and the added burden upon public assistance. The unleashed vengeance of the mountain shows that all general and

particular interests must unite to check the ruin of the plains and the unconscious suicide of the highlanders."[76]

The writings of the forester Lucien-Albert Fabre provide a variation on the
theme of social crisis by relating alpine emigration to colonization—both *by*
French peasants and *of* their places of origin. Fabre's numerous pamphlets
blended outrage over alpine depopulation, deforestation, and the presence of
foreigners in the mountains of France. The greatest absurdity, for Fabre, lay in
the transfer of people between France and North Africa. Again that unsettling
proximity: alpine peasants left with hopes of obtaining cheap or free land in Algeria, while Algerians were coming to replace the alpine *chasseurs* in the French
army. The laws of adaptation proved the foolishness of the pattern: "This
magic transfer of arms adapted for centuries to their labors, to climates, and to
environments entirely dissimilar, this swap as bold as it is ironic, between the
inhabitants of our snowy alpages and those of the torrid bush of Africa, seems
brilliant in the administrative spheres of the *Grande* and the *Petite Patrie*. This
is the magic key to the triple impasse—pastoral, colonial, and electoral."[77]

In this "double and violent uprooting" Fabre criticized both the state's expropriation of land from French peasants and confiscation of land from "Arabs
guilty of having defended their possessions with too much tenacity." But his
defense of the Algerian stopped there; Fabre marshaled theories of "adaptation"
largely to express his worry over the increasing Algerian presence in the army.
The loss of a native alpine population meant the loss of proverbially good soldiers (similar in quality to Swiss and Scottish highlanders); it was not "from the
black army, certainly excellent in Africa where it is 'adapted,' that we will ever
ask the services that the country awaits from the white army of the alpine corps,
recruited among our montagnards."[78] But Fabre reserved his most biting
racism for the Spanish and Italian shepherds in the mountains of France, evoking images that others continued to deploy in criticizing French shepherds: "we
estimate that the first task to pursue is to expel the parasites from the mountains
and the montagnards—the transhumants, beasts and people, these maleficent
tramps of pastoralism, who are unable to root themselves anywhere."[79] "Root-
edness" was, of course, becoming less and less characteristic of the French montagnards themselves, yet Fabre clung to the myth of the alpine family to express
this very loss, accentuating Le Play's now supremely appropriate metaphor of
the tree that founded the concept of "stem family." What had deforestation and
expropriation brought but "the rapid atrophy of most of the stem families
which are now deprived of their youngest branches, the most vivacious, the
most apt to perpetuate the taking of root"?[80]

By contrast, a final passage from Lucien-Albert Fabre illustrates the ambivalence toward the presence of people in the forest felt by this forester, writer for the CAF's *La Montagne,* and supporter of associationist pedagogy. The passage reveals Fabre's politics and the influence of Le Play and strongly suggests the science of ecology's inheritance of old social metaphors, especially in its early twentieth-century focus on "communities" and "assemblages"; his words also imply that though the forest is essentially social, it contains a society of life forms excluding human beings. Fabre was, in any case, more eloquent in depicting this kind of forest than the harmonious sylvo-pastoral world that otherwise preoccupied him:

> In the heart of forests, a multitude of infinitesimal and ephemeral plants, bacteria, saprophytes, cryptogams, vegetate on or in the soil, under the powerful dome that the privileged class of trees develops; this proletarian mass lives in mutual benefit with the ligneous aristocracy which shelters it. Certainly, this "social" milieu has nothing of the equality that was the ideal of Plato and those who, in his wake, take interest in the same chimeras. Nature, wiser and more cooperative, assures the endurance of vegetal associations: the humble micorrhizae and the majestic tree live in perpetual and necessary symbiosis; they defy time and the elements, on a soil always *protected* and fertilized, where the profuse and salubrious waters are automatically stored in order to assure the indefinite prosperity of the "association," and the easy life of he who exploits it.[81]

The human comes in only at the end, as an individual "exploiter," whereas the real society lies in the forest, in its nature. Between these two poles, there is little room for the society of peasants.

Fabre's writings crystallize the hand-wringing over alpine depopulation, the real and symbolic costs of the colonial mission, and the fundamental ambivalence toward all pastoral peoples. This is not to suggest that all the players in this chapter labored under precisely the same contradictions, but it is at least clear that private associations did not contribute a great deal of coherence to discussions of the "forest question." If there is some continuity to this varied discourse, it might be that these spokespersons had reached beyond the limited concept of deforestation and seized upon the more troubling notion of desertification. A loss of vegetation and a loss of humanity were now seen as part of the same process, named desertification and signaling the demise of civilization. After all, as the Larousse etymological dictionary tells us, *désert* comes from the Latin *desertus,* meaning "abandoned."[82] The French obsession with deserts played into the larger obsession with national decline, so acute in the supposed Belle Epoque when it was Germany that possessed the military edge, the demographic edge, and the lush, homogeneous coniferous forests. For certain, France lay somewhere between Germany and North Africa.

But the most enduring legacy of the associations in alpine France has to do with urban appropriation. Whether one takes the ACAM's Leçons de choses or the ANIB's Fête de l'arbre, it is, to borrow Nicholas Green's words, a particular urban "mode of apprehension, both of the world and of oneself" that shines through the associations' efforts.[83] This mode of apprehension derived, in most cases, not from local knowledge of the mountains but rather from a textbook view of the ideal alpine landscape existing in the interests of the bourgeoisie. In a short pamphlet detailing the geography, climate, and vegetation of the Pyrenees for the benefit of members of the Club Alpin Français, Henri Gaussen, Ariégeois though he was, implicitly celebrated the depopulation of the Pyrenees: "one of the charms of the Pyrenees is that there one can find pure and smiling nature."[84]

On one level, associational activities depended (like Green's *natura naturans*) on the peasants' disappearance as active, thinking agents. Private initiatives in forestry and pastoral improvements thus echoed the promotion of tourism; the Touring-Club neatly spans these complementary tendencies. The montagnard might be useful to the tourist, but only if he fulfilled arduous requirements; otherwise, his insalubrious villages might be a hazard to the mountain climber and skier. As early as 1881, for example, the Tarentaise (Savoie) section of the Club Alpin Français published a set of regulations stipulating the minimal qualifications for mountain guides. To become a guide in the Tarentaise, one had to be a native of the valley or of the Beaufort or Flumet valleys, be at least twenty-one years old and of robust complexion, exercise all civil and political rights, be able to "justify one's good behavior," know how to read and write, and know the names of all passes and summits in the region; finally, one had to have already made several ascents. Though findable, this type was hardly typical of the average Savoyard peasant in the 1880s. And aside from the rare hotel keeper whose establishment lived up to alpinists' standards, the sorts of people one was most likely to find in the mountains had become superfluous and irrelevant to the needs of tourists.[85]

On another level, associations had to reckon with the montagnard once they developed deeper interests in preservation and restoration. In the end, alpine people were liberated from associational agendas through both their own reticence toward didacticism and a contradictory discourse about them that neutralized any possibility of a single-minded, rationalizing project. A glimmer of understanding lay in the linkage of cultural and natural degradation; unfortunately, bourgeois contempt for alpine people lent artificiality to the alarm over alpine desertification. Many montagnards did, of course, leave, but whatever else it shows, emigration also illustrates autonomous action in the face of objectification. By the same token, the lives of those who stayed hardly remained static in the first decades of the twentieth century. Although it would be foolish to deny the impacts of tourism on alpine France, those impacts have had regional specificity. Following concluding remarks, a final consideration of Ariégeois and Savoyard trajectories is in order.

Conclusion

I went then with a tranquil step to look for some wild place in the forest, some deserted place where nothing showing the hand of man would be a sign of servitude and domination.
—*Jean-Jacques Rousseau*

Nothing is more beautiful than a tree, Alain Le Goff likes to say. The poor man does not possess a single tree of his own, but all those that he can see with his eyes are his partners in Creation's great game.
—*Pierre-Jakez Hélias*

In Jean Giono's fable *The Man Who Planted Trees*, the reforestation of a broad upland area, "where the Alps thrust down into Provence," brings ecological and social health to a forsaken landscape. The effort is individual and silent, the agent unknown to most of the thousands of people who ultimately benefit from it: a shepherd named Elzéard Bouffier collects acorns and beechnuts, sorting and planting them decade after decade, experimenting with birch later in life. He is a man connected to neither community nor state, motivated only by a "magnificent generosity."[1]

Bouffier's forests have a magical beauty; they are so seemingly "natural" that a state forester mistakes them for a spontaneous growth. Beginning in 1910, Bouffier has planted a forest of approximately eleven by three kilometers by the end of World War I. His young trees cause water to flow through once-arid hills. The shepherd continues his silent work. With the forests, signs of social regeneration appear: people come to reoccupy and restore abandoned villages, such as Vergons, an alpine hamlet. From a population of three people in 1913, Vergons grows to twenty-eight by 1945. People have moved up from the plains, "bringing youth, motion, the spirit of adventure." Two world wars have passed and provided the counterpoint to regeneration: Bouffier shows off clumps of birch that he planted while the narrator was fighting in Verdun; he is even oblivious to the brief threat to his forests posed by the prevalence of wood-burning generators in cars during the second war. "The shepherd had seen nothing of it. He was thirty kilometers away, peacefully continuing his work, ignoring the war of '39 as he had ignored that of '14."[2]

Giono does allow the state and peasants to appear in some familiar ways, and his portrayal accentuates the positive. The state, fittingly, appropriates Bouffier's forests, but officials recognize a good thing: "In 1935 a whole delegation came from the Government to examine the 'natural forest.' There was a high official from the Forest Service, a deputy, technicians. There was a great deal of ineffectual talk. It was decided that something must be done and, fortunately, nothing was done except the only helpful thing: the whole forest was placed under the protection of the State, and charcoal burning prohibited. For it was impossible not to be captivated by the beauty of those young trees in the fullness of health, and they cast their spell over the deputy himself." Giono portrays villages of a few charcoal makers, whose communities languish prior to Bouffier's miracle. Living rude lives and driven to violence by penury and isolation, these people nevertheless transform themselves in response to their renewed land; the "former population" become "unrecognizable now that they live in comfort."[3] Canaan has replaced the desolate uplands.

Jean Giono's story proves the mythical possibilities of reforestation, as powerful as those of deforestation. The historical version of reforestation in France neither begins with total desolation nor ends with Canaan. It is striking that none of this history echoes in *The Man Who Planted Trees*—there is no technocratic vision of rationalized landscape, *territoire aménagé*; no contestation between the state and communities; no financial or technical vicissitudes in the Eaux et Forêts; no rural people reclaiming possession through many strategies. Nor do we find a discussion of public utility in Giono's tale, for no "public" is involved in reforestation, just Elzéard Bouffier and his seeds.

Far from containing a myth of regeneration, the history of alpine restoration in France finds an ambiguous place between the two common narrative structures in environmental history—progress and declension. Environmental historians have recognized the mostly declensionist tendency of their field, parallel but not equivalent to the declensionism in environmentalist discourse. Histories of ecological restoration would seem to fall outside of this dilemma: no matter how limited or misguided in perspective, acts of restoration, rigorously defined, must carry seeds of renewal. But such histories should also address what may be a more fundamental question in environmental history: the question of social and cultural differences in humanity's relations to nature. Just as environmental degradation carries strong social components, so do acts of restoration, yet the full import of these components cannot be grasped without attention to the meanings ascribed to nature. A key to synthesis in environmental history may lie in questions that address meaning, such as those proposed by William Cronon: "What do people care most about in the world they inhabit? How do they use and assign meaning to that world? . . . How do people struggle with each other for control of the earth, its creatures, and its meanings?"[4]

To France's peripheral mountains, state officials ascribed meanings that remained stable through the nineteenth century and into the twentieth. A mountain "at risk" and posing threats to lowland areas had become a controlling image by the early nineteenth century; policies grounded in this perception held upland and lowland in strict opposition to each other. Early Third Republic legislators restrained the image by focusing concern on specific areas of "evident and present danger." Yet, as I have argued, foresters chafed under the limitations that recognition of only localized danger placed on their work; at times violating the restoration law of 1882, they ultimately won an amendment that vindicated the older perception of global risk. Their logic incorporated new metaphors evoking human illness: images of "open wounds" date from at least the 1870s, and the mutilation of both people and trees in World War I added further resonance to the idea of sickness. In language that became banal, foresters criticized local and temporary "cures" and called for "prevention" that would take the whole alpine organism into account.

"Mountain," for rural society in both the Alps and the Pyrenees, indicated high-altitude pastures, but peasants perceived their alpine habitat less as a series of juxtaposed spaces (cultivated fields, forest, pastures) than as land modeled by overlapping practices, primarily farming and pasturing. Whereas juxtaposed spaces, like tire-et-aire forest management, lent themselves to demarcation by property lines, overlapping practices within a large space, like jardinage, corresponded to possession in the sense of both communal property and use rights.

This complex and humanized mountain lost ground, literally, to a process of pseudo-naturalization: in defining the mountain by its protective role, the RTM envisioned and, in many places, created a rationally forested and engineered mountain. Forester-engineers channeled torrents away from their banks by means of elegant masonry barriers, drained excess water from slopes, shored up dry ravines against the gushing waters of the future, and planted forests sometimes at higher elevations than trees could grow. In other words, they fashioned "nature" with artificial props. Unlike some critics of restoration ecology who accuse the entire undertaking of "faking nature," I find reason in Alan McQuillan's defense that a restored ecosystem may well become "capable of adapting to changing environmental conditions in an evolutionary process so as to maintain its identity without collapse."[5] The moral problem, rather, at the heart of restoration in France was its exclusion of alpine society; indeed, it became a practical problem as well for the Eaux et Forêts, for it beckoned contestation.[6]

The advent of alpine tourism reinforced the peasantry's erasure: in France as in the United States, the logic of outdoor recreation demanded that indigenous inhabitants be pushed aside, or transformed, in the search for pure "nature." Fledgling tourists' associations adopted older problematics, outsiders' anxieties over agro-pastoralism and deforestation; Eaux et Forêts officials became prominent on their councils and committees. Before the mountain could be "naturalized" for climbers, hikers, and skiers, associations spent much energy and initiative exorcising the demon of deforestation by trying to change the behavior of alpine peasants. For several decades after 1900, uneasy combinations of criticism, solicitude, condescension, and racism colored the objectifications of uplanders by bourgeois civil society. The latter's achievements, however, remained largely rhetorical.

Tourists and their associations construed the mountain as a place of leisure, but they did not radically question the process of pseudo-naturalization launched by the state. Official and vernacular meanings of the mountains related to each other through contestation over the meaning of public utility. Although policies of reforestation followed by restoration consummated, in theory, a long-term shift from communal to state management of alpine forests, the state still had to reckon with communes and seek their cooperation. Stated otherwise, the politics of restoration forced the state to include a largely peasant population within the "public" of public utility. Even if peasants could not be persuaded to "love trees" in the same way as foresters trained at Nancy, they had to be convinced that restoration, in whatever guise, lay in their interests. Spokespersons for private associations articulated this before the Eaux et Forêts did, though it was from the state that alpine communes won compromise. Through the regrassing law of 1864, améliorations pastorales (notwithstanding its limited success), pasturing concessions in the 1920s and 30s, the maintenance of use rights, and other gains, inhabitants of the upland communes made a forced entry into the public sphere originally formulated to exclude them.

The case studies in this book center deliberately on communes that resisted meanings and agendas coming from the state. Though Massat and Jarrier may be less than representative in the successes they achieved, they are fully representative of the multicolored palette of politics that rural communes used to safeguard the material and symbolic value of their resources. The two cases reveal different sections of a political spectrum: Jarriens did not turn the struggle over the commune's portion of the Lower Arc perimeter (a project, it is important to repeat, that would have confiscated nearly all of the inhabitants' communal and private pastures) into an electoral battle, unlike their expression of differences over secular education in the same years. Instead, they clandestinely destroyed seedlings and markers, and they manipulated land prices. By contrast, in a long-standing conflict over possession, residents of the rural hamlets of Massat, Biert, and Le Port marshaled tactics that included popular revolt, intimidation, mass meetings, electoral politics, and the manipulation of private property. It would be artificial to classify the case of Jarrier as "resistance" and that of Massat as "politics." They were both political struggles, a notion that acquires far more power as a fundamental category of human life if it is broadened to include all strategies by which groups of people defend their vital interests.

French peasants had far to go in making their voices heard by the representatives of a managerial culture that had great resources at its disposal. The state has, of course, remained intimately involved in the urban appropriation of the mountain; if anything, the whole history of restoration puts the state at the forefront of the trend. As Gérard Collomb has noted, urban representations of alpine landscapes continue to form the basis of management plans largely conceived for the benefit of tourists, "an urban population led to look for and consume at once the resources of this nature and the images of these [alpine] societies."[7] For its part, the RTM has provided essential tools for the transition from an agricultural to a touristic economy in Savoie; founded to protect lowland agriculture, cities, and navigable rivers, the RTM now serves the interests of tourists, who are more exacting of the state and less patient with mud, blocked roads, and avalanches than were peasants. In recent years, the overburdened and underfunded RTM has begun a campaign to return primary responsibility for "the system of protection" to rural communes.[8]

The historical irony attached to the RTM's increasing reliance on rural communes parallels one sequel to restoration—the story of French national parks. A brief evocation of this story reveals, as well, a final contrast between Ariège and Savoie. Created in 1963, Savoie's National Park of the Vanoise became the first such entity conforming to the 1960 charter for national parks; covering more than fifty-six thousand hectares, it encompasses most of the Vanoise range between the Tarentaise and Maurienne Valleys. The Touring-Club and Club Alpin Français originally sponsored the project, and the mayor of Bonneval-sur-Arc, Gilbert André (a CAF member), carried it forward in the 1950s and left a strong imprint on its outcome: of equal importance to the protection of nature, cultural and recreative roles figured prominently in the decreed purposes of the park. More broadly, Denys Pradelle, the ministry of construction's *chargé de mission* for the Vanoise initiative, explained the park as a unifying framework for "agriculture, tourism, artisanal activity, [and] national educational establishments."[9] The 1960 charter allowed the creation of vast peripheral zones around national parks; in the case of the Vanoise, the zone includes all or portions of twenty-nine communes. Unlike the purported ecological buffer zones formed by national forests ringing national parks in the United States, this area was to be the object of economic and cultural development in order to facilitate access to the park, provide amenities, and (primarily or incidentally, depending on the spokesperson) develop the alpine economy.

In effect, the decline of pastoralism has oriented development almost exclusively toward tourism. And though supporters of the Vanoise and other parks recognize the alpages as central to the ecological heritage of France's alpine peripheries, their maintenance has not only been rendered difficult by the dwindling numbers of pastoralists, but the *purpose* of their maintenance—like that of forests and wildlife—has been cast as the interest of urban tourists. As one report on the park has proclaimed, "it is necessary to conserve the ecological capital which urbanites need more and more."[10] In this optic, the remaining peasants have become vital "gardeners of the mountain." As a further irony, a law passed in 1972 grants subsidies to owners of *vaches tondeuses*, "shearing cows," whose munching of alpine grasses has gained official recognition for helping to prevent avalanches: longer, ungrazed grasses provide slicker surfaces for masses of moving snow. Avalanches, of course, primarily threaten skiers and their resorts. With respect to the long-term economic benefits of tourism to alpine communes, Collomb's evidence from Lanslebourg and Lanslevillard in the upper Maurienne suggests that the national park, at any rate, remains peripheral to local economic and cultural life. In the Southern Alps as well, evidence from the early 1970s showed a similar pattern of "modernization without development," or investment in tourism that largely bypassed local needs.[11]

Whereas Savoyard communes have lived with high expectations and mixed judgments of the National Park of the Vanoise, the Ariégeois fully rejected plans for a National Park of Ariège. Formally proposed only in 1973, the park would have included nearly all the uplands of the department from east to west, stretching from the Spanish border in the south to an erratic northern boundary designed to exclude most inhabited areas. Treading carefully, the administrative council planned not only to spare communes the limitations imposed by the park but also to allow fishing and the hunting of wild boar and izard (the Pyrenean chamois) within its borders. Opponents of the park included the communist and socialist parties, hunters' organizations, and even L. P. Galy-Gasparrou, mayor of Massat and descendent of the old notable and political family from the town. Ultimately, the socialists, who held a balance of power in Ariège, mounted an offensive against the park and stymied its realization: in Michel Chevalier's estimation, socialist authorities feared the loss of jurisdiction that the joint administrative council would suffer in the park's peripheral zone, thus the loss of political influence over the sixty or so communes in the region. But the socialists' apprehensions over the larger consequences of the park have perhaps been vindicated by results in and around the National Park of the Western Pyrenees—an influx of tourists accompanied by demographic decline.[12] In a consummation of Ariégeois history, local powers held the state at bay in the uplands, nearly 150 years after the War of the Demoiselles.

The story of these two national parks, tolerated at arm's length in Savoie, rejected in Ariège, cannot but suggest continuities shaped by history and geography: Savoie, more industrial, more open to outside influences, its Maurienne and Tarentaise Valleys scoured by trade and migration since the Middle Ages, versus Ariège, more rural and isolated yet, paradoxically, home to a longer history of contentious relations with the French state, especially regarding that *lieu de pouvoir,* the forest.[13]

Of course, Ariège has not been immune from sources of transformation that have altered life for Savoyards; this can hardly be true of a department that has lost 35 percent of its population since the beginning of the century. The Ariégeois well know that outsiders will continue to play a central role in shaping their destinies. It is reasonably safe to predict that the European Union, with its growing store of agricultural, regional, and environmental policies, will hold sway over many initiatives in Ariège and Savoie. Already, Article Nineteen, a regulation issued by the European Commission in 1985, means to elevate rural incomes while encouraging agricultural practices that promote ecological balance and maintain a visually interesting landscape; it represents an attempt, then, to articulate the goals of agriculture, environmentalism, and tourism. Thus far, its implementation in Ariège appears to show that "gardening the mountain" may serve pastoralists' interests. Just as state foresters had rehabilitated jardinage by 1930, Article Nineteen has revalorized use rights and traditional pastoral practices.[14] The present French government itself has proposed the first major modification in 150 years of the legal procedure that spawned much of the contentious politics of reforestation and restoration—the notorious *déclaration d'utilité publique* that can lead to expropriation—in order to open it to more local, democratic debate.[15] Though they augur well for people in the uplands, all of these measures will be lived and interpreted unpredictably and differently. To others' conceptions of law and *natura naturans,* rural society will continue to respond with strategies that reflect the humanization of forest and mountain. The French story of restoration is hardly exceptional in revealing little consensus of social vision, whether one looks at the forest or the trees; it is much less an example of "how not to do it" than a reminder of the complicated alliance of society and nature in the forest.

Notes

INTRODUCTION

1. See Tucker and Richards, "Global Economy and Forest Clearance," as well as Tucker and Richards, *Global Deforestation and the Nineteenth-Century World Economy.*

2. From less than 11 million hectares in 1914, the forested area of France grew to more than 14 million hectares by the 1980s. Corvol, "La forêt" 688, 728.

3. Plaisance, "L'emprise des forêts françaises," 199, 204–7.

4. Harrison, *Forests: The Shadow of Civilization,* 120.

5. Bloch's *French Rural History* is an essential source for the history of use rights, communal property, and enclosures in France. The difficulties of codifying, not to mention interpreting, customary practices in twentieth-century France are well represented in *Une France coutumière,* ed. Louis Assier-Andrieu, whose work attests to the vitality of local usages while analyzing their broader social and juridical contexts. See also Christian Fruhauf's monograph on capitalist appropriation of the forest in the pays de Sault (mostly in the department of Aude): *Forêt et société.* The history of the English enclosure movement provides fertile ground for cross-cultural comparison. For some contrasting views see Wordie, "Chronology of English Enclosure, 1500–1914"; Allen, *Enclosure and the Yeoman;* Kerridge, *The Agricultural Revolution;* and Chambers and Mingay, *Agricultural Revolution.*

6. For a helpful set of ideas about popular contention, see Tilly, *The Contentious French.* For the growing literature on more subterranean forms of resistance, a good place to start is James Scott's précis, "Everyday Forms of Resistance." A more empirical discussion of "anonymous" resistance can be found in Thompson, "Crime of Anonymity."

7. Chabrol, "L'oeuvre des forestiers français"; Fourchy, "Un centenaire oublié," 40. For essential if neutral background on reforestation, see Devèze, *La Forêt et les communautés rurales.*

8. Corvol, *L'Homme aux bois.* See also Kalaora, *Forêt et société au XIXe siècle;* Larrère et al., "Reboisement des montagnes et systèmes agraires"; Nougarède, *L'Administration forestière face à une société montagnarde;* and Kalaora and Savoye, *La Forêt pacifiée.* For contemporary foresters' perspectives, see Combes, "Restauration des terrains en montagne"; Crécy, "La politique de prévention"; and Crécy, "L'histoire de la RTM."

9. An excellent exception is an article by Monique Barrué-Pastor on conflicts over alpine restoration in two valleys of Haute-Garonne: "Les aménageurs face aux communautés."

10. Evans, "Ecology of Peasant Life in Western Europe," 237.

11. Lehning, *Peasant and French,* 107.

12. Maurice Agulhon, "Attitudes politiques" and "Les paysans dans la vie politique."

13. P. McPhee, *Politics of Rural Life,* 9.

14. Ibid., 141. McPhee neatly divides the historians of this subject into three schools: those who proceed from social and economic structures to politics, inspired by André Siegfried's original model of electoral geography (1913); those who explain politicization by means of a model of cultural diffusion (having found little evidence of socioeconomic change in their regions of study); and those who have closely examined the political process and the diffusion of ideology from urban centers to rural areas. An initial exploration of these schools should include the following works: Vigier, *La Seconde République dans la région alpine;* Agulhon, *La République au village;* Corbin, *Archaïsme et modernité en Limousin au XIXe siècle;* Merriman, *Agony of the Republic;* Margadant, *French Peasants in Revolt;* Berenson, *Populist Religion and Left-Wing Politics in France, 1830–1852.* Though he displaced politicization and modernization in general into the late nineteenth century, Eugen Weber quite explicitly relied on a diffusion model in his discussions of "archaic" rural politics in *Peasants into Frenchmen: The Modernization of Rural France, 1870–1914.* See also Weber, "Comment la Politique Vint aux Paysans," an article that yields a more nuanced chronology of politicization than that in Weber's earlier work.

15. Ryden, *Mapping the Invisible Landscape,* 38.

16. Bazire and Gadant, *La Forêt en France,* 25–26. The departmental figures date from 1989, the national figure from 1991.

17. According to official statistics for 1878, the first year in which parallel figures exist for the two departments, Ariège received a rating of 33 percent forest cover, Savoie 22 percent; forest represented 17 percent of the surface area of all of France. See Administration des Forêts, *Statistique forestière* (1878). Both departments lost forest in the last quarter of the nineteenth century, before beginning uninterrupted gains in the twentieth. Nearly all authors on the topic doubt the accuracy of forest statistics prior to the mid-nineteenth century. For some interesting guesswork with regard to Savoie, see Palluel-Guillard, "Les Forêts de Savoie depuis le XVIIIe siècle."

18. Palluel-Guillard, "Les Forêts de Savoie," 25; Chevalier, *La Vie humaine dans les Pyrénées ariégeoises*, 504–5.

19. The richness of forest history in Lozère can be glimpsed in Galzin, "Déboisement et plantation de châtaigniers en Cévennes"; Poujol, "Le Rôle de la forêt dans le début de la guerre des camisards"; and from the same volume, Pourcher, "La Forêt: Espace global et espace conflictuel." A fascinating case study of a major reforestation effort is presented by Nougarède, Poupardin, and Larrère, "Le reboisement de RTM de l'Aigoual, en Cévennes."

20. Chevalier, *L'Ariège*, 15–21.

21. Veyret and Veyret, *Atlas et géographie des Alpes françaises*, 21–35, 52–56, 108–9, 148–50.

22. Salvador, "Le département de l'Ariège au point de vue forestier," 221, 241–42; Chevalier, *L'Ariège*, 22.

23. Bazire and Gadant, *La Forêt en France*, 45–46; Gensac, "La forêt en Savoie, approche écologique," 8–9.

24. Chevalier, *L'Ariège*, 90. See also the articles by Henri Gaussen (1937): "Climat et végétation des Pyrénées ariégeoises" and "Les forêts de l'Ariège et du Salat."

25. Veyret and Veyret, *Atlas et géographie des Alpes françaises*, 65; Plaisance, *La Forêt française*, 311; Gensac, "La forêt en Savoie, approche écologique," 8–9; Père Robert Fritsch, "La forêt savoyarde, réceptacle de plantes en survie," 9–13.

26. For a French understanding of truncated ecosystems and rural space, see the useful article by Bertrand, "Pour une histoire écologique de la France rurale."

27. Chevalier, *La Vie humaine*, 151–56, 171–78.

28. Guichonnet, *Histoire et civilisation des Alpes*, 2:53–54; Marnézy, *Maurienne, terre humaine*, 47–48.

29. Chevalier, *La Vie humaine*, 217–30; Arbos, *La Vie pastorale dans les Alpes françaises*, 107, 113; Palluel-Guillard et al., *La Savoie de la Révolution à nos jours*, 170–75; "Enquête sur la situation et les besoins de l'agriculture," 22 M 1 2, ADS.

30. Although he does not treat the mountains of France, McNeill's *The Mountains of the Mediterranean World* is essential reading for an understanding of the vulnerabilty of alpine agriculture, especially ch. 4.

31. Soulet, *Les Pyrénées au XIXe siècle*, 2:166; Chevalier, *La Vie humaine*, 519. See Oliver Rackham's discussion of woodland pasturing in "Savanna in Europe."

32. Lovie, "Les ressources forestières de la Savoie," 742; Daubrée, *Statistique et atlas des forêts de France*, 178. The overall proportion of communal forest in Savoie has declined over the past 250 years due to an increased forest cover largely in private hands; the *extent* of communal forest has in fact risen since around the mid-nineteenth century. Palluel-Guillard, "Les forêts de Savoie," 36. The survey of 1878 is not a good index of communal property, since it combines forests belonging to communes and departments in a single figure. Communal property accounted for much nonforested land as well; an inquiry of 1863 listed Savoie as second only to Hautes-Alpes in proportion of communal property. See Arbos, *La Vie pastorale dans les Alpes françaises*, 75.

33. Chevalier, *La Vie humaine*, 187, 764; Administration des Forêts, *Statistique forestière*, 17. This figure had hardly changed by 1912; see Daubrée, *Statistique et atlas des forêts de France*, 71.

34. For an exhaustive account of use rights in Ariège, see *Les Droits d'usage en Ariège,* especially vol. 1. See also the astute juridical and social analysis of Assier-Andrieu in "La coutume dans la question forestière."

35. Arbos makes a claim for a long historical equilibrium between pasture and forest in the northern Alps, even though Savoyard communities themselves began to clamor for restrictions on cutting by the fifteenth century. The humidity of the northern Alps favored the growth of forests *and* grasses, effectively limiting the extent of cutting. See Arbos, *La Vie pastorale dans les Alpes françaises,* 41–49.

36. Lovie et al., *Savoie: Ecologie, économie, art, littérature, langue, histoire, traditions populaires,* 75.

37. Vidal de la Blache, *Tableau de la géographie de la France,* 263; Arbos, *La Vie pastorale dans les Alpes françaises,* 388.

38. Inspector in Foix to conservator in Toulouse, 28 October 1843, Dossier 1: "Constitution du périmètre; projet général," RTM Ariège.

39. Métailié, "Les incendies pastoraux dans les Pyrénées centrales."

40. My analysis of pastoral systems derives largely from the comprehensive studies by Philippe Arbos and Michel Chevalier.

41. Chevalier, *La Vie humaine,* 285–91.

42. Arbos was unable to locate a clear determining factor in the locations of these patterns of pastoralism in Savoie, though he explored the roles of soil types, topography, climate, property, labor, and even varieties of cheese. Private property structured pastoralism only in the pre-alpine Bauges district. Arbos, *La Vie pastorale dans les Alpes françaises,* 70, 415–523.

43. Castillon, *Histoire d'Ax et de la Vallée d'Andorre,* 101–2.

44. Vidal de la Blache, *Tableau de la géographie de la France,* 263.

1. FORESTS, THE STATE, AND ALPINE COMMUNES

1. *Les Eaux et Forêts du 12e au 20e siècle,* 53, 55, 88–91, 162; Clarenc, "Le code de 1827," 297.

2. Devèze, *La Forêt et les communautés rurales,* 206.

3. The 1669 ordinance did not positively prescribe tire-et-aire as much as it assumed its use, allowing much variation for individual forests. *Les Eaux et Forêts du 12e au 20e siècle,* 163–64; Huffel, *Economie forestière,* 3:48–50.

4. *Les Eaux et Forêts du 12e au 20e siècle,* 155, 157; *French Forest Ordinance of 1669,* 121–25, 141.

5. Clarenc, "Le code de 1827," 308; *Les Droits d'usage en Ariège,* 1:4–5.

6. One such title was the charter granted in 1245 by Roger VII, count of Foix, permitting the inhabitants of the Consulate of Ax to dispose of the mountains and forests of the district "less as users than as masters." See Clarenc, "Le code de 1827," 307, and Municipal Council of Ax, 2 October 1838, F 10 1664, AN.

7. Devèze, *La Forêt et les communautés rurales,* 207; *Les Eaux et Forêts du 12e au 20e siècle,* 269–270; Buttoud, "Les projets forestiers de la Révolution."

8. P. M. Jones, *The Peasantry in the French Revolution,* 128–37; Garaud, *La Révolution et la propriété foncière,* 378; Corvol, "L'affirmation de la propriété communale," 161–64. Chapter 6, "A Revolution in Property," of William H. Sewell's *Work and Revolution in*

France, 114–42, remains one of the most lucid comparisons of Old Regime concepts of property and the absolute, individualistic notions concretized in Revolutionary legislation. .

9. The Directory suspended the decree of 1793 on 9 June 1796. Ogé, "Appropriation communautaire et/ou appropriation étatique," 131–32; Jones, *Peasantry in the French Revolution,* 137–54.

10. Woronoff, "La 'dévastation révolutionnaire' des forêts."

11. Ibid., 50–51; see also Woronoff's conclusion to *Révolution et espaces forestiers,* 257–58. E. Allen, in "Deforestation and Fuel Crisis in Pre-Revolutionary Languedoc," offers a rather deterministic account of fuel shortages and the onset of the Revolution in rural France.

12. Peter McPhee makes a valuable contribution to this discussion in *Revolution and Environment in Southern France,* even though he focuses on clearances in the largely non-forested Corbières. See also Bloch, *French Rural History,* 18–19; Bourgenot, "L'histoire humaine des forêts françaises"; Corvol, *L'Homme aux bois,* 300; Ogé, "Appropriation communautaire et/ou appropriation étatique," 127–29.

13. Mormiche, "La notion d'aménagement forestier," 134.

14. See Gordon Robinson's discussions of forest management and silviculture in *Forest and the Trees,* 59–69.

15. In his classic treatise of 1926, Huffel defined *aménagement* as the "operations destined to improve [forests'] production, and especially to order it." Huffel, *Economie forestière,* 4–7.

16. Robinson, *Forest and the Trees,* 61.

17. In *Forests: The Shadow of Civilization,* 122–23, Robert Harrison singles out the "subjection of forests to mathematical analysis" as the essential feature of German forestry, an analysis that aided both in calculating volumes of wood and in planting trees in straight rows.

18. Huffel, *Economie forestière,* 59, 171; Devèze, *La Forêt et les communautés rurales,* 167.

19. Devèze, *La Forêt et les communautés rurales,* 172, 175.

20. Richez, "Science allemande et foresterie française," 232–46.

21. Scott, *Seeing Like a State,* 11–22.

22. *Les Eaux et Forêts du 12e au 20e siècle,* 163 n. 3; Huffel, *Economie forestière,* 49.

23. Huffel, *Economie forestière,* 155–57.

24. Ibid., 53–54, 109–110; Sahlins, *Forest Rites,* 51–54.

25. Huffel, *Economie forestière,* 54, 205.

26. Dralet, *Description des Pyrénées,* 2:78, 80.

27. Natural regeneration shows the turn toward silviculture by shifting focus to reproduction by seed-bearing trees left in the cut parcel. James, "A History of Forestry and Monographic Forestry Literature," 17; Reed, *Forests of France,* 48.

28. Quoted in Richez, "Science allemande et foresterie française," 243.

29. *Les Eaux et Forêts du 12e au 20e siècle,* 304–5.

30. Ibid., 308–13; Buttoud, "L'état forestier," 216–18.

31. The administration did implement a system of bonuses in hopes of reinforcing forest guards' zeal. See Buttoud, "L'état forestier," 218.

32. Corvol, *L'Homme aux bois,* 189–90.

33. Ibid., 192–94. Over time, signs of unity in the corps triumphed over signs of internal hierarchy: in 1875 guards were accorded gray trousers with green trim, and by 1914 all members of the forestry corps wore the *képi,* the cap of the French military.

34. *Les Eaux et Forêts du 12e au 20e siècle,* 477; Devèze, *La Forêt et les communautés rurales,* 237–40, 242; Corvol, *L'Homme aux bois,* 247–48 (quotation is from 247); James, "A History of Forestry and Monographic Forest Literature," 29.

35. For an excellent introduction to the lives of forest guards, see Buttoud, "L'état paternel," 113–35.

36. Quoted in *Les Eaux et Forêts du 12e au 20e siècle,* 479.

37. Bourdeaux, *Code forestier et code rural,* article 90.

38. Quoted in Corvol, *L'Homme aux bois,* 259.

39. Bourdeaux, *Code forestier,* article 110.

40. Ibid., articles 63, 111, and 118; Garaud, *La Révolution et la propriété foncière,* 376–77. Cantonnement pertained only to use rights in wood, however; rights to graze cattle, gather acorns, and run pigs in the forest could be extinguished only through direct payment to the holder of the rights and in the absence of a decision by the prefectorial council that these rights were of absolute economic necessity. Yet existing rights to both grazing and wood became subject to regulation; henceforth the Forêts would oversee deliveries of wood in addition to determining the number of cattle that could graze in which portion of a forest for how long a season. Pasturing rights on land considered nonforested, however, have been subject to cantonnement according to laws passed in 1790 and 1792 that were not abrogated by the Forest Code. These legal measures pertain to the case of Massat (see Chapter 4). See *Les Droits d'usage en Ariège,* 1:100, 115.

41. Documents relating to the cantonnement of the forest of Ax-les-Thermes are located in F 10 1664, AN.

42. Bourdeaux, *Code forestier,* Title 10.

43. The 1859 law allowed foresters to negotiate legal settlements with suspects prior to a definitive judgment. Ibid., Titles 11 and 12.

44. Soulet, *Les Pyrénées au XIXe siècle,* 2:163.

45. Justice of the Peace from the canton of Ax-les-Thermes to Prefect, 12 April 1850, 7 P 69, ADA.

46. Viazzo, *Upland Communities,* 89–93; Palluel-Guillard et al., *La Savoie de la Révolution à nos jours,* 129–30, 262; Soulet, *Les Pyrénées au XIXe siècle,* 2:29–46; Arbos, *La Vie pastorale dans les Alpes françaises,* 217.

47. Soulet, *Les Pyrénées au XIXe siècle,* 2:508.

48. Arbos, *La Vie pastorale dans les Alpes françaises,* 221.

49. See Dralet's assertions that forge owners were not to blame for the devastation of Pyrenean forests, as well as his rational but flawed argument that the forests could provide for the needs of industry as well as subsistence and give a yearly surplus of wood. Dralet, *Description des Pyrénées* 2:132–34, 143–44.

50. Bonhote and Fruhauf, "Métallurgie au bois et espaces forestiers," 459–74. For a photograph and description of a catalan forge, see Dejean and Dejean, *L'Ariège d'autrefois,* 126–27.

51. See Soulet's discussion of popular contestation over the commons, *Les Pyrénées au XIXe*

siècle, 2:126–39; Clarenc, "Riches et pauvres," 307–15. According to Arbos, Alpine communes withstood pressures to sell, partition, and usurp the commons relatively well; the revolutionary laws allowing partition had negligible effects in Savoie. Arbos, *La Vie pastorale dans les Alpes françaises*, 78–80.

52. *Les Eaux et Forêts du 12e au 20e siècle*, 482–83.

53. Clarenc, "Le Code de 1827," 312–13, 316; Soulet, *Les Pyrénées au XIXe siècle*, 2:170–71.

54. Vigier notes that by the end of the July Monarchy, peasants in the Briançonnais (Hautes-Alpes) were paying less in taxes than in fines for forest crimes. Vigier, "Les troubles forestiers," 128–29, 132.

55. Soulet, *Les Pyrénées au XIXe siècle*, 2:502–15.

56. Ibid., 2:610–15.

57. Merriman, "Demoiselles of the Ariège," 109.

58. Sahlins, *Forest Rites*.

59. Soboul, *Problèmes paysans de la révolution*, 274–88; see also P. McPhee, *Politics of Rural Life*, 50, 82–83.

60. Quoted in Clarenc, "Riches et pauvres," 312.

61. Merriman, "Demoiselles of the Ariège," 104–7; Soulet, *Les Pyrénées au XIXe siècle*, 2:168.

62. Soulet, *Les Pyrénées au XIXe siècle*, 2:628–34; P. McPhee, *Politics of Rural Life*, 81; quotation is from Soboul, *Problèmes paysans de la révolution*, 309.

63. Coquerelle, "Les droits collectifs," 356; Soulet, *Les Pyrénées au XIXe siècle*, 2:624.

64. Coquerelle, "Les droits collectifs," 354, 356.

65. Soulet, *Les Pyrénées au XIXe siècle*, 2:625–26.

66. Ibid., 621–22, 625, 635; Clarenc, "Riches et pauvres," 314–15. In *Pays de Sault: Les Pyrénées audoises au XIXe siècle* 90–91, Christian Thibon attempts to correlate "red" voting with areas of private forest domains and conservative voting with the existence of state forests in an area of Aude close to Ariège. This hypothesis fails to account for the voting in much of upland Ariège, the home of extensive state forests.

67. Margadant, *French Peasants in Revolt*, esp. chs. 2 and 3 and the conclusion. See also P. McPhee, *Les Semailles de la république*, 377.

68. Margadant, *French Peasants in Revolt*, 46; Soulet, *Les Pyrénées au XIXe siècle*, 2:634–36; Bercé, *Revolt and Revolution in Early Modern Europe*, 1.

69. St.-Ybars, "De la Question forestière dans l'Ariège," 7, 9, 14, 24–25. At least one similar manifesto issued from an Alpine department: J.-P.-A. Fabre, writing as the former mayor of Meironnes (Basses-Alpes), penned his *Des Habitants des montagnes considérés dans leurs rapports avec le régime forestier* (1849) also as a diatribe against the rigors of the Forest Code and a reminder of the newly won electoral power of the peasantry. His epigraph read, "The forest regime, for the alpine inhabitant, is a permanent state of siege."

70. "Observations d'un agent forestier sur la brochure de M. Latour de St. Ybars intitulée: 'De la Question forestière en Ariège,'" n.d., 7 P 3, ADA.

71. Guichonnet, *Histoire de la Savoie*, 396.

72. Guichonnet, *Histoire et civilisation des Alpes*, 1:298.

73. Guichonnet, *Histoire de la Savoie*, 392.

74. In 1852 Savoyards vehemently opposed Cavour's free trade agreement with France. Ibid., 368, 370–71, 388; Palluel-Guillard et al., *La Savoie de la Révolution à nos jours*, 96–97.

75. Guichonnet, *Histoire de l'annexion*, 53–54.

76. Palluel-Guillard et al., *La Savoie de la Révolution à nos jours*, 108; Guichonnet, *Histoire de l'annexion*, 54. For a more parallel comparison with the Pyrenees in 1848, see Vigier, *La Seconde République dans la région alpine*, on the departments of Isère, Drôme, Hautes-Alpes, Basses-Alpes, and Vaucluse. Relative differences vis-à-vis the Pyrenees include the very recent (1845–47) stiffening of the Forest Code in the Alps and the attenuation of forest troubles by August 1848, but similar violence toward forest guards had erupted soon after the change of regime in February. Vigier argues that the Second Republic left the faintest political traces in the upland areas of the Alpine region, a conclusion that poses a contrast to the more left-leaning Pyrenean uplands. See 1:48–50, 204–5, 270; 2:414, 440–41.

77. Palluel-Guillard et al., *La Savoie de la Révolution à nos jours*, 109. Whereas the suffrage included one in forty inhabitants in Savoie, only one in sixty-five could vote in Piedmont and Genoa and one in seventy-two in Sardinia.

78. Guichonnet, *Histoire de l'annexion*, 58–59; Palluel-Guillard et al., *La Savoie de la Révolution à nos jours*, 117; Guichonnet, *Histoire de la Savoie*, 389.

79. Guichonnet, *Histoire de la Savoie*, 394–96. A compromise achieved the incorporation of the northern provinces by allowing a free trade zone, in existence since 1816, between them and Geneva.

80. Guichonnet, "De la Restauration," 378; Palluel-Guillard et al., *La Savoie de la Révolution à nos jours*, 152, 129–30, 145–46, 153–54; 160–61; Guichonnet, *Histoire de la Savoie*, 376–77.

81. Quoted in Weber, *Peasants into Frenchmen*, 489. See also Weber's anecdote about the Savoyard who insulted a gendarme in 1873 with the epithets, "I don't give a damn about you, you are French, I hate the French, I've never been French and never will be!," 103.

82. "Circulaire à Messieurs les Maires" 12 June 1861, F 10 2317, AN.

83. Quoted in Lovie, "Les ressources forestières," 747.

84. Palluel-Guillard et al., *La Savoie de la Révolution à nos jours*, 260; Lovie, "Les ressources forestières," 746, 754.

85. Palluel-Guillard, "Les forêts de Savoie depuis le XVIIIe siècle," 27.

86. Palluel-Guillard et al., *La Savoie de la Révolution à nos jours*, 247. After the first lottery for military service in 1861, 10 percent of the men chosen evaded service. In 1867 a law abolished the school taxes about which peasants had complained since the annexation.

2. "A QUESTION ALMOST POLITICAL"

1. Jean-Paul Bozonnet even suggests that nineteenth-century fears of deforestation posed as a "scientific substitute for the mythical primitive catastrophe that destroyed ecological paradise." See Bozonnet, *Des monts et des mythes*, 96.

2. Early in his regime Napoleon III personally launched the reforestation of another forty thousand hectares in the Sologne, a project under way since the Restoration, and created the vast program of fixing the sand dunes of the Landes through reforestation in 1857. See *Les Eaux et Forêts du 12e au 20e siècle*, 581.

3. Mornet, *Le Sentiment de la nature*, 58, 259–87.

4. Schama, *Landscape and Memory,* 447–66, 490–93, emphasis in original.

5. Picon, "L'idée de nature," and Desailly, "Perception et gestion du risque."

6. Hallam, *Great Geological Controversies,* 40–41.

7. Greene, *Geology in the Nineteenth Century,* 73–75.

8. Briffaud, "Le rôle des catastrophes naturelles," 135–38, 141.

9. Desailly, "Perception et gestion du risque," 43–44; Briffaud, "Le rôle des catastrophes naturelles," 143. Engineers' fixation on regulating the flow of water downstream was in keeping with their passion for building canals, which received the backing of the state for much of the nineteenth century. See Smith, "Longest Run."

10. The distinction was only partial because nineteenth-century foresters tended to exaggerate by deeming every act of land clearance an act of deforestation. See Corvol, *L'Homme aux bois,* 39–40. See also Devèze, *La Forêt et les communautés rurales,* 185–86; Bourguet, "L'image des terres incultes."

11. *Les Eaux et forêts du 12e au 20e siècle,* 507.

12. Among others, the engineer J. A. Fabre's *Essai sur le thème des torrents et des rivières* (1797) preceded Surell's work in its focus on the relations among deforestation, flooding, and erosion. See Grove, *Green Imperialism,* 259.

13. Surell, *Etude sur les torrents des Hautes-Alpes,* 1, 152.

14. Ibid., 156, 172–73, 228–29, 276–77. It is likely that Surell emphasized the importance of soil conservation because of the visibility of erosion in Hautes-Alpes. Indeed, he distinguished conditions pertaining in Hautes-Alpes from those in other mountainous areas of France. Not only were the southern Alps highly prone to short, violent storms, but they were also formed mostly of unstable layers of sedimentary rock. See 121, 127–28. Surell's evidence of the particularity of Hautes-Alpes stands in contrast to his argument for the reforestation of all of alpine France.

15. Ibid., 194; Lorentz, "Reboisement des montagnes"; V. Legrand, *Rapport sur le reboisement des montagnes,* quoted in Ogé, "Les prémices de la politique de restauration," 12.

16. Corvol, *L'Homme aux bois,* 291.

17. Antoine, Desailly, and Métailié, "La chronologie des crues," 7, 13, 23–28. These authors, admitting the paucity of regional studies of climate, draw upon a comparison with the "little ice age" of the seventeenth century for an explanation: replacing the usual weather patterns that travel across France from the Atlantic, a series of polar or subtropical anticyclones in the nineteenth century produced cold winters, droughts alternating with heavy rain in the summers, and dramatic contrasts in temperature, providing the conditions for violent, repeated storms. One might date the series of catastrophic floods from the 1840s: in his 1842 report on the Alps and the Pyrenees, Lorentz ("Reboisement des montagnes," 14) referred to devastating floods of the Rhône and the Saône in 1840. The Rhône flooded again in 1843.

18. Gorce, *Histoire du Second Empire,* 2:40–41.

19. *Le Moniteur,* 16 February 1857; quoted in Gorce, *Histoire du Second Empire* 2:41.

20. Corvol, *L'Homme aux bois,* 314–15. In the construction of natural disasters as "national" phenomena, Pierre Fourchy emphasizes the access of prefects and subprefects—fonts of information about local conditions—to central power and the diffusion of forestry personnel into each chef-lieu de canton or commune. Fourchy, "Un centenaire oublié," 21–

22. See also Désert, "Prospérité de l'agriculture," 232–33.

21. The reforestation of alpine France had nearly become law in the 1840s. The Chambre des Pairs of the July Monarchy (1830–1848) debated bills in 1843 and 1847, both of which partially foreshadowed the 1860 law. The bill of 1843 carried the ambitious goal of reforesting three hundred thousand hectares of communal lands not yet under the forest regime and another eight hundred thousand hectares of pasture that were; proposed by Director General Legrand, whom Napoleon III reappointed to the post in 1851, the 1847 project provided discretionary power and methods of financing reforestation that the legislators of 1860 adopted. Fourchy, "Un centenaire oublié," 26; Corvol, *L'Homme aux bois,* 321, 330–31.

22. Puton, *Code de la législation forestière,* 393–400.

23. Surell, *Etude sur les torrents des Hautes-Alpes,* 199.

24. Ibid., 283.

25. "Loi du 28 juillet 1860, relative à la mise en valeur des Marais et des Terres incultes appartenant aux Communes," 7 P 2, ADA.

26. *Le Moniteur Universel,* 21 July 1860.

27. Napoleon III's legislative corps was not the first in modern French history to be preoccupied with marshes: under Napoleon Bonaparte, a law of 1807 led to significant drainage of primarily shallow marshes. By 1860, most had been drained and transformed into rich meadowland. According to Jean-Laurent Rosenthal, half of the increase in pasture between 1837 and 1862 was due to the reclamation of marshes. See Rosenthal, *Fruits of Revolution,* 53–56.

28. *Le Moniteur Universel,* 21 July 1860.

29. Kalaora and Savoye, "Aménagement et ménagement," 310.

30. A precedent for the connection between reclamation and reforestation lay in the 1857 law directed at the departments of Gironde and Landes. It conceptualized the planting of Maritime pine trees as a means of "reclaiming" the sand dunes that stretched over the immense territory of western Gascony, a clear precursor to the 1860 laws. See Sutton, "Reclamation of Wasteland," 286. According to Sutton, this law dealt a blow to the pastoral interests in the Landes.

31. Report by an engineer of the Service hydraulique, Ponts et Chaussées, 5 November 1862, F 10 2315, AN.

32. Combes, "Restauration des terrains en montagne," 93.

33. Dubourdieu, "Les forêts de montagne," 33–35.

34. Combes, "Restauration des terrains en montagne," 92.

35. Surell, *Etude sur les torrents des Hautes-Alpes,* 230.

36. Browne, *Secular Ark,* 44–46.

37. Ibid., 53–54.

38. Fourchy, "Un centenaire oublié," 22.

39. Soutadé, "La Limite supérieure de la forêt," 168. See as well the other contributions in the volume in which this essay appears, the publication of a colloquium devoted to questions of forests and altitude.

40. Soutadé, "Passage de la forêt à la pelouse ou à la lande"; Combes, "Restauration des terrains en montagne," 99.

41. Corvol, *L'Homme aux bois,* 305; Combes, "Restauration des terrains en montagne," 102.

42. Métailié, "Aux origines des améliorations pastorales," 97.

43. Ibid., 100–2.

44. Fourchy, "Un centenaire oublié," 33. Experimenting with species resulted in a clear favorite—the hardy and adaptable Silvester pine, but Maritime pine did well in light soils, Aleppo pine in calcareous soils and near the Mediterranean, and Atlas cedar in the Midi. To a lesser extent, foresters also planted deciduous trees, especially oak and ash, and experimented with grasses and native plants (juniper, berberis, sainfoin, and lucern, to name a few) in areas too erosive to support trees. See the report by Vicaire to the minister of finance in *Le Moniteur Universel,* 20 February 1864.

45. Vicaire, "Reboisement des montagnes," 10 January 1862, 7 P 2, ADA.

46. *Le Moniteur Universel,* 20 February 1864; Circular no. 77, "Exécution de la loi du 28 juillet 1860 sur le reboisement des montagnes," 17 August 1860, 6 P 38, ADS.

47. Eighteen forty-three was one of the years in which a legislative project to reforest the mountains failed in the Chambre des Pairs. Circular No. 535 bis, 14 July 1843; General Guard to Inspector in Foix, 14 October 1843, Dossier 1, RTM Ariège.

48. *L'Ariégeois,* 13 July 1861, 4; 17 July 1861, 3; Paul Troy to Director General, 8 September 1862, AGRI 4429, AN.

49. Fourchy, "Un centenaire oublié," 34. The high percentage of lands reforested by communes in 1861—82 percent—was significantly higher than the proportion of forest owned by communes in all of France.

50. Vicaire, "Reboisement des montagnes."

51. Director General to Prefect of Ariège, 13 June 1863, 7 P 2, ADA; report by Director General to Minister of Finance, *Le Moniteur Universel,* 20 February 1864.

52. Prefect of Ariège to Minister of Finance, 16 November 1861, AGRI 4429, AN.

53. Conservator in Toulouse to Director General, 2 January 1862, AGRI 4429, AN.

54. Prefect to Director General, 8 February 1862 and 14 March 1863; Conservator to Director General, 20 February 1862, AGRI 4429, AN. Prefect of Ariège to Prefect of Ain, 12 October 1864, 7 P 2, ADA.

55. Director General to Minister of Finance, *Le Moniteur Universel,* 20 February 1864.

56. Ibid.

57. *Supplément au Moniteur universel,* 29 May 1864, F 10 2314, AN.

58. Puton, *Code de la législation forestière,* 400–3.

59. See, e.g., Fourchy, "Un centenaire oublié," who comments that the law on regazonnement received little practical application (38–39); for a different interpretation see Crécy, "La politique de prévention." Crécy asserts that foresters used the law of 1864 as a mechanism to improve pastures, achieving "spectacular results."

60. Bonnet, "La Restauration des terrains en montagne," 8, 15, 72, 82.

61. Ibid., 99–100.

62. "Les habitants de la commune de Auzat, canton de Vicdessos, département de l'Ariège, à Sa Majesté l'Empereur Napoléon III," 15 December 1862, AGRI 4429, AN.

63. Ibid.

64. Conservator in Toulouse to Director General, 31 March 1863, AGRI 4429, AN.

65. Bonnet, "La Restauration des terrains en montagne," 137–38.

66. M. Doumenjou to Director General, Conservator, and Prefect, undated (found among documents dating 1871–72), 7 P 3, ADA.
67. Conservator's reports to the Conseil Général, 5 July 1875 and 17 June 1876, 7 P 3, ADA.
68. Ibid., 15 July 1869 and 5 July 1872. Frédéric Ogé finds that the Conseil Général of Ariège consistently supported the large livestock owners and opposed reforestation; throughout the nineteenth century, the council also hesitated to evict goats, "the poor man's cow," from the forest, remained critical of the Forest Code, and did not formally admit the role of forests in preventing some natural disasters until after World War I. See Ogé, "Le Conseil Général de l'Ariège," 6–10.
69. Conservator's reports to the Conseil Général, 7 P 3, ADA.
70. Zeldin, *Political System of Napoleon III,* 135–42.
71. Conservator in Toulouse to Director General, 7 January 1869, F 10 1659, AN; Conservator's reports to the Conseil Général, 8 June 1874; 17 June 1876, 7 P 3, ADA.
72. Conservator's reports to the Conseil Général 1867–1876, 7 P 3, ADA. Between 1867 and 1869, inhabitants of Goulier committed approximately 2,020 of the 2,641 forest crimes in the Inspection of Foix.
73. Conservator's reports to the Conseil Général, 25 May 1868 and 15 July 1869, 7 P 3, ADA.
74. Conservator's report to the Conseil Général, 10 August 1871, 7 P 3, ADA.
75. Report by Sub-Inspector in Saint-Girons, 16 December 1870 and 19 December 1870; Conservator to Prefect, 9 January 1871; Sub-Prefect in Saint-Girons to Prefect, 26 January 1871, 7 P 13, ADA.
76. Conservator's report to the Conseil Général, 5 July 1872, 29 June 1872, and 23 June 1877, 7 P 3, ADA.
77. Larrère et al., "Reboisement des montagnes et systèmes agraires," 28.
78. Conservator in Toulouse to Director General, 2 January 1862, AGRI 4429, AN.
79. Buttoud, "L'état paternel," 121.
80. Conservator's report to the Conseil Général, 15 July 1869, 7 P 3, ADA.
81. Palluel-Guillard, "Les Forêts de Savoie depuis le XVIIIe siècle," 23–24.
82. Lovie, "Les ressources forestières de la Savoie," 750; Director General to Prefect, 12 November 1860, 6 P 38, ADS.
83. Conservator par interim to Prefect, 22 February 1862; "Compte rendu des travaux de 1862," March 1863, Administration des Forêts, Reboisement des montagnes, 6 P 45, ADS.
84. Reforestation reports from 1861 to 1921 can be found in 6 P 45, ADS, and 7 P 2, ADA; Lovie, "Les ressources forestières de la Savoie," 757; Mignerot, *Notice forestière du département de la Savoie,* 1887, 34 DF 3, AN, 12, 29.
85. Palluel-Guillard et al., *La Savoie de la Révolution à nos jours,* 248.
86. Quoted in Prefect of Savoie to Minister of Industry, Commerce, and Agriculture, 21 October 1861, F 10 2317, AN. See this early version of the "tragedy of the commons" thesis in the work of the conservator and former Nancy school professor Auguste Mathieu, first published in 1864: *Le Reboisement et le regazonnement des Alpes.*
87. Prefect of Savoie to Minister of Industry, Commerce, and Agriculture, 21 October 1861, F 10 2317, AN.
88. Palluel-Guillard et al., *La Savoie de la Révolution à nos jours,* 162.

89. Prefect to Minister of the Interior, 12 July 1861, 6 P 45, ADS.

90. Conservator to Prefect, 15 December 1860, 6 P 45; Report by the Conservator for 1882, 6 P 36, ADS.

91. Conservator to Prefect, 25 September 1860, 6 P 38, ADS.

92. Inspector in Moûtiers to Conservator in Chambéry, 9 July 1861; Conservator to Prefect, 15 July 1861, 6 P 45, ADS.

93. Report by general guard in Moûtiers, 10 September 1861, 6 P 35, ADS.

94. Inspector in Moûtiers to Conservator, 18 September 1861, 6 P 35, ADS; Lovie, "Les ressources forestières de la Savoie," 753; Mougin, *Les Forêts de Savoie*, 746.

95. Report from the meeting of 4 June 1864 of the Société Générale d'Agriculture du département de la Savoie, 28 June 1864; Conservator's response, 4 July 1864, 6 P 45; Direction Générale des Forêts, "Note pour Monsieur le Préfet de la Savoie," 21 May 1863, 6 P 40, ADS.

3. SISYPHUS IN SAVOIE

1. For brief accounts of the genesis of the "law of 4 April 1882, relative to the Restoration and Conservation of Alpine Lands," see Corvol, *L'Homme aux bois*, 335–37, and *Les Eaux et Forêts du 12e au 20e siècle* (1987), 542–43.

2. Corvol, *L'Homme aux bois*, 343, 361, 374.

3. Not only were the reforestation and regrassing laws of 1860–64 abrogated, but all properties acquired under the aegis of those laws were to be returned to their original owners or incorporated within new perimeters and purchased by the state within three years. See the *loi du 4 avril 1882 relative à la Restauration et à la Conservation des Terrains en Montagnes* in Puton, *Code de la législation forestière*, 431–32.

4. Ibid., 425–33.

5. Tétreau, *Commentaire de la loi du 4 avril 1882*, 45, 51.

6. In 1887 the state opened a credit of 11,500,000 francs in order to pay for acquisitions up front. By the end of the nineteenth century, the state had invested 25,000,000 francs (38 percent of the restoration budget) in acquisitions alone for 163,000 hectares of land, distributed between the Alps (113,611 h.), the massif Central (37,868 h.), and the Pyrenees (11,495 h.); according to Andrée Corvol, only 53 percent of this land was ever reforested, and at the time it represented just under half of what the state wished to acquire. See Corvol, *L'Homme aux bois*, 350, 360; Restauration et conservation des terrains en montagne, *Compte rendu sommaire des travaux de 1860 à 1900*, 3, 32; *Les Eaux et Forêts du 12e au 20e siècle*, 557.

7. Crécy, "La politique de prévention," 3.

8. See Marchand, *Les Torrents des Alpes et le pâturage;* Thierry, *Restauration des montagnes;* Chabrol, "L'oeuvre des forestiers français," 342–43.

9. Fron, *Economie sylvo-pastorale*, 149–55. See also detailed descriptions of the repertoire of *ouvrages de correction* in Mougin, *La Restauration des Alpes*, 198–206.

10. Conservator's reports to the Conseil Général of Savoie, 25 April 1881 and 17 May 1882, 6 P 36, ADS. For more on restoration *avant la lettre*, see *Les Eaux et Forêts du 12e au 20e siècle*, 578n.

11. Kuss, *Restauration et conservation des terrains en montagne,* 10.

12. Demontzey, *Traité pratique,* xix, 3. Viollet-le-Duc had published an article on alpine reforestation in the journal *XIXe Siècle* in 1879.

13. Demontzey, *Traité pratique,* 47–49; quotation is from Demontzey, "La correction des torrents et le reboisement des montagnes," 494. Indicative of the ongoing popularity of reforestation, the words *reboisement* and *gazonnement* figured in an 1880 draft of the law debated in the Senate. See "Discours prononcés par M. Michel. Séances des 1er et 5e juillet 1880. Projet de loi relatif à la restauration et à la conservation des terrains en montagne," *Journal Officiel,* 2 and 6 July, 1880.

14. Demontzey, "La correction des torrents," 495.

15. Doumenjou, *Question forestière,* 33.

16. Chapelain, *Notice sur le projet,* 9, 17–18.

17. In 1912 (a year otherwise marked by the commune's resentment toward the RTM), the municipal council of Jarrier even voted six francs for the purchase of *Les Torrents de la Savoie,* "considering the great usefulness of this work." Municipal council of Jarrier, 17 March 1912, communal archives of Jarrier.

18. Röhrich, "Le monde surnaturel dans les légendes alpines," 25, 33.

19. "Etat nominatif des habitants de la commune de Jarrier," 10 January 1877, M 196, ADS; Dequier and Viallet, *Un Village en Maurienne,* 18.

20. See the introduction for a description of pastoral systems in Savoie.

21. Gaillard, "Jarrier, commune mauriennaise," 18. Dequier and Viallet (*Un Village en Maurienne,* 276) stress that Jarriens have practiced this cycle of migration more fully in the twentieth century; in the mid-nineteenth century, the higher population of Jarrier limited the extent to which all members of the family took part in it. From 925 residents in 1876, the population of Jarrier grew slightly toward the end of the nineteenth century; a sustained period of population loss through emigration followed between 1901 and 1931. By 1936, 586 people lived in Jarrier, and the census listed only eighteen hamlets. See "Etat nominatif des habitants," 30 March 1936, M 196, ADS.

22. In 1887 nearly 30 percent of forested land in Savoie was private property; communes possessed nearly all of the remaining 70 percent of forest. See Mignerot, *Notice forestière,* 34 DF 3, AN.

23. Dequier and Viallet, *Un Village en Maurienne,* 90, 223–30; Marnézy, *Maurienne, terre humaine,* 40–41; Meilleur, "La forêt dans l'économie traditionnelle montagnarde," 126–30.

24. Dequier and Viallet, *Un Village en Maurienne,* 80, 276.

25. Ibid., 75–76, 94, 229–231; Marnézy, *Maurienne, terre humaine,* 32.

26. Dequier and Viallet, *Un Village en Maurienne,* 277–81; Marnézy, *Maurienne, terre humaine,* 38.

27. Van Gennep, *Du berceau à la tombe,* 71–73.

28. Dequier and Viallet, *Un Village en Maurienne,* 264–67, 280.

29. Dequier, *De bouche à oreille,* 103, 111, 183. On rates of endogamy, see the *registres d'Etat civil,* 1865–1939, communal archives of Jarrier.

30. Dequier and Viallet, *Un Village en Maurienne,* 40–41.

31. Ibid., 15; see Eisbacher and Clague, "Destructive Mass Movements in High Mountains," 97, for a geological portrait of Jarrier. In chapter 3 of *The Control of Nature,* John McPhee provides graphic descriptions of debris flows from the San Gabriel mountains overlooking the Los Angeles basin, furnishing a useful basis of comparison between two managerial cultures in similar ecological situations.

32. Mougin, *Les Torrents de la Savoie,* 1122.

33. Dequier and Viallet, *Un Village en Maurienne,* 41–42, 46.

34. Ibid., 269–70; Hermann, *Architecture et vie traditionnelle,* 69.

35. Municipal council of Jarrier, November 1861; Sub-prefect in Saint-Jean-de-Maurienne to Prefect, 24 November 1861, Communal archives, Jarrier 001, ADS.

36. Reports by the Conservator in Chambéry to the Conseil Général of Savoie, 25 April 1881 and 17 May 1882, 6 P 36, ADS.

37. Elisée Reclus, quoted in Malte-Brun, *Savoie,* 24.

38. Commune of Saint-Jean-de-Maurienne, statutes, Service hydraulique, Ponts et Chaussées, 27 April 1865, 6 P 216, ADS.

39. Assistant Inspector in Jarrier, summary information on the Bonrieu torrent, 23 February 1882, Lower Arc perimeter, diverse documents, Dossier A2 [hereafter Dossier A2], Bonrieu torrent of Jarrier, RTM Savoie; reconnaissance report by Phal, Kuss, and Cugnet, 7 July 1891, Lower Arc perimeter, Jarrier series, Perimeter Project, Dossier B [hereafter Dossier B], Bonrieu torrent of Jarrier, RTM Savoie.

40. General reconnaissance report on the Lower Arc perimeter by Phal, Kuss, and Cugnet, 7 July 1891, Lower Arc perimeter, Dossier Général d'affaires diverses [hereafter General Dossier]; reconnaissance report on Jarrier by Phal, Kuss, and Cugnet, 7 July 1891, Dossier B, Bonrieu torrent of Jarrier, RTM Savoie.

41. General reconnaissance report, General Dossier.

42. Municipal council of Albiez-le-Jeune, 4 December 1892, 6 P 330, ADS.

43. Municipal council of Jarrier, 4 December 1892, 6 P 330, ADS; Distribution of total area, Jarrier, 7 July 1891, Dossier B, Bonrieu torrent of Jarrier, RTM Savoie.

44. Sub-Prefect in Saint-Jean to Prefect, 26 January 1889; Mayor of Jarrier to Inspector in Saint-Jean, 7 February 1889; Sub-Prefect to Prefect, 28 February 1889; Conservator to Prefect, 12 March 1889; Citizens of Jarrier to Prefect, 18 November 1889; Sub-Prefect to Prefect, 26 November 1889; Sub-Prefect to Prefect, 20 October 1890, 6 P 35, ADS; Dequier and Viallet, *Un Village en Maurienne,* 231–33. Quotation is from Citizens of Jarrier to Prefect.

45. Mayors in the canton of Modane to Prefect, 2 February 1889, 6 P 35, ADS.

46. *L'Autorité,* 17 February 1889.

47. Growing republicanism and a decline in clerical influence characterized even some of the isolated cantons of the Maurienne and the Tarentaise from the 1870s. See Palluel-Guillard et al., *La Savoie de la Révolution à nos jours,* 304.

48. Mayors in the canton of Modane to Prefect, 2 February 1889; Sub-Prefect to Prefect, 11 April 1889, 6 P 35, ADS.

49. Information concerning the floods of 22 August 1891 and 9 September 1892, Lower Arc perimeter, Floods, Dossier J [hereafter Dossier J], Bonrieu torrent of Jarrier, RTM Savoie.

50. Note to the commissioners, Lower Arc perimeter, n.d., General Dossier, RTM Savoie.

51. Municipal council of Jarrier, 7 January 1894, 6 P 136, ADS.

52. Municipal council of Jarrier, 1 August 1897, Lower Arc perimeter, Jarrier series, acquisitions, Dossier C [hereafter Dossier C], Bonrieu torrent of Jarrier, RTM Savoie.

53. Report by M. Luze, 3 May 1904, General Dossier, Bonrieu torrent of Jarrier, RTM Savoie.

54. Report by Mougin, 23 September 1897, Dossier C, Bonrieu torrent of Jarrier, RTM Savoie; Report by Kuss, 28 February 1898, 30 DF 82, AN.

55. Report by M. Luze, 24 March 1901; report by Conservator Cochon, 2 August 1902, 6 P 333, ADS.

56. Report by M. Luze, 1 December 1900, Documents d'Affaires Diverses, Dossier A1 [hereafter Dossier A1], Bonrieu torrent of Jarrier, RTM Savoie.

57. Report by Conservator Cochon, 10 March 1904, 6 P 216, ADS.

58. Conseil Général, 17 April 1901, General Dossier, Bonrieu torrent of Jarrier, RTM Savoie.

59. Report by Mougin, 17 March 1906, 6 P 216, ADS.

60. Mougin's opinion following reports by M. de Luze, 25 November 1905, Dossier A2, and 29 December 1905, Contrôle des travaux, Dossier K [hereafter Dossier K], Bonrieu torrent of Jarrier, RTM Savoie.

61. Combes, "Restauration des Terrains en Montagne," 102; Eisbacher and Clague, "Destructive Mass Movements in High Mountains," 97.

62. Report by M. Montmayeur to the Conseil Général, April 1909, 6 P 216, ADS.

63. Report by the Agriculture Commission on the complementary perimeter for the Lower Arc, Chamber of Deputies, 10 March 1910, Dossier B, Bonrieu torrent of Jarrier, RTM Savoie. In 1914, Paul Mougin dedicated his tome *Les Torrents de la Savoie* to David, who was by then minister of agriculture.

64. Rambaud and Vincienne, *Les Transformations d'une société rurale,* 56–57; Ariès, *Histoire des populations françaises,* 290–92. Owing to natural increase, the overall population of Jarrier declined somewhat less dramatically though still significantly—18 percent between 1901 and 1911. "Etat nominatif des habitants de la commune de Jarrier," Department of Savoie, M 196, ADS.

65. Municipal council of Jarrier, 1 November 1908; municipal council of Saint-Pancrace, 6 November 1908, Dossier B, Bonrieu torrent of Jarrier, RTM Savoie.

66. Municipal council of Jarrier, ibid.

67. Report by Joseph Ruau on the complementary perimeter for the lower Arc, Chamber of Deputies, 16 December 1909, Dossier B, Bonrieu torrent of Jarrier, RTM Savoie.

68. Opinion of the inquiry commissioner, 30 October 1908 and 10 November 1908, Dossier B, Bonrieu torrent of Jarrier, RTM Savoie.

69. Municipal council of Jarrier, 1 January 1911, communal archives of Jarrier.

70. Mayor of Jarrier to Conservator, 20 May 1909; Inspector Mougin to Conservator, 28 May 1909, Dossier A2, Bonrieu torrent of Jarrier, RTM Savoie.

71. Reports by General Guard Martin, 30 November 1907 and 30 October 1908; Report by Paul Noël, 8 October 1910, Contrôle des travaux—Régie, Dossier L [hereafter Dossier L], Bonrieu torrent of Jarrier, RTM Savoie.

72. Prefect to Sub-Prefects in Savoie, 20 January 1898, 6 P 361, ADS.

73. Municipal council of Jarrier, 29 December 1907; Conservator to Prefect, 13 November 1908, 6 P 361, ADS.

74. Reports by Martin, 24 September 1908 and 25 March 1909; mayor of Jarrier to Prefect, 19 December 1908, 6 P 361, ADS.

75. Reports by Noël, 9 August 1909 and 15 August 1911, Dossier A2, Bonrieu torrent of Jarrier, RTM Savoie.

76. Joint Inspector Paul Noël, General project for the restoration of the basin of the Bonrieu torrent of Jarrier, 8 May 1913, Dossier H, Bonrieu torrent of Jarrier, RTM Savoie, 79–80, 93.

77. Ibid., 84.

78. Neither they nor Noël himself, in his 1913 report, brought attention to the fundamental geological character of the area, the bedrock-debris slump extending fifty meters down. It can safely be assumed that geologists did not elucidate this problem until later in the century. For Noël's emphasis on humidity and lateral erosion, see his report of 5 December 1912, Dossier K, Bonrieu torrent of Jarrier, RTM Savoie.

79. Noël, General project, 96.

80. Ibid., 90.

81. According to Paul Mougin's figures, peasants in the ten Alpine departments sold land to the RTM for an average price of eighty-nine francs per hectare in the first decade of the twentieth century and for ninety-seven francs between 1909 and 1914. Mougin, *La Restauration des Alpes*, 454.

82. Noël, General project, 93–94.

83. Nominal role of the inhabitants of Jarrier, 25 March 1911, M 196, ADS.

84. Noël, General project, 95.

85. Ibid., 101–13.

86. Dequier and Viallet, *Un Village en Maurienne*, 94–95.

87. Report by Joint Inspector Alteirac, 3 November 1919, Dossier L, Bonrieu torrent of Jarrier, RTM Savoie.

88. See the data codified by Mougin in *La Restauration des Alpes*, 446–53.

89. Dequier and Viallet, *Un Village en Maurienne*, 220–22.

90. Rambaud and Vincienne, *Les Transformations d'une société rurale*, 227–28.

91. The expression is Marnézy's, *Maurienne, terre humaine*, 71; Rambaud and Vincienne, *Les Transformations d'une société rurale*, 144–53.

92. Dequier and Viallet, *Un Village en Maurienne*, 98.

93. Rambaud and Vincienne, *Les Transformations d'une société rurale*, 134–35.

4. THE PATRIMONY OF THE POOR

1. See Chapter 1 for a full description of the mechanisms and significance of cantonnement. The countess of Sabran invoked the primitive version of cantonnement allowed by Colbert's Forest Ordinance of 1669.

2. This synopsis of the prehistory of the "Affair of the Mountains" is drawn from two complementary accounts: see Servat, *Histoire de Massat*, 102–21, and Galy-Gasparrou, "La

Vérité sur la question des montagnes de Massat," 9–15, 24 April 1900, Zo 17[14,] ADA. I wish to thank Peter Sahlins for providing me with both sources.

3. Michel Chevalier, the eminent historical geographer of the Ariège, saw fit to summarize the affair in one paragraph in his 1,060-page opus; see Chevalier, *La Vie humaine dans les Pyrénées ariégeoises,* 340.

4. Soulet, *Les Pyrénées au XIXe siècle,* 2:604, 606.

5. Vigier, "Les troubles forestiers," 128.

6. Sub-Prefect to Prefect, 28 December 1861, 7 P 17, ADA. More than one historian has noted that "Demoiselles" reappeared several times during the 1860s as well as during the period 1870–72, acting out their grievances against forest guards and forge owners.

7. See, for example, Roquemaurel and Delpla to Minister of the Interior, 1 June 1864, 2 O 43, and Sub-Prefect to unknown, 17 May 1867, 7 P 13, ADA, in which the latter suspects the property owners' rhetorical use of the phrase "insurrection of the demoiselles."

8. Report by Brigadier Peyrat, 24 February 1897, 2 O 47, ADA.

9. Soulet, *Les Pyrénées au XIXe siècle,* 2:605.

10. Witness the mass assemblies convoked by the *Tard Avisés* of the Limousin and Périgord in the 1590s: see Bercé, *History of Peasant Revolts,* 71–106.

11. Prefect of Ariège, "Mémoire sur le département de l'Ariège," 4 October 1834, 1 J 439, ADA.

12. Ruffié, *Massat,* 4.

13. Margadant, *Urban Rivalries in the French Revolution,* 228.

14. Chevalier, *La Vie humaine,* 81.

15. Loubet, "Etude géographique," pt. 1: "Etude physique," 43.

16. Chevalier, *La Vie humaine,* 354.

17. Ibid., 241, 291, 298, 313, 317, 320, 363.

18. Ibid., 410–15; Loubet, "Etude géographique," pt. 2: "Etude humaine," 210–12.

19. Chevalier, *La Vie humaine,* 413, 447–51. Some livestock from Massat, namely the non-milk-producing cows, took part in transhumance, driven each summer to the pastures of the upper Ariège basin.

20. Clarenc, "Riches et pauvres," 309; Coquerelle, "Les droits collectifs," 350; Sahlins, *Forest Rites,* 94.

21. Chevalier, *La Vie humaine,* 664, 671, 673; Soulet, *Les Pyrénées au XIXe siècle,* 1:149. In this demographic context, it is worth mentioning that Ariège, of all departments, was the most severely affected by the cholera epidemic of 1854, suffering an average mortality rate of 4.3 percent. Cholera reappeared in the Massat Valley as late as 1893.

22. Loubet, "Etude géographique," pt. 2, 189–90; Salies, *Quand l'Ariège changea de siècle,* 106–9; Chevalier, *La Vie humaine,* 674, 677–80, 683–86, 688; 10 M 1, ADA. The revenues of seasonal migrants came close to those of the inhabitants engaged in cattle raising in 1865.

23. Galy-Gasparrou, "La Vérité sur la question des montagnes de Massat," 15–16; Delpla and Roquemaurel to Minister of the Interior, 1 June 1864, 2 O 43, ADA.

24. Weill, *Droit civil,* 19–20, 32.

25. Contracts and judicial decisions can maintain indivision, however, or be forced if the property does not lend itself to partition, as in the cases of common walls or hedges. Ibid., 181–87.

26. Weill notes that "public moral persons" can also own private property and that commonly owned lands of a commune might be considered either the "private domain of the commune" or a "special" form of collective property. Ibid., 187–92. See also Garaud, *La Révolution et la propriété foncière*, 386.

27. *Code civil des Français*, 408; Weill, *Droit civil*, 318, 327, 338–39, 352–53, 379.

28. Soulet, *Les Pyrénées au XIXe siècle*, 2:102–6; Loubet, "Etude géographique," pt. 2, 195, 198.

29. Chevalier, *La Vie humaine*, 328–29; Soulet, *Les Pyrénées au XIXe siècle*, 2:116.

30. Chevalier, *La Vie humaine*, 333–34, 338–39.

31. Galy-Gasparrou, "La Vérité sur la question des montagnes de Massat," 15.

32. Ibid., 17; Chevalier, *La Vie humaine*, 177 n 5, 190 n 1; Sub-Prefect to Prefect, 8 April 1853, 2 O 42, ADA. Chevalier notes the people of Le Port's usage of the phrase "les messieurs de Massat," referring to all inhabitants of the bourg, in 1850. The syndical commission was an administrative structure that preceded the intercommunal syndicate, the latter authorized by law in 1890; both forms served the purpose of managing interests or properties shared by two or more communes. See Rivéro, *Droit administratif*, 335, 337.

33. Municipal council of Le Port, 14 February 1855, 2 O 42, ADA.

34. Mayor of Massat and President of syndical commission to Prefect, 19 June 1855, 2 O 42; President of syndical commission to Sub-Prefect, 7 February 1862, 7 P 17, ADA.

35. Galy-Gasparrou, "La Vérité sur la question des montagnes de Massat," 17.

36. Report by two gendarmes, brigade of Massat, based on the declaration of private forest guard Gabriel Sable, 11 May 1867; Sub-Prefect to "my dear colleague," 17 May 1867, 7 P 13, ADA; Galy-Gasparrou, "La Vérité sur la question des montagnes de Massat," 18–19.

37. Delpla and Roquemaurel to Minister of the Interior, 1 June 1864, 2 O 43, ADA.

38. Imperial Prosecutor in Saint-Girons to Sub-Prefect, 1 June 1867, 7 P 13, ADA.

39. Report by M. Serval, Inspector General, concerning the verification of service by M. Guinier, Inspector in Foix, tour of 1882, F 10 7026, AN.

40. Extending the forest regime to more communal forests remained, for example, out of the question: "Politics has never played a role more contrary to the interests of the forest," ibid. See also the report by M. Bédel, Inspector General, concerning the verification of service by M. Bernard, Inspector in Toulouse, tour of 1879, F 10 7023, AN.

41. Report by M. Serval, Inspector General, concerning the verification of service by M. Jacques, Inspector in Saint-Girons, tour of 1882, F 10 7026, AN.

42. Sébastien, *Rivières d'Ariège*, 18–19, 22. Sébastien notes the plea by alpine shepherds, who suffered much loss of livestock, that their fines for forest crimes be reimbursed.

43. General reconnaissance report by MM. Guary (Conservator), Vaultrin (Inspector), and Bentajou (Joint-Inspector), 25 August 1887, Salat perimeter, RTM, AGRI 4429, AN.

44. Report by M. Serval, Inspector General, concerning management, reforestation, works of all sorts, etc., tour of 1882, F 10 7026, AN.

45. Ibid.

46. The assumption that reigned throughout these negotiations was that the state would acquire the land and then proceed to reforest it, anticipating the state expenditures authorized by the law of 1882 on the restoration and conservation of alpine lands. Reports by Forest Inspector Boixo, 1 and 7 April 1862; municipal council of Biert, 12 October 1862;

municipal council of Le Port, 12 October 1862; municipal council of Massat, 9 December 1862; Conseil Général, 29 August 1863; Minister of Finance to Prefect, 8 December 1863, 7 P 17, ADA.

47. Report by M. Watier, Forest Inspector in Toulouse, 29 October 1902, 15 DF 22, AN; Galy-Gasparrou, "La Vérité sur la question des montagnes de Massat," 19–20.

48. Report by Guary, Vaultrin, and Bentajou, 22 August 1887, Salat Perimeter, Massat, AGRI 4429, AN.

49. Ibid.; see also the reports on Biert and Le Port.

50. Report by Loze (Conservator), Watier (Inspector), and d'Ussel (General Guard), 17 December 1903, perimeter revision, Salat Perimeter, AGRI 4429, AN.

51. Report by Guary, Vaultrin, and Bentajou, 22 August 1887, Salat Perimeter, Le Port, AGRI 4429, AN.

52. General reconnaissance report, 25 Aug. 1887, Salat Perimeter, RTM, AGRI 4429, AN.

53. Reports by M. Serval, F 10 7026, AN.

54. For a detailed argument against communal ownership, see Justice of the peace in Massat to Prefect, 1 August 1854, 7 P 69, ADA.

55. Galy-Gasparrou, "La Vérité sur la question des montagnes de Massat," 11, 16. Soulet alludes to a clan, most likely the Galy-Gasparrous, that held an iron grip on professional life in Massat. Soulet, *Les Pyrénées au XIXe siècle*,1:377.

56. Salies, *Quand l'Ariège changea de siècle*, 234.

57. Prefect to Minister of Agriculture, 4 February 1888; Galy-Gasparrou to Prefect, 1 February 1888, 7 P 128, ADA.

58. Report by M. Bentajou, General Guard, 15 September 1886; Galy-Gasparrou to Sub-Prefect, 18 March 1887; Prefect's report to the Conseil Général, 2nd Session, 1887, 2 O 47, ADA.

59. A "citadel of socialism" by the 1980s, Ariège began its electoral identification with the left in the legislative elections of 1849. Though a slight presence at the turn of the century, socialism made significant inroads in the department during the interwar years; by 1936, all three deputies from Ariège were socialist. As Michel Chevalier notes, "Symbolic of the decline of the radicals has been the effacement of the great Galy-Gasparrou family, republican notables and radicals from the Massat valley." Chevalier, *L'Ariège*, 159 n 8.

60. Sub-Prefect to Mayor of Massat, 23 May 1903, 15 DF 22, AN.

61. Special commission of the Chemins de Fer in Oust to Prefect, 1 March 1897, 2 O 47, ADA.

62. Municipal council of Massat, 11 May 1873, 5 K 355, ADA.

63. Special commission of the Chemins de Fer, 1 March 1897, 2 O 47, ADA.

64. Report by General Guard M. Griess, 6 November 1898, 15 DF 22, AN.

65. Municipal council of Massat, 20 December 1896; handwritten note signed by fifteen members of the municipal council of Massat, 21 February 1897, 5 K 355, ADA.

66. Galy-Gasparrou, "La Vérité sur la question des montagnes de Massat," 24.

67. Galy-Gasparrou, "La Vérité sur la question des montagnes de Massat," 24–25.

68. Sub-Prefect in Saint-Girons to Prefect, 27 December 1899, 2 O 47, ADA.

69. Report by Lieutenant Claustre, gendarmerie commander in Saint-Girons, "on the events which have brought a certain agitation to the commune of Massat," 9 July 1899, 1 J 57, ADA.

70. Ibid.
71. Special commission of the Chemins de Fer, 1 March 1897, 2 O 47, ADA.
72. *La Dépêche,* 15 February 1897, 2 O 47, ADA. Though little socialist press existed locally, at the turn of the century newspapers and activists from Toulouse began to make numerous inroads in Ariège; see Salies, *Quand l'Ariège changea de siècle,* 424–25. For the links between small property, common rights, and socialist politics in the Third Republic, see Judt, *Socialism in Provence.*.
73. *Express du Midi,* 20 November 1899, 2 O 47, ADA.
74. Notice from the proprietors of the woods and mountains of Massat, Biert, and Le Port, 11 May 1899, 2 O 47, ADA.
75. Transcript of the public session of the Court of First Instance in Saint-Girons, 18 February 1901, 5 K 357, ADA.
76. Ibid.; Report by gendarmes Bonnel, Carol, and Hayron[?], 1 August 1900, 2 O 47, ADA.
77. Report by the sergeant commanding the supplementary force in Massat, 31 August 1900, 2 O 47, ADA.
78. Report by Alexis Suère, Jean-Pierre Servat, and Baptiste Abadie, 24 October 1898, 15 DF 22, AN.
79. Report by brigadier Saint-Agne, commander in Massat, 17 July 1899, 2 O 47, ADA.
80. Report by Saint-Agne, 26 February 1900, 2 O 47, ADA.
81. Report by Saint-Agne, 19 March 1900, 2 O 47, ADA.
82. Key material for these years of the affair can be found in 2 O 47, 1 J 57, and 5 K 357, ADA, as well as 15 DF 22, AN.
83. Sub-Prefect to Prefect, 25 July 1900, 2 O 47, ADA.
84. Lefort, "La question des montagnes," *Le Réveil du Saint-Gironnais,* 1 March 1903.
85. Letter from Galy-Gasparrou, *La Dépêche,* 11 May 1900, 2 O 47, ADA; editorial by Galy-Gasparrou, *Le Républicain du Saint-Gironnais,* 25 April 1902. In this editorial the Radical Republican slipped in his diagnosis of the danger represented by the inhabitants of Massat: on one hand, they were political enemies of the Republic; on the other, they showed an "invincible atavism" in their will to recover their possessions, posing a threat to order through their "excitation" and "very vitality."
86. For a description of the repertoire of typical 14 July celebrations between 1880 and 1914, see Sanson, *Les 14 juillet, fête et conscience nationale,* 92–100, and Chapter 1 of Rearick, *Pleasures of the Belle Epoque.*
87. Salies, *Quand l'Ariège changea de siècle,* 188, 191.
88. Report by Saint-Agne, 14 July 1900, 2 O 47, ADA.
89. Ibid.
90. This act of appropriation raises Eugen Weber's question, "Who Sang the Marseillaise?" Since most of the men who had put the "peasant government" into power were peasants themselves, it is likely that some—most?—spoke in patois most of the time; it will be remembered that speeches at the mass meetings had been spoken in patois. On the other hand, it is also likely that enough people in the mayor's crowd were conversant in French to give a credible rendition of the Marseillaise, an eminently "urban song," as Weber notes, and to allow the rest to follow along. See Weber, "Who Sang the Marseillaise?," 161–73.

91. Report by Saint-Agne, 14 July 1900, 2 O 47, ADA.
92. Rearick, *Pleasures of the Belle Epoque*, 19–23.
93. For Sanson, both "republican myth" and "revolutionary potential" continued to infuse the popular festival of 14 July in the late nineteenth century. Sanson, *Les 14 juillet, fête et conscience nationale*, 56–63.
94. "Pétition adressée à la Chambre des Députés et au Sénat par les Propriétaires des Montagnes," 5 November 1900, 3530/22, ADH-G.
95. Ibid.
96. Sub-Prefect to Prefect, 2 March 1901, 2 O 47, ADA. See also 5 K 357, ADA, for the civil case against the communes and its outcome.
97. Municipal council of Le Port, 6 July 1901; Prefect to Minister of the Interior, 17 August 1901; Sub-Prefect to Prefect, 4 January 1902; President of the Council of State to Prefect, 14 January 1910, 2 O 48; Report by M. Caster, Forest Inspector in Saint-Girons, 16 April 1912, 7 P 23; Accounts of the syndical commission of Massat–Le Port, 1911, 1 O 687, ADA. It was only after Galy-Gasparrou once again became president of the syndical commission that he himself steered authorization for the repurchase through the Council of State.
98. Prefect to Minister of Agriculture, 27 September 1902; Director General to Conservator in Toulouse, 24 October 1902; Minister of Finance to Minister of Agriculture, 15 November, 1902, 15 DF 22, AN.
99. Report by Watier, Inspector in Toulouse, and list of fires in Massat, Biert, and Le Port, 6 June 1903, 3530/23, ADH-G.
100. Report by Watier, 13 March 1903, 15 DF 23, AN; Report by Inspector A. Campagne, 29 June 1908, 3530/23, ADH-G.
101. Opinion of Inspector A. Campagne, 4 July 1908, and other documents in 7 P 20, ADA. In 1917 the state agreed to furnish the seedlings for reforestation that the inhabitants would undertake themselves after a new communal syndicate acquired the land from Loubet.

5. OLD AND NEW IN THE EAUX ET FORÊTS

1. *Les Eaux et Forêts du 12e au 20e siècle*, 565–66.
2. Ibid., 557–58.
3. Restauration et conservation des terrains en montagne, *Compte rendu sommaire des travaux*, 5–7, 32; Fabre, *Restauration et nationalisation du sol en haute montagne*, 3.
4. Guénot, *Les Inondations de 1897*, 2, 5.
5. Ibid., 1, 13, 16.
6. Buffault, *Insuffisance de notre législation*, 16–19.
7. Ibid., 19. See an earlier formulation of this argument in Forest Inspector Paul de Boixo's *Les Forêts et le reboisement dans les Pyrénées-Orientales* (1894).
8. Fabre, *L'Idée forestière*, 17.
9. Ibid., 18–19, emphasis in original.
10. In "Deep Play in the Forest," chapter 2 of *Forest Rites*, Peter Sahlins explores feminine images of the Ariégeois forest and the "ambivalence of the male peasantry's simultaneous identification with the forest and their 'marital' possession of it." Sahlins, 59.

11. Fabre, "L'Idée forestière" 4, 10, 15, emphasis in original. Colbert's Forest Ordinance of 1669 continued to resonate for foresters in the twentieth century. In 1926 Forest Inspector Marcel Paillié praised the return of an explicitly economic take on the forest: "we are managing, as in Colbert's time, to envisage the public utility of the forest as a function of its ligneous production." Paillié, *L'Etat et la propriété forestière*, 42.

12. Fron, *Economie sylvo-pastorale*, 2, 4–5. Fron estimated that firewood still accounted for three-quarters of the production of French forests.

13. Importations et exportations de bois communs (pour la France), 1946, 30 DF 163, AN; Asselain, *Histoire économique de la France*, 182.

14. Fron, *Economie sylvo-pastorale*, 161. See the *Statistique forestière* of 1878; Daubrée, *Statistique et atlas des forêts de France;* and the pamphlet *L'Office National des Forêts: Une entreprise au service du public* for comparative statistics.

15. Buffault, *Insuffisance de notre législation*, 8–9, 12, 34.

16. *Les Eaux et Forêts du 12e au 20e siècle*, 638–39; Bourdeaux, *Code forestier*, 52–54.

17. The revision of 1913 continued the provision of subsidies for voluntary reforestation, and all obligatory projects had to be sanctioned by a law (a point amended in 1933, allowing a decree by the Council of State to suffice). See articles 2 and 5 in Bourdeaux, *Code forestier*, 131–32.

18. *Les Eaux et Forêts du 12e au 20e siècle*, 578; Bourdeaux, *Code forestier*, 131.

19. "Situation d'Avant Guerre," n.d., Eaux et Forêts dossier, 30 DF 163, AN.

20. *Les Eaux et Forêts du 12e au 20e siècle*, 626; Fussell, *Great War and Modern Memory*, 37. According to General Director Dabat's report of 1917, France's average annual production of construction wood was 6,712,156 cubic meters. Dabat, "La production ligneuse de la France et la guerre," 30 September 1917, 30 DF 163, AN, 2.

21. "Les exploitations forestières pour les besoins des armées," 1918, 30 DF 163, AN.

22. Ibid., 2–6.

23. "La production ligneuse de la France et la guerre," 9–11. "Notre domaine forestier et la guerre," 43; Clout, *After the Ruins*, 30–31. Susan Lanier-Graham also cites the lower figure of 494,000 acres (200,000 hectares) of destroyed forest in *Ecology of War*, 19.

24. "Restauration des forêts dévastées par la guerre," General Direction of the Eaux et Forêts, 14 December 1918, 30 DF 163, AN, 2–3; David is quoted in *Les Eaux et Forêts du 12e au 20e siècle*, 627.

25. "La production ligneuse de la France et la guerre," 18–22.

26. "Restauration des forêts dévastées par la guerre," 4–5; "Notre domaine forestier et la guerre," 44.

27. "La production ligneuse de la France et la guerre," 26; "Restauration des forêts dévastées par la guerre," 8–9.

28. Salvador, "Simples notes sur l'aménagement et l'exploitation des forêts pyrénéennes françaises," 71–72.

29. Mougin, *Les Forêts de Savoie*, 750.

30. Corvol, *L'Homme aux bois*, 460–61. Minister of Agriculture Méline had used the language of protection in 1897: He refused the request of Ariège's Conseil Général that the state alienate some state lands that might be put to agricultural purposes, arguing that land in the state's possession constituted zones safe from erosion and thus an "efficacious

means of protection." See Prefect's report to the Conseil Général, first session of 1898, 7 P 69, ADA.

31. Mougin, "Les forêts de protection en Savoie," 557.

32. Quoted in Kalaora and Savoye, *La Forêt pacifiée,* 65.

33. Buffault, *Insuffisance de notre législation,* 19, quoting Gorse, *La Question du reboisement.*

34. See Leynaud, *L'Etat et la nature,* 19–20.

35. Bourdeaux, *Code forestier,* 140.

36. Prefect of Savoie to Minister of the Interior, 5 November 1920, 6 P 352, ADS.

37. Chamber of Deputies, *session extraordinaire* of 1921, 22 December 1921, 6 P 352, ADS.

38. "Note remise par M. Bouvet, Président du groupe forestier de la Chambre des Députés," Ibid.

39. Opinion of the various collectivities, assemblies, and authorities, n.d., 22 DF 7, AN.; Report to the Special Commission . . . relating to the classification of protective forests, 25 March 1926, 6 P 340, ADS.

40. See especially the dossier on the commune of Bramans, as well as those on Héry-sur-Ugine, Saint-Nicolas-La-Chapelle, and Termignon, 22 DF 7, AN.

41. Palluel-Guillard et al., *La Savoie de la Révolution à nos jours,* 354.

42. Municipal council of Bramans, 14 June 1925, 6 P 340, ADS.

43. Report by General Guard Sarlit, Eaux et Forêts, 10 April 1933; Mayor and municipal council of Termignon, 14 February 1933; Mayor to Prefect, 4 March 1933, 6 P 340, ADS.

44. Decree from the Ministry of Agriculture, 15 September 1932, 6 P 340, ADS.

45. On the growing industrial and commercial economy of the Savoie during the interwar years, as well as urban densification, see Palluel-Guillard et al., *La Savoie de la Révolution à nos jours* 359–71.

46. Municipal council of Rogalle, 11 April 1926, 7 P 25, ADA.

47. Foresters' tendencies to stretch the applicability of the Chauveau law (seen earlier with respect to the 1882 law in both Ariège and Savoie) also arose in the context of an instruction from the director general of the Eaux et Forêts in 1922: Using the 1920 floods in the Maurienne as a justification, he urged conservators to submit degraded communal forests to the forest regime. For much of the nineteenth century, the advanced degradation of a communal forest had constituted a reason not to submit it to the state's management—notwithstanding the imperatives of restoring mountain slopes. See Director General to Conservator in Toulouse, 27 January 1922, and Conservator to Prefect of Ariège, 4 February 1922, 7 P 69, ADA.

48. Conseil Général, 2 October 1925 and 30 September 1926; report by the prefectorial commission on protective forests, 10 March 1926, 7 P 25, ADA.

49. Relying on the *Inventaire forestier national* of 1978, Michel Chevalier claims that the forested surface of Ariège grew from 27 to 34 percent of the department between 1900 and 1950. Chevalier, *L'Ariège,* 87. Galy-Gasparrou's 1925–26 micro-observation of this phenomenon is highly plausible.

50. Conseil Général, first session of 1926, 7 P 25, ADA.

51. Conseil Général, second session of 1926, 30 September 1926, 7 P 25, ADA.

52. Minister of Agriculture, decrees, 29 June and 23 August 1927; prefecture of Ariège, 25 March 1927, 7 P 25, ADA; Géneau, "Les forêts de protection," 657.

53. Municipal council of Termignon, 14 February 1933; Dossier on the commune of Flumet, n.d., 22 DF 7, AN.

54. For an example of the administrative state's imprint on communal space in these years, see Boucharlat, Cadenne, and Gachet, "Espace et communauté."

55. These percentages, based on Daubrée's 1912 figures for forest cover, are undoubtedly too high since they would not reflect the natural reforestation that had taken place between 1912 and the time that protective forests were designated in the late 1920s. See Daubrée, *Statistique et atlas des forêts de France*, 71.

56. See 6 P 325 and 6 P 359, ADS, for correspondence regarding these requests into the early 1930s. Municipal council of Montagny, 26 March 1932, 6 P 325, ADS.

57. Guicherd, *L'Agriculture du département de la Savoie*, 192.

58. Municipal council of Le Bois, 22 December 1937, 6 P 359, ADS.

59. Conservator Sorney to Prefect of Savoie, 23 January 1931, 6 P 360, ADS.

60. Conservator in Chambéry to Director General, 3 November 1921; quotation is from a report by General Guard Messines, 13 February 1926; Report by Inspector Rochebrune, 25 June 1927, F 10 2390, AN.

61. Report by General Guard Parlier, 6 July 1931; Conservator to Director General, 23 April 1932; quotation is from a report by General Guard Plagnat, 28 March 1933, F 10 2390, AN.

62. Report by Inspector Caster, 28 November 1925, 7 P 37, ADA; Report by Conservator Salvador, 21 January 1936, F 10 2381, AN.

63. Report by Salvador, 21 January 1936, F 10 2381, AN

64. Fournié, *Code officiel des usages locaux*, articles 104, 106–110.

65. Broilliard, *Le Traitement des bois en France*, 644–45, 652–53.

66. Salvador, "Simples notes," 63, 69. See also a prewar article whose author struggles to find the mathematical formulas for calculating the possibility of a forest submitted to jardinage: de Fonteny, "Notes sur l'aménagement des futaies jardinées," 193–204.

6. THE COERCION OF PEDAGOGY

1. Rabouille, *Du Rôle de l'Administration*, 9.

2. Ibid., 3. The reacquisition of Alsace and Lorraine, as well as state purchases made since World War I, added 556,000 hectares to the Eaux et Forêts' jurisdiction, or 17 percent of the territory under its control in 1913.

3. Ibid., 14.

4. Green, *The Spectacle of Nature*, 6.

5. Specifically, mayors, members of the clergy, primary school teachers, gendarmes, customs officials, forest guards, and rural policemen could join the Société free of charge if they promised to plant at least five trees a year. Société des Amis des Arbres, Statutes, Title III, Article 14, May 1895, 6 P 328, ADS.

6. Ibid.

7. The key bridge between the two groups lay in the person of E. Cardot, who presided over the Touring-Club's Commission on Grasses and Forests and became general secretary of the Société des Amis des Arbres in 1909. Corvol, *L'Homme aux bois*, 458. The

ethos of European touring clubs is well presented in Bertho-Lavenir, "Normes de comportement et contrôle de l'espace," 69–87.

8. On the sociocultural basis of alpinism, see Collomb, *Du bon usage de la montagne*, 51–56, 68–70, who draws upon Gaston Bachelard's psychology of ascension as well as Pierre Bourdieu's theory of the production of artistic taste. For a broader cultural analysis of alpinism, see Schama, *Landscape and Memory*, 447–513.

9. Quoted in Collomb, *Du bon usage de la montagne*, 71; Mestrallet, "Histoire de l'alpinisme en Savoie," 21.

10. Collomb, *Du bon usage de la montagne*, 71–73. The Touring-Club initiated the Comité National des Sentiers de Grande Randonnée in 1947, thus spurring the construction of the famous numbered trails that traverse France. See Mestrallet, "Histoire de l'alpinisme en Savoie," 32.

11. Corvol, *L'Homme aux bois*, 458; Puyo, "Les expériences sylvo-pastorales," 14. Though not as much as the Touring-Club, the Club Alpin Français took at least some interest in reforestation. See Note from Fodéré Barnabé of the CAF to Prefect of Savoie, 19 January 1912; Report by M. Lefranc, Joint Inspector in Saint-Jean-de-Maurienne, 24 January 1912, 6 P 336, ADS.

12. Société des Amis des Arbres, Statutes, 1895, 6 P 328, ADS, 2, 4.

13. Descombes, *La Mise en pratique*, 6; Touring-Club de France, *Conférence sur le déboisement*, 21.

14. Bauby, *Le Reboisement et les conditions économiques*, 10; Puyo, "Les expériences sylvo-pastorales," 35.

15. Buffault, "L'évolution forestière," 57–60.

16. Fron, *Economie sylvo-pastorale*, 163; Touring-Club de France, *Conférence sur le déboisement*, 28.

17. Corvol, *L'Homme aux bois*, 454. Over time, the Eaux et Forêts did respond to the example set by the associations, as well as Buffault's admonition to become teachers. Foresters in Savoie were teaching courses in silviculture and pastoral economics at the Normal School in Albertville and the Agricultural School in Moûtiers by 1928. They had also begun to give peripatetic lectures through the forests for Savoyard students. See Conservator to Prefect, 27 October 1928, 6 P 360, ADS.

18. Corvol, *L'Homme aux bois*, 455, 537 n 6. See also Corvol, "Transformation of a Political Symbol," 465–66.

19. President of the ANIB to Prefect of Savoie, 20 April 1927, 6 P 360, ADS. Bulletin of Primary Instruction, "Fête de l'Arbre," 14 October 1927, 6 P 328, ADS.

20. ANIB, *La Fête de l'arbre*, 1927, 6 P 328, ADS.

21. Ibid.

22. Demorlaine, "L'importance stratégique des forêts et la guerre," 25–30. Hugh Clout points out that sentiment in the northern departments favored the restoration of arable land over reforestation in the former red zone. See Clout, *After the Ruins*, 261–72.

23. ANIB, *La Fête de l'arbre*, 1927.

24. ANIB, *La Fête de l'arbre*, 1929, 6 P 328, ADS. Similarly patriotic rhetoric lies scattered throughout the associational literature. Dr. Jeannel of the Société des Amis des Arbres had written as early as 1894 that it was "patriotic sentiment, the love of native soil" that had

guided the Société since its birth. In many documents, deforestation becomes the denudation of "our lovely France" or of "French soil." The slogan of the ACAM, appearing on its
letterhead was, indeed, "Sauver la terre de la patrie"—to save the soil of the fatherland.

25. Municipal council of Saint-Marcel, 14 December 1927, 6 P 328, ADS. The issue of cost,
for example, cannot be taken too literally, because the Eaux et Forêts had, since 1860,
provided seedlings for voluntary reforestation at extremely low prices. The ANIB reminded mayors of this service.

26. ANIB, *La Fête de l'arbre*, 1931, 6 P 328, ADS.

27. Campardon, *Les Améliorations pastorales*, 6.

28. Report by Inspector Chiriat, 10 July 1866; Conservator to Prefect of Ariège, 22 August
1883, 7 P 21, ADA.

29. Report by Joint Inspector in Ax-les-Thermes, 24 September 1890; Report by Conservator in Toulouse, 18 June 1895 and 6 July 1896, 7 P 21, ADA.

30. Conservator to Prefect of Ariège, 22 August 1883; Report by Conservator in Toulouse, 18
June 1895, 7 P 21, ADA. See also Mathieu, *Le Reboisement et le regazonnement des Alpes*,
11–13.

31. Campardon, *Les Améliorations pastorales*, 7–9, 13, 16–20.

32. Cavaillès, "L'association pastorale dans les Pyrénées," *Le Musée Social* (1910), and M. Al-
icot, *Compte rendu de la 1ère séance du IIe Congrès de l'aménagement des montagnes* (1907),
both cited in Puyo, "Les expériences sylvo-pastorales," 10–12. These contemporary observations echo in Harriet G. Rosenberg's analysis of creameries in Abriès (Hautes-
Alpes). See *A Negotiated World*, 126–28.

33. Direction Générale des Forêts, *Restauration et conservation des terrains en montagne*, 214.

34. Descombes, *La Question forestière et pastorale;* Association Centrale pour l'Aménagement des Montagnes, Notice, n.d., 6 P 45, ADS. This document reveals the touristic appeal of the ACAM, as well: members of the association enjoyed, among other things,
discounts on hotel rooms and half-price tickets for travel to the annual congress, which
involved a month-long sojourn in the Pyrenees.

35. Kalaora and Savoye, *La Forêt pacifiée*, 110; Puyo, "Les expériences sylvo-pastorales,"
20–22.

36. Corvol, *L'Homme aux bois*, 414. In *La Forêt pacifiée*, Kalaora and Savoye discuss the influence of Frédéric Le Play's functional sociology on three generations of foresters in the
mid- to late-nineteenth century. In a minor work written in 1840, *Des forêts considérées
dans leur rapport avec la constitution physique du globe et l'économie des sociétés*, as well as
in the more widely read *Les Ouvriers européens* and *La Réforme sociale en France*, Le Play
drew correlations between the extent of social stability and the presence of forest in
given regions, positing the health of forests as a chief indicator of the state of society.
His ideas drew the attention of a small group of foresters—twenty-two between 1864
and 1914—who reconceived their mission in the mountains as a duty to work for pastoral peoples, improving their forests and pastures in their interests, not the interests of
the state. Jean-Yves Puyo notes that prominent "social foresters" attended the ACAM's
three conferences on alpine management, held in Bordeaux (1905, 1907) and Pau (1906),
the latter advertised as the "first international conference on alpine management." Puyo,
"Les expériences sylvo-pastorales," 32–34.

37. Kalaora and Savoye, *La Forêt pacifiée*, 110–13; Fontaine, *Le Voyage et la mémoire*.

38. ACAM, *Notice*, c. 1913, 6 P 328, ADS. The Eaux et Forêts actually subsidized the ACAM's first project, carried out in la Géla (Hautes-Pyrénées), on condition that forestry personnel supervise the work. The mere sighting of a brigadier, however, inflamed the local population and caused Descombes to sever formal ties with the administration. Puyo, "Les expériences sylvo-pastorales," 23.

39. Descombes, *La Mise en pratique du reboisement*, 6; Kalaora and Savoye, *La Forêt pacifiée*, 96–97, 110–11; ACAM, *Notice*. De Sailly contributed his own diatribe against the state's encroachment on private forests in his pamphlet *La Déforestation de la France* (1908).

40. ACAM, *Notice*.

41. Quoted in Métailié, "Aux origines des améliorations pastorales dans les Pyrénées," 99. Métailié also notes that the decline in transhumance had begun with the century, whereas Descombes claimed to have led the way toward its abolition.

42. See articles by Briot in the *Annuaire de la Société Française d'Economie Alpestre* 1 (1921): 3–35 and 3 (1923): 92–95. In the first issue Briot in fact criticized the 1882 restoration law for its "old-regime" understanding of *réglementation* as *police* and *surveillance*.

43. Anonymous, "Les sociétés d'économie alpestre" *L'Economie alpestre* 10 (1930): 21–26. The organization changed its name to Fédération Française de l'Economie Alpestre in 1928, its review acquiring the title *L'Economie alpestre*. See also Rosenberg, *A Negotiated World*, 116–21.

44. Gaussen, "Le rôle de la Fédération d'Economie Montagnarde," *Annales de la Fédération Pyrénéenne d'Economie Montagnarde* 1 (1932): 25.

45. Briot, "Fondation de la Société et Assemblées Générales," *Annuaire de la Société Française d'Economie Alpestre* 1 (1921): 31–33.

46. "Concours d'architecture montagnarde [etc.]," *Annales de la Fédération Pyrénéenne d'Economie Montagnarde* 2 (1933): 141–52.

47. "Société Centrale d'Agriculture de la Savoie: Année 1937, concours d'alpages," *L'Economie alpestre* 18–19 (1938–39): 34–79; Report by M. Messines, Inspector in Chambéry, 5 March 1937, 6 P 325, ADS.

48. "Société Centrale d'Agriculture de la Savoie: Rapport sur le concours des alpages, 1930," *L'Economie alpestre* 11 (1931): 71.

49. "Société Centrale de l'Agriculture de la Savoie: Année 1932: Concours d'alpages," *L'Economie alpestre* 12 (1932): 47–52; quotation is from the obituary for François Rey, *L'Economie alpestre* 13 (1933): 124.

50. Briot, "Rapport moral," *L'Economie alpestre* 17 (1937): 9. In addition to critics such as Briot, mainstream figures within the Eaux et Forêts echoed such an orientation. In a standard textbook on alpine restoration used at the Nancy school, Claudius Bernard played down the fact of alpine depopulation as follows: "what matters above all is that the alpine areas fulfill, without ruining themselves or causing the ruin of other [areas], the role that they must play in the national economy." Bernard, *Cours de restauration des montagnes*, 421.

51. Gaussen, "Congrès de 1936 à Ax-les-Thermes: Rapport général," *Annales de la Fédération Pyrénéenne d'Economie Montagnarde* 5 (1936): 274, 278; Gaussen, "L'oeuvre des forestiers aux Pyrénées françaises," 411, 414. See also Métailié, "Aux origines," 100.

Though less commonly, other writers advocated heavy industrialization for the Pyrenees. Speaking at the second congress of the ACAM in 1907, Joint Inspector of the Eaux et Forêts Philippe Bauby (who on the same occasion frowned upon the associations' "neophyte ardor") declaimed: "When industry develops, pastoralism declines and the forest phase begins." See Bauby, *Le Reboisement*, 42.

52. Gaussen, "Congrès de 1936," 284–86; Gaussen, "La question forestière aux Pyrénées," 213–14.

53. Prochaska, "Fire on the Mountain," 232–34; Corvol, *L'Homme aux bois*, 369–70, 523 n 48.

54. Prochaska, "Fire on the Mountain," 239–41, 244. The French government promulgated a separate Forest Code for Algeria in 1903. Although modeled on the French Forest Code, the Algerian Forest Code contained harsher provisions regarding expropriation as well as severe measures pertaining to forest fires, including mandatory watch duties for all able-bodied men in the form of corvée labor. See Bourdeaux, *Code forestier*, 99–125. A translation of the Algerian Forest Code can be found in Woolsey, *French Forests and Forestry*, 161–208, though it contains several translation errors.

55. Trolard, *La Forêt: Conseils aux indigènes.*

56. Doumenjou, *Etudes sur la révision du code forestier*, vii, 264–97.

57. Ibid., vii; Trolard, *La Question forestière algérienne devant le Sénat*, 10, 28.

58. Osborne, *Nature, the Exotic, and the Science of French Colonialism*, 163.

59. At first glance, this opposition seems to provide a striking counterpoint to Robert Harrison's well-crafted argument in *Forests: The Shadow of Civilization* that irreducible antagonisms between "forests" and "civilization" form a thread running throughout Western thought. The forests promoted by associations in the twentieth century, however, were not "barbaric" forests but rather "enlightened" forests, highly managed and expunged of sacredness, wolves, bears, and peasants. See Harrison, especially chapter 3, "Enlightenment," 106–52.

60. Guénot, *Les Inondations de 1897*, 15; Touring-Club de France, *Conférence sur le déboisement*, 11–12.

61. *Le Courrier des Bois*, 10 December 1924, 6 P 328, ADS.

62. Attenborough, *First Eden*, 117–18; McNeill, *Mountains of the Mediterranean World*, 310.

63. Boutilly, "Les forêts en Algérie," 63–66.

64. Fron, *Economie sylvo-pastorale*, 17.

65. Fabre, *Les Incendies pastoraux*, 2–3. Chapter 1 of Eugen Weber's *Peasants into Frenchmen* contains ample nineteenth-century depictions of French peasants as savages.

66. Descombes, *La Mise en pratique*, 7.

67. Roquette-Buisson, *La Question forestière dans les Pyrénées*, 6; Touring-Club de France, *Conférence sur le déboisement*, 25.

68. Buffault, *Insuffisance de notre législation*, 3–4. The very methodology of the social foresters—who borrowed Le Play's form of the regional monograph in their studies of the "Savoyard type" or the "Auvergnat highlander"—lent itself to racial stereotyping. See Kalaora and Savoye, *La Forêt pacifiée*, 56–57. Along these lines, guides for tourists pointed to the positive characteristics of peasants by referring to race: a 1927 guide to Ariège touted the department as a good place to see the "vigorous and sane race of

highlanders." See *Les Pyrénées ariégeoises: Guide thermal et touristique* (1927), 20 J 4, ADA, 4.

69. *Le Courrier des Bois,* 10 December 1924, 6 P 328, ADS.
70. See Bourguet, "Race et folklore," 802–23.
71. Doumenjou, *Question forestière,* 28.
72. Soulet, *Les Pyrénées au dix-neuvième siècle,* 2:29–46.
73. Viazzo, *Upland Communities,* 89–93.
74. Palluel-Guillard et al., *La Savoie de la Révolution à nos jours,* 129–30, 262.
75. Descombes, *La Mise en pratique,* 9.
76. Descombes, *La Question forestière et pastorale,* 12.
77. Fabre, *La Fuite des populations pastorales françaises,* 14. See also his *L'Exode du montagnard et la transhumance du mouton en France.*
78. Fabre, *Restauration et nationalisation,* 6. As one might expect, a current of thought did promote the alpine peasants' colonizing as well as military potential. Guinier argued in 1890 that intensive bovine pasturing would both speed the recuperation of superfluous alpine pastures and keep the human population of the mountains overly abundant, thereby providing France with cheap colonies and fit soldiers. Just as the alpine glaciers fed watercourses in warm weather, so alpine people should feed the crucial currents of emigration to the colonies. See E. Guinier, *La Question des montagnes.*
79. Fabre, *L'Exode du montagnard,* 24.
80. Fabre, *Restauration et nationalisation,* 5.
81. Fabre, *Sur l'achèvement de la restauration des montagnes en France* (first congress of the ACAM, 1906), 7, emphasis in original.
82. *Dictionnaire étymologique* (Paris: Librairie Larousse, 1964), 230.
83. Green, *The Spectacle of Nature,* 71.
84. Gaussen, "Les Pyrénées," 11.
85. See Hudry, "Le Club Alpin Français," 334.

CONCLUSION

1. Giono, *The Man Who Planted Trees,* 7, 26.
2. Ibid., 32, 34, 38.
3. Ibid., 28, 38.
4. Cronon, "A Place for Stories," 1376.
5. McQuillan, "Making Restoration Work," 278.
6. For a striking parallel to the French case, see José D. García Pérez's work on twentieth-century reforestation in Spain. Similar failures have stemmed from the effects of technocratic planning and implementation, but the author has proposed and himself used the method of Participatory Rural Appraisal to ensure the participation of communities in conceiving and carrying out restoration projects. García Pérez, "The Promotion of Participation in Planning for Soil and Water Conservation Through Reforestation."
7. Collomb, "Images du changement," 154.
8. On these and other issues facing the present-day RTM, see Combes, "Restauration des

terrains en montagne," and Feuvrier, "Risques naturels et restauration des terrains en montagne."

9. Préau, "Le Parc National de la Vanoise," 405. For a brief general history of French national parks, see Leynaud, *L'Etat et la nature.*

10. Jean Brocart, *Pour que la montagne vive* (1975), quoted in Bozonnet, *Des monts et des mythes*, 193.

11. Lienert, "Genèse du paysage alpine," 6; Collomb, *Du bon usage,* 140–44; Rosenberg, Reiter, and Reiter, "Rural Workers in French Alpine Tourism."

12. Chevalier, *L'Ariège,* 135–43.

13. The expression is Frédéric Ogé's; see "Appropriation communautaire et/ou appropriation étatique," 132.

14. Barrué-Pastor and Fournié, "La montagne ariégeoise entre friche et paysage."

15. See *Le Monde* 11 July 1997, and *Le Moniteur,* 22 August 1997.

Bibliography

ARCHIVAL SOURCES

Archives Nationales: Centre d'accueil et de recherche, Paris
F 10: Eaux et Forêts

1645: Forêts domaniales, Ariège, 1830–70
1659: Commissions de cantonnement, 1857–65
1664: Forêts domaniales, cantonnements des droits d'usage, Ariège, 1844–74
2314: Mise en valeur des communaux, législation, 1860–80
2315: Mise en valeur des communaux, reconnaissance générale, Ariège, 1861–64
2317, 2318: Mise en valeur des communaux, Savoie, 1861–1900
2381: Autorisations de pacage des bêtes à laine dans les forêts et bois communaux soumis au régime forestier, 1939–42
2390: Autorisations de parcours et de pâturage dans les forêts et terrains domaniaux, Savoie, 1860–1943

Archives Nationales: Centre des archives contemporaines, Fontainebleau
AGRI 4429

Box no. 6, reboisement, Ariège, 1862–1903

F 10: Eaux et Forêts

7021: Inspection générale, départements de la chaîne des Alpes, 1885

7023: Inspection générale, Haute-Garonne et Ariège, 1879
7026, 7029: Inspection générale, Ariège, 1882, 1885

10 DF 9: Statistiques du département (1888), améliorations pastorales (1900), Ariège
15 DF: Forêts domaniales

22: Massat, montagnes, 1898–1904
23: Salat, périmètre, 1877–1904

22 DF 7: Forêts de protection, Savoie, 1921–32
24 DF 20: Forêts domaniales, Ariège: Auzat, 1858–1959
30 DF: Questions économiques

82: Reboisement, Savoie
163: Statistiques générales, 1890–1948
166: Crise forestière, 1930–37

34 DF 3: Notice forestière, Savoie, 1887

Archives Départementales de l'Ariège, Foix
4 E Massat M: Etat civil, mariages, 1860–1890
1 J 57: Agitation au sujet des pâturages des montagnes de Massat, 1899
1 J 439: Mémoire sur le département de l'Ariège, 1834
20 J 4: Tourisme et loisirs, 1907–27
5 K 350 (Massat, Biert, Le Port, 1879), 354–355 (Massat, 1806–58, 1863–1901), 357 (Le Port, 1863–1903): Conseil de préfecture; recours de particuliers ou de communes
5 M 72.2–72.3: Rapports sur la situation générale du département de l'Ariège, 1920–36
10 M 1, 3: Tableau de la population du département de l'Ariège, 1861–1935; Dénombrement de la population, Massat, 1876
7 M 11: Inondations du 23 juin 1875
1 O 687: Syndicats intercommunaux, Massat, Biert, Le Port (1853–1933), Massat, Le Port (1911–40)
2 O 42 (1853–58), 43 (1864), 47 (1856–1904), 48 (1901–10): Administration communale, biens communaux, etc., Massat, Biert, Le Port
7 P: Eaux et Forêts

2: Instructions générales, circulaires, 1862–1921
3: Rapports du conservateur au Conseil Général, 1817–1918
5–6: Recensement agricole des bois et forêts, 1929
13: Dévastation des bois, 1867, 1870–71
15–18: Reboisement, 1854–98
20: Restauration des terrains en montagne, 1902–35
21–23: Travaux d'améliorations pastorales, 1880–1922
25: Forêts de protection, 1924–28
37: Location de pâturages, droit de parcours, 1919–40
46: Forêts domaniales, liste de communes
69: Forêts communales, régime forestier, 1828–1922
128: Forêts domaniales, Massat, 1835–1930

447: Foudre, inondations, 1931–38

451–52: Renseignements statistiques, 1850, 1876, 1904–1910, 1922

4 T 35: Rapports sur les causes présumées des variations subites de l'atmosphère du fait du reboisement, 1821

8 U: Tribunal de première instance de Saint-Girons

685–708: 1886–1926 Jugements correctionnels, causes de l'Administration des Eaux et Forêts, 1886–1926

729: Coupes de bois, outrages et menaces . . . violences envers gardes forestiers, 1870–71

Zo 17^{14}: "La vérité sur la question des montagnes de Massat," 1900

L'Ariégeois, 1861

Le Républicain du Saint-Gironnais, 1902

Le Réveil du Saint-Gironnais, 1903

Archives Départementales de la Savoie, Chambéry

Archives communales, Jarrier

001: Affaires forestières

002, 004: Bois et biens communaux

Cadastre, Jarrier, 1898

M 70: Inondations, 1927–28

M 196: Population, canton de Saint-Jean-de-Maurienne, 1877–1936

22 M ^{1} 2: Enquête sur la situation et les besoins de l'agriculture, 1866

6 P: Eaux et Forêts

35: Délits forestiers, 1861–1920

36–37: Affaires forestières soumises au Conseil Général, 1874–1920

38: Régime forestier; défrichement, opposition, 1860–1874

40: Améliorations pastorales, pâturage, 1862–1923

45: Reboisement des montagnes, affaires diverses, 1861–1923

46: Reboisement, périmètre de l'Arc Supérieur

136: Forêt communale, Jarrier, 1890–96

216: Syndicat du Bonrieu, 1864–1875; torrents, reboisement, 1903–19

325: Améliorations pastorales, 1908–39

328: Association pour l'aménagement de la montagne, 1913–21; fête de l'arbre, 1928–31

330–33: Périmètre de l'Arc Inférieur, 1901–16

336: Travaux de reboisement, 1901–32; aménagement de forêts, 1921–28

340: Forêts de protection, 1922–35

352: Inondations, 1920–21

359: Reboisement, 1877–87; contenance des forêts de Savoie, 1735–1909; glissement de terrains, 1937–38

360: Affaires diverses, 1907–44

361: Réglementation de pâturages communaux, 1908–30

362: Rapports annuels des conservateurs, 1904–34

363: Travaux de reboisement et d'amélioration, 1914–33

L'Autorité, 1889

Archives Départementales de la Haute-Garonne, Toulouse
3530: Projet de périmètre du Salat

    22: 1886–1900
    23: 1887–1930

Archives du Service de Restauration des Terrains en Montagne de l'Ariège, Foix
Dossier sur les crues de 1897
Dossier 1

    Reboisement des montagnes, 1843–59
    Périmètre du Salat, projet général, 1903

La Dépêche du Midi, 1937

Archives du Service de Restauration des Terrains en Montagne de la Savoie, Chambéry
Périmètre de l'Arc Inférieur, Torrent du Bonrieu de Jarrier
Jarrier

    Dossier général d'affaires diverses, 1890–1920
    Dossiers A1, A2: documents d'affaires diverses, 1882–1911
    Dossier B: projet de périmètre, 1891–1910
    Dossier C: acquisitions, 1897
    Dossier H: projet général, 1913
    Dossier J: crues, 1885–1931
    Dossier K: contrôle des travaux—entreprise, 1905–07, 1935
    Dossier L: contrôle des travaux—régie, 1905–46
    Etats généraux: forêt domaniale de l'Arvan, 1906–77

Saint-Pancrace

    Dossier B: projet de périmètre

Greffe du Tribunal de Grande Instance, Foix
Registres d'Etat civil: Mariages, Massat, 1893–1940

Archives communales de Jarrier, Savoie
Registres d'Etat civil: Mariages, 1865–1939
Registres des délibérations du conseil municipal, 1911–22

PUBLISHED PRIMARY SOURCES

Journals
Annales de la Fédération Pyrénéenne d'Economie Montagnarde, 1932–36
Annuaire de la Société Française d'Economic Alpestre, 1921–28
L'Economic alpestre, 1928–39
Le Moniteur universel, 1857, 1860, 1864

Books and Articles

Administration des Forêts. *Statistique forestière*. Paris: Imprimerie Nationale, 1878.

Bauby, Philippe. *Le Reboisement et les conditions économiques en montagne*. Bordeaux: Imprimerie Commerciale et Industrielle, 1907.

Bernard, Claudius. *Cours de restauration des montagnes*. Nancy: Ecole Nationale des Eaux et Forêts, 1927.

Bourdeaux, Henry, ed. *Code forestier et code rural*. Paris: Librairie Dalloz, 1938.

Boutilly, V. "Les forêts en Algérie." *L'Illustration economique et financière*, special issue, "L'Algérie 1830–1930" (1930): 63–66.

Broilliard, Charles. *Le Traitement des bois en France: Estimation, partage et usufruit des forêts*. 3d ed. Paris and Nancy: Berger-Levrault, 1911.

Buffault, Pierre. "L'Evolution forestière." *REF* 58, 3 (1920): 57–60.

———. *Insuffisance de notre législation en matière de conservation et de restauration des forêts*. Bordeaux: Imprimerie G. Gounouilhou, 1902.

Campardon, M. *Les Améliorations pastorales dans l'Ariège et la Haute-Garonne*. Paris: Imprimerie Nationale, 1900.

Castillon, H. *Histoire d'Ax et de la Vallée d'Andorre*. Toulouse: Ansas, 1851.

Chapelain, P. C. *Notice sur le projet de périmètre de l'Arc Supérieur*. Chambéry: Imprimerie Chatelain, 1886.

Code civil des Français: Edition originale et seule officielle. 1804. Reprint, Paris: Librairie Duchemin, 1974.

Code forestier et code rural. Paris: Librairie Dalloz, 1938.

Daubrée, Lucien. *Statistique et atlas des forêts de France*. Paris: Imprimerie Nationale, 1912.

de Boixo, Paul. *Les Forêts et le reboisement dans les Pyrénées-Orientales*. Paris: J. Rothschild, 1894.

de Fonteny, Bizot. "Notes sur l'aménagement des futaies jardinées." *RFF* 52, 7 (1913): 193–204.

de Gorsse, Ernest. *La Question du reboisement dans les pays de Comminges*. Saint-Gaudens, 1899.

Demontzey, Prosper. "La correction des torrents et le reboisement des montagnes." *REF* 29 (1890): 485–502.

———. *Traité pratique du reboisement et du gazonnement des montagnes*. 2d ed. Paris: J. Rothschild, 1882.

Demorlaine, J. "L'importance stratégique des forêts et la guerre." *REF* 57, 1 (1919): 25–30.

Descombes, Paul. *La Mise en pratique du reboisement*. Bordeaux: Imprimerie G. Gounouilhou, 1906.

———. *La Question forestière et pastorale*. Foix: Typographie et lithographie Veuve Pomiès, 1907.

Direction Générale des Eaux et Forêts. *Restauration et conservation des terrains en montagne*. 3 vols. Paris: Imprimerie Nationale, 1911.

Doumenjou, Hippolyte. *Etudes sur la révision du code forestier: Les reboisements en France et en Algérie*. Paris: J. Baudry, 1883.

———. *Question forestière: Critique du projet de loi de l'application de l'expropriation pour cause d'utilité publique aux reboisement et gazonnement des montagnes.* Foix: Typographie et lithographie Pomiès, 1877.

Dralet, Etienne. *Description des Pyrénées.* 2 vols. Paris: Arthus Bertrand, 1813.

Fabre, J.-P.-A. *Des Habitants des montagnes considérés dans leurs rapports avec le régime forestier.* Marseille: Imprimerie Senés, 1849.

Fabre, Lucien-Albert. *L'Exode du montagnard et la transhumance du mouton en France.* Lyon: A. Rey, 1909.

———. *La Fuite des populations pastorales françaises.* Paris: Société d'Economie Sociale, 1909.

———. *L'Idée forestière sur le versant septentrional des Pyrénées.* Bagnères-de-Bigorre: Imprimerie Dominique Bérot, 1902.

———. *Les Incendies pastoraux et les associations dites 'forestières' dans les Pyrénées centrales.* Third congress of the Sud-Ouest navigable. Narbonne, 28 May 1904, 3 pp.

———. *Restauration et nationalisation du sol en haute montagne.* Excerpt from *La Houille Blanche* (March 1911), 8 pp.

———. *Sur l'achèvement de la restauration des montagnes en France.* Bordeaux: Imprimerie Commerciale et Industrielle, 1906.

Fournié, Léonce. *Code officiel des usages locaux à caractère agricole ayant force de loi dans le département de l'Ariège.* Foix: Imprimerie J. Fra, 1935.

French Forest Ordinance of 1669. Translated by John Croumbie Brown. London: Simpkin, Marshall, 1883.

Fron, A. *Economie sylvo-pastorale: Forêts, pâturages et prés-bois.* Paris: Librairie Hachette, 1907.

Gaussen, Henri. "L'oeuvre des forestiers aux Pyrénées françaises." *RGPSO* 3 (1932): 385–414.

———. "Les Pyrénées." Excerpt from *Manuel d'alpinisme du Club Alpin Français,* n.p., n.d.

———. "La question forestière aux Pyrénées." *RGPSO* 1 (1930): 205–14.

Géneau, G. "Les forêts de protection: L'application de la loi Chauveau." *REF* 65, 12 (1927): 656–57.

Giono, Jean. *The Man Who Planted Trees.* Translator unknown, 1954. Reprint, Chelsea, Vt.: Chelsea Green, 1985.

Guénot, S. "Le déboisement des Pyrénées: De la gravité et de l'opportunité du sujet," *Bulletin de la Société de Géographie de Toulouse* 2 (March–April 1899): 160–75.

———. *Les Inondations de 1897 et les effets du déboisement des Pyrénées.* Marseille: Secrétariat de la Société de Géographie de Toulouse, 1899.

Guicherd, Jean, ed. *L'Agriculture du département de la Savoie.* Dijon: Imprimerie Bernigaud & Privat, 1930.

Guinier, E. *La Question des montagnes.* Grenoble: Imprimerie F. Allier Père et Fils, 1890.

Huffel, G. *Economie forestière.* Vol. 3. Paris: Librairie Agricole de la Maison Rustique, 1926.

Joly de Sailly, R. *La Déforestation de la France.* Besançon: Typographie et Lithographie Jacquin, 1908.

Kuss, Charles. *Restauration et conservation des terrains en montagne: Eboulements, glissements et barrages.* Paris: Imprimerie Nationale, 1900.

Latour de Saint-Ybars, M. *De la question forestière dans l'Ariège.* Toulouse: Typographie de Bonnal et Gibrac, 1849.

Lorentz, Bernard. "Reboisement des montagnes: Les Alpes et les Pyrénées." *Annales forestières* (1842): 13–22.

Malte-Brun, V. A. *Savoie: Géographie, histoire, statistique, administration.* 1882. Reprint, Les Editions du Bastion, 1979.

Marchand, M. L. *Les Torrents des Alpes et le pâturage.* 2d ed. Paris: Imprimerie Nationale, 1876.

Mathieu, Auguste. *Le Reboisement et le regazonnement des Alpes.* 2d ed. Paris: Imprimerie Nationale, 1875.

Mougin, Paul. "Les forêts de protection en Savoie." *REF* 52, 18 (1913): 545–57.

———. *Les Forêts de Savoie.* Paris: Imprimerie Nationale, 1919.

———. *La Restauration des Alpes.* Paris: Imprimerie Nationale, 1931.

———. *Les Torrents de la Savoie.* Grenoble: Grands Etablissements de l'Imprimerie Générale, 1914.

"Notre domaine forestier et la guerre." *Bulletin de la Société Forestière de Franche-Comté et Belfort* 13 (1919): 43–46.

L'Office National des Forêts: Une entreprise au service du public. Paris: Office National des Forêts, 1988.

Paillié, Marcel. *L'Etat et la propriété forestière en montagne.* Paris: Presses Universitaires de France, 1926.

Puton, A. *Code de la législation forestière.* Paris: J. Rothschild, 1883.

Les Pyrénées ariégeoises: Guide thermal et touristique. Union Thermale et Touristique de l'Ariège, 1927.

Rabouille, Georges. *Du rôle de l'Administration: De la situation des officiers des Eaux et Forêts.* Poitiers: Imprimerie Marc Texier, 1935.

Restauration et conservation des terrains en montagne. *Compte rendu sommaire des travaux de 1860 à 1900.* Paris: Imprimerie Nationale, 1900.

Roquette-Buisson, Comte. *La Question forestière dans les Pyrénées.* n.d., 15 pp.

Ruffié, M. *Massat: Chansons, danse, usages et charte communale.* Foix: Imprimerie-Librairie Gadrat Ainé, 1889.

Salvador, Jean. "Simples notes sur l'aménagement et l'exploitation des forêts pyrénéennes françaises." *RGPSO* 1 (1930): 58–74.

Surell, Alexandre. *Etude sur les torrents des Hautes-Alpes.* 1841. Reprint, Paris: Dunod, 1870.

Tétreau, A. *Commentaire de la loi du 4 avril 1882 sur la restauration et la conservation des terrains en montagne.* Paris: Paul Dupont, 1883.

Thierry, E. *Restauration des montagnes, correction des torrents, reboisement.* Paris: Librairie Baudry, 1891.

Touring-Club de France. *Conférence sur le déboisement, la restauration et la mise en valeur des terrains en montagne.* Paris, n.d.

Trolard, M. *La Forêt: Conseils aux indigènes.* Algiers: Imprimerie de l'Association Ouvrière P. Fontana, 1883.

———. *La Question forestière algérienne devant le Sénat.* Publications de la Ligue du Reboisement de l'Algérie. Algiers: Imprimerie Casablanca, 1893.

Troy, Paul. *Etude sur les moyens de faciliter l'exécution de la loi du 28 juillet 1860 sur le reboisement des montagnes.* Paris, 1861.

SECONDARY SOURCES

Agulhon, Maurice. "Attitudes politiques" and "Les paysans dans la vie politique." In *Histoire de la France rurale,* edited by Georges Duby and Armand Wallon, 3:143–75, 357–81. Paris: Editions du Seuil, 1976.

———. *La République au village: Les populations du Var de la Révolution à la IIe République.* Paris: Editions du Seuil, 1979.

Allen, Edward A. "Deforestation and Fuel Crisis in Pre-Revolutionary Languedoc, 1720– 1789." *French Historical Studies* 13 (1984): 455–73.

Allen, Robert C. *Enclosure and the Yeoman: The Agricultural Development of the South Midlands, 1450–1850* Oxford: Clarendon, 1992.

Antoine, Jean-Marc, Bertrand Desailly, and Jean-Paul Métailié. "La chronologie des crues et phénomènes torrentiels dans les Pyrénées (XVIIIe–XXe siècles)." In *Le Torrent et le fleuve: Risques, catastrophes et aménagement dans les Pyrénées et leur piémont. Fin XVIIe–XXe siècles,* 6–30. Centre Interdisciplinaire de Recherche sur les Milieux Naturels et l'Aménagement Rural, 1991.

Arbos, Philippe. *La Vie pastorale dans les Alpes françaises.* Paris: Armand Colin, 1922.

Ariès, Philippe. *Histoire des populations françaises.* Paris: Editions du Seuil, 1971.

Asselain, Jean-Charles. *Histoire économique de la France du XVIIIe siècle à nos jours.* Paris: Editions du Seuil, 1984.

Assier-Andrieu, Louis. "La coutume dans la question forestière: La lutte d'une communauté des Pyrénées catalanes françaises (1820–28)." *RFF,* special issue (1980): 149–59.

———, ed. *Une France coutumière: Enquête sur les "usages locaux" et leur codification.* Paris: CNRS, 1990.

Attenborough, David. *The First Eden: The Mediterranean World and Man.* Boston: Little, Brown, 1987.

Badré, Louis. *Histoire de la forêt française.* Paris: Arthaud, 1983.

Barrué-Pastor, Monique. "Les aménageurs face aux communautés: La RTM dans les vallées d'Oô et du Larboust." In *Le Torrent et le fleuve: Risques, catastrophes et aménagement dans les Pyrénées et leur piémont. Fin XVIIe–XXe siècles,* edited by Jean-Marc Antoine, 165–203. Centre Interdisciplinaire de Recherche sur les Milieux Naturels et l'Aménagement Rural, 1991.

Barrué-Pastor, Monique, and Valérie Fournié. "La montagne ariégeoise entre friche et paysage: Un consensus illusoire?" *Etudes Rurales* 141–42 (1996): 109–23.

Bazire, Pierre, and Jean Gadant. *La Forêt en France.* Paris: La Documentation Française, 1991.

Bercé, Yves-Marie. *History of Peasant Revolts: The Social Origins of Rebellion in Early Modern France.* Translated by Amanda Whitmore. Ithaca: Cornell University Press, 1990.

———. *Revolt and Revolution in Early Modern Europe.* Translated by Joseph Bergin. New York: St. Martin's, 1987.

Berenson, Edward. *Populist Religion and Left-Wing Politics in France, 1830–1852.* Princeton: Princeton University Press, 1984.

Bertho-Lavenir, Catherine. "Normes de comportement et contrôle de l'espace: Le Touring Club de Belgique avant 1914." *Le Mouvement Social,* 178 (1997): 69–87.

Bertrand, Georges. "Pour une histoire écologique de la France rurale." In *Histoire de la France rurale,* edited by Georges Duby and Armand Wallon, 1:37–113. Paris: Editions du Seuil, 1976.

Bloch, Marc. *French Rural History: An Essay on Its Basic Characteristics.* Translated by Janet Sondheimer. Berkeley: University of California Press, 1966.

Bonhote, Jérôme, and Christian Fruhauf. "Métallurgie au bois et espaces forestiers pyrénéens dans l'Aude et l'Ariège." *RGPSO* 61 (1990): 459–74.

Bonnet, Joël. "La Restauration des terrains en montagne dans le bassin du Vicdessos." Ph.D. diss., University of Toulouse le Mirail, 1985.

Boucharlat, Alain, Ivan Cadenne, and Louis-Jean Gachet. "Espace et communauté: L'institution de l'espace dans une commune de montagne: Saint-Jean-d'Arves (Savoie)." In *La Montagne face au changement: Observation du changement social et culturel,* 117–36. Grenoble: Centre Alpin et Rhodanien d'Ethnologie, 1984.

Bourgenot, L. "L'histoire humaine des forêts françaises: Quelques considérations sur les siècles qui ont précédé la Révolution de 1789." *Comptes rendus de l'Académie agricole française* 73 (1987): 79–86.

Bourguet, Marie-Noëlle. "L'image des terres incultes: La lande, la friche, le marais." In *La Nature en Révolution,* edited by Andrée Corvol, 15–29. Paris: L'Harmattan, 1993.

———. "Race et folklore: L'image officielle de la France en 1800." *Annales: Economies, sociétés, civilisations* 31 (1976): 802–23.

Bozonnet, Jean-Paul. *Des monts et des mythes: L'imaginaire social de la montagne.* Presses Universitaires de Grenoble, 1992.

Briffaud, Serge. "Le rôle des catastrophes naturelles: Cas des Pyrénées centrales." In *La Nature en Révolution,* edited by Andrée Corvol, 134–44. Paris: L'Harmattan, 1993.

Browne, Janet. *The Secular Ark: Studies in the History of Biogeography.* New Haven: Yale University Press, 1983.

Burns, Michael. *Rural Society and French Politics: Boulangism and the Dreyfus Affair, 1886–1900.* Princeton: Princeton University Press, 1984.

Buttoud, Gérard. *Les Conservateurs des Eaux et Forêts sous la IIIe République.* Nancy: INRA, 1983.

———. "L'état forestier face au droit nouveau." In *Révolution et espaces forestiers,* edited by Denis Woronoff, 216–22. Paris: L'Harmattan, 1988.

———. "L'état paternel: Les gardes forestiers au XIXe siècle face à leur administration." In *Jalons pour une histoire des gardes forestiers,* 113–35. Paris: CNRS and INRA, 1985.

———. "Les projets forestiers de la Révolution." *RFF* 35 (1983): 9–20.

Chabord, Marie-Thérèse, and Jean Le Pottier. *Inventaire des dossiers relatifs à l'application du régime forestier aux forêts non domaniales.* Paris: Ministère de l'Agriculture, Direction des Forêts, 1984.

Chabrol, Paul. "L'oeuvre des forestiers français dans la restauration des terrains en montagne, et plus particulièrement dans les Pyrénées de la Haute-Garonne et de l'Ariège." *Pirineos,* 33–34 (1954): 333–63.

Chambers, J. D., and G. E. Mingay. *The Agricultural Revolution, 1750–1880.* London: Batsford, 1969.

Charry, Jean-Claude. "La restauration des terrains en montagne, vue des Pyrénées." *RGPSO* 59 (1988): 29–34.

Chevalier, Michel. *L'Ariège.* Editions Ouest-France, 1985.

———. *La Vie humaine dans les Pyrénées ariégeoises.* Paris: Génin, 1956.

Clarenc, Louis. "Le code de 1827 et les troubles forestiers dans les Pyrénées centrales au milieu du XIXe siècle." *Annales du Midi* 77 (1965): 293–317.

———. "Riches et pauvres dans le conflit forestier des Pyrénées centrales vers le milieu du XIXe siècle." *Annales du Midi* 79 (1967): 307–15.

Clout, Hugh. *After the Ruins: Restoring the Countryside of Northern France After the Great War.* Exeter: University of Exeter Press, 1996.

Collomb, Gérard. *Du bon usage de la montagne.* Paris: L'Harmattan, 1989.

———. "Images du changement: Agriculture et tourisme en Beaufortain." In *La Montagne face au changement: Observation du changement social et culturel,* 137–54. Grenoble: Centre Alpin et Rhodanien d'Ethnologie, 1984.

Combes, François. "Restauration des terrains en montagne: Du rêve à la réalité." *RFF* 41 (1989): 91–106.

Coquerelle, Suzanne. "Les droits collectifs et les troubles agraires dans les Pyrénées en 1848." *Congrès National des Sociétés Savantes* 78 (1953): 345–63.

Corbin, Alain. *Archaïsme et modernité en Limousin au XIXe siècle, 1845–1880.* 2 vols. Paris: Marcel Rivière, 1975.

Corvol, Andrée. "L'affirmation de la propriété communale." In *Révolution et espaces forestiers,* edited by Denis Woronoff, 159–67. Paris: L'Harmattan, 1988.

———. "La Forêt." In *Les France.* Vol. 3 of *Les Lieux de mémoire,* edited by Pierre Nora, 672–737. Paris: Gallimard, 1992.

———. *L'Homme aux bois: Histoire des relations de l'homme et de la forêt, XVIIIe–XXe siècles.* Paris: Fayard, 1987.

———. "The Transformation of a Political Symbol: Tree Festivals in France from the Eighteenth to the Twentieth Centuries." *French History* 4, 4 (1990): 455–86.

———, ed. *La Nature en Révolution.* Paris: L'Harmattan, 1993.

Crécy, Louis. "L'histoire de la RTM: Quelques réflexions d'un praticien." *RGPSO* 59 (1988): 17–27.

———. "La politique de prévention des risques naturels en montagne depuis 150 ans." *Congrès National des Sociétés Savantes* 108 (1983): reprint, 8 pp.

Cronon, William. "A Place for Stories: Nature, History, and Narrative." *Journal of American History* 78 (1992): 1347–76.

Dejean, Max, and Denise Dejean. *L'Ariège d'autrefois.* Le Coteau: Horvath, 1988.

Dequier, Daniel. *De bouche à oreille: Contes et récits de la tradition orale en Maurienne.* Apremont: Editions Curandera, 1988.

Dequier, Daniel, and Jean-Henri Viallet. *Un Village en Maurienne: Jarrier.* Saint-Avre: Imprimerie Roux, 1985.

Desailly, Bertrand. "Perception et gestion du risque: Les ingénieurs et les crues méditerranéennes." In *La Nature en Révolution,* edited by Andrée Corvol, 41–45. Paris: L'Harmattan, 1993.

Désert, Gabriel. "Prospérité de l'agriculture." In *Histoire de la France rurale*, edited by Georges Duby and Armand Wallon, 3:221–53. Paris: Editions du Seuil, 1976.

Devèze, Michel. *La Forêt et les communautés rurales, XVIe–XVIIIe siècles: Recueil d'articles*. Paris: Publications de la Sorbonne, 1987.

Les Droits d'usage en Ariège. 2 vols. Foix: Chambre d'Agriculture de l'Ariège, 1983.

Dubourdieu, J. "Les forêts en montagne et leurs fonctions multiples." *RFF* 34 (1982): 32–39.

Duby, Georges, and Armand Wallon, ed. *Histoire de la France rurale*. 4 vols. Paris: Editions du Seuil, 1976.

Dupont, René. "Les forêts du Saint-Gironnais avant la guerre des Demoiselles." *RGPSO* 3 (1932): 355–67.

Les Eaux et Forêts du XIIe au XXe siècle. Paris: CNRS, 1987.

Eisbacher, G. H., and J. J. Clague. "Destructive Mass Movements in High Mountains: Hazard and Management." *Geological Survey of Canada*. Paper 84–16 (1984): 97–98.

Evans, Estyn. "The Ecology of Peasant Life in Western Europe." In *Man's Role in Changing the Face of the Earth*, edited by William L. Thomas Jr., 217–39. Chicago: University of Chicago Press, 1956.

Feuvrier, Jean-Pierre. "Risques naturels et restauration des terrains en montagne: Un siècle d'histoire, son actualité en Savoie." *L'Histoire en Savoie*, special issue (September 1985): 265–72.

Fontaine, Laurence. *History of Pedlars in Europe*. Translated by Vicki Whittaker. Cambridge, U.K.: Polity, 1996.

———. *Le Voyage et la mémoire: Colporteurs de l'Oisans au XIXe siècle*. Lyon: Presses Universitaires de Lyon, 1984.

Fourchy, Pierre. "Un centenaire oublié: Les lois du 28 juillet 1860 et 8 juin 1864 sur le reboisement et le gazonnement des montagnes." *RGA* 51 (1963): 19–41.

Fritsch, Père Robert. "La forêt savoyarde, réceptacle de plantes en survie." In *La Forêt de Savoie*, edited by P. Gensac, 9–13. Montmélian: Imprimerie Arc-Isère, 1983.

Fruhauf, Christian. "Administration forestière et populations dans les Pyrénées: De la compréhension au mépris." *RGPSO* 60 (1989): 425–34.

———. *Forêt et société: De la forêt paysanne à la forêt capitaliste en pays de Sault sous l'ancien régime*. Paris: CNRS, 1980.

Fussell, Paul. *The Great War and Modern Memory*. Oxford: Oxford University Press, 1975.

Gaillard, Emile. "Jarrier, commune mauriennaise: Les remues hivernales et l'habitat." *Revue de Savoie* 1 (1943): 17–23.

Galzin, Jacques. "Déboisement et plantation de châtaigniers en Cévennes." *Annales du Parc national des Cévennes* 3 (1986): 7–70.

Garaud, Marcel. *La Révolution et la propriété foncière*. Paris: Recueil Sirey, 1958.

García Pérez, José D. "The Promotion of Participation in Planning for Soil and Water Conservation Through Reforestation: A Case Study of Guadalajara (Spain)." In *European Woods and Forests: Studies in Cultural History*, edited by Charles Watkins, 191–214. Wallingford and New York: CAB International, 1998.

Gaussen, Henri. "Climat et végétation des Pyrénées ariégeoises." *RGPSO* 8 (1937): 350–63.

———. "Les forêts de l'Ariège et du Salat." *RGPSO* 8 (1937): 364–75.

Gensac, P. "La forêt en Savoie, approche écologique." In *La Forêt de Savoie*, edited by P. Gensac, 7–9. Montmélian: Imprimerie Arc-Isère, 1983.

Gorce, Pierre. *Histoire du Second Empire.* 7 vols. Paris: Librairie Plon, 1905.

Green, Nicholas. *The Spectacle of Nature: Landscape and Bourgeois Culture in Nineteenth-Century France.* Manchester: Manchester University Press, 1990.

Greene, Mott T. *Geology in the Nineteenth Century: Changing Views of a Changing World.* Ithaca: Cornell University Press, 1982.

Grove, Richard H. *Green Imperialism: Colonial Expansion, Tropical Island Edens, and the Origins of Environmentalism, 1600–1860.* Cambridge: Cambridge University Press, 1995.

Guichonnet, Paul. *Histoire de l'annexion de la Savoie à la France (et ses dossiers secrets).* Roanne: Editions Horvath, 1982.

————, ed. *Histoire de la Savoie.* Toulouse: Edouard Privat, 1973.

————. *Histoire et civilisation des Alpes.* 2 vols. Toulouse: Privat/Payot, 1980.

Hallam, A. *Great Geological Controversies.* 2d ed. Oxford: Oxford University Press, 1989.

Harrison, Robert Pogue. *Forests: The Shadow of Civilization.* Chicago: University of Chicago Press, 1992.

Hermann, Marie-Thérèse. *Architecture et vie traditionnelle en Savoie.* Paris: Berger-Levrault, 1980.

Hudry, Abbé Maurius. "Le Club Alpin Français, Section de Tarentaise, 1875–1914." In *La Sociabilité des Savoyards: Actes du XXIXe Congrès des Sociétés Savantes de Savoie,* 328–36. Montmélian: Imprimerie Arc-Isère, 1983.

Hunt, David. "Peasant Politics in the French Revolution." *Social History* 9 (1984): 277–99.

James, N. D. G. "A History of Forestry and Monographic Forestry Literature in Germany, France, and the United Kingdom." In *The Literature of Forestry and Agroforestry,* edited by Peter McDonald and James Lassoie, 15–44. Ithaca: Cornell University Press, 1996.

Jones, P. M. *The Peasantry in the French Revolution.* Cambridge: Cambridge University Press, 1988.

Judt, Tony. *Socialism in Provence, 1871–1914: A Study in the Origins of the Modern French Left.* Cambridge: Cambridge University Press, 1979.

Kalaora, Bernard. *Forêt et société au XIXe siècle: La sève de Marianne.* Ardon: Laboratoire d'Economies et de Sociétés Rurales, 1980.

Kalaora, Bernard, and Antoine Savoye. "Aménagement et ménagement: Le cas de la politique forestière au XIXe siècle." *Congrès National des Sociétés Savantes* 113 (1988): 307–28.

————. *La Forêt pacifiée: Les forestiers de l'Ecole de Le Play, experts des sociétés pastorales.* Paris: L'Harmattan, 1986.

Kerridge, Eric. *The Agricultural Revolution.* New York: A. M. Kelley, 1968.

Lanier-Graham, Susan. *The Ecology of War: Environmental Impacts of Weaponry and Warfare.* New York: Walker, 1993.

Larrère, Raphaël, A. Brun, Bernard Kalaora, Olivier Nougarède, and Denis Poupardin. "Reboisement des montagnes et systèmes agraires." *RFF,* special issue (1980): 20–36.

Lehning, James R. *Peasant and French: Cultural Contact in Rural France During the Nineteenth Century.* Cambridge: Cambridge University Press, 1995.

Leynaud, Emile. *L'Etat et la nature: L'exemple des parcs nationaux français.* Florac: Parc National des Cévennes, 1985.

Lienert, Leo. "Genèse du paysage alpin." *Le Courrier du mois* (February 1987): 4–8.

Loubet, Jean-Louis. "Etude géographique d'un milieu montagnard: Les communes du Port et de Massat (Pyrénées Ariégeoises)." Parts 1 and 2. *Société Ariégeoise des Sciences, Lettres et Arts* 33 (1978): 5–43; 34 (1979): 187–263.

Lovie, Jacques. "Les ressources forestières de la Savoie pendant les premières années du régime français." *RGA* 49 (1961): 741–59.

————. *La Savoie dans la vie française de 1860 à 1875.* Paris: Presses Universitaires de France, 1963.

Lovie, Jacques, et al. *Savoie: Ecologie, économie, art, littérature, langue, histoire, traditions populaires.* Le Puy: Christine Bonneton, 1978.

Margadant, Ted W. *French Peasants in Revolt: The Insurrection of 1851.* Princeton: Princeton University Press, 1979.

————. "Tradition and Modernity in Rural France During the Nineteenth Century." *Journal of Modern History* 56 (1984): 667–97.

————. *Urban Rivalries in the French Revolution.* Princeton: Princeton University Press, 1992.

Marnézy, Alain. *Maurienne, terre humaine.* Montmélian: Imprimerie Arc-Isère, 1984.

McNeill, J. R. *The Mountains of the Mediterranean World: An Environmental History.* Cambridge: Cambridge University Press, 1992.

McPhee, John. *The Control of Nature.* New York: Farrar, Straus, and Giroux, 1989.

McPhee, Peter. *The Politics of Rural Life: Political Mobilization in the French Countryside, 1846–1852.* Oxford: Oxford University Press, 1992.

————. *Revolution and Environment in Southern France: Peasants, Lords, and Murder in the Corbières, 1780–1830.* Oxford: Oxford University Press, 1999.

————. *Les Semailles de la république dans les Pyrénées-Orientales, 1846–1852.* Perpignan: Les Publications de l'Olivier, 1995.

McQuillan, Alan G. "Making Restoration Work: The Ethics of Restoration Ecology, or, Why Postmodernists are Not the Enemy." In *Making Protection Work: Proceedings of the 9th Conference on Research and Resource Management in Parks and in Public Lands,* edited by David Harmon, 274–79. Hancock, Mich.: George Wright Society, 1997.

Meilleur, Brien. "La forêt dans l'économie traditionnelle montagnarde." In *La Forêt de Savoie,* edited by P. Gensac, 125–35. Montmélian: Imprimerie Arc-Isère, 1983.

Merriman, John. *The Agony of the Republic: The Repression of the Left in Revolutionary France, 1848–1851.* New Haven: Yale University Press, 1978.

————. "The Demoiselles of the Ariège, 1829–1831." In *1830 in France,* edited by John Merriman, 87–118. New York: New Viewpoints, 1975.

Mestrallet, Michèle. "Histoire de l'alpinisme en Savoie." *L'Histoire en Savoie,* special issue (June 1988): 1–40.

Métailié, Jean-Paul. "Aux origines des améliorations pastorales dans les Pyrénées." *Production Pastorale et Société* 18 (spring 1986): 91–105.

————. "Les incendies pastoraux dans les Pyrénées centrales." *RGPSO* 49 (1978): 517–26.

Mormiche, André. "La notion d'aménagement forestier." *RGPSO* 55 (1984): 129–40.

Mornet, Daniel. *Le Sentiment de la nature en France de Jean-Jacques Rousseau à Bernardin de Saint-Pierre.* 1907. Reprint, New York: Burt Franklin, 1971.

Nougarède, Olivier. *L'Administration forestière face à une société montagnarde.* Orléans: INRA, 1983.

Nougarède, Olivier, Denis Poupardin, and Raphaël Larrère. "Le reboisement de RTM de l'Aigoual, en Cévennes: Epopée dissidente ou expérience d'avant-garde" *RGPSO* 59, (1988): 111–24.

Ogé, Frédéric. "Appropriation communautaire et/ou appropriation étatique de la forêt sous la Révolution." In *Propriété et Révolution*, edited by Geneviève Koubi, 127–33. Paris: CNRS, 1990.

———. "Le Conseil Général de l'Ariège et la 'question du bois' de l'an VIII à 1914." In *Actes du CTHS de Poitiers* (1986): 6–10.

———. "Le personnel de l'administration forestière de l'Ariège, du Second Empire à la Première guerre mondiale." In *Jalons pour une histoire des gardes forestiers*, 139–44. Paris: CNRS and INRA, 1985.

———. "Les prémices de la politique de restauration des terrains en montagne." *RGPSO* 59 (1988): 9–15.

Osborne, Michael A. *Nature, the Exotic, and the Science of French Colonialism*. Bloomington: Indiana University Press, 1994.

Palluel-Guillard, André. "Les forêts de Savoie depuis le XVIIIe siècle." In *La Forêt de Savoie*, edited by P. Gensac, 23–37. Montmélian: Imprimerie Arc-Isère, 1983.

Palluel-Guillard, André, Christian Sorrel, Guido Ratti, Antoine Fleury, and Jean Loup. *La Savoie de la Révolution à nos jours, XIXe–XXe siècle*. Rennes: Ouest-France, 1986.

Picon, Antoine. "L'idée de nature chez les ingénieurs des Ponts et Chaussées." In *La Nature en Révolution*, edited by Andrée Corvol, 117–25. Paris: L'Harmattan, 1993.

Plaisance, Georges. "L'emprise des forêts françaises et son explication." *Congrès national des sociétés savantes* 88 (1963): 197–223.

———. *La Forêt française*. Paris: Denoël, 1979.

Poujol, Robert. "Le rôle de la forêt dans le début de la guerre des camisards," in *La Forêt et l'homme en Languedoc-Roussillon*, 49–56. Montpellier: Dehan, 1984.

Pourcher, Yves. "La Forêt: Espace global et espace conflictuel. La Lozère aux XVIIIe et XIXe siècles," in *La Forêt et l'homme en Languedoc-Roussillon*, 95–108. Montpellier: Dehan, 1984.

Préau, Pierre. "Le Parc National de la Vanoise, banc d'essai d'une politique d'aménagement de la montagne." *RGA* 52 (1964): 393–436.

Prochaska, David. "Fire on the Mountain: Resisting Colonialism in Algeria." In *Banditry, Rebellion, and Social Protest in Africa*, edited by Donald Crummey, 229–52. London: James Currey, 1986.

Puton, A. *Code de la législation forestière*. Paris: J. Rothschild, 1883.

Rackham, Oliver. "Savanna in Europe." In *The Ecological History of European Forests*, edited by Keith J. Kirby and Charles Watkins, 1–24. Wallingford: CAB International, 1998.

Rambaud, Placide, and Monique Vincienne. *Les Transformations d'une société rurale: La Maurienne (1561–1962)*. Paris: Armand Colin, 1964.

Rearick, Charles. *Pleasures of the Belle Epoque*. New Haven: Yale University Press, 1985.

Reed, J. L. *Forests of France*. London: Faber & Faber, 1954.

Richez, Jean-Claude. "Science allemande et foresterie française: L'expérience de la rive gauche du Rhin." In *Révolution et espaces forestiers*, edited by Denis Woronoff, 232–46. Paris: L'Harmattan, 1988.

Rivéro, Jean. *Droit administratif.* Paris: Librairie Dalloz, 1962.

Robinson, Gordon. *The Forest and the Trees: A Guide to Excellent Forestry.* Washington, D.C.: Island, 1988.

Röhrich, Lutz. "Le monde surnaturel dans les légendes alpines." *Le Monde alpin et rhodanien: Revue régionale d'ethnologie* 1 (1982): 25–41.

Rosenberg, Harriet. *A Negotiated World: Three Centuries of Change in a French Alpine Community.* Toronto: University of Toronto Press, 1988.

Rosenberg, Harriet, Randy Reiter, and Rayna R. Reiter. "Rural Workers in French Alpine Tourism: Whose Development?" *Studies in European Society* 1 (1973): 21–38.

Rosenthal, Jean-Laurent. *The Fruits of Revolution: Property Rights, Litigation, and French Agriculture, 1700–1860.* Cambridge: Cambridge University Press, 1992.

Ryden, Kent C. *Mapping the Invisible Landscape: Folklore, Writing, and the Sense of Place.* Iowa City: University of Iowa Press, 1993.

Sahlins, Peter. *Forest Rites: The War of the Demoiselles in Nineteenth-Century France.* Cambridge: Harvard University Press, 1994.

Salies, Pierre. *Quand l'Ariège changea de siècle.* Tarascon-sur-Ariège: Editions Résonances, 1982.

Salvador, Jean. "Le département de l'Ariège au point de vue forestier." *Annales de la Fédération Pyrénéenne d'Economie Montagnarde* 5 (1936): 216–63.

Sanson, Rosemonde. *Les 14 juillet, fête et conscience nationale, 1789–1975.* Paris: Flammarion, 1976.

Schama, Simon. *Landscape and Memory.* New York: Alfred A. Knopf, 1995.

Scott, James. "Everyday Forms of Resistance." In *Everyday Forms of Peasant Resistance,* edited by Forrest D. Colburn, 3–33. Armonk, N.Y.: M. E. Sharpe, 1989.

———. *Seeing Like a State: How Certain Schemes to Improve the Human Condition Have Failed.* New Haven: Yale University Press, 1998.

Sébastien, Michel. *Rivières d'Ariège: Eaux et inondations.* Foix: Centre Départemental de Documentation Pédagogique, 1985.

Sébillot, Paul. *La Flore.* Vol. 6 of *Le Folklore de France.* 1904–06. Reprint, Paris: Editions Imago, 1985.

———. *La Terre et le monde souterrain.* Vol. 2 of *Le Folklore de France.* 1904–06. Reprint, Paris: Editions Imago, 1985

Servat, J. M. *Histoire de Massat.* Foix: Gadrat, 1936.

Sewell, William H., Jr. *Work and Revolution in France.* Cambridge: Cambridge University Press, 1980.

Smith, Cecil O. "The Longest Run: Public Engineers and Planning in France." *American Historical Review* 95 (June 1990): 657–92.

Soulet, Jean-François. *Les Pyrénées au XIXe siècle.* 2 vols. Toulouse: Eché, 1987.

Soutadé, G. "La Limite supérieure de la forêt: Résumé et synthèse des travaux." In *La Limite supérieure de la forêt et sa valeur de seuil,* 167–74. Prada: Terra Nostra, 1982.

———. "Passage de la forêt à la pelouse ou à la lande: Problèmes de réversibilité et de gestion de la montage: Discussion." In *La Limite supérieure de la forêt et sa valeur de seuil,* 26–30. Prada: Terra Nostra, 1982.

Sutton, Keith. "Reclamation of Wasteland During the Eighteenth and Nineteenth Centuries." In *Themes in the Historical Geography of France,* edited by Hugh D. Clout, 247–300. London: Academic, 1977.

Thibon, Christian. *Pays de Sault: Les Pyrénées audoises au XIXe siècle: Les villages et l'état.* Paris: CNRS, 1988.

Thompson, E. P. "The Crime of Anonymity." In *Albion's Fatal Tree,* edited by Douglas Hay et al., 255–308. New York: Pantheon, 1975.

Tilly, Charles. *The Contentious French.* Harvard University Press, 1986.

Tucker, Richard B., and John F. Richards. "The Global Economy and Forest Clearance in the Nineteenth Century." In *Environmental History: Critical Issues in Comparative Perspective,* edited by Kendall E. Bailes, 577–85. Lanham: University Press of America, 1985.

Tucker, Richard B., and John F. Richards, eds. *Global Deforestation and the Nineteenth-Century World Economy.* Duke Press Policy Studies. Durham: Duke University Press, 1983.

Vallerant, Jacques. "La permanence du changement: Techniques et savoir-faire dans les sociétés rurales des Alpes du Nord." In *La Montagne face au changement: Observation du changement social et culturel,* 107–16. Grenoble: Centre Alpin et Rhodanien d'Ethnologie, 1984.

Van Gennep, Arnold. *Du berceau à la tombe.* Vol. 1 of *En Savoie.* Chambéry: Librairie Perrin, 1916.

Veyret, Paul, and Germaine Veyret. *Atlas et géographie des Alpes françaises.* Paris: Flammarion, 1979.

Viazzo, Pier Paolo. *Upland Communities: Environment, Population, and Social Structure in the Alps Since the Sixteenth Century.* Cambridge: Cambridge University Press, 1989.

Vidal de la Blache, Paul. *Tableau de la géographie de la France.* 1903. Reprint, Paris: Hachette, 1979.

Vigier, Philippe. *La Seconde République dans la région alpine: Etude politique et sociale.* Paris: Presses Universitaires de France, 1963.

———. "Les troubles forestiers du premier XIXe siècle français." *RFF,* special issue (1980): 128–35.

Weber, Eugene. "Comment la Politique Vint aux Paysans: A Second Look at Peasant Politicization." *American Historical Review* 87 (1982): 357–89.

———. *Peasants into Frenchmen.* Stanford: Stanford University Press, 1976.

———. "Who Sang the Marseillaise?" In *The Wolf and the Lamb: Popular Culture in France from the Old Regime to the Twentieth Century,* edited by Jacques Beauroy, Marc Bertrand, and Edward T. Gargan, 161–73. Saratoga, Calif.: Anma Libri, 1976.

Weill, Alex. *Droit civil: Les biens.* 2d ed. Paris: Dalloz, 1974.

Woolsey, Theodore, Jr. *French Forests and Forestry.* New York: John Wiley and Sons, 1917.

Wordie, J. R. "The Chronology of English Enclosure, 1500–1914." *Economic History Review* 36, no. 4 (1983): 483–505.

Woronoff, Denis. "La 'dévastation révolutionnaire' des forêts." In *Révolution et espaces forestiers,* edited by Denis Woronoff, 44–52. Paris: L'Harmattan, 1988.

Wright, Gordon. *France in Modern Times.* 4th ed. New York: W. W. Norton, 1987.

Zeldin, Theodore. *The Political System of Napoleon III.* New York: W. W. Norton, 1958.

Index

Administration des Forêts: created, 30–31; and War of the Demoiselles, 42, 43; and Second Republic, 44, 45, 46; relations with Ponts et Chaussées, 57; and science, 65; and local knowledge, 69; in Ariège, 74–77, 135–36; and communal property, 79; in Savoie, 77–81, 103; in Massat, 136, 137–39, 152–54; change of name to Eaux et Forêts, 155; mentioned *passim*, 3–155. *See also* Eaux et Forêts

Agro-sylvo-pastoralism: in Ariège and Savoie, 10, 14–19, 197–98, 224*n42;* in Alps and Pyrenees, 13, 17, 29, 66, 130, 224*n35;* reforestation and, 57; in Jarrier, 96, 114–15, 234*n21;* in Massat, 128–30; in Algeria, 200, 201; associations' criticisms of, 204–5; decline of, 217; and Article Nineteen, 219

Algeria, 199–204, 208

Alpes-Maritimes, 90, 194

Alpinism, 53–54, 182, 184–85, 210. *See also* Tourism

Alps: literacy in, 5; deforestation of, 9, 50, 51; geology, topography, climate of northern, 11–12; agro-sylvopastoralism in, 13, 17, 29, 66, 224 *n35;* demography of, 38, 206–7; Romanticism and, 53; catastrophism and, 57; restoration of, 92, 119, 156, 158, 175; and tourism, 184, 218; foresters' perceptions of, 197; and fears of desertification, 201. *See also* Savoie

Ariège: vegetation in, 9, 13, 222*n17,* 244*n49,* 245*n55;* agro-sylvo-pastoralism in, 10, 14–18; geography of, 11; climate of, 12; settlement types in, 14; during French Revolution, 25; demography of, 38, 195; metallurgy in, 39, 42; electoral politics in, 44–45, 240*n59;* coup of *1851* in, 45; reclamation in, 63; pastoral improvements in, 66, 191–92; reforesta-

Ariège (*cont.*)
tion in, 66, 67–71, 136–37; use rights
in, 70, 135, 171, 178–79; restoration
in, 127, 136–38; flood of *1875* in, 136,
137; and Fête de l'Arbre, 190; defeat
of national park in, 218. *See also*
Pyrenees
Association Centrale pour l'Aménagement des Montagnes (ACAM): relation to state and other associations,
186, 193–94, 248*n38;* projects, 194–95;
assumptions about peasantry, 204, 205,
207; legacy of, 210; and tourism,
247*n34;* mentioned, 196
Association Nationale et Industrielle du
Bois (ANIB), 187, 188, 189, 190, 210
Associations: interest in forestry, 182–83;
pedagogical goals of, 186–190; patriotic
rhetoric of, 246–47*n24. See also* names
of associations
Audiffred Law, 161
Auzat (Ariège), 18, 71–74, 76, 137

Basses-Pyrénées, 43, 192, 194
Biert (Ariège), 133–42 *passim,* 147, 148,
151, 154, 216
Biogeography, 64–65
Briot, Félix, 195, 198
Buffault, Pierre, 158, 160, 166, 186, 205

Cantonnement. *See* Use rights
Catastrophism, 54–55, 57
Cévennes, 10, 29
Chauveau law on protective forests: ori-
gins and definition, 165, 166–67; appli-
cation in Savoie and Ariège, 167–74;
and restoration, 171, 244*n47*
Chevandier de Valdrôme, Eugène, 59, 71
Civil Code, 125, 131–32, 143
Civil Society of the Mountains of Massat,
125, 134, 135, 142, 146–52 *passim*
Club Alpin Français, 184–85, 193, 195,
196, 210, 217
Communal property: and reclamation

law of *1860,* 61–62; in Savoie, 78–79,
223*n32;* and restoration, 92; in Massat,
123; partition of, 227*n51*
Couserans (Ariège), 128, 130, 133, 136, 137

Deforestation: global, in nineteenth century, 1; in French Revolution, 25;
dogma among nineteenth-century
foresters, 52, 65; as distinct concept, 55;
in Surell's work, 56; of Massat valley,
122; of Algeria, 201–3
Delpla, Jean-Jules-Isidore, 123, 131, 134, 135
Demontzey, Prosper, 90, 91, 105, 110, 183,
185
Descombes, Paul, 193–99 *passim,* 204,
207
Desertification, 209, 211
Dieu, Hippolyte, 78, 79, 81
Doumenjou, Hippolyte, 74, 92, 201
Dralet, Etienne, 29–30, 46, 158, 226*n49*

Eaux et Forêts: origins of, 22; demise in
1790, 24; in Massat, 152–54; name
changed from Administration des
Forêts, 155; and mobilization during
World War One, 162; and appropriation of communal property, 173; communes' solicitations of, 174–75; and
grazing concessions, 175, 178; added re-
sponsibilities of, 181–82; involvement
with associations, 183, 186–87, 193–98
passim; and education, 247*n17;* and
alpine depopulation, 248*n50. See also*
Administration des Forêts
Ecole Nationale des Eaux et Forêts, 30, 33,
51, 65

Fabre, Lucien-Albert, 158, 159, 208–9
Fédération Française de l'Economie
Alpestre. *See* Société Française d'Eco-
nomie Alpestre
Fédération Pyrénéenne d'Economie
Montagnarde, 195, 196, 197
Fête de l'Arbre, 187–90, 210